A Primer on Property Tax

A Primer on Property Tax

Administration and Policy

Edited by

William J. McCluskey

Built Environment Research Institute
University of Ulster
UK

Gary C. Cornia

Marriott School of Management
Brigham Young University
USA

Lawrence C. Walters

Romney Institute of Public Management
Brigham Young University
USA

A John Wiley & Sons, Ltd., Publication

Wiley-Blackwell is an imprint of John Wiley & Sons, formed by the merger of Wiley's global
Scientific, Technical and Medical business with Blackwell Publishing.

Registered *Office*
John Wiley & Sons, Ltd, The Atrium, Southern Gate, Chichester, West Sussex, PO19 8SQ, UK

Editorial Offices
9600 Garsington Road, Oxford, OX4 2DQ, UK
The Atrium, Southern Gate, Chichester, West Sussex, PO19 8SQ, UK
2121 State Avenue, Ames, Iowa 50014-8300, USA

For details of our global editorial offices, for customer services and for information about
how to apply for permission to reuse the copyright material in this book please see our
website at www.wiley.com/wiley-blackwell.

Library of Congress Cataloging-in-Publication Data

A primer on property tax : administration and policy / edited by William J. McCluskey,
Gary C. Cornia, Lawrence C. Walters.
    p. cm.
  Includes bibliographical references and index.
  ISBN 978-1-4051-2649-6 (cloth)
1. Property tax. 2. Property tax—Law and legislation. I. McCluskey, William J.
II. Cornia, Gary C. III. Walters, Lawrence C.
  HJ4113.P75 2013
  336.22–dc23

                    2012029010
A catalogue record for this book is available from the British Library.

  ISBN: 978-1-405-12649-6

Wiley also publishes its books in a variety of electronic formats. Some content that appears
in print may not be available in electronic books.

Cover design by Steve Flemming
Cover image courtesy of iStockPhoto

1 2013

Contents

About the Contributors

Claudia M. De Cesare is an adviser for the Secretariat of Finance in the municipality of Porto Alegre, Brazil. She is a member of the Teaching Faculty of the Lincoln Institute of Land Policy and a Member of the Advisory Board of the International Property Tax Institute (IPTI). She has written several publications on property taxation and valuation for taxation purposes, as well as working as a course developer and editor. Among other initiatives, she was the creator of the Capacity Building Program to Improve the Performance of the Property Tax in Brazil, coordinated by the Lincoln Institute and the Ministry of the Cities. She is a Civil Engineer, holds a Masters degree in real estate valuation by Universidade Federal do Rio Grande do Sul (UFRGS) and holds a Ph.D. degree awarded by the University of Salford, England.

Gary C. Cornia is the Dean of the Marriott School of Management at Brigham Young University. He is the past president of the National Tax Association and has served as State Tax Commissioner in Utah. He has been a visiting Fellow at the Lincoln Institute of Land Policy and a visiting Scholar at the Andrew Young School of Policy at Georgia State University. He has published a variety of articles on state and local tax policy, decentralization and property tax. He received his Ph.D. from The Ohio State University.

Peadar Davis is a Chartered Surveyor and lecturer at the University of Ulster, with specific teaching and research interests in valuation, appraisal and asset management. In 2009, he was awarded a Ph.D. by the University of Ulster, specializing in simplified property tax systems. He has been involved in research into property valuation, local government finance and property taxation policy in several jurisdictions including Northern Ireland, Kosovo, Uganda and Egypt. He previously managed a complex, mixed portfolio of office, retail (notably shopping centres), industrial and residential properties.

Riël Franzsen is Professor and Director of the African Tax Institute, University of Pretoria. Previously he was professor in the Department of Mercantile Law at the University of South Africa. In 1990, he obtained a doctorate from the University of Stellenbosch, South Africa. He is a co-founder of the African Tax Institute (ATI), which was established in 2002 to undertake capacity development in the areas of tax policy and tax administration in the public sector in Africa. He is a member of the Advisory Board of the International Property Tax Institute (IPTI) and has acted as an advisor to The People's Republic of China, Democratic Republic of the Congo, Egypt, Indonesia, Rwanda, South Africa,

Tanzania and Uganda, as well the World Bank on especially property tax issues. He has acted as an instructor on property taxation for the IMF and the Lincoln Institute of Land Policy.

Martin Haran is a Senior Research Fellow within the Real Estate Initiative at the University of Ulster. He was awarded a first class Honours degree in Business and Financial Management from the University of Ulster. In 2008, he graduated with a Ph.D. from the University of Ulster with specialisms in financial modelling. Principal research and teaching interests comprise business finance, economic competitiveness, real estate finance, financial modelling and investment performance. He has authored a number of industry and academic papers in the areas of real estate finance, financial modelling, real estate investment, regeneration, planning and property.

Yu-Hung Hong is a Senior Fellow at the Lincoln Institute of Land Policy. He earned his Ph.D. in Urban Development and Masters in City Planning from the Department of Urban Studies and Planning at the Massachusetts Institute of Technology (MIT). At the Lincoln Institute, he focuses his research on issues related to property rights and obligations, land management tools and local public finance. He is a visiting faculty in the Department of Urban Studies and Planning at MIT, teaching budgeting, fiscal policy evaluation, urban public finance in developing countries and advanced public finance seminars.

Roy Kelly is a Professor of the Practice of Public Policy Studies, Sanford School of Public Policy, Duke University. Previously, he spent 19 years at Harvard University teaching local government finance, tax analysis and project evaluation. He has over 25 years of experience teaching, designing and implementing reforms on fiscal decentralization, local finance and property taxation in Asia, Africa, Latin America and eastern Europe. He served as resident advisor in Tanzania, Cambodia, Kenya and Indonesia and has worked on property tax reforms in Albania, Argentina, Bahamas, Cambodia, Dominican Republic, Egypt, Indonesia, Kenya, Malawi, Mexico, Nepal, Poland, Russia, South Africa, Tanzania and Uganda.

Harry Kitchen is Professor Emeritus in the Economics Department at Trent University, Peterborough, Ontario, Canada. Over the past 20 years, he has completed more than 100 articles, reports, studies and books on issues relating to local government expenditures, finance and governance in Canada and abroad. In addition, he has served as a consultant or advisor for a number of municipal and provincial governments in Canada, the federal government, foreign governments in Russia and China and private sector organizations.

William J. McCluskey is Reader in Real Estate and Valuation at the University of Ulster where he received his Ph.D. in Real Estate Valuation in 1999. He has held various international positions including Visiting Professor of Real Estate at the University of Lodz, Poland, Professor of Property Studies at Lincoln

University, Christchurch, New Zealand and is currently Visiting Professor in Real Estate at University of Technology Malaysia. His main professional and academic interests are in the fields of real estate valuation, developing automated valuation methods and property tax policy. In addition, he has been an invited instructor in real estate at the African Tax Institute and the Lincoln Institute of Land Policy: China Programme. He is a faculty member of the Lincoln Institute of Land Policy and founding Board Member of the International Property Tax Institute.

Michael McCord is a Lecturer at the University of Ulster. He was awarded a BSc degree in the field of Geography and Economics from Queens University, Belfast. In 2010 he graduated with a Ph.D. from the University of Ulster. His main teaching and research interests comprise property market analysis, property statistics, spatial econometrics and financial modelling. In addition he has published several industry and academic papers.

David McIlhatton is a research officer at the University of Ulster. He was awarded a BSc degree in geography, postgraduate degree in geographic information systems (GIS) and a Ph.D. in GIS and spatial modelling from the University of Ulster. He has actively researched in the area of GIS and real estate appraisal for a number of years demonstrating the real business benefits that linking location with data can bring to organizations. More recently, he has engaged in developing and implementing GIS based asset management tools for both academic and non-academic purposes. He is a member of a number of professional organizations, including being an executive committee member of the Association of Geographic Information.

John L. Mikesell is Chancellor's Professor of Public and Environmental Affairs at Indiana University. His research focuses on sales and property taxation, tax administration and revenue forecasting, and his textbook *Fiscal Administration* is widely used in graduate public administration programmes. He has been a David Lincoln Fellow in Land Value Taxation with the Lincoln Institute for Land Policy and Senior Research Fellow, Peking University – Lincoln Institute Center for Urban Development and Land Policy, Beijing, People's Republic of China. He holds a B.A. from Wabash College and M.A. and Ph.D. in economics from the University of Illinois-Urbana.

Frances Plimmer holds a Master of Philosophy degree and was awarded a Ph.D. in 1999. She was Research Professor at Kingston University until 2006 and with the Research Department at the College of Estate Management. She was the editor of *Property Management* from 1994 to 2010. She is a member of the RICS' Research Advisory Board. She is the UK delegate and chair of FIG's Commission 9 (Valuation and Real Estate Management). She has an international research reputation and written and presented widely on the subjects of valuation, property taxation compulsory acquisition and professional education and qualifications.

Jay K. Rosengard is Lecturer in Public Policy at Harvard Kennedy School with over 30 years of experience in the design, implementation and evaluation of development policies and programmes throughout Asia, Africa and Latin America. His areas of expertise include public finance and fiscal policy, tax and budget reform, municipal finance and management, intergovernmental fiscal relations, banking and financial institutions, microfinance and public administration. He is currently Director of the Mossavar-Rahmani Center for Business and Government's Financial Sector Program, which focuses on the development of bank and non-bank financial institutions. In addition, he is a Faculty Affiliate of both the Ash Center for Democratic Governance and Innovation and the Center for International Development.

Enid Slack is the Director of the Institute on Municipal Finance and Governance at the Munk School of Global Affairs at the University of Toronto. Her research interests include property taxes, the finance and governance of large metropolitan areas, infrastructure financing and intergovernmental fiscal arrangements. Recent publications include *A Tale of Two Taxes: Reforming the Property Tax in Ontario* (co-authored with Richard Bird and Almos Tassonyi), *International Handbook of Land and Property Taxation* (co-edited with Richard Bird, 2004) and *UN Habitat Guide to Municipal Finance (2009)*. Enid is a member of the Advisory Board of the International Property Tax Institute (IPTI).

Martim Smolka is a Senior Fellow and Director of the Latin American and the Caribbean Program and Co-chairman of the International Department at the Lincoln Institute of Land Policy. He graduated from the Pontifical Catholic University of Rio de Janeiro with an M.A. and then was awarded a Ph.D. in Regional Science from the University of Pennsylvania, USA. He was a Faculty Member and Professor of the Urban and Research and Planning Institute (IPPUR) at the Federal University of Rio de Janeiro, a co-founder and president of the Brazilian National Association for Research and Graduate Studies on Urban and Regional Planning (ANPUR). He has authored many publications on the functioning of urban land markets and in particular informal land markets and their consequences to regularization policies, on intra-urban structuring and the dynamics of property markets in Latin American cities.

Lawrence C. Walters is the Stewart Grow Professor of Public Management at the Romney Institute of Public Management, Brigham Young University, USA. His teaching includes courses on land and real estate taxation at the Institute for Housing and Urban Development Studies, Erasmus University, Rotterdam, Netherlands. He has over 40 publications on public policy and management topics, several of which have received national awards for excellence. He has just completed a property tax policy guide for developing countries sponsored by UN-Habitat and a book on managing 'wicked' environmental problems. He received his Ph.D. from the Wharton School at the University of Pennsylvania.

Kurt Zorn is Associate Vice-Provost for Undergraduate Education and a Professor in the School of Public and Environmental Affairs (SPEA) at Indiana University Bloomington. He also serves as Indiana University's Faculty Athletics Representative to the Big Ten and the NCAA. His research interests focus on state and local public finance, tax policy, transportation safety, economic development and gaming. He has conducted research, consulted and taught in the general area of tax policy and fiscal decentralization in a number of international settings including Egypt, Bosnia-Herzegovina, the Russian Federation, China and Taiwan and the United Arab Emirates.

Foreword

February 2012

The property tax is an important revenue source for local governments across the world, although the relative reliance on it varies widely. There are also substantial differences across countries in the structural and administrative components of the property tax. To operationalize the property tax requires a mix of choices regarding design issues such as: what property will be taxed – land, improvements, personal property; what is the basis of the tax – market value, rental value, area or something else; who will the tax be imposed on – owner or user; what will the tax rate structure be – a flat rate or rates that differ by value, type or location of property; and what options will be available to enforce collection, for example foreclosures. Developing administrative procedures involves addressing such tasks as: identifying the property to be taxed; determining the taxable basis of each property; identifying the taxpayer for each property; setting the tax rate or rates; invoicing the tax payer; and collecting the tax.

The chapters in this book explore in detail the choices regarding both the structure and administration of the property tax, drawing on the extensive knowledge that the authors have acquired in studying property taxes around the world. The chapters provide a wide-ranging treatment of the design choices and administrative tasks, both in terms of the breadth of design options and administrative tasks covered and the depth of the discussion. The authors describe the range of design choices, discuss the associated issues and the advantages and disadvantages for each and present the criteria to help choose among the options. Regarding administration, the chapters offer in-depth discussion of the administrative tasks and how they can be addressed efficiently and effectively. There is consideration of such extraordinary policy and administrative issues as the taxation of public leasehold property and informal settlements, the use of GIS technology and forecasting revenue capacity. Not only do the chapters provide extensive discussion of the options, they provide insightful discussions of implementation issues. The chapters are also rich in examples of the choices that have been made in various countries for each of these design issues and administrative tasks.

In Chapter 1, Harry Kitchen provides an introduction to, and an overview of, the property tax and an initial discussion of many topics and issues inherent with the property tax. Kitchen starts with a discussion of the role that the property tax should play in local government finance. Given the characteristics of the property tax, for example its relatively immobile base, Kitchen develops the argument that the property tax is the ideal tax for local governments. But, the primary focus of the chapter is on issues associated with the assessment of property and the setting of the tax rate. Determining the assessment involves a series of critical tasks. Kitchen discusses the importance of each of these tasks, the difficulties involved in accomplishing the tasks, the implications if the tasks are not appropriately carried out, and how the procedures actually used differ across countries. Kitchen then explores the issues associated with selecting the property tax rate structure (namely a flat rate, or rates that vary with type, use or value of the property), the tax rate (for example, which government should set the rate, should there be limits on the rate, etc.), and the economic consequences of these decisions. Kitchen provides a summary of the debate over the incidence of the property tax, namely the conflicting views that the property tax is a distortionary tax on capital or is a non-distortionary benefit tax, and the role of relief programmes in altering the distribution of the property tax burden.

The two aspects of the property tax that are perhaps most central to its implementation concern the choices over the types of property that are going to be taxed and the basis on which the tax liability is determined. Riël Franzsen and William McCluskey explore these key policy decisions in Chapter 2 in the context of value-based property tax systems. As Franzsen and McCluskey point out, there are many different types of property that might be included in the property tax base, many different ways that property value might be defined, for example, annual value, capital value, land value, etc., and alternative methods for determining market value. The authors provide an extensive discussion of the many issues associated with making decisions among these alternatives, along with a presentation of the advantages and disadvantages of each alternative. Franzsen and McCluskey explain the many conditions that must be present in order for a value-based system to be successfully implemented. To illustrate the options, the authors present many examples of the choice that specific countries have made.

Public finance economists and others who study the property tax have some 'ideal' system in mind that they use as a standard in evaluating existing property tax systems. It is not exactly earth shattering to note that to the extent decisions regarding the structure of the property tax are made by government officials who are influenced by the views of citizens; politics affects the policies associated with the property tax. In Chapter 3, Enid Slack considers the features of a good or ideal property tax system and describes how politics has resulted in a property tax that does not correspond to what students of the property tax consider the best structure. Slack explores why and how politics has influenced the design of the property tax and how its unpopularity has led to 'property tax revolts'. Slack discusses the policy choices that have been made as a result of these revolts and the resulting implications for the property tax systems. As Slack points out, this conflict between what is considered the ideal system and what politics demands must be recognized in designing or reforming the property tax.

A major issue that countries face is whether the property tax should be administered centrally or locally. This is a very important question since it goes to the heart of fiscal decentralization and to the quality of tax administration. In Chapter 4, John Mikesell extensively explores the advantages, disadvantages and experiences with centralized and decentralized administration of the property tax. He first considers the reasons why centralized administration might be preferred, giving examples of how various countries administer the property tax. He then discusses decentralized administration, giving examples of countries in which local governments have successfully administered the property tax. Based on his analysis Mikesell concludes that local administration is preferred, but points out the major dilemma associated with decentralization of administration, namely, the presumed greater competency associated with the central administration offset by the lack of incentive for the central government to perform well since there are no revenue consequences. The solution, in Mikesell's view, is to provide the training and technical assistance to local governments necessary for them to become competent.

Establishment of the tax rate or rates is a critical issue and involves addressing two questions. First, should the tax rate be set centrally or locally? Second, should there be one rate, or should the rate be allowed to differ between types, uses, ownership or value of property? These are the issues that Kurt Zorn addresses in Chapter 5, which also includes a survey of how these questions are answered in various countries. For each question, Zorn discusses the issues involved and presents the arguments for and against having the tax set centrally and having multiple tax rates. Zorn concludes that for fiscal decentralization to be successful, local governments need to have control over the property tax rate. Regarding the second question, Zorn comes down on the side of a one-rate system, pointing out how simplicity and transparency are compromised with classification systems.

Once the tax rate has been set, the next step in administering the property tax is the politically difficult one of collecting the revenue. Ultimately, the objective of the property tax system is the mobilization of revenue. Some see the key to collection being a mechanism for the enforcement of the collection of the revenue, e.g., penalties and ultimately foreclosure for non-payment. But in Chapter 6, Roy Kelly takes a much broader view of revenue collection and enforcement, positing that in performing all of the administrative steps, property tax agencies should view themselves as tax collectors. Kelly makes the case that the collection process should begin with property tax administration that is seen as efficient and high quality, that yields tax liabilities that are considered fair and equitable and that ends with the appropriate methods to enforce collection. Kelly identifies the steps that governments can take to improve the mobilization of property tax revenue, and provides rich details on how to design an effective property tax collection system, from assessing the tax liability to the process for seizing property for non-payment of the property tax. He also describes how various countries have done this, and points out the pitfalls to avoid in trying to implement such a system.

As Slack suggests in Chapter 3, scholars of the property tax can design an ideal property tax system but that actual systems differ from the ideal. Furthermore, changes come through reform of existing property tax systems rather than implementation of a new system *de novo*. Reforming existing tax systems is not a matter of waving a magic wand and transforming the current system into one that scholars consider the ideal. Jay Rosengard has thought deeply about not just what the characteristics of an ideal system are, but also about the practical aspects of reforming existing property tax systems. In Chapter 7, Rosengard explores how to go about reforming existing property tax systems, or in his words, how 'to make an existing property tax less taxing'. Rosengard discusses the primary rationales for reform, namely improving fiscal performance, social equity, economic efficiency and administrative cost-effectiveness, and presents four guidelines that should be followed in conducting property tax reform, for example, simple trumps optimal. He also discusses the principal strategic choices that reformers face. To assist those who might engage in a property tax reform, he documents the frequent mistakes in reforming the property tax and the common elements of successful reform, and presents a review of what has been learned from several attempted reforms. Rosengard notes that while there is no formula for ensuring success in attempting to reform a property tax system, past efforts provide guidance to future attempts.

While it is common for students of the property tax to think in terms of policies and administrative structures and procedures, it is important to realize that the property tax must be enshrined in law. What the law says about what is taxable property, about the definition of property, about the rights of taxpayers and so on has important ramifications for the performance of the property tax, including the consistency of the application of the tax, its fairness, bureaucratic discretion, and so on. In Chapter 8, Frances Plimmer explores the issues associated with enshrining the property tax in law and the relationship between the law, regulations and the desired outcomes of the property tax systems, including fairness, behavioural changes, economic growth and so on. These legal issues include the definition of property, the meaning of value, the identification of ownership, the application of tax relief and the treatment of land occupied by squatter populations (a topic discussed in detail in Chapter 12). As Plimmer points out, all aspects of the property tax must be contained in law, they cannot be inferred and the legislation must be such that the tax achieves the desired outcomes. Getting the tax right starts with getting the law right.

While the first eight chapters discuss practical aspects of the design of the property tax and its administration, Chapter 9, by Gary Cornia, provides an extensive discussion of the principles or criteria that should be used in deciding on how reliant a government should be on the property, and used as guides in designing property tax policies and administration. The list of criteria that Cornia provides goes well beyond the typical list of principles for a good tax that includes equity, efficiency and simplicity. Cornia's list adds such factors as the need for subnational governments to have a revenue source for which they can control the design and implementation; the need for revenue that is stable and permanent; and a tax that captures some of the benefits from improved infrastructure. These criteria are fundamental to decisions regarding the use and design of the property tax. Cornia develops the arguments as to why these criteria should be adhered to in designing or reforming the property tax, and discusses the advantages and disadvantages of the property tax in the context of the criteria.

The first nine chapters are concerned with relatively broad topics associated with the design, implementation and administration of the property tax. Chapters 10–15, on the other hand, each focus on relatively specific or specialized matters concerning the property tax. In the first of these chapters, Lawrence Walters explains how to estimate the revenue potential of the property tax. In a jurisdiction or country in which there are assurances that the value of taxable property is accurately measured, forecasting revenue or revenue potential is relatively simple. But in countries in which property escapes the tax net, or assessed values are not a reliable measure of actual property values, measuring revenue potential is much more complex and difficult. It is the task of estimating the potential revenue in such situation, both for the country and for local governments, that Walters considers in Chapter 10. After explaining the concepts of fiscal capacity and fiscal effort, Walters presents and discusses each of the steps – and the required data associated with each step – that are necessary to derive an estimate of the revenue potential of the property tax. Knowing the revenue potential of the property tax is important in evaluating the design and administration of the property tax, and thus the estimation methods that Walters presents are a key to the evaluation process.

Chapters 11 and 12 discuss the treatment of what might be considered unique property. In Chapter 11, Yu-Hung Hong considers the largely overlooked issue of the taxation of public leasehold property in transitional countries, while in Chapter 12 Martin Smolka and Claudia De Cesare consider informal property in developing countries. In transitional countries, it is a common practice to lease public property to the private sector. A major question is whether the government can impose a tax on such leased property. Consideration of this issue is complicated by the fact that there is substantial variation across countries in how lease payments are structured, including the relationship between the lease payment and market value, and whether the lease includes both land and improvements. Hong considers three significant issues associated with imposing property taxes on public lands and buildings that are leased to private firms and individuals. One of the basic issues is the conceptual consistency of applying a tax that is generally associated with private ownership of property to the lease of public property, and whether the public will find it acceptable and thus would actually pay the tax. The second issue is whether a tax on leasehold property would be borne by the private sector or would simply result in a reduction in lease payments. To address this question Hong presents a theoretical approach to the incidence of a tax on public leasehold property, noting that the answer depends on the extent to which the property tax is capitalized into the value of the leasehold property. The third issue that Hong explores is that taxing the lessee of public leasehold property requires valuing the lease and finding a way to establish taxable values using a technique equivalent to mass appraisal, an issue that has been given little previous attention. Hong notes that the value of the lease will depend on the terms of the lease, including its duration and whether rental value is based on fair market rent or the actual contract rent. Given the desire to use property taxation in transitional countries, Hong's analysis of these issues is important.

Major cities in developing countries contain large informal settlements, which pose difficult issues regarding the application of the property tax since tenure rights are at best obscure and the state of improvements is in continuous flux. In Chapter 12, Smolka and De Cesare document that process and magnitude of the development of informal settlements and then explore the questions and issues associated with applying the property tax to these settlements. Smolka and De Cesare address the many facets of the most basic of questions, namely should these properties be taxed at all, given the presumptions that residents do not have an ability-to-pay and that determining the property's value and assigning liability are impossible. Smolka and De Cesare explore the feasibility of taxing these properties and conclude that is both possible and desirable, and thus should be part of the property tax base. They develop the argument that a well-designed property tax system that is applied to informal settlements could be a part of a more effective urban policy. In particular, the tax revenue generated from the settlement could be devoted to the provision of infrastructure and public services in the settlements, which now receive little in the way of public services or government investments. In addition, the property tax could reduce the land distortions that are observed in informal settlements.

In the mid-19th century, state governments in the USA changed their property taxes from a mixed system of per unit and *ad valorem* taxes to one based on market value. However, over the past four decades alternative concepts of value have been adopted, such as value in use and acquisition value. And, as transitional and developing countries have adopted property taxes they have relied on non-market property tax systems. In Chapter 13, William McCluskey and Riël Franzsen explore non-market value property tax systems, describing each of the alternatives, discussing the advantages and disadvantages of each and providing details of how such systems function in several different jurisdictions. Non-market value systems, which include systems in which the tax is based on the area and/or the use of the property, are generally adopted when reliable market values are not available. The chapter also explores hybrid systems, for example banding and acquisition value systems, in which some monetary value other than current market value is used as the basis for the tax. While the major advantage of these systems is their simplicity, McCluskey and Franzsen point out the many drawbacks of such systems.

One of the primary objectives of property tax administration is to appraise property so that the resulting values closely reflect market value, and to do so in a cost-effective manner. The approach that is increasing being used to determine market value for property tax purpose is computed assisted mass appraisal (CAMA), which is the focus of Chapter 14, written by William McCluskey, Peadar Davis, Michael McCord, David McIlhatton and Martin Haran. The authors begin with a description of the main concepts that must be considered in using mass appraisal systems in general and CAMA in particular. There are many different modelling paradigms that can be used for property tax appraisal purposes. The authors explain each of these systems, which include automated appraisal systems including rule based expert systems, artificial neutral networks, fuzzy rule-based systems, multiple regression techniques, comparable sales analysis and adaptive estimation procedure. Multiple regression modelling is the traditional approach used in CAMA systems. The authors provide a real world example of the application of CAMA system that uses multiple regression modelling and discuss the issues that have to be addressed in using this technique.

Chapter 15 by Peadar Davis, Michael McCord, David McIlhatton and Martin Haran examines the use of geographic information systems (GIS) in appraising property. While most people who study property taxation have some sense of what GIS is, it is likely that few know how GIS can be incorporated in CAMA systems. This chapter assists in closing that gap, by providing an extensive discussion of the potential use of GIS in property tax appraisal and administration. After describing GIS, the authors explain how GIS can play an important role in CAMA systems. As they note, GIS systems are no longer just mapping methodologies, but now involve advanced analytical capabilities. Linking GIS and CAMA is not a trivial exercise, and the authors discuss the many issues associated with integrating GIS and CAMA. The authors describe the several benefits that GIS provides to appraisal systems, including increased efficiency and accuracy, and present an example that is helpful in seeing the benefit of using GIS in the mass appraisal of property.

David L. Sjoquist
Professor of Economics
and
Dan E. Sweat Scholar Chair in
Educational and Community Policy
Georgia State University

Introduction

William J. McCluskey, Gary C. Cornia and Lawrence C. Walters

For thousands of years, governments around the world have levied taxes based on land. It may seem odd, therefore, to include in the title of a book on property taxation the word 'primer'. Surely by now, it might be argued, governments understand how land and improvements can be taxed to achieve policy goals without introducing unreasonable burdens, distortions or inequities. Unfortunately, as is amply demonstrated in the chapters in this volume, such is not the case. In fact, governments across the globe are in one of three circumstances: they largely ignore taxes tied to land; they struggle to maintain efficient and effective property tax systems in the face of dynamic markets and political resistance; or they face the even more daunting task of building an effective property tax system where no such system currently exists. Increasingly, countries are coming to realize both the revenue potential and the policy advantages of land-based taxes. The result is that the countries in the first set are probably dwindling in number, while the latter two sets are increasing in size over time.

One observable result is that the variability across countries in property tax collections as a percentage of gross domestic product (GDP) is much higher in wealthy countries than it is in other countries. To be sure, the average reliance on the property tax is higher overall in wealthier countries. But this higher average masks the fact that collections range from nearly nothing in countries such as Kuwait, Luxembourg and Switzerland to well over 2 per cent of GDP in countries such as Canada, France, the UK and the USA. The performance of the property tax in middle- and low-income countries is much more consistent, but it is, for the most part, consistently low. Yields well below ½ per cent of GDP are very common and yields above 1 per cent of GDP are rare indeed.

Without question, advocates and administrators of the property tax in industrialized countries face very different challenges from their counterparts in developing countries. The variation observed among the world's wealthiest countries is certainly attributable in part to policy choices – many of which may have been made decades or even centuries ago. But such choices are also made in a context that is a product of the complexity associated with property tax policy and administration.

The basic idea underlying nearly all taxes on land is that the tax should be a function of the productive capacity of the land (and often permanent improvements). While historically capacity may have been measured in quantities of food or other commodities produced, it is now most frequently measured as capital market value (or some proxy), thus maintaining a clear conceptual link between taxable value and property productivity. But markets are dynamic and real estate values may move dramatically within short periods of time in response to changing market perceptions. Tracking these changes and incorporating them appropriately into estimates of taxable value are daunting administrative tasks requiring both human and financial resources and the political will to keep tax rolls up to date.

In many instances, these administrative functions are not carried out as effectively as they might be. As a consequence, official records containing key property information are not always complete and up to date. Even if records are current, dynamic market conditions, lack of resources and political resistance may combine to yield taxable values which are badly out of date and which no longer reflect current market judgments of property value. When property values are updated and taxes levied, those subject to the tax may launch time-consuming and expensive appeals and public protests. And for a variety of political reasons, policymakers may choose to overuse tax exemptions that erode the tax base. Ultimately, effective administration of the property tax requires the sustained commitment of a country's political leaders. Policy leaders must frame and sanction a sound and practical legal framework. They must commit sufficient resources to administer the system efficiently and effectively. Finally, they must uphold the administrative and judicial officials who are charged with levying and collecting the tax. The chapters in this volume describe best practice in both policy and administration, but these must be coupled with political commitment if the property tax system is to be seen as fair, and if it is to realize its potential as a revenue source.

The issues in middle- and low-income countries include all those facing more industrialized countries, especially concerns about the level of political support from senior political leaders. But their efforts are often complicated by additional unique challenges as well. In many instances, property rights are ambiguous by western standards, and formal systems for recording property rights are incomplete. Many such countries experience inadequate formal property markets and underdeveloped market-sustaining institutions (e.g. mortgage markets), limiting the ability to base taxable value on readily available market information. At the same time, many of these countries face rapidly increasing urbanization and growth in informal settlements. All too often, the resources to mount, reform or maintain a viable property tax system are severely lacking.

A recent UN-Habitat publication (Walters, 2011) stresses that implementing a practicable property tax system in such an environment should be informed by four considerations:

1. The system should reflect and be sensitive to the accepted institutions and traditions related to **land and property rights**. In this context, two distinctions are central. The first is whether land is seen as a tradable economic commodity or whether land is viewed as fundamental to achieving other basic human rights. The other important property right question is whether

or not individual private ownership of land is widely accepted. Given any combination, it is possible to design a workable property tax system, but these distinctions will affect who should be obligated to pay the tax and what options are available to administrators in pursuing tax avoiders.

2. Implementing a property tax system requires a fiscal cadastre, and a practical system must reflect the realities of the current formal and informal **systems for registering and defending land rights**. In many cases, this will require a fiscal cadastre that is separate from the legal cadastre. There are examples where less formal fiscal cadastres have provided a path for landholders to regularize their interests and transition to fully registered legal ownership. The key is to link as closely as possible the interests of the administrators and the taxpayers.

3. The property tax system should also attend carefully to **market conditions** in different locations and for different types of property. As noted previously, in many less developed countries, formal land markets are underdeveloped. In such cases, attempting to base the property tax on market values can only lead to frustration and failure. But there are other options as discussed in Chapter 2 by McCluskey and Franzsen.

4. The system must be designed with a thought to the **administrative capacity** of government agencies that will be charged with implementing the property tax. Overall administration will likely need to be divided between levels of government and between different agencies, as suggested in Mikesell's Chapter 4. And the information requirements for the system should be tailored to the resources available for administering the tax.

While the challenges of designing and implementing a property tax system are significant and vary somewhat based on the particular country context, ongoing tensions between certain aspects of the property tax and its administration also bear mentioning here. They are explored more fully in the chapters which follow. These tensions will arise in virtually every context and are not likely to be permanently resolved in any setting. Rather the balance must be revisited and renewed, perhaps with modifications, time and time again over the years.

The first such tension involves the balancing of administrative costs and operational effectiveness. The property tax is not a simple or inexpensive tax to administer. It requires expertise and judgment on the part of administrators. Even if governments employ private consultants to do much of the work of managing the cadastre, valuing property, generating tax bills and even collecting the tax, managing the system requires competent public employees with enough expertise to ensure that adequate quality is maintained. But there is always a temptation to increase the net yield from the tax by reducing administrative costs. Reassessment cycles are often delayed. Staff may not be as well trained as the job requires. Budgets for equipment and information sources may be cut back. In the short run, these may have both fiscal and political benefits, but they undermine the integrity and effectiveness of the system. Before long, values are out of date, cadastres are inaccurate, collection rates begin to fall and the system loses legitimacy in the eyes of the public.

A second source of tension lies in two competing political objectives. Public finance economists, including those represented in this volume, argue that transparency in a tax system leads to improved governance. Public officials are more accountable and responsive if the public understands clearly what the cost of government is and what each household is expected to pay. For this reason, the visibility of the property tax is often touted as one of its advantages. On the other hand, that very visibility often makes the property tax very unpopular, as Rosengard notes in his chapter. So there is a temptation to reduce the clarity of the property tax system by such practices as allowing valuations to become outdated or by using classification schemes that change the effective tax rate for different types of property. In the minds of some public officials, the property tax would be more politically acceptable to the public if it were less clear and visible. Thus, there is an ongoing tension between transparency and political acquiescence.

A third tension exists between the policy goal of promoting some degree of buoyancy in the tax system and a desire for certainty on the part of taxpayers. Faced with rising costs and expanding demands for service improvements, public officials are inclined to favour revenue sources which grow more or less automatically with the economy in a region. Failure to build in this buoyancy means that over time, the revenue source becomes less and less relevant as a foundation for funding services. Thus, property taxes based on escalating market values can be attractive because they yield additional revenue without raising the tax rate. The public, on the other hand, desires certainty. Businesses and households want to be able to predict with a high degree of accuracy exactly what their tax obligation will be in the future. Both businesses and households tend to favour stable valuations and stable tax rates. The tension becomes most clear and strident following revaluations or other significant adjustments in the property tax base. If public officials fail to adjust tax rates to hold revenues relatively constant, public protest is often the result. But even if rates are reduced overall, there may well be a significant tax shift between regions or property classes that affects some taxpayers much more than others. If this tension between a desire for buoyancy by public officials and a desire for stability by taxpayers is not recurring, it likely means that taxpayers have prevailed and the tax is losing relevance as a funding source.

The final tension to be mentioned is that between earmarking tax revenues for a particular purpose versus placing all funds in a common general fund. Experience suggests that public acceptance of a property tax is greatly enhanced if the public understands exactly what infrastructure or service improvements will result if the tax is paid. This argues strongly for earmarking the tax for those specific purposes. On the other hand, public finance theory tends to favour placing tax revenues in a general fund from which a broad range of public services can be funded. Such an approach grants to public officials greater flexibility in managing the affairs of government. In this instance, fostering public acceptance and support should perhaps trump finance theory more often than it does.

The chapters that follow are organized loosely around what some have termed the property tax revenue identity. This expression recognizes that the actual revenue collected through the property tax is a function of

- how the property to be taxed and its taxable value are legally defined
- how property is actually valued (valuation rate)
- what the tax rate is
- the proportion of the total property in a jurisdiction that actually appears on the fiscal cadastre (coverage) and
- the actual collection rate.

Of these five factors, three are the result of administrative practices: the valuation rate, the coverage and the collection rate. Defining the tax base and setting the tax rate are largely policy considerations. In the chapters that follow, some authors approach particular elements in this revenue identity, such as rate setting or collection practices (Chapters 1–6). Others paint with a broader brush and focus on policy issues or structural design considerations (Chapters 7–10). Finally, some of the chapters focus on more specialized topics, such as computer-assisted mass appraisal or how property owned by the government but leased to private entities should be treated by the tax system (Chapters 11–15). In combination, the chapters present a rich and detailed understanding of property tax practices around the world.

This brief discussion has pointed out that when local history and conditions combine with the inherent challenges in designing and implementing a property tax, variations in policy choices and administrative practices are inevitable. That some choices and practices are superior to others has also become apparent over the years. The purpose of this volume is to introduce the reader to both the options and the better alternatives, where possible. Selection and implementation of strategies and techniques will of course require some degree of adaptation to local conditions. And it might well be asked whether when all is said and done, a tax that only raises 1–3 per cent of GDP is worth the effort and political fallout. If the property tax is seen as a national tax, the answer may well be no. Income and value added taxes quite likely have higher yields with fewer administrative challenges, but as a mainstay in local revenue sources, the property tax is a critical element. Our strong belief is that the property tax represents a key element in providing a solid foundation and stable funding source for basic public services.

Reference

Walters, Lawrence, 2011, *Land and Property Tax: A Policy Guide*. Nairobi, Kenya: United Nations Human Settlements Programme.

1

Property Tax: A Situation Analysis and Overview

Harry Kitchen

Introduction

Property taxation is the backbone of municipal finance in most developed countries, and has been for some time. More recently, it has played an increasingly important role in financing local government services in a number of developing and transitional countries. Over the years, and regardless of the country, property tax has not been without controversy on a variety of issues and it still faces substantial controversy on a number of fronts. Many of these are discussed in this chapter, which is separated into a number of sections. The first lays out the role that property taxes should play in financing municipal services. The second provides data on the relative importance of property taxes as a generator of local revenue in a range of countries. Then we note the base for property taxation in the same countries. The next section covers a number of important and controversial issues in assessment including the identification of property; the importance of establishing uniform assessment practices; the responsibility for assessment; the frequency with which it should take place; the importance of an appeals mechanism; and mass appraisal as an assessment technique. Then we look at a number of issues around property tax rates, in particular, responsibility for setting the tax rate; limits on property tax rates; variable tax rates versus uniform rates; taxation of business properties; exporting the tax on commercial and industrial properties; property taxes and urban sprawl; responsibility for tax

A Primer on Property Tax: Administration and Policy, First Edition.
Edited by William J. McCluskey, Gary C. Cornia and Lawrence C. Walters.
© 2013 Blackwell Publishing Ltd. Published 2013 by Blackwell Publishing Ltd.

billing and collection; and other land and property related taxes used by local governments. Then we turn to the often mentioned and frequently maligned incidence of the property tax and whether property tax relief schemes should be used to remove some of the alleged regressivity of the property tax. The final three sections cover Senior the politics of the property tax; some speculations on the future of the property tax, and a final summary.

Role for property taxes

Local governments in every country supply a range of goods and services; from those that exhibit mainly 'private good' characteristics, such as water, sewage, solid waste, electricity, and some recreation, to those that exhibit mainly 'public good' characteristics, such as local roads and streets, street lighting and sidewalks, police and fire protection, neighbourhood parks, libraries, land use planning, sometimes social services and public education. For services with mainly 'private good' characteristics, individual beneficiaries can be identified, income redistribution is not a primary goal, and spillovers are unlikely to exist. For these services, user fees are the most appropriate financing tool. They are relatively easy to administer and, if properly designed, they are efficient, accountable, transparent and fair in their impact on taxpayers.

For services providing mainly collective or 'public good' benefits (specific beneficiaries cannot be identified), user fees are inappropriate. Instead, these should be funded from a local tax imposed on residents (or exported to the same extent services are) with necessary adjustments through the use of grants to account for spillovers; that is, benefits from these services that spill over into neighbouring communities should be funded from something other than a local tax. For services that are partially private and partially public, a combination of user fees and local taxes may be appropriate.

While there may be some debate over the criteria that should be satisfied in setting a local tax, it is generally agreed that the property tax meets the criteria for a good local tax better than the alternatives of personal income or consumption based taxes. Its tax base is largely immobile. Revenue is generally predictable and stable in that it does not vary with the cyclical swings in economic activity as much as personal income and consumption based tax revenues. The part of the tax that is on residential property is unlikely to be exported. It is highly visible and fair as long is it covers the cost of providing those services that provide collective benefits to the local community. If the property tax is a local tax only (senior levels of government not involved), harmonization problems and wasteful tax competition should not be a problem. A potential downside of a local property tax is that it may be more expensive to administer than other local taxes (income, sales, fuel, for example) that could be 'piggybacked' onto existing federal or regional taxes. This, however, may be a small price to pay if local governments are to have autonomy and flexibility in setting tax policy – important ingredients of responsible, efficient and accountable local governments (McClure, 2001; Bird, 2001; Bird and Slack, 2004b; and Bird and Bahl, 2008).

Importance of the property tax

Today, municipal or local governments in many countries – but not every country – rely on some form of property tax to generate revenues for funding local public services. The relative importance of the property tax, of course, varies from country to country. It depends on the range of services funded by the tax, the distribution of expenditure responsibilities between the local government and the senior levels of government, the relative importance of grants from senior levels of government, the ability of the local government to administer a local tax, and so on. Table 1.1 illustrates the importance of property tax revenues for 25 countries chosen from different parts of the world. In Built Environment Research Institute general, property taxes represent the highest percentage of local revenues in Organization for Economic Co-operation and Development (OECD) and Latin American countries, and the lowest percentage in Asian and central and eastern European countries. Countries in Africa tend to fall between these two extremes.

Choice of tax base

There is no uniform property tax base or method of assessment that applies in every country. In some countries, the tax base is land only. In a few countries, only buildings constitute the tax base. In most countries, however, both land and buildings are taxed. For an indication of where each tax base is used and its frequency of use, see Table 1.2 which lists the tax base and method of assessment in the same 25 countries as are reported in Table 1.1.

The basis for assessment is wide-ranging. In some countries, it is based on market value; in others, it is based on site value; and in others, it is rental value. In some countries, the value is based on building area and property area – this is referred to as unit value (Youngman and Malme, 2000). In a few countries, a mix of these approaches is employed. Since these assessment bases are discussed in a separate chapter in this book, they are not discussed in detail here. A simple observation from this comparison is that valued based assessment systems and market value, more specifically, are deemed to be superior to area based systems in countries where there are fully functional property or real estate markets. Here, market values can be determined. Where property or real estate markets are not fully developed such as in developing and transitional economies or where there are a number of impediments to their operation, area based assessment may be preferred. As these countries develop and real estate markets emerge, however, a move to a value based system is often their eventual goal compulsory acquisition.

Table 1.1   Reliance on property taxes by local governments

Countries	Types of property tax	Property tax as % of local revenues
OECD		
Australia	State land tax; municipal rates	37.7[1]
Canada	Property tax	53.3
Germany	Land tax	15.5
Japan	Fixed property tax	25.5
United Kingdom	Council tax (local tax on residential property); Business rates (central tax on non-residential property)	33.0[2]
Central and eastern Europe		
Hungary	Building tax; plot tax; communal tax	13.6[3]
Latvia	Real estate tax	18.2[4]
Poland	Urban real estate tax; agricultural tax; forest tax	9.7
Russia	Land tax; individual property tax; enterprise assets tax	7.0
Ukraine	Land payments and taxes	9.3
Latin America		
Argentina	Property tax	35.0[5]
Chile	Property tax	35.1[6]
Colombia	Unified property tax	35.0[7]
Mexico	Property tax	58.7[8]
Nicaragua	Property tax	6.4
Asia		
China	Urban and township land use tax; house property tax; urban real estate tax; farm land occupation tax	4.9
India	Property tax	7.0–41.0[9]
Indonesia	Land and building tax	10.7
Philippines	Real property tax	13.4
Thailand	Buildings and land tax; land development tax	1.4
Africa		
Guinea	Rental value tax on housing; local business taxes	32.0
Kenya	Property rates	15.0
South Africa	Rates on property	21.0
Tanzania	Local building tax; national land rents	4.0
Tunisia	Rental value tax on housing; tax on unbuilt land; local business tax	32.4

Notes:
[1] Includes only local taxation and not the state tax on land.
[2] Includes the local council tax and the local share of national non-domestic rates.
[3] Includes other local taxes such as a tourism tax.
[4] Percentage of local taxes.
[5] This refers only to the municipal tax. There is also a property tax at the provincial level.
[6] The property tax is a national tax earmarked for local governments; 40% of revenues remains with municipalities where property is located.
[7] Property taxes as a percentage of total Colombian local taxes.
[8] Percentage of municipal taxes.
[9] The range depends on the state.
Source: Bird and Slack (2004a)

Table 1.2   Tax and assessment bases

Country	Tax base	Basis of assessment
OECD:		
Australia	Land or land and improvements	Market value or rental value or combination
Canada	Land and improvements (sometimes machinery included)	Market value
Germany	Land and improvements; farm properties also include machinery and livestock	Market value (rental income/construction costs); area in former GDR
Japan	Land, houses, buildings, and tangible business assets	Market value
United Kingdom	Land and improvements; some plant and machinery	Market value for residential; rental value for non-residential
Central and eastern Europe:		
Hungary	Unimproved value (plot tax); buildings (building tax)	Area or adjusted market value
Latvia	Land and buildings	Market value
Poland	Land, buildings and structures	Area
Russia	Land for land tax; structures for property tax; assets for enterprise property tax	Area; inventory value of structures; value of assets
Ukraine	Land	Area
Latin America		
Argentina	Land and buildings	Market value
Chile	Land and improvements	Area by location for land; construction value for buildings
Colombia	Land and buildings	Market value
Mexico	Land and buildings	Market value
Nicaragua	Land, buildings and permanent improvements	Cadastral value
Asia		
China	Occupied land; land and improvements	Area; market value or rental value
India	Land and improvements	Mostly annual rental value; limited use of area and market value
Indonesia	Land and buildings	Market value
Philippines	Land, building, improvements and machinery	Market value
Thailand	Land and improvements (buildings and land tax); land (land development tax)	Rental value; market value

(Continued)

Table 1.2   (*cont'd*)

Country	Tax base	Basis of assessment
Africa		
Guinea	Land and buildings	Rental value
Kenya	Land (but can use land and improvements)	Area; market value; or a combination
South Africa	Land and/or improvements	Market value
Tanzania	Buildings, structures or limited development	Market value (or replacement cost, if market value not available)
Tunisia	Land and improvements (rental housing tax); land only (tax on unbuilt land)	Area; rental value

Source: Bird and Slack (2004a)

Issues in assessment

Regardless of the assessment base used, its success depends on five critical parts of the assessment process: identifying the property; achieving uniformity in assessment; responsibility for undertaking assessment; frequency of reassessment; and having an effective appeals mechanism. This section concludes with a discussion of an increasingly popular and productive assessment technique – mass appraisal.

Property identification

All taxable properties must be identified and described on the assessment roll with each property assigned a roll number. This number is important for linking assessment information with tax billing and property transfer records (Slack, 2001). The assessment roll or fiscal cadastre should include the address of the property, its owner, building and lot size in square metres (feet) or hectares (acres), a definition of property boundaries (using cadastral maps), the age of the building and information on renovations or improvements. This information will be used to assign an assessed value to the property, especially if the tax base is market value and the property has not recently been sold. Furthermore, this information should be reported in a consistent way and a process should be established to update assessment annually or as frequently as administratively possible. Once assessed values have been determined, local tax rates must be set, tax bills issued, responses must be made to assessment appeals, taxes must be collected, and arrears must be addressed.

Property identification is often difficult in developing countries and transitional economies (Dillinger, 2002; and Malme and Youngman, 2000). For example, maps for property identification may not exist; property ownership data may not be provided because of disputes over who owns what; information on improvements may be missing; building permit information may not be provided to the taxing authority; tax records may be identified by taxpayer and not by property; land and building records may be maintained by different agencies and not linked; computerized tax records may not exist because of the expense; and tax records may be considered secret (see many of the case studies reported in Bird and Slack, 2004a).

Uniformity in assessment

If property taxes are to be fair in their application, they must be based on assessments that are uniform within each taxing jurisdiction. Uniformity in assessment practices is especially important, for example, if the assessment base in a two-tier local government system is used to apportion the costs of upper tier services consumed by residents and businesses in the lower tier municipalities. Here, failure to assess all lower tier municipalities in a uniform manner will lead to inequities and distortions in local tax practices because the lower tier municipalities that are over assessed will very likely be taxed for public services used by those lower tier municipalities that are under assessed. Also, if a role of provincial/state/regional grants to municipalities is to redistribute income, then the assessed value of property within the municipality is likely to be the major, if not the sole, component of the grant base. If assessment practices are not uniform, the redistributive mechanism inherent in these grants will not work as intended.

Uniformity is most easily achieved when the assessment function is centralized at the regional/state/provincial level if not at the central or federal level. This is the practice in a number of countries reported in Table 1.3. At the very minimum, this means that all assessors must use a standard assessment manual where all details of the assessment practice and procedures are spelled out. As well, assessors should be required to attend training courses and pass clearly defined educational standards before becoming property assessors. This is the current practice in Canada as it is in other countries that have fully developed property assessment systems.

Uniformity in assessment means that all properties must be assessed in the same way; that is, residential, commercial, industrial, farm, government, properties of charitable organizations and not-for-profit agencies, and so on. In most countries, the practice of exempting certain properties or applying differential assessment rates to others lowers the tax base and creates potential problems. Lower assessment rates are often used to provide special treatment for farmland. This ranges from assessing farmland at its value as a farm rather than its value as land for other purposes (Canada, Japan and Mexico), to taxing farmland at lower rates (Colombia, India and Thailand), to exempting farm land from taxation (United Kingdom, Nicaragua, Guinea, South Africa, Tanzania and Tunisia), and a variety of other measures (Bird and Slack, 2004a).

Table 1.3 Assessment and appeals

	Responsibility for assessment	Frequency of reassessment	Appeals mechanism
OECD			
Australia	State government for state and local taxes	Different in each state; ranges from annual to 7 years	State commissioner; courts
Canada	Generally provincial	Different in different provinces	Provincial review board; provincial courts
Germany	Local government	By law, every 6 years (actually use price adjusted 1964 values)	Changes in standard assessment are rare
Japan	Local governments based on a uniform national formula	Every 3 years; annuxxally for business assets	Valuation Council and Review Committees
United Kingdom	Central government	No revaluations on residential; 5 years for non-residential	Valuation tribunals; High Court
Central and eastern Europe			
Hungary	Local governments	At local discretion; infrequent	n.a.
Latvia	Central government	Every 5 years	Head of local govt. council
Poland	Local governments (using information in central registry)	Annual	Local council; regional appeal board, Administrative Appeals Court
Russia	Central government	n.a.	No appeal mechanism
Ukraine	Central government – state tax admin.	n.a.	n.a.
Latin America			
Argentina	Provincial and local governments	Periodic adjustments	Formal appeal procedures at both govt. levels
Chile	National tax administration with local input	Between 3 and 5 years but often postponed	Internal Tax Service; Special Appeals Court on Property Valuation; Supreme Court
Colombia	Local governments	Every 5 years	Cadastral Division; petition tax administration
Mexico	State and local governments jointly	Annual	Fiscal authority; judicial branch
Nicaragua	National tax administration	Infrequent	n.a.

Asia			
China	Local tax office directly under the state council	Once a year for urban real estate tax	Committee
India	ILocal authorities; some state assessment authorities	Periodic revision of assessments	Appellate Authority; appeal against revision
Indonesia	Central tax department	Every 3 years (annual in cases of rapid development)	Objections to Directorate of Property Tax
Philippines	Provincial and Local governments	Every 3 years	Local and Central Boards of Appeal
Thailand	Local governments	Every 4 years	n.a.
Africa			
Guinea	Central government	n.a.	n.a.
Kenya	Local governments	Every 10 years, but generally longer	Objections handled by local councils
South Africa	Local governments	Every 4 or 5 years, but not always done	Valuation board and valuation appeal board
Tanzania	Local authorities (funded by central government)	Every 5 years (or longer if approved by Minister)	Appeals Tribunal
Tunisia	Urban municipalities within nationally set ranges	Every 10 years with annual updates	Appeals on tax rate categories

Source: Bird and Slack (2004a)

In some countries, special treatment is also accorded to managed forest lands (Canada and Poland, are two examples). This treatment takes a number of forms. In some Canadian provinces, for example, forest lands are exempt from property taxation; in others, they are taxed at a fixed amount per hectare; in still others their assessment is fixed in value (Kitchen, 2002).

There is also variation in the way in which mines and mineral resources are treated for property tax purposes. As with forest lands, they are sometimes exempt from property taxation, either because they are not assessed or because the property tax does not apply. Other times, mines along with underground improvements and minerals are assessed and subject to property taxation (Kitchen, 2002).

In some countries, special assessment rules apply to electrical, telecommunications and natural gas distribution systems; railway property other than land and buildings; and pipelines. Depending on the country and the utility, valuation may be based on assessed property value, gross revenue or gross receipts for natural gas, electricity distribution, cable television and other telecommunications; pipe length and/or diameter for pipelines; and length of tracks or tonnage per kilometre for railways. 'Rights of ways' owned by utilities and railways are sometimes taxed at a fixed rate per acre/hectare.

Most countries provide additional exemptions from property taxation. Some of these are mandated by senior levels of government and others are discretionary. Those that are most likely to be mandated include exemptions for properties owned and occupied by governments, universities, colleges, public hospitals, penal institutions, churches and cemeteries, and properties owned by charitable institutions. Public parks, roads, schools, public libraries, foreign embassies and property owned by international organizations also tend to be exempt from property taxes.

Exemptions create a number of problems or potential problems. First, they reduce the tax base and thus increase taxes on taxable properties or lead to a lower level and quality of local public services than would otherwise be the case. Second, for properties owned by senior levels of government, universities, colleges, public hospitals and penal institutions, payments-in-lieu of property taxes are often provided, although these payments are often less than the property taxes would be if they were permitted (Kitchen, 2002). Third, the policy of exempting properties or assessing them at a value that is less than other properties is discriminatory and unfair, leading to a mix of land use that may be different from the mix that would exist under equal treatment of all properties. If it is possible to make a sound case for the preferential treatment of certain organizations, then these organizations should be rewarded directly through a system of grants or through the application of differential tax rates (discussed below) applied to a uniform assessment base. In either case, such subsidization would be more transparent and subject to review and amendment by elected representatives according to their interpretation of the public interest (Kitchen, 1992).

Fourth, where owners/managers of taxed properties face higher costs than owners/managers of exempt properties, this differential will have implications for competition among businesses, and between businesses and government (Kitchen and Vaillaincourt, 1990). Fifth, differential tax treatment of properties almost always has a distortionary impact on location and other economic decisions made by firms and governments.

Because of problems such as these, virtually all suggestions for property tax reform have recommended that exempt properties be subject to full assessment so that the value of the exemption is known. For properties where payments in lieu of taxes are appropriate, the payment should be equivalent to the taxes that would be collected under a uniform and equitable property tax system. For exempt properties where payments in lieu are not appropriate, serious considera-tion should be given to terminating their exempt status unless it can be estab-lished that there is a worthy public policy interest in retaining the exemption.

To ensure that the assessment system operates effectively and fairly there are at least two things that must be avoided: capping or freezing assessment and utilizing preferential assessments. Capping or freezing is almost always a response to rapid increases in assessed property values. In fact, this was a major reason why two provincial governments in Canada (Nova Scotia and Prince Edward Island) imposed a freeze on property assessment. While this practice seems to be politically palatable in the short run, it is simply bad policy and bad practice. It leads to inequities and distortions during the period of the cap or freeze and it is inclined to have suicidal political consequences when the cap or freeze is removed. During the freeze, inequities exist because individuals whose property values increase relatively little pay proportionately more in property taxes than individuals whose property values increase by a larger proportion. This translates into the poor (as defined by property values) paying proportion-ately more and the rich paying proportionately less for local services.

Distortions may also arise because there is an incentive for individuals whose property values have increased the most to put pressure on local councils to increase expenditure, knowing that they will pay proportionately less to fund these additional services when compared with those individuals whose property values have increased very little.

After a cap or freeze is removed or properties are reassessed after a number of years, significant increases in some property values will be required to put all properties on a level playing field. This, in turn, will lead to more criticism, more complaints, the possibility, or even probability, of the province introduc-ing more bad policies and practices to, once again, calm the critics.

Finally, if property values are increasing quickly, property owners are better off. If they are better off, why should they not pay taxes to reflect this? If the concern is that these taxpayers are income poor even though they are asset rich, there are property tax relief schemes that are available to assist taxpayers. One that is becoming more and more important in some countries is a 'reverse mortgage' – the homeowner continues to live in the house and when the house eventually sells, back taxes plus interest on these taxes are paid. A more common option for rapidly fluctuating property values is to introduce a three-year moving average to smooth out rapid changes in assessment and property taxes. This is not without problems, however, because properties with escalating prices do not pay their fair share of taxes during the increase and they are over-taxed when properties are decreasing in value.

   Since uniformity in assessment is a critical component of any properly functioning assessment system, special treatment should not be granted to certain property types; in particular, waterfront and vacation properties should not be given special consideration as some ratepayer groups in Canada, for example, have been advocating. These properties should (must) be assessed in the same manner and on the same base as other residential properties in every municipality. To do otherwise would be to grant them favourable treatment vis-à-vis other properties, and unfairly lower their share of property taxes paid to fund local services. Generally, the response of special interest groups is that they do not receive as many services as the rest of the community. If this is true, the local council can and should use variable tax rates to capture service differentials.

Responsibility for assessment

Reliance on a centralized uniform assessment manual is critical, but the way in which the assessment is carried out may also be important. In Canada, for example, assessors work for a variety of employers. In some provinces, they work for the province; in others, they work for an independent province-wide assessment authority; in another province, they work for a province-wide non-profit corporation; and in a couple of provinces, municipalities hire their own assessors. Differences in the effectiveness of using local rather than provincial or region wide assessors has been studied in at least one US study where it was concluded that county or regional rather than local assessors produced more uniform residential assessments.

   In addition, a centralized agency (region-wide) responsible for assessment has a further advantage. It is able to benefit from economies of scale that might not be available to each municipality if each were to carry out its own assessment (Sjoquist and Walker, 1999). Alternatively, economies of scale might also be achieved by contracting out the assessment function (Bell, 1999).

   Table 1.3 shows the level of government responsible for assessment in 25 countries. In about half of these countries, the assessment function is essentially local, and in the other half, it is regional or central. Even where assessment is listed as a local responsibility, most of these countries do as they do in Canada – they work from a standardized assessment manual that is uniform across a province/state/region or country.

   In the majority of countries, responsibility for assessment rests with at least one level of government. In a few countries, generally those that are relatively poor with little tax administrative capacity, self assessment may be the practice. Here, property owners assess their own property and pay a tax based on this assessed value. Hungary, Tunisia and Thailand are examples of countries that have self assessment systems (for a discussion of self assessment systems, see

Bird and Slack, 2004a). A major problem with this approach is that unless there are significant and effective penalties for non-reporting and under-reporting, it is almost certain to lead to under estimates of property values with the more expensive properties carrying a higher rate of underestimation than lower price properties. Not only is this unfair, it erodes the size of the tax base leading to higher tax rates and/or lower levels of service than would otherwise be the case (Bird and Slack, 2004a).

Frequency of assessment

If the assessment base is to be fair and productive, periodic valuations and revaluations must be undertaken to ensure that assessment is kept up to date. In value based systems, a shorter time frame for reassessment is preferred because this helps in maintaining the legitimacy of the tax base and it reduces the risk of sudden and dramatic changes in tax burdens that often arise when reassessments are conducted sporadically and infrequently (Bird and Slack, 2004a).

Indexing the assessment base (between infrequent reassessments) to keep up with inflation, as is done in some countries, is not as equitable as conducting frequent property reassessments. Indexing all properties by the same factor (consumer price index or some other index) fails to capture the differential rates at which individual properties change in value. On the other hand, giving up some fairness may be a small price to pay if there are insufficient resources to conduct reassessments on a fairly regular basis. Furthermore, indexing that captures relative price changes by location and type of property could minimize some of the large assessment changes that might otherwise occur at the time when properties are actually reassessed.

Table 1.3 shows the range in the frequency of reassessing properties. Although there are exceptions, the legislated interval for reassessing properties is generally reported to be from 3 to 10 years. In practice, however, the interval is frequently longer. In Canada over the past decade, most provinces have moved to more frequent and up-to-date reassessments – some provinces now do them annually, most others every three or four years but many are moving towards annual reassessment.

Appeals mechanism

An important component of a well-run assessment system is an effective appeals mechanism. In other words, taxpayers should have an avenue for appealing their assessment if they feel it has been incorrectly determined. In most cases, this starts with a reassessment by the assessment authority to correct factual errors and resolve minor differences of opinion over the value of the property. If differences cannot be resolved, the taxpayer should be able to proceed to a higher authority, generally made up of valuation experts. In some countries, there may be a further stage whereby the appeal could go to a specialized tax court. Table 1.3 records the assessment appeals bodies in 25 countries.

Assessment technique

When reassessment based on market values is done frequently (yearly, every second year, or even every third year), it is not possible for property assessors to reassess each piece of residential property on such a frequent basis. This would require too many assessors and it would be too expensive. This shortfall, however, can be overcome with mass appraisal techniques for residential properties. Indeed, this approach is becoming more and more common in countries relying on frequent property reassessments.

Mass appraisal makes use of a multiple regression statistical package. It predicts the market value of properties from known values of other variables associated with these properties (such as living area, lot size, location, availability of garage, age of building, number of bathrooms, and so on). This technique examines properties that have actually sold and identifies the statistical relationship between a number of features of these properties and their selling price. This statistical relationship is used to estimate the price for properties that have not sold recently.

This approach does not eliminate the need for traditional property assessors and assessment practices. Indeed, property assessors are necessary for examining a certain number or properties yearly and for assisting in developing and improving the computer-assisted mass appraisal (CAMA) models that identify property features affecting price. Property assessors are also needed for assessing properties that display anomalies from the regular pattern and for handling property assessment appeals. What mass appraisal does do is to permit more frequent assessment updates without a physical inspection of all properties.

In many countries, assessment agencies now use software packages for mass appraisals. Where this technique is used, local assessors can quickly analyse thousands of sales and use this information to estimate market values for properties that have not recently sold. It has definitely improved the quality and frequency of reassessment and permitted municipalities to have much more up-to-date assessment rolls.

Summary

A uniform assessment system is necessary if one is to establish a tax base that is fair, transparent and accountable. Uniformity is more likely achieved if a few practices are followed. First, within a region, state, or province, all assessors work from a standard assessment manual that is updated frequently to reflect changing market conditions. Second, assessors should be required to pass specific education and training programmes on assessment practices and procedures. Third, although the evidence is sketchy, assessors working for centralized assessment agencies seem to be more successful (because they are more likely to work at arm's length) than those working for municipalities in achieving uniformity in assessment. Fourth, the more frequent the reassessment, the fairer the assessment system, leading to fewer surprises for taxpayers, fewer complaints and fewer appeals. Fifth, there should be an effective appeals mechanism in place to correct for perceived inequities in the assessment system. Finally, wherever possible, mass appraisal techniques should be used to improve the quality of the assessment system and to minimize the cost of the assessment process.

Issues with property tax rates

Assessment is the first major component of the property tax system and setting the local tax rate is the second major component. In countries where local governments set their own property tax rate, the first step is for the local government to determine its expenditure requirements or needs. The second step is for the local government to subtract all non-property tax revenues (grants, user fees, charges, permits and so on) from spending requirements, leaving the amount that is to be funded from the property tax. The third step is to divide the required property tax revenues by the property tax base to get the property tax rate. This rate, while easy to calculate, is not free of controversy, especially as it is applied in most countries. The following discussion covers a number of issues around tax rates.

Setting the property tax rate

In some countries, tax rates are set locally, although limits are sometimes imposed by senior levels of government; in others they are set by senior levels of government. In Japan, Latvia, Ukraine, Chile, Nicaragua, China, Thailand, Guinea and Tunisia, rates are basically set by a senior level of government. In Hungary, Poland, Russia, Colombia and the Philippines, rates are set by local governments but within limits imposed by a senior level of government (Bird and Slack, 2004a).

On the established theme that the most transparent, efficient and accountable local government is one that is responsible for raising its own revenue, it follows that local governments should be responsible for setting their own tax rates. Failure to permit and require this means that the close link between decisions over revenue generation and expenditure decisions is lost. In those countries where the tax base is determined by an independent assessment authority or where it is the responsibility of a senior level of government, responsibility for local rate setting is particularly important.

Where a two-tier system of local government exists and where both tiers rely on the property tax, the upper tier should set its tax rate independently of the tax rate set by the lower tier. For each level of government, the tax rate should be high enough to generate sufficient revenues (beyond those generated by user fees, grants from senior levels of government, and other local revenues including permits, licences, and so on) to cover the cost of local public services that each level provides. Each tier should also use variable tax rates (described below) if service levels and standards vary across the municipality or jurisdictional area.

Limits on property tax rates

The practice of imposing tax limits on municipal governments by a senior level of government is more prominent in some countries than in others. In the USA, for example, a number of state governments have imposed limits on tax rates for local government (O'Sullivan, 2001; Brunori, 2007). In Canada, provincial governments have not placed limits on the general municipal tax rate although some provinces have legislated the amount by which commercial/industrial tax rates must differ from the residential rate.

Limits on tax rates are intended to control and restrict the growth in municipal government spending and hence, property taxation. Recent research on the success of these limits has addressed three main questions. First, have property tax limits reduced property tax revenues? Based on the evidence, the answer is yes. Property tax revenues have declined in constant dollars if not in current dollars. In California, proposition 13 led to an immediate decrease of about 45 per cent. In Massachusetts, the initial impact was a decrease of 18 per cent (Clemens *et al.*, 2003). Overall in the USA, it has been estimated that local property taxes per capita fell by 3 per cent after tax limits were imposed (Shadbegian, 1999).

Second, have reductions in property tax revenues been offset by increases in other local revenues? The evidence here is not as compelling but it does indicate that other local revenue sources have generally been substituted for property tax decreases (O'Sullivan, 2001; Brunori, 2007). Greater reliance is now placed on local user fees, permits, licences, and so on.

Third, have property tax limits affected input choices (administrative staff versus service providers such as police officers and firefighters) and quantities of output produced by local governments? The evidence here is mixed. Some studies found that local governments responded to tax limits by cutting proportionately more of their administrative costs while others found that local governments responded by cutting proportionately more of their service costs. Similar variations in results were noted for output. Some studies found that municipalities produced roughly the same quantity of services with less revenue while other studies noted that private sector provision had replaced public provision of local services (O'Sullivan, 2001).

Property tax limits also have another major impact. They curtail the decision-making power of municipal governments because they reduce the municipal sector's flexibility and capacity to raise its own revenue. This is particularly worrisome if it means that local governments cannot provide sufficient revenues to provide local public services that are desired or wanted by local citizens.

Analytical arguments supporting property tax limits for local governments are generally weak unless, of course, they are necessary to prevent property tax exporting (discussed below). This arises when local governments levy higher taxes on industries, believing that the ultimate tax burden will be borne by non-residents (Boadway and Kitchen, 1999).

In general, however, locally elected councils should be responsible for setting local property tax rates. They are in the best position to determine what citizens want and need. Furthermore, if these councils are unresponsive to local wishes, they are likely to be voted out of office at the next municipal election. Also, the comparatively large number of municipalities in every country means that local tax rates are set in a competitive environment; that is, every municipality is aware of its neighbouring jurisdiction's tax rates and unwilling to have its rate differ noticeably from its neighbours for fear of losing businesses and people. The literature tells us that property tax differentials play a role in intra-regional location decisions – hence the reason why municipal governments compete with their neighbours to control property taxes. This tax competition works to control tax rates and it permits the municipality to make its own spending and taxation decisions without the restrictive controls of a senior level of government. Finally, the implementation and use of municipal performance measures would be much more effective and efficient in controlling the spending behaviour of local governments than are tax limitations.

Variable tax rates versus uniform rates

The issue here is whether a local taxing jurisdiction should apply a single uniform property tax rate to all properties within its taxing jurisdiction or whether different (variable) tax rates should be used, that is tax rates that vary with the cost of servicing different properties by type or by location within a municipality or rates that may vary for other reasons. The evidence suggests that a number of countries have one tax rate for all properties. Others have tax rates that differ by property class, or that differ by assessment practices, or that differ because of tax relief for specific classes of property (Bird and Slack, 2004a). In most cases where variable rates are used, properties are assessed at a uniform percentage of market value (100 per cent, or 80 per cent, or some other fixed percentage) and differential rates are applied to the assessed values. In a few countries – the Philippines, for example – differentiation is achieved by applying a uniform tax rate to properties that are assessed at different percentages of value (Guevara, 2004).

Many countries have introduced, perhaps unwittingly, differentiation through the use of graduated tax rates. This has been achieved by exempting low-value properties from taxation, or as in some provinces in Argentina, by using tax rates that increase with the value of the property (Rezk, 2004). Rural parts of some countries have attempted to apply progressive land taxes to the property holdings of individuals. This has generally failed because of administrative difficulties in assembling the information, especially when the landowner owns property in different jurisdictions. Achieving differentiation in any way other than through differential tax rates leads to a property tax system that is less visible, and therefore less accountable and transparent, and considerably more difficult to understand than one that assesses all properties in a uniform manner and applies differential tax rates.

Traditionally and historically in Canada, as in most other countries with a history of property taxation based on property values, the practice has been to apply a single tax rate to all residential properties and a higher tax rate to commercial and industrial properties. More recently in Canada, but not everywhere, this practice has changed. All municipalities in the provinces of Alberta, British Columbia and Ontario are now permitted to use variable property tax rates. Some other countries have also moved in this direction.

Variable tax rates should be designed to capture cost differences across properties, property types and municipalities or neighbourhoods within a city (municipality) or city-region. For example, if some properties or property types are more expensive to service, a case can be made for using differential property tax rates. Here, higher tax rates are assigned to properties that are more expensive to service.

Variable tax rates have a number of advantages (Slack, 2002a; Kitchen 2002). First, they are fair on the basis of benefits received as long as the rates are set to capture the cost of municipal services used up by different property types or property location. Second, they are efficient if designed to recover the cost of local public services consumed – no incentive would exist for a household or firm to alter its behaviour or location to avoid the tax as long as it matched the cost of services used up. Third, they are efficient as long as higher tax rates apply to tax bases that are most inelastic in supply. Since residential property has an inelastic tax base when compared with commercial and industrial property (it can move to other municipalities and to other countries), this calls for higher tax rates on residential properties than on commercial and industrial properties, a practice that is almost never followed as is noted in the next section. Fourth, variable tax rates have a further advantage in that they could be used to distort decisions deliberately to achieve certain municipal land use objectives. For example, if higher tax rates slow development, and lower tax rates speed up development, a deliberate policy to develop certain neighbourhoods instead of others might be achieved through different tax rates for different locations.

Taxation of business properties

The taxation of business properties (commercial and industrial) at higher tax rates than residential properties is a common practice across countries (Bird and

Slack, 2004a). Not only does it consist of higher property tax rates on these properties, it often consists of a number of other property related charges that have no relationship to services received or to property value.

Higher property taxation of commercial and industrial properties is generally done in one of two ways: either through the practice of assessing business properties at higher values than residential properties with the same tax rate applied to both property types; or through the simple application of higher tax rates on business properties. Higher taxation of business properties creates a number of efficiency and equity concerns. Efficiency in municipal service levels will not be achieved if revenues collected from property taxes on business properties are used to subsidize services consumed by the residential sector. Since service levels in any municipality are driven primarily by the demands of the residential sector (they vote), their subsidization means that the residential tax rate will be less than it would be in the absence of the subsidy, and an oversupply of municipal services could follow. Equity is not achieved either if those benefiting from the services are not paying full costs.

This heavy taxation of the non-residential sector has been addressed in three Canadian studies that compared the property tax paid by non-residential properties with the cost of municipal services consumed by these properties. All studies (Kitchen and Slack, 1993; KPMG, 1995; MMK Consulting Inc., 2004) found that the residential sector, when compared with the non-residential sector, is the recipient of proportionately more benefits from local government services (social services, elementary and secondary education, libraries, recreational facilities, etc.). The studies concluded that, when combined with higher effective property tax rates paid by the non-residential sector, the commercial/industrial sector is over-taxed and the residential sector under-taxed. Beginning in 1995, the city council in Vancouver (Canada) did something to correct this. It shifted, over the ensuing five years, some of its tax burden from the commercial and industrial sector onto the residential sector. More recently, the provincial government in Ontario announced that tax increases beyond the range of fairness (Kitchen, 2002) – established as a standard that is defined by taking the ratio of commercial/industrial taxes to single dwelling residential property taxes – must be imposed on the residential sector and not on the commercial/industrial sector.

At least one study in the USA found similar results. Specifically, it was estimated that the 'business related' share of combined state and local expenditures in the USA is about 13 per cent, although there is considerable variation from state to state (Oakland and Testa, 1995). These businesses, however, pay proportionately more of the state and local taxes.

Further concerns with the over-taxation of the commercial/industrial sector arise because this tax represents a fixed charge that must be paid. The tax is fixed in the sense that it is unrelated to the value of municipal services used or profits earned. As long as the tax rate is more than necessary to cover the marginal cost of municipal services consumed or if there are no economic rents for it to capture, resources will be allocated inefficiently. This over-taxation of the non-residential sector can lead to less economic activity, lower output, fewer jobs and a less competitive business environment (Ottawa, 1998).

There is also an issue of whether this over-taxation plays a role in location decisions. Since firms and businesses generally locate where they can maximize their profits, the provision of fiscal inducements such as lower property taxes can influence a firm's location decision in the same way as the reduction in other production costs may play a role. The impact of property tax differentials depends on a number of factors including the size of the differential between competing municipalities and whether this differential is sufficient to offset differentials in other costs or market factors.

While it is uniformly accepted that the cost of doing business is an important factor in location decisions, there is less consensus on the role played by property taxes in this decision. The evidence, most of which is drawn from the USA, suggests that property tax differentials are relatively unimportant in inter-municipal or inter-regional location decisions but do play an important role in intra-municipal or intra-regional location decisions (Kitchen and Slack, 1993). Higher effective property tax rates on commercial and industrial properties in one municipality within a region or area when compared with neighbouring municipalities create incentives for firms and businesses to locate in the lower taxed municipalities. In the extreme, one might expect these property tax differentials to produce a heavy (why not total?) concentration of firms and businesses in the lower taxed jurisdictions. In other words, intra-municipal tax competition could be potentially destructive if it led to a race to have the lowest tax rates. A study on municipalities in the province of British Columbia (Canada) examined this issue and concluded that while there is some evidence that municipalities react to tax increases of their neighbours, there is no widespread destructive competition for capital (Brett and Pinkse, 2000). Similar studies in the USA, however, have concluded that property tax competition among neighbouring municipalities is much more prevalent and widespread (Brueckner and Saavedra, 2001).

In reality, the extent to which firms and businesses respond to property tax differentials depends on many factors. These include, for example, the importance of being in the core of the region or area for business reasons; the opportunity to shift the tax differential on to consumers (of the final service or product), employees and owners; and the enhanced amenities that may be offered by a 'downtown location.'

In a US study of individual office buildings in downtown Chicago, it was found that 45 per cent of property tax differentials was shifted forward onto tenants as higher gross rents per square foot and 55 per cent was borne by owners (McDonald, 1993). The reality that some firms are willing to pay a premium to locate in the downtown core suggests that those firms benefit from 'economic rents' created by that location. For example, large financial institutions may benefit from a downtown location. Taxing these rents is efficient from an economics standpoint because it will not impact on the location decision. It is difficult to know, however, the extent of the economic rent. In other words, it is difficult to know at what rent (or property tax) a firm will choose to move out of the downtown location.

There are at least two more positive effects that would arise from shifting the relative tax burden away from the business sector (Damus *et al.*, 1987; Devarajan *et al.*, 1980). First, a reduction in the relative property tax burden on this sector reduces the potential for exporting the property tax to non-residents (see discussion in the next section). Second, since there is some evidence suggesting that capital invested in real property is, on average, taxed at higher rates than capital invested in other factors of production, at least in Canada, the variation in capital tax rates is reduced if this burden is altered. On balance, the reduction in tax exporting and the decrease in the variance in tax rates could result in an improved allocation of resources for the Canadian economy as a whole and overall efficiency gains (Economic Council of Canada, 1987).

A major defence of the over-taxation of business properties is provided by municipal officials and some taxpayers and it is as follows. Since businesses can deduct all expenses incurred in earning income (including business taxes) for their corporate income tax base, and since owner-occupiers of residential dwellings are not allowed similar deductions, it has been suggested that an extra tax on business is legitimate in that it attempts to even out the disparities in taxes that would otherwise exist on these two different categories of taxable property. While it is true that owner-occupiers are not able to deduct property taxes, it is also the case that owner-occupiers are not required to include in taxable income either imputed income from their owner-occupied dwellings or, in most countries, capital gains earned on the disposal of their principal residences (Boadway and Kitchen, 1999). Such exclusion is similar to a deduction from income for tax purposes (as in the case of the tax on businesses) in that both reduce the taxable economic income of the taxpaying unit. On this basis, it is difficult to make a case for a higher tax rate on commercial and industrial properties.

Concern over the kinds of distortions noted above with the property tax on commercial and industrial properties has prompted at least one suggestion for reform in Canada (Bird and Mintz, 2000; Bird and Slack, 2004b; Bird and Wilson, 2003). Specifically, it has been argued that revenues from a portion of the non-residential property tax should be replaced with revenues from a new business value tax (BVT). This BVT would be a value-added tax. It would be levied on business income. It would be on production and not consumption. This would make it an origin-based, not a destination-based tax; hence, it would tax exports and not imports. Further, it is suggested that it be a provincial tax, with municipalities having the opportunity to set local rates that are 'piggy-backed' onto the provincial rate. The province could even impose limits on local surcharges to prevent excessive locational distortions. Because the BVT is a value-added tax (essentially sales less cost of goods purchased), it would eliminate a number of the distortions created by the current over-taxation of business property. This type of local business tax is used in Germany and Japan.

Exporting commercial and industrial property taxes

The opportunity for the commercial/industrial sector to export its property tax burden onto residents of other municipalities has the potential for misallocating resources and lowering municipal accountability. Of course, the ability of a firm to export will depend on the elasticity of demand for the exported product.

Tax exporting refers to situations in which some portion of the local tax burden is borne by people who live elsewhere, either through a change in relative commodity prices or in a change in the net return to non-locally owned factors of production (inputs in the production process). For example, if higher effective tax rates on commercial and industrial properties lead to relatively higher prices charged on the sale of that community's exports to other communities, the taxing jurisdiction will have effectively shifted part of its tax burden onto residents of other communities. If the commercial/industrial property tax in every jurisdiction is exported to some extent, those jurisdictions exporting relatively more of the tax will be better off than those jurisdictions exporting relatively less. In particular, if the burden of this tax is shifted from residents of high income jurisdictions to those of low income jurisdictions, the distribution of income among jurisdictions is worsened. Furthermore, this runs counter to equalization schemes of senior levels of government that are aimed at redistributing resources (income) from relatively high income jurisdictions to relatively low income jurisdictions.

There is limited evidence on tax exportation. One Canadian study on a sample of large municipalities in Ontario is somewhat dated (Thirsk, 1982) but it is all that we have. It concluded that the degree of exportation ranged from a low of 16 per cent of the commercial/industrial tax burden to a high of 106 per cent. More than this, relatively rich municipalities had relatively high exporting rates whereas relatively poor municipalities had relatively low tax exporting rates. This tax exporting resulted in an implicit transfer from relatively low income municipalities to relatively high income municipalities.

Furthermore, when the commercial/industrial sector exports its tax burden, municipal government accountability is weakened because the direct link between the municipal government responsible for local services and the ultimate person/agency/body paying the tax is missing.

Property taxes and urban sprawl

Since the tax is levied on property, any investment that increases the value of the property (such as any improvements including an increase in density) will subject it to a higher tax. For this reason, higher property taxes are expected to discourage density. If, on the other hand, higher property taxes reflect higher levels of service, it is unlikely that there would be any impact on location or land use. To the extent that the allocation of service costs is based on property values and not on services consumed, some taxpayers pay more or less for services than the benefits they receive.

An extensive literature in Canada and the USA suggests that spatial factors do affect the costs of development (Marchand and Charland, 1992; Transit Cooperative Research Program, 1998; Brueckner, 2001). In particular, the density of development and its location with respect to existing services influence the costs of providing services. For example, 'hard' services such as sidewalks, roads and water and sewer mains cost less to provide in denser neighbourhoods. With water, a pipe is laid down the centre of a street and individual service lines extend from the water main to each building. In high-density neighbourhoods, there are more dwelling units per kilometre of water main over which to spread the costs. Furthermore, increasing the distance from central infrastructure facilities such as water and sewage treatment plants will increase costs.

An efficient property tax would thus reflect the higher costs associated with providing services in less dense developments. This would generally mean that property taxes based on services received should be higher in suburban municipalities than in the core. If property taxes are higher in the core and service provision less costly, the property tax creates an incentive to move to less dense developments (Slack, 2002b).

Responsibility for property tax billing and collection

Before property taxes may be collected, each taxing jurisdiction is generally responsible for making sure that the tax role is prepared, tax liability is established for each property (the tax bill) and ensuring that the tax bills are distributed to all property owners. In some countries, these functions are all handled by the jurisdiction that sets the tax rate. In other countries, municipalities set their own tax rates with the remainder of the activities handled by another level of government (regional or state) or a private sector institution (banks, for example). To illustrate, the tax role is often prepared by a region-, state- or province-wide agency (discussed above); tax billing and collection are often done by the taxing jurisdiction but there is no reason why this need be the case. Tax billing and collection benefit from economies of scale; hence, these two functions could be handled by a private sector institution or by a larger unit of government. In the province of Ontario in Canada, for example, all regional and county governments (upper tier) set their own taxes independently of the tax rates set by the local municipalities (lower tier). The local municipalities then send out combined tax bills and collect both upper and lower tier taxes. This practice has been around for years and has been fiercely defended in the face of proposals to migrate billing and collection to the upper tier in order to take advantage of economies of scale. Furthermore, billing and collection is an administrative function and has nothing to do with policy setting or decision making; hence, there is no reason why billing and collection need to rest with the taxing jurisdiction that sets the tax rate.

Tax collection is usually, but not always, a local government function. If the property tax is not paid by a specific due date, interest charges and a late-payment penalty are generally charged. If payment is not forthcoming after a considerable period of time, the property may be seized and sold to pay all delinquent taxes and penalties. Such sales are rare, however. A more effective enforcement mechanism, especially in countries with well defined legal systems for property ownership and transfers, involves preventing the transfer of legal title to the property (either through a sale or gift) until all past property taxes and penalties have been paid.

Tax arrears can be a serious problem for some countries because they lower the revenues generated by the property tax. The larger the uncollected taxes, the lower the effectiveness of the property tax system in generating revenues to fund local public services. Large tax arrears create higher taxes on those properties that pay their taxes and/or lead to fewer local public services than should otherwise be the case.

Other land and property related taxes used by local governments

In addition to the property tax, there are a number of additional land based taxes that are employed in virtually every country. The range of charges is extensive. It includes development charges, special assessments and value capture levies on the property tax base for financing local infrastructure. It also includes land transfer taxes, capital gains taxes, stamp duties, inheritance taxes, value-added taxes, and so on. Except for the first three listed above that have fiscal merit, there is no solid economic rationale for the rest.

One that is fiscally appropriate is often called a development charge, or lot levy, or exaction. It is used to recover the off-site costs of capital infrastructure required to service new development or growth. Where these are used, they almost always include the growth-related cost of infrastructure for water supply, sewage treatment, trunk mains and roads. Depending on the country and municipality, they may also include growth-related infrastructure costs for general administration, police, fire, recreation and cultural facilities (Kitchen, 2002).

A development charge or lot levy corresponds best to the benefits-received principle when the costs and benefits of the infrastructure for each property can be determined. An efficient development charge must cover the full cost of delivering the service: a capacity component which covers the capital cost of constructing the facility, plus a location or distance/density charge that reflects the capital cost of extending the service to properties or neighbourhoods.

The most efficient development charges are those that vary by type of property (residential, commercial or industrial), neighbourhood and distance from source of supply, so that each charge captures the extra cost of the infrastructure required to service the new growth. Most Canadian municipalities, however, do not use variable charges. Instead, they impose identical charges on all properties of a particular type, regardless of location. While administratively convenient, this practice levies the same charge on residential dwellings in low-density neighbourhoods as on it does on residential dwellings in high-density neighbourhoods. This occurs even though the marginal cost per property of infrastructure projects in low-density areas is higher, which can lead to urban sprawl (Slack, 2002a). Likewise, similar charges to properties that absorb different amounts of resources, because of factors such as terrain or soil type, will encourage development in the wrong places. While it may be naive to expect municipal officials to calculate the infrastructure cost for each new property, costs could and should be calculated for each new development area or neighbourhood, to discourage inefficient patterns of development (Kitchen, 2006).

The second type of charge that has fiscal merit is some form of special assessment or land betterment tax that has the capacity to collect taxes from property owners who are beneficiaries of specific local public services. In the USA and Canada, these charges are common; elsewhere, they are far less common. A special assessment is a specific charge added to the existing property tax to pay for improved capital facilities that border on them. The charge is based on a specific capital expenditure in a particular year, but may be spread over a number of years (Tassonyi, 1997). Projects financed in this way include construction or reconstruction of sidewalks, streets, water mains or storm sewers. The justification is that an owner of an abutting property will benefit from the local improvement and should, therefore, help fund it.

Municipalities use several types of special assessments, and the correctness of the apportionment depends upon the base for assessment. The most common base, foot frontage of each benefiting property, is appropriate for projects whose cost per property increases with the width of the lot. For projects such as parks, whose benefits accrue to particular areas or blocks within a community, the best approach may be zone assessment, under which all properties in the serviced area pay the same share. Other possible bases for special assessments, such as lot size, or charging each property based on their increase in value, are less satisfactory than foot frontage and zone assessments. A sensible approach is to split the cost of improvements that benefit an abutting property and the public at large by charging the bordering properties, for example, 40–60 per cent of the total construction costs, with the municipality raising the balance. The challenge is to match the share assigned to abutting properties with the marginal benefit to those properties.

The third type of charge is a value capture levy. It can be designed to recover the increase in land value arising from a public investment. Municipal spending on public infrastructure and subsequent zoning decisions can increase the commercial value of holdings of private landowners. Value capture levies are justified if the public investment creates windfall gains for the private developer. The levy permits the municipality to capture (some of) the economic rents accruing to the private sector that have been created by this local infrastructure spending.

The value may be captured in a variety of ways including a requirement that the developer provide various facilities and infrastructure or cash, in return for being permitted to undertake the development that the new municipal infrastructure facilitates and makes profitable. Value may also be captured through a tax on commercial revenues generated by property abutting the infrastructure. Alternatively and more likely, a special annual tax on property could be levied on value added (Tassonyi, 1997). This would be relatively easy to implement and administer, although care would be required in estimating the value added to the property as a result of the public infrastructure (Kitchen, 2008). Value capture levies are most suitable for mega-projects such as rapid transit expansion. Also, large developers could negotiate to provide transit construction improvements.

The other charges noted earlier in this section that municipalities sometimes use are much more difficult to justify on any kind of benefits based principles. Land transfer taxes, for example, may be relatively easy to administer, but they are a very bad local tax. A land transfer tax is levied at the time of sale of a property and usually is calculated as a percentage of the value of the property transferred. The tax, which must be paid before the transfer is registered, is like a sales tax payable by the purchaser and is calculated as a percentage of the purchase price. A number of variations on land transfer taxes exist. For example, the tax rate sometimes increases with the value of the property; in some cases, taxes are higher on non-residents.

Since this tax bears no relationship to the benefits received for local services, it imposes a burden on those who buy property, while placing no burden on those who remain in their existing property. Not only is this tax unfair in its distributional impact, it reduces house sales and house prices and impedes household mobility (Dachis *et al.*, 2008). The tax also provides an incentive for those who remain in their houses to demand municipal services knowing that they will be disproportionately paid for by those who buy property.

Like the land tax, most of the remaining charges bear no relationship to the value of local public services consumed by the owners or occupiers of different properties. A major problem with overcharging properties for local public services is the distortions and inefficiencies that are created, many of which are described above. Also, these charges will, in all likelihood, lead to lower business investment, reduced economic activity, and fewer jobs than could otherwise be the case. This is not a desirable outcome, especially for developing and transitional economies who are trying to grow and improve their standard of living.

Incidence of the property tax

The legal incidence of the property tax is on the owners of real property. The emphasis in this chapter, however, is on economic incidence – the tax's final resting place. Every tax creates an incentive for those paying the tax to try and avoid it, either by attempting to shift its burden to another economic agent (for example, from the owner to the tenant in the case of rental properties or from the producer to the consumer or the factor of production in the case of the tax on commercial and industrial properties) or by shifting resources into other, less heavily taxed activities, or by shifting one's activity to other, less heavily taxed jurisdictions. The following discussion focuses on who pays the property tax and a range of property tax relief measures that are used in a number of countries.

Who pays it?

Local council meetings, taxpayer discussions and newspaper reports on local government revenue issues frequently focus on the incidence of the property tax and more specifically, on its so-called regressivity – a tax is regressive if it absorbs a greater percentage of the income of lower income individuals or households than of higher income individuals or households. Indeed, most municipal officials, taxpayers and some analysts believe that the property tax is regressive, though a number of studies have disputed this. Determining the incidence of the property tax, or of any tax, is an empirical matter, and any empirical study of the property tax must begin with assumptions about the tax's distributional impact on taxpayers. These assumptions can be derived, however, only after one has decided on the role for the property tax (see Dahlby, 1985, for an excellent summary of the assumptions used in the tax incidence literature and how these assumptions affect the incidence pattern). Is it a benefits tax that falls on a property's consumption of municipal services? Or is it unrelated to benefits received and more likely to be a tax on capital? Each of these views is summarized here.

If it is a benefits tax?

One view is that the property tax approximates a benefit tax and, as such, encourages the right sort of fiscal decisions by local governments and taxpayers. Benefit taxation, it is argued, promotes efficient public decisions because taxpayers will oppose any programmes or services whose costs exceed its benefits (Fischel, 2000; 2001). Benefits from local public programmes and their costs in terms of property tax liabilities tend to be capitalized into property values. That is to say, the benefits of low crime rates and good public parks or sound local infrastructure on the one hand, and of low property tax rates, on the other, will manifest themselves in higher market values.

To understand how property tax capitalization can work, consider the case of two neighbouring cities, X and Y. The two cities are identical in every respect (structure, demography and provision of local public services) except one: property taxes are higher in City Y. If taxpayers (residential and non-residential) are aware of this property tax differential and respond to it, it becomes capitalized into lower property values in the higher taxed city (City Y) vis-à-vis the lower taxed city (City X). The following numerical example illustrates how capitalization works. Consider two houses (A in one municipality and B in another municipality) that are identical in every respect except for their property tax liability. Property taxes on house A exceed those on house B by $2,000. Higher property taxes on A mean that the imputed net return (imputed gross return minus operating costs including property taxes) on this property is $2,000 less than the imputed net return on B. If the rate of return on investments in general (as reflected in the interest rate) is currently 10 per cent, this translates into a $20,000 difference in property values ($2,000 divided by 0.10).

As long as differences in property taxes are capitalized into differences in property values, the tax provides no incentive to live or locate in one municipality over another and in that sense, is efficient. Recent evidence suggests that considerable capitalization of property taxes occurs in cities in the USA (Zodrow, 2001a; Fischel, 2001). In Canada, there have been two empirical studies of the capitalization of residential property tax differentials into residential property values. The first was completed in the 1970s and the second in the early 1980s and the results may no longer be relevant. For what it is worth, the first study, based on housing data for London, Ontario, found no evidence of capitalization (Chinloy, 1978). The second study, based on similar data for 27 communities within the city of Edmonton, Alberta, found some capitalization (Shah, 1989).

If the property tax were a true benefits tax designed to fund local government services, the tax price of a service would equal the marginal benefit from the service and there would be no incentive to move to one municipality to another in order to minimize the net tax burden (municipal expenditures minus municipal taxes). Given a number of jurisdictions large enough to ensure the satisfaction of every level of demand for public services and perfectly mobile consumers/ taxpayers who vote with their feet, net tax burdens would be the same across all municipalities. In this scenario, the property tax is like a user fee in that it covers the cost of municipal services consumed and involves no redistribution of income – local residents bear the full burden of any increase in property taxes, and since the tax falls on housing, it is regressive. The regressivity arises because the tax is a flat percentage rate on the values of dwelling units; since lower income households spend more on housing relative to income than higher income households spend, it follows that they spend relatively more on property taxes as well. The question that lingers, however, is whether this way of considering the tax burden is in fact a valid one.

If it is a capital tax?

An alternative conceptual view of the property tax (often called the 'new view') is that it is a tax on capital and, as such, a source of distortion in housing markets and in local fiscal decisions (Zodrow, 2001a; Zodrow, 2001b). The fact that the tax base includes structures and other improvements to land discourages improvements; the result is an underutilization of land in the sense that the amount of capital used per unit of land is less than the economically efficient amount. Also, since the tax is on capital, it is progressive; that is, it claims a higher percentage of income from higher income individuals than it claims from lower income individuals. This arises because higher income households own a disproportionately large share of the stock of capital.

Which is the preferred view?

There is no clear cut answer to this question. Both views have their theoretical strengths and weaknesses and both have been tested empirically with varying results (Kitchen, 2002). Also, both have their supporters and both have their detractors. After considering the evidence on property tax incidence, it is impossible to say whether the property tax is regressive or not. In all likelihood, it is less regressive than it is said to be by the strongest proponents of the benefits tax view but not as progressive as it is said to be by many proponents of the capital tax view. In any case, a more fundamental question is whether on not one should really be concerned about the regressivity of the property tax? The answer is not likely because the property tax funds a bundle of municipal services that provide collective benefits to the local community. Hence, the tax should be structured so that it is allocatively (economically) efficient, accountable and transparent, as discussed earlier in this chapter. Concerns about the distributional impacts of the property tax are important, but they should be handled through property tax relief schemes or, more generally, through income transfer programmes that are targeted for the truly needy (Boadway and Kitchen, 1999).

Property tax relief programmes

Property tax relief programmes are intended to reduce the property tax burden on specific individuals in specific circumstances. Reliance on one or more of these programmes is motivated by a perception that the property tax is regressive (takes proportionately more income from low income individuals than from high income individuals) – an issue that has been the subject of many studies and debates for a number of years without any firm conclusion or direction (Kitchen, 2002; Kitchen, 1992; Duncombe and Yinger, 2001). In spite of the uncertainty over whether or not the property tax is regressive, municipal governments and their senior counterparts in countries where a property tax is used almost always assume that it is regressive. This has produced a variety of programmes including those described here. While this description concentrates on the Canadian schemes or potential schemes, it is also indicative of those used in other countries.

   Property tax credits are used in five Canadian provinces (Quebec, Ontario, Manitoba, Alberta and British Columbia). The credit is designed so that its value varies inversely with personal income tax liability; that is, as income tax liability increases, the value of the credit, which is subtracted from personal income taxes payable, declines.

One comprehensive analysis of the Ontario refundable property tax credit programme suggested that the property tax credit is progressive in its impact on taxpayers; that is, it provides relatively greater benefits to low income households vis-à-vis high income households (Bird and Slack, 1978). A similar conclusion was noted some years later in a study completed for the Fair Tax Commission in Ontario (Ontario, 1993). While property tax credits are likely to be progressive, especially if they are refundable, they are not problem free. For example, when a tax credit exceeds tax liability, the tax is refundable if the government reimburses the taxpayer for this difference. It is non-refundable if the government does not refund this difference. A problem exists because residents pay their property taxes during the year, yet they do not receive the tax credit until their income tax return has been filed early in the following year. This practice can create liquidity problems for income-poor taxpayers because of the relatively long wait between payment of property taxes and receipt of the tax credit.

Furthermore, given the uncertainty over whether or not the property tax is regressive, the property tax credit could more appropriately be analysed as part of the general income-transfer programme in province, region or state, and not as a credit specifically designed to offset property tax liability. Indeed, it is unlikely that many taxpayers see any link between property taxes paid and the ensuing tax credit. After all, the credit for property taxes paid in one year is not available until the income tax return is filed in the following year.

When it is considered as a component of the state income-transfer system, one could question whether the property tax credit, which is designed to provide more relief to those with more wealth (higher property values), generates the desired income redistributional results. To some, it may seem strange to have an income distribution system that provides more relief for taxpayers with more wealth.

In summary, uncertainty over regressivity of the property tax and the tendency to provide relief that varies directly with property values argues strongly in favour of eliminating property tax credits and using other components of the state, region or provincial government's income-transfer system to improve inequities in the overall distribution of income. Indeed, the analysis of the province of Ontario's property tax credit programme referred to above concluded that it is 'difficult to argue convincingly that the property tax credit system ... has been either terribly successful or terribly needed' (Bird and Slack, 1978).

Tax deferral programmes are not widely used, although local governments in some countries have the power to implement them for specific taxpayers. Also, they are sometimes implemented by a more senior level of government. For example, in the province of British Columbia in Canada, a province-wide tax deferral programme for senior citizens and handicapped individuals operates. And in the province of Ontario, a deferral scheme is mandatory for low-income seniors and the disabled to alleviate any tax burden arising from increased taxes due to reassessment.

Under a tax deferral programme, the owner of the property is permitted to defer some or all of his/her property taxes on an annual basis. Depending on the programme, the lost revenue will be made up from revenue provided by a senior level of government or from general revenues of the municipality itself. The amount of the tax deferred becomes a lien against the property and is payable to the senior level of government or the municipality when the property is transferred. Also, there is usually, but not always, an interest charge applied to the deferred taxes.

There are a number of implications arising from the use of tax deferral schemes. First, if one's ability to pay taxes is measured by a combination of income and wealth where the property tax is viewed as a proxy for a tax on wealth, then a taxpayer who is asset rich but income poor could use this scheme to reduce his/her tax burden. In fact, tax deferral schemes can be especially useful in alleviating cash flow problems for income deficient taxpayers.

Second, and more critically, eligibility for most tax deferral programmes is restricted by age (seniors) and sometimes, disability. While one may be critical of age or disability dependent eligibility requirements for any income transfer scheme, it may be administratively practical to impose restrictions of this sort. Otherwise, if this programme were expanded to include everyone, there could be a significant increase in the number of applicants with the ensuing result that loans (tax deferrals plus interest charges on them) would be outstanding for a much longer period of time. According to some municipal officials, this would be administratively more complicated and costly (Slack, 1989).

Grants, designed to remove some of the property tax burden, are provided to eligible homeowners and/or renters in some countries. The value of the grant usually varies inversely with income and/or is given according to whether or not potential recipients are elderly or in receipt of welfare assistance. In the province of New Brunswick in Canada, for example, grants are the only property tax credit scheme while in other provinces (e.g. Alberta and Manitoba), grants are used in conjunction with tax credits. In British Columbia and Ontario, tax credits, deferrals and grants are used for various purposes.

As a mechanism for transferring income, the grant should be evaluated in the same way as any other component of the overall provincial income-transfer scheme. By comparison with current property tax credit schemes, the disbursement of grants could be more directly linked with the payment of or reduction in property tax liability. Also, it is frequently easier to direct grants to specific individuals especially in smaller communities where hardship cases are more quickly identified, even though it may be more complex administratively to operate than the tax credit programme.

Exempting individuals from property taxes as is done for certain taxpayers under specific circumstances in the provinces of Newfoundland and Nova Scotia in Canada effectively removes the burden of funding local services from these taxpayers and shifts the costs on to other taxpayers. This differs from grants in that the individuals do not receive actual cash payments from the province but its impact is similar to that where grants, reductions, cancellations or refunds completely offset property tax payments. Exempting property differs from tax deferrals in that taxes are simply postponed under the latter scheme while they are not payable under the former.

Where the exemption is available to people over a certain age only (senior citizens, for example), these exemptions, as a tax relief measure, may be deficient because they fail to consider the ability of the recipient to pay taxes. Similar deficiencies may exist where the criteria for exempting property for owner-occupiers is based strictly on taxpayer's income, and ignores property values.

Reducing, cancelling or refunding property taxes is generally associated with special circumstances, usually with poverty or illness. These programmes last for one year, and taxpayers are required to apply for them annually. The lost revenues are absorbed out of general municipal revenues. These programmes are used infrequently and appear to operate more appropriately in smaller municipalities where it is easier to identify worthy recipients.

Assessment credits are not used as widely as the other programmes but they have been suggested as a possible mechanism for relieving the property tax burden on residential properties. This scheme involves the removal of a fixed amount (determined by the local council) of market value assessment from property taxation. It works quite simply. After all properties are assessed at market value, a fixed amount of assessment is deducted from the total assessed value (similar to allowing personal income tax exemptions in a personal income tax system). Use of assessment credits applied to each piece of property would convert the property tax into a progressive tax rate. While this may appear to have merit on the surface, it would be a suspect device unless all properties owned by any particular individual were aggregated. Use of assessment credits would also result in a reduced assessment base overall. When compared with the system before the assessment credit is introduced, an equivalent amount of property tax dollars would be generated, then, through the imposition of higher property tax rates. For those properties with relatively low assessed values, the value of the assessment exemption would offset the higher tax rates and these taxpayers would be better off financially. For properties with relatively high values, the higher tax rates would more than offset the taxes saved from the availability of the assessment credit, and these taxpayers would be worse off financially. As a relief mechanism, the assessment credit, which is the same dollar value for all residential property owners, is deficient because it is based on the assessed value of property and not on the property owner's total ability to pay (Slack, 1989).

Summary

While tax relief for people who are deemed to have insufficient ability to pay is an important policy objective of governments, there is some question whether local governments ought to be using property tax relief instruments for income redistribution purposes. There are at least three objections to these instruments at the municipal level. First, the available evidence is not conclusive on whether or not the property tax is regressive. If it is not regressive, there is little basis for providing relief to reduce any alleged regressivity.

Second, if the tax is considered as a tax on one component of wealth (namely, property values), there may be limited support for granting property tax relief on the basis of the taxpayers income. In other words, if some recipients are asset rich and income poor, the real issue is whether people with significant assets should get relief from property tax payments, under any circumstances. Third, if taxpayers are not required to pay for local services they use, there is every incentive for them to demand larger quantities than is allocatively efficient.

Briefly, then, greater dependence on province-wide, region-wide, state-wide or nationwide income transfer schemes could more appropriately handle the income distribution issue (greater overall equity in the tax system based on ability to pay) while greater use of tax deferral schemes could handle the liquidity problem for asset wealthy homeowners. Recent trends towards the increased use of reverse mortgages, especially for elderly homeowners, can do a great deal to alleviate property tax burdens as well (Shan, 2009).

Politics of the property tax

Despite the merits of the property tax as a good tax for local governments, it is one of the most unpopular taxes in many countries. Its high visibility, though a positive virtue by any tax policy measure, and uneven assessment practices are largely responsible for its unpopularity.

The property tax is determined annually with payment generally made on a yearly, semi-annual or quarterly basis. Each single tax payment is almost always larger than any other single tax payment and is, therefore, highly visible. Furthermore, the payment is not based on the amount of one's income (as with the personal income tax) nor is it triggered by the exchange of money for a specific good or service (as with consumption based taxes). At the same time, taxpayers often question where this money is being spent. They tend to forget that property tax revenues are necessary to fund those services that provide collective benefits to the local municipality (roads, streets, sidewalks, street lighting, fire and police protection, neighbourhood parks, libraries, public recreation and so on) and because of this, the link between taxes paid and services received is often ignored. Ironically, it is this visibility that has made the property tax one of the most efficient taxes in use. Increases are often met with public resistance so decision makers have a strong incentive to provide local services in a responsible and efficient manner.

Unfair assessment practices still exist although they tend to be less prevalent than in the past. Policies to shift part of the tax burden from the non-residential (commercial/industrial and industrial) to the residential sector – recent practice in some places and generally a good policy decision – have been perceived as a problem by many residential taxpayers. Moreover, it is the residential taxpayer who votes, not the non-residential taxpayer. The summation of concerns such as these have led to the growing unpopularity of the property tax.

This unpopularity is behind a number of policy initiatives to alleviate taxpayer criticism. Among others, this includes property tax limits; assessment freezes or phasing-in of assessment increases; use of exemptions; shifts to user fees and specific charges; and reliance on tax relief schemes.

Property tax limits take many forms. In the USA, for example, 34 state governments have imposed property tax rate limitations on local governments. These prevent the rates from exceeding a predetermined level; for example; proposition 13 in California is the most notorious and it set the property tax rate at 1 per cent. Twenty-nine states in the USA also impose property limits on the extent to which property tax revenues can increase. These range from 2 per cent in Arizona to 15 per cent in Delaware (Brunori, 2007). Another 12 states have imposed limits on increases in assessed property values. In California, reassessment of properties can only occur at the time of sale or resale. Between sales, assessment may only increase by 2 per cent per year. In Michigan, reassessment is restricted to the lesser of 5 per cent or the inflation rate (O'Sullivan, 2001; Brunori, 2007).

Market value assessment has been criticized on the ground that rapid increases in market values may increase property taxes beyond taxpayers' ability to pay them. California tried to address the volatility problem by updating assessments to market value only when the property is sold and increasing assessment, thereafter, by 2 per cent annually. In the UK, every property was assessed at its market value in April 1991 and placed into one of eight valuation bands (Slack, 2004). The higher the band, the higher the tax rate. A property is not reassessed once it has been placed in a higher band. Changes in value do not affect a property's assignment to a given band unless the size of the property changes. Two provinces in Canada have restricted annual residential assessment increases – one to the rate of inflation until the property is sold at which time a new assessed value is established (Nova Scotia) and the other until time of sale (Prince Edward Island). A third province (Ontario) recently switched from annual reassessments to a four-year reassessment cycle with a phase-in of changes over the four intervening years.

Such tax and assessment limits while popular politically almost always generate serious short- and long-run consequences. In general, they are unfair and inefficient in their impact and often create distortions that are hard to overcome in the long run. Such limits, however, have created at least one positive outcome. Local governments, in many places, have turned to alternative revenue sources for funding some of their services. For example, there has been a trend towards greater reliance on user fees for funding solid waste collection and disposal; increased reliance on fuel taxes for public transit and transportation and even congestion or toll charges in some large cities and metropolitan areas (Kitchen, 2008).

Also, there is really no solid argument for continuing with property tax exemptions as was discussed above. Finally, concern over assessment volatility and property tax increases should not be addressed through limitations or restrictions on either, but rather through income transfers targeted to the poor of specific income tax relief programmes.

Future for the property tax

Perhaps the most certain thing that can be said about the property tax is that it is here to stay! Except for the Scandinavian countries where local property taxes do not exist, it has been the mainstay of municipal finance systems in virtually every industrialized and developed country for many decades and will continue to be there in the future. More recently and as functioning real estate markets have developed, its importance has grown in China, Russia and many eastern European countries.

Its strength lies in its solid attributes for funding local services – the tax base is immobile; the revenue yield is largely predictable and stable; the residential portion is unlikely to be exported; it is highly visible and fair as long is it covers the cost of providing those services that provide collective benefits to the local community; and if it is only a local tax (senior governments not involved), harmonization problems and wasteful tax competition are seldom a problem. This, however, does not mean that it is the only tax that will be used by many local and municipal governments in the future. There are solid arguments for giving cities and large metropolitan areas access to more than one tax as long as the local governing body sets the tax rate (Kitchen and Slack, 2003; Kitchen, 2004, 2008). This includes access to the personal income tax (either employee or resident based) and it includes access to one or more consumption based taxes (e.g. general sales, fuel taxes, motel and hotel occupancy taxes). Indeed, local governments, especially cities and large metropolitan areas in many countries, currently have access to more than one local tax (OECD, 2009) and this trend is likely to continue.

At the same time, there is every reason to believe that initiatives to impose assessment and property tax limits will continue. While these often create fiscal problems for local governments, one positive effect could be a movement to a greater reliance on user fees and charges as long as the fee and charge structure is efficiently and fairly designed. Indeed, this has happened in many places and seems to be growing.

Summary

For a variety of reasons, a local property tax is a good tax. There is, however, no uniform property tax base or method of assessment that applies in every country. In some countries, the tax base is land only. In a few countries, only buildings constitute the tax base. In most countries, however, both land and buildings are taxed. The basis for assessment is also wide ranging. In some countries, the value of the tax base is determined by market value, or site value. In other countries, the value is based on building area and property area – this is referred to as unit value. In a few countries, a mix of these approaches is employed in determining value.

Of these possible tax bases, valued based assessment systems and market value, more specifically, are deemed to be superior to area based systems in countries where there are fully operational property or real estate markets. Here, market values can be determined. Where property or real estate markets are not fully developed such as in developing and transitional economies or where there are a number of impediments to their operation, area based assessment is likely to be superior.

The success of any assessment system depends on a number of critical parts. A uniform assessment system is needed if one is to establish a tax base that is fair, transparent and accountable. Uniformity is more likely achieved if a few practices are followed. First, within a region, state or province, all assessors work from a standard and uniform assessment manual that is updated frequently to reflect changing conditions. Second, assessors should be required to pass specific education and training programmes on assessment practices and procedures. Third, although the evidence is sketchy, assessors working for centralized assessment agencies seem to be more successful (because they are more likely to work at arm's length) than those working for municipalities in achieving uniformity in assessment. Fourth, the more frequent the reassessment, the fairer the assessment system, leading to fewer surprises for taxpayers, fewer complaints and fewer appeals. Fifth, there should be an effective appeals mechanism in place to correct for perceived inequities in the assessment system. Finally, wherever possible, mass appraisal techniques should be used to improve the quality of the assessment system and to minimize its impact on costs.

The second major component of the property tax system is the tax rate. Here, it is generally conceded that each level of government (metropolitan and local, for example) should be responsible for setting its own property tax rate(s). Variable tax rates should be used when the cost of providing municipal services varies by property type and location. Variable rates, when compared with a uniform rate, are more likely to discourage urban sprawl and to minimize the extent to which the local property tax is exported to other jurisdictions.

Business properties (commercial and industrial) should not be over-taxed vis-à-vis residential properties. Limits (by a senior level of government) should not be imposed on tax rates set by local governments unless they are to prevent local taxing authorities from imposing unnecessarily high rates on commercial and industrial properties vis-à-vis residential properties or unless they are to protect the policy interests of a more senior level of government.

Tax billing and collection is an administrative function that benefits from economies of scale and should, therefore, be administered on a regional basis. Other land based taxes should not be used by local government unless they are designed to fund the costs of capital infrastructure needed to service specific properties or neighbourhoods, or unless these charges fund higher service levels or more services for specific properties or neighbourhoods.

Uncertainty over whether or not the property tax is regressive suggests that extreme caution should be exercised before specific property tax relief schemes are introduced. The property tax should be viewed as a tax that funds a bundle of local government services that provide collective benefits to the local community. To the extent that it imposes an unfair tax burden on lower income households, this tax burden should be treated in the same way that every other income distributional concern should be treated; that is, relief should come in the form of a comprehensive tax relief scheme administered by the regional or central government and not a property tax relief scheme directed at specific property owners and implemented by local governments.

Although politics plays a role in the structure of every tax, the visibility and general unpopularity of the property tax has made it one of the most politicized taxes in almost every country where it exists. This has led to the introduction of exemptions, assessment freezes and property tax limits. All of these serve to make the property tax less efficient, less transparent, less accountable and more inequitable than it should be. As for the future of the property tax, it is here to stay. It will continue to be an important source of revenue for local governments in most countries over the next few decades.

References

Bell, M. (1999) *An Optimal Property Tax: Concepts and Practices*. World Bank Paper, Washington DC: World Bank.

Bird, R.M. (2001) *Subnational Revenues: Realities and Prospects*. Washington DC: World Bank Institute.

Bird, R.M. and Bahl, R. (2008) *Subnational Taxes in Developing Countries: the Way Forward*. Institute for International Business Paper No. 16, Toronto: Joseph L. Rotman School of Management, University of Toronto.

Bird, R.M. and Mintz, J.M. (2000) Tax Assignment in Canada: A Modest Proposal. In: Lazar, H. (ed.), *Canada: the State of the Federation 1999/2000*, Kingston: Queen's University, Institute of Intergovernmental Relations, 261–292.

Bird, R.M. and Slack, E. (1978) *Residential Property Tax Relief in Ontario*. Ontario Economic Research Council Studies, Toronto: University of Toronto Press.

Bird, R.M. and Slack, E. (2004a) Land and Property Taxation in 25 countries: a Comparative Review. In: Bird, R.M. and Slack, E. (eds.), *The International Handbook of Land and Property Taxation*, Northampton, MA: Edward Elgar Publishing Limited, 19–56.

Bird, R.M. and Slack, E. (2004b) *Fiscal Aspects of Metropolitan Governance*. International Tax Program Paper 0401, Toronto: Joseph L. Rotman School of Management, University of Toronto.

Bird, R.M. and Wilson, T.A. (2003) *A Tax Strategy for Ontario*. Research paper 32. prepared for the Panel on the role of government in Ontario, available at: http://www.law-lib.utoronto.ca/investing/index.htm

Boadway, R.W. and Kitchen, H.M. (1999) *Canadian Tax Policy*. 3rd edition, Toronto: Canadian Tax Foundation.

Brett, C. and Pinkse, J. (2000) The Determinants of Municipal Tax Rates in British Columbia. *Canadian Journal of Economics*, 33(3): 695–714.

Brueckner, J.K. (2001) Property Taxation and Urban Sprawl. In: Oates, W.E. (ed.), *Property Taxation and Local Government Finance*, Cambridge, MA: Lincoln Institute of Land Policy, 153–175.

Brueckner, J.K. and Saavedra, L.A. (2001) Do Local Governments Engage in Strategic Property-Tax Competition? *National Tax Journal, LIV* (2): 203–229.

Brunori, D. (2007) *Local Tax Policy: A Federalist Perspective*. 2nd Edition, Washington DC: The Urban Institute Press.

Chinloy, P. (1978) Effective Property Taxes and Tax Capitalization. *The Canadian Journal of Economics*, 11: 740–750.

Clemens, J., Fox, T., Karabegovic, A., LeRoy, S. and Veldhuis, N. (2003) *Tax and Expenditure Limitations: The Next Step in Fiscal Discipline*. Critical Issues Bulletin, Vancouver: The Fraser Institute.

Dahlby, G.B. (1985) The Incidence of Government Expenditures and Taxes in Canada: A Survey. In: Vaillaincourt, F. (ed.), *Income Distribution and Economic Security in Canada*, Collected Research Studies of the Royal Commission on Economic Union and Development Prospects for Canada, Vol. 1, Toronto: University of Toronto Press, 111–151.

Dachis, B., Duranton, G. and Turner, M (2008) Sand in the Gears: Evaluating the Effects of Toronto's Land Transfer Tax. *Commentary No. 277*, Toronto: C.D. Howe Institute.

Damus, S., Hobson, P. and Thirsk, W. (1987) *The Welfare Effects of the Property Tax in an Open Economy*. Discussion Paper No. 320, Ottawa: Economic Council of Canada.

Devarajan, S., Fullerton, D. and Musgrave, R.A. (1980) Estimating the Distribution of Tax Burdens: A Comparison of Different Approaches. *Journal of Public Economics*, 13: 155–82.

Dillinger, W. (2002) *Urban Property Tax Reform Guidelines and Recommendations*. Washington DC: The World Bank.

Duncombe, W. and Yinger, J. (2001) Alternative Paths to Property Tax Relief. In: Oates, W.E. (ed.), *The Economics of Fiscal Federalism and Local Finance* Cheltenham, UK: An Elgar Reference Collection, 243–194.

Economic Council of Canada (1987) *The Taxation of Savings and Investment*. Research Report, Ottawa: The Economic Council of Canada.

Fischel, W.A. (2000) Homeowners, Municipal Corporate Governance, and the Benefit View of the Property Tax. *National Tax Journal, LIV* (1): 157–173.

Fischel, W.A. (2001) Municipal Corporations, Homeowners and the Benefit View of the Property Tax. In: Oates, W.E. (ed.), *Property Taxation and Local Government Finance*, Cambridge, MA: Lincoln Institute of Land Policy, 33–77.

Guevara, M. (2004) Real Property Taxation in the Philippines. In: Bird, R.M. and Slack, E. (eds.), *The International Handbook of Land and Property Taxation*, Northampton, MA: Edward, Elgar Publishing Limited,152–159.

Kitchen, H. (1992) *Property Taxation in Canada*. Toronto: Canadian Tax Foundation.

Kitchen, H. (2002) *Municipal Revenue and Expenditure Issues in Canada*. Toronto: Canadian Tax Foundation.

Kitchen, H. (2004) *Financing City Services: A Prescription for the Future*. AIMS 'Urban Future Series', Atlantic Institute for Market Studies, Halifax: Nova Scotia, 1–48.

Kitchen, H. (2006) A State of disrepair: How to Fix the Financing of Municipal Infrastructure in Canada. *Commentary*, C.D. Howe Institute, Toronto.

Kitchen, H. (2008) *Financing Public Transit and Transportation in the Greater Toronto Area and Hamilton: Future Initiatives*, available at: www.rccao.com

Kitchen, H. and Slack, E. (1993) *Business Property Taxation*. Government and Competitiveness Project Discussion Paper No. 93–24, Kingston, Ontario: Queen's University, School of Policy Studies.

Kitchen, H. and Slack, E. (2003) Special Study: New Finance Options for Municipal Governments. *Canadian Tax Journal*, 51(6). 2215–2275.

Kitchen, H. and Vaillaincourt, F. (1990) The Federal Grants-in-Lieu Program: An Assessment. *Canadian Tax Journal*, 38(4): 928–936.

KPMG, (1995) *Study of Consumption of Tax Supported City Services*. Report for the City of Vancouver, mimeograph.

Marchand, C. and Charland, J. (1992) *The Rural Urban Fringe: A Review of Patterns and Development Costs*. Toronto: Intergovernmental Committee on Urban and Rural Research.

McDonald, J.F. (1993) Incidence of the Property Tax on Commercial Real Estate: The Case of Downtown Chicago. *National Tax Journal*, 46(2), 109–120.

Malme, J.H. and Youngman, J.M. (2000) *The Development of Property Taxation in Economies in Transition*. Washington DC: The World Bank.

McClure Jr., C.E. (2001) The Tax Assignment Problem: Ruminations on How Theory and Practice Depend on History. *National Tax Journal*, LIV (2): 339–363.

MMK Consulting Inc. (2004) *Consumption of Tax Supported Municipal Services in the City of North Vancouver for the 2003 Tax Year, and Consumption of Tax Supported Municipal Services in the District of North Vancouver for the 2003 Tax Year*. Reports prepared for the North Shore Waterfront Industrial Association.

Oakland, W.H. and Testa, W.A. (1995) *Community Development-Fiscal Interactions: Theory and Evidence from the Chicago Area*. Working Paper 95-7 Chicago: Federal Reserve Bank of Chicago.

OECD (2009) *Revenue Statistics 1965–2008*. Organization for Economic Co-operation and Development, Paris.

Ontario (1993) *Fair Taxation in a Changing World: Report of the Ontario Fair Tax Commission*. Toronto: University of Toronto Press in cooperation with the Ontario Fair Tax Commission.

O'Sullivan, A. (2001) Limits on Local Property Taxation: The United States Experience. In: Oates, W.E. (ed.), *Property Taxation and Local Government Finance*, Cambridge, MA: Lincoln Institute of Land Policy: 177–200.

Ottawa, (1998) *Report of the Technical Committee on Business Taxation*. Ottawa: Department of Finance.

Rezk, E. (2004) Taxes on land and property in Argentina. In: Bird, R.M. and Slack, E. (eds.), *The International Handbook of Land and Property Taxation*, Northampton, MA: Edward, Elgar Publishing Limited, 281–285.

Shadbegian, R.J. (1999) The effect of tax and expenditure limitations on the revenue structure of local government, 1962–1987. *National Tax Journal*, 52(2): 221–238.

Shah, A.M. (1989) A Capitalization Approach to Fiscal Incidence at the Local Level. *Land Economics*, 65(4): 359–375.

Shan, H. (2009) *Reversing the Trend: The Recent Expansion of the Reverse Mortgage Market*. Working Paper 2009–42, Finance and Economics Discussion Series, Washington DC: Divisions of Research & Statistics and Monetary Affairs, Federal Reserve Board.

Sjoquist, D.L. and Walker, M.B. (1999) Economies of Scale in Property Tax Assessment. *National Tax Journal*, 52(2): 207–220.

Slack, E. (1989) *An Analysis of Property Tax Relief Measures and Phase-in Mechanisms*. Toronto: Task Force on Reassessment in Metropolitan Toronto, mimeograph.

Slack, E. (2001) *Alternative Approaches to Taxing Land and Real Property*. Washington, DC: The World Bank Institute, mimeograph.

Slack, E. (2002a) Property Tax Reform in Ontario: What Have We Learned? *Canadian Tax Journal*, 50(2): 576–85.

Slack, E. (2002b) Municipal Finance and the Pattern of Urban Growth. *Commentary*, Toronto: D.D. Howe Institute.

Slack, E. (2004) Property taxation in the United Kingdom In: Bird, R.M. and Slack, E. (eds.), The *International Handbook of Land and Property Taxation*, Northampton, MA: Edward, Elgar Publishing Limited, 81–90.

Tassonyi, A. (1997) Financing Infrastructure in Canada's City-Regions. In: Hobson, P.A.R. and St-Hilaire, F. (eds.), *Urban Governance and Finance: A Question of Who Does What*. Montreal: Institute for Research on Public Policy, 171–200.

Thirsk, W.R. (1982) Political Sensitivity Versus Economic Sensibility: A Tale of Two Property Taxes. In: Thirsk, W.R. and Whalley, J. (eds.), *Tax Policy Options in the 1980s*, Canadian Tax Paper No. 66, Toronto: Canadian Tax Foundation, 384–440.

Transit Cooperative Research Program (1998) *The Costs of Sprawl Revisited*. Washington, DC: National Academy Press.

Youngman, J. and Malme, J. (2000) *An International Survey of Taxes on Land and Buildings*. Netherlands: Kluwer Law and Taxation Publishers.

Zodrow, G.R. (2001a) Reflections on the New View and the Benefit View of the Property Tax. In: Oates, W.E. (ed.) *Property Taxation and Local Government Finance*, Cambridge, MA: Lincoln Institute of Land Policy, 79–111.

Zodrow, G.R. (2001b) The Property Tax as A Capital Tax: A Room with Three Views. *National Tax Journal*, 54(1): 139–156.

2

Value-Based Approaches to Property Taxation

Riël Franzsen and William J. McCluskey

Introduction

One of the key policy decisions in respect of the implementation of a property tax is the one on an appropriate tax base. It is as much a political as a policy decision because it will ultimately have to be defined in the law. In unitary states (e.g. Indonesia, Jamaica, Kenya, South Africa, UK) the tax base or bases are generally determined in a national law, whereas in federal countries (e.g. Canada, USA) it is determined in terms of state/provincial laws.

In many respects the choice of an appropriate (or less appropriate) tax base is a function of several criteria including history, culture, politics and administrative expediency (Almy, 2001). As will be discussed in Chapter 3, the choice of tax base is a critical policy decision which should ideally be based primarily on the available property-related data.

There are generally three value-based approaches in determining a tax base for the property tax:

- capital improved value
- capital unimproved value
- annual value.

A Primer on Property Tax: Administration and Policy, First Edition.
Edited by William J. McCluskey, Gary C. Cornia and Lawrence C. Walters.
© 2013 Blackwell Publishing Ltd. Published 2013 by Blackwell Publishing Ltd.

This is, to some extent, an over-simplification because there are several examples of jurisdictions and countries that utilize more than one basis at the same time (Bahl and Linn, 1992; Bird and Slack, 2004; Franzsen and McCluskey, 2005). Typically, you can find residential property taxed on one basis, and commercial, industrial and agricultural property taxed on a different basis (McCluskey, 1991).

Apart from the traditional value-based approaches mentioned above, there are also countries or jurisdictions (within countries) utilizing non-value approaches, or approaches which can best be described as 'hybrid' approaches, to determine an appropriate property tax base. These non-value approaches, of which the area-based approach (Bell *et al.*, 2008; Malme and Youngman, 2001; McCluskey *et al.*, 1998) is the most common, are discussed in some detail in Chapter 13.

This chapter is divided into several sections: a general overview of tax bases, market valuation approaches as the basis for the property tax, the concept of market value, traditional valuation methods; and finally some conclusions are drawn.

Overview of property tax bases

Scope of the property tax base

Only a few countries (e.g. Georgia) or taxing jurisdictions (a number of states in the USA) include movable (i.e. personal) property, such as aircraft, boats and yachts, in the base of their annual property tax. The vast majority of countries or jurisdictions will levy property tax only on immovable (i.e. real) property. In the remainder of this chapter property tax bases will be discussed with reference to taxes levied only on immovable property.

Although immovable property in principle provides a broad tax base, the definition of, for example, 'property' or 'land' may indeed broaden or narrow the actual scope of the tax (Bahl, *et al.*, 2010; Bahl, 2009). In South Africa, for example, 'property' and 'owner' are broadly defined. There are only a few exclusions (i.e. property categories not included in the tax base by law) and exemptions (i.e. property included in the base and in principle taxable, but fully or partially exempted by applying a zero or lower tax rate). In contrast, Tanzania's local government and property tax laws allow for significant exclusions (e.g. vacant land) and exemptions (all government-owned property), which narrow the tax base materially.

From 1993, the property tax in Sweden has been levied only on residential property (Youngman and Malme, 1994) and since 1978 only non-residential properties were taxed in the Republic of Ireland, although a residential property tax is to be reintroduced (Commission on Taxation, 2009). In some countries, for example India and Pakistan (Bahl and Wallace, 2010), owner-occupied properties are taxed, but at a materially lower rate. The issue of classified rates, also referred to as differential taxation, is dealt with in Chapter 5.

Nature of the tax base

The relevant property-tax-related laws in some countries may allow local authorities to select an appropriate tax base from two or more options (e.g. Australia, Kenya, Malaysia, Namibia, New Zealand and Swaziland) (Olima, 2005). For example, local authorities in New Zealand are allowed to use capital improved value, unimproved land value or annual rental value, whereas local authorities in Namibia may choose among area, capital improved value or site value, or the value of land and buildings separately.

In many countries the law will define a single property tax base, for example Brazil, Estonia, Indonesia, Philippines and South Africa (Rosengard, 1998). However, there are also countries where different tax bases may be utilized with reference to the use of the property, for example Barbados, Niger, St Lucia, Trinidad & Tobago and the UK (Franzsen and McCluskey, 2005; McCluskey *et al.*, 2010). In a few countries different tax bases are used within a single taxing jurisdiction, on the basis of:

- location: for example, in shires in Western Australia, urban properties are taxed on the basis of annual rental values and rural properties on the basis of unimproved land values (Franzsen, 2005)
- use: for example in the the UK, residential properties are taxed on the basis of capital values and non-residential properties on the basis of annual rental values (Hills and Sutherland, 1991; McCluskey, 1999)
- whether developed or undeveloped: for example in Côte d'Ivoire where the former is taxed on the basis of annual rental value and the latter on the basis of capital value (Tayoh, 2009)
- category of ownership: for example Niger, where property belonging to individuals are taxed on the basis of annual rental value, but properties owned by legal entities on the basis of a capital (book) value (Hassane, 2009)
- simply because not all properties are yet reflected in the valuation roll: for example, in most cities and towns in Tanzania, properties not on the valuation roll are taxed on the basis of a calibrated flat tax, which allows for some differentiation in respect of size, use and location (McCluskey and Franzsen, 2005).

Across developed and developing countries alike, a variety of tax bases are presently utilized, for example:

- simple flat taxes on the basis of ownership (or occupation), without reference to size or value, e.g. Ireland, Malawi
- simple area- or adjusted-area-based taxes, e.g. Bosnia, Burundi, Democratic Republic of the Congo, Hungary, India, Israel, Poland, Tajikistan (Szalai and Tassonyi, 2004; Zorn et al, 2000; Rochlickova, 1999; Peteri and Lados, 1999)
- unimproved land value or site value taxes, e.g. Australia, Estonia, Fiji, Jamaica, Kenya (McCluskey, 2005)
- taxes on building value only, e.g. Ghana, Tanzania

- land value and building value taxes (i.e. split-rate taxes), e.g. Grenada, Namibia, Swaziland (Franzsen and McCluskey, 2005), and some counties in Virginia and Pennsylvania in the USA (Bowman and Bell, 2004; Bourassa, 2009)
- capital improved value taxes, e.g. Australia, Brazil, Cameroon, Canada, Colombia, New Zealand, South Africa, USA
- Annual value taxes, e.g. Australia, Egypt, France, Ghana, India, Malaysia, New Zealand, Singapore, Uganda, UK (Rao and Ravindra, 2002).

Selection of tax base

Why a country uses a particular basis for its property tax can often be explained by its historical origins. Many countries that were former British or French colonies retained and still maintain an annual rental value system. However, with the passing of time, property markets in countries generally and in cities more specifically evolve, often creating potential disjoints between the current property tax basis as provided for in the law and the current status of the property market. This may result in a system that is somewhat dysfunctional (e.g. Freetown, Sierra Leone and Mumbai, India). However, in some countries the historically inherited system has indeed been adapted or reformed to align itself more appropriately with the current legal, political and/or socio-economic conditions applying in the relevant country, state or city. Recent reforms in a number of cities in India that have replaced their dilapidated annual value systems with calibrated area-based systems (Rao, 2008) and the rather perverse migration from a market value to an acquisition value base system in California in 1978 (Youngman and Malme, 1994) can be cited as examples.

The absence or paucity of reliable transaction evidence and lack of valuation assessment skills are major issues in many developing countries (McCluskey and Plimmer, 2007). Despite these realities, some countries have recently abolished their primarily area-based systems and implemented value-based property tax, for example Sierra Leone (2004), Rwanda (2011) and Cameroon (2007). In contrast, annual value taxation was retained as preferred tax base in recent reforms in Uganda (2005) and Egypt (the new law was passed in 2008, but will likely only be implemented in 2013) – despite the lack of valuation skills in these two countries.

In jurisdictions where property markets are relatively efficient, and the required levels of skill exist to determine credible property values on a signifi-cant scale on a regular basis, annual value or capital improved value approaches may indeed present themselves as the preferred options. Not surprisingly, annual and capital value systems are common in developed countries. Rather surprisingly, *ad valorem* systems are also common in developing countries (e.g. Argentina, Brazil, Colombia, Fiji, Ghana, Indonesia, Malawi, Philippines, South Africa and Sri Lanka). A number of countries in central and eastern Europe (e.g. Estonia, Latvia, Lithuania, Moldova, Slovenia) (McCluskey and Bevc, 2007;

Bevc, 2000) and central Asia (Armenia, Kazakhstan) have already adopted, or are in the process of implementing, a value-based property tax system (McCluskey and Plimmer, 2007).

Value-based approaches

Annual value systems

As mentioned above, a number of countries with a British (e.g. Australia, Belize, Guyana, Hong Kong, India, Malaysia, New Zealand, Singapore, St Lucia and Uganda) or French (e.g. Chad, Côte d'Ivoire, Mauritius, Niger, Senegal and Tunisia) colonial history utilize an annual value property tax system.

In Côte d'Ivoire, an annual value system is used for developed parcels, whereas a capital value system is used for undeveloped parcels (Tayoh, 2009). In Uganda, the 1979 law was replaced with a new law in 2005, retaining the annual value system. Given that there are fewer than 50 valuers in this country with a population in excess of 30 million, it is doubtful that the system will be able to function properly outside the capital city of Kampala (Franzsen, 2010). In Egypt, the outdated property tax legislation which provides for three taxes, was replaced in 2008 by a new law providing for one, consolidated tax with annual value as tax base. It was foreseen that revenue from property tax would increase sevenfold within the first two years of implementation (Amin, 2010). The new tax has been met by severe political resistance, resulting in a compulsory value threshold of 1 million Egyptian pounds. As a result it is estimated that less than 5 per cent of properties in Egypt will actually be liable for the new tax (Amin, 2010). At the other end of the scale, Singapore and Hong Kong operate modern and dynamic rental value systems and comprehensive revaluations occur annually.

An annual rental value system relies on arm's length rental transactions for all property types. The basis of an *ad valorem* property tax should be closely aligned to the operation of the property market. If an active residential rental market that results in sufficient rental evidence exists, it could support annual rental value assessments. For example, Hong Kong and Singapore have well-functioning rental markets for both residential and non-residential property. In Hong Kong, for example, a reference tenement approach to value is adopted in respect of high-rise apartments and condominiums. This involves the valuation of the most typical type of unit in a block; other units are then valued in line with the typical unit, but subject to some adjustments for location (floor), aspect, size, presence of elevators and other amenities such as balcony. Retail, office and industrial property that are relatively homogeneous, are valued on the basis of standardized values reflecting the specific street location, shopping centre, age and condition.

In the UK, however, the rental market is only used for purposes of non-residential properties. Given the high percentage (in excess of 70 per cent) of owner-occupied properties in the residential market, the council tax is based on capital values (DoE, 1991; DoETR, 1998).

Western Australian cities and shires use 'gross rental value' (GRV) as its tax base for urban property (Franzsen, 2005). The Office of the Valuer General of Western Australia provides the City of Perth with a valuation roll every three years. Previously the City of Perth categorized properties into seven property classes. However, with effect from 1 July 2011 (i.e. from the 2011–12 financial year), only four property classes, namely residential, commercial, office and vacant, have been determined. The tax rates for 2011–12, based on the GRVs, are as follows: residential: 3.7 per cent; office: 2.5 per cent; vacant: 5 per cent; and commercial: 4.6 per cent. Apart from the above differential rates, and irrespective the value of a taxable property, a minimum rate of ASD 560 applies.

The City of Melbourne, in the State of Victoria, Australia, uses a 'net annual value' (NAV) approach. The City of Melbourne is the only jurisdiction in the state of Victoria that uses differential tax rates in combination with its NAV tax base. In 2010–11 the residential tax rate was 4.4 per cent, and for non-residential property the tax rate was 5.2 per cent. Values for commercial properties are based on actual rental market evidence, whereas the NAV of a residential property in the City of Melbourne is a mandatory 5 per cent of that property's capital value. In other words, the valuer must determine the capital value of residential properties to determine the NAV. A general revaluation is done every two years (CoM, 2011).

Advantages

Mass appraisal could be used effectively for homogenous condominium and high-rise apartment type properties. An annual value approach provides a reasonable proxy for benefits received in respect of people-related services, such as libraries, clinics, recreational facilities (McCluskey *et al.*, 2010).

Disadvantages

Especially in developing countries there is lack of clarity in the relevant laws on how vacant land should be accommodated and, where there is rent control, whether market rent or regulated rent should be used as the base (Bahl and Wallace, 2010). Determining a notional market rent for owner-occupied property may also be difficult (Bahl and Wallace, 2010). As Bahl and Wallace (2010) also points out, an annual value basis does not fit well in a system where other property-related taxes (e.g. property transfer taxes and capital gains taxes) are based on capital values.

Capital value systems

The notion of capital value can be considered from two perspectives, namely that of 'improved' capital value, and that of 'unimproved' capital value (Bahl, 1998). In simplest terms the former values both land and buildings or improvements to land while the latter only values the land ignoring the improvements. As mentioned already, the basis of an *ad valorem* property tax should be closely aligned to the property market. If an active capital market exists from which sufficient evidence of market prices can be obtained, it could support a property tax system based on capital value assessments.

'Market value', 'assessed value' and 'cadastral value' are just some of the terms encountered in the context of capital value systems. Relatively few jurisdictions value to 100 per cent of 'market value' for purposes of the property tax.

In the context of capital value systems, a number of different tax base options exist:

- 'unimproved land value' or 'site value' – where only the value of land is used, in other words improvements are generally ignored for tax purposes
- building value only – where land values are ignored and only the value of building and other improvements are considered for tax purposes
- land value and building value as separate taxable objects – where the value of both land and buildings are determined independently and taxed independently
- capital improved value – where the total value of the property is determined (whether improved or vacant).

Each of these options will now be reviewed.

Unimproved land value or site value systems

Systems based on unimproved land values or site values are presently used in a number of developed countries (e.g. Australia and New Zealand), countries in transition (e.g. Estonia) and developing countries (e.g. Fiji, Jamaica, Kenya, Papua New Guinea and Solomon Islands). It is also used in a number of cities in countries where another system is predominant, for example, Belmopan (Belize), Mexicali (Mexico) and Harare (Zimbabwe).

A key issue in the context of land value tax systems is the concept of 'unimproved land'. At the turn of the 19th century and early in the 20th century, there were still large tracts of undeveloped land in countries such as Australia, New Zealand and South Africa where the use of land value taxation was extensive. The original concept of unimproved land was based on the physical state of the land as it existed prior to any human development. Over time the so-called 'virgin' or 'prairie' state of the land became problematic (McCluskey *et al.*, 2010) as it became increasingly difficult for valuers to determine the value of property as if in its original state, given the nature of certain types of improvements (e.g. levelling) that have been made to properties have effectively merged with these properties (Franzsen and McCluskey, 2008). In many jurisdictions in countries such as Australia, New Zealand and South Africa the problem was addressed by inserting appropriate definitions of 'unimproved land value' or 'site value' in the relevant valuation (and taxation) legislation. Strangely, the state of Queensland, Australia, only addressed this issue as recently as 2010, acting on the recommendations of the Queensland *Statutory Valuation Reform Review* (2010).

The Queensland Land Valuation Act, 2010 now defines 'site value', 'site improvements', 'non-site improvements' and 'unimproved value of improved land' as follows:

19. What is the site value of improved land
1. If land is improved, its site value is its expected realisation under a bona fide sale assuming all non-site improvements for the land had not been made.
2. However, the land's site value is affected by any other relevant provisions of this chapter.

23. What are *site improvements*
1. *Site improvements*, to land, means any of the following done to the land—
   a. clearing vegetation on the land;
   b. picking up and removing stones;
   c. improving soil fertility or soil structure;
   d. if the land was contaminated land as defined under the *Environmental Protection Act 1994*—works to manage or remedy the contamination;
   e. restoring, rehabilitating or improving its surface by filling, grading or levelling, not being irrigation or conservation works;
   f. reclamation by draining or filling, including retaining walls and other works for the reclamation;
   g. underground drainage;
   h. any other works done to the land necessary to improve or prepare it for development.
2. However, a thing done as mentioned in subsection (1)—
   a. is a site improvement only to the extent it increases the land's value; and
   b. ceases to be a site improvement if the benefit was exhausted on the valuation day.
3. Also, excavating the land for any of the following is not a site improvement—
   a. footings or foundations;
   b. underground building levels.
Example of an underground building level—
an underground car park
4. In this section—
clearing vegetation on land—
   a. means removing, cutting down, ringbarking, pushing over, poisoning or destroying in any way, including by burning, flooding or draining; but
   b. does not include destroying standing vegetation by stock or lopping a tree.

24. What are *non-site improvements*
1. *Non-site improvements*, to land, means work done, or material used, on the land other than a site improvement.
2. The work done or material used is a non-site improvement whether or not it adds value to the land.

25. Working out the value of site or non-site improvements
1. This section applies if, under this division, it is necessary to work out the value of site improvements or non-site improvements (the *existing improvements*) to or on the land to decide its site value or unimproved value.
2. The value of the actual improvements is the lesser of the following—

    a. the added value the existing improvements give to the land on the valuation day, regardless of their cost;

    b. the cost that should have reasonably been involved in effecting on to the land, on the valuation day, improvements of a nature and efficiency equivalent to the existing improvements.

  3. In this section—***added value***, of non-site improvements, includes the value of any commercial hotel licence whose value has been included in the land's value.

26. What is the unimproved value of improved land

  1. If land is improved, its unimproved value is its expected realisation under a bona fide sale assuming all site improvements and non-site improvements on the land had not been made.

  2. However, the land's unimproved value is affected by any other relevant provisions of this chapter.

As stated by Condon (2011), municipalities in Queensland now use the new site value methodology to value non-rural land, while still retaining the unimproved value methodology to value rural land. Given the context of Queensland, approximately 95 per cent of residential land in Queensland has not been significantly affected by the change in valuation methodology. However, for other types of land such as industrial estates that have been heavily filled, retained or levelled have seen the value of these improvements now included in the value of the relevant properties. These changes reflect the difference in value between the land in its natural state (i.e. unimproved value) and its current state (i.e. site value) (Condon, 2011).

Given that improvements are excluded from the tax base, land value systems rely extensively on the comparative sales method of valuation. In Jamaica, the factors important in determining assessed value are the area of the parcel, location, use, zoning, topography and shape. Sales are analysed to develop so-called 'standard enclosure values' for predetermined enclosures. These values are then applied to all parcels located within the relevant enclosures. The values are then adjusted to reflect differences between the individual parcels and the standard enclosure value. Given the homogeneity of parcels within specific locations, much of the land sales analysis is still done manually, although the use of automated valuation processes and geographic information systems (GIS) is increasing. GIS is especially used to identify parcels and for purposes of valuation quality control.

Despite statutory definitions for 'unimproved value' or 'site value', land value taxation present challenges, such as:

(i) Obtaining land-only data

    Conceptually many commentators, valuers and taxpayers apparently find it problematic to ignore the existing improvements on land in determining a taxable value.

(ii) Few land sales

    This is probably the most often levelled criticism against the use of a land-value tax system – especially in heavily built-up areas where there are few if any vacant plots and thus a lack of empirical sales data to use as evidence of land values (McCluskey and Franzsen, 2004; Franzsen, 2009).

(iii) Excluding buildings reduces equity

Especially in urban areas, the greater proportion of the total value of an improved property would generally be in the improvements effected to the land, rather than the land itself. However, this is not necessarily the case. In jurisdictions where suitable land for development is scarce (e.g. due to geographic features or zoning) or where other property-specific locational factors (e.g. river frontage or exceptional views) are evident, the land to improvement ratio may differ significantly.

For these reasons it can indeed be argued that excluding improvements reduces the equity of the property tax.

(iv) Loss of transparency

Arguably the majority of taxpayers have an intuitive notion of the value of their property; in other words they would have a fair sense of what a property would fetch in the market place. Thus a tax which excludes an important but undeterminable proportion of the 'market value' for purposes of determining a property's taxable value is difficult to explain. The result is that the tax becomes less transparent.

Advantages

Given a few exceptions, the physical attributes of land remain constant, which makes a land value tax less costly to maintain (Franzsen and McCluskey, 2008) than one which includes the valuation of buildings and other improvements. Furthermore, the tax burden should be borne more heavily by landowners, which makes it more progressive (Bahl, 1998). It may provide a simple solution in rural areas (Bahl and Wallace, 2010).

Disadvantages

Especially in heavily built-up areas, it may become exceedingly difficult to determine pure land values – i.e. to determine an acceptable division of value between the land and building components of a property (Bahl, 1998; McCluskey and Franzsen, 2004). Furthermore, given a narrow, less buoyant base, higher nominal tax rates are required, which may be politically problematic (Bahl, 1998; Bahl and Wallace, 2010), as is the exclusion of significant wealth inherent in buildings. Furthermore, it does not fit in with property transfer taxes based on total values (Bahl and Wallace, 2010).

Building value only systems

In some countries, for example Ghana and Tanzania, where land cannot be privately owned and belongs to the state, the property tax is levied only on the value of buildings and other improvements. In both Ghana and Tanzania, buildings are valued on a depreciated replacement cost basis.

Subsection 96(9) of the Local Government Act, 1993, of Ghana defines the tax base as follows:

> Subject to subsection (11) of this section, the rateable value of premises shall be the replacement cost of the buildings, structures and other development comprised in the premises after deducting the amount which it would cost at the time of the valuation to restore the premises to a condition in which they would be as serviceable as they were new; except that the rateable value shall not be more than fifty percent of the replacement cost for the premises of an owner occupier and shall not be less than seventy-five percent if the replacement cost in all other cases.

Subsection 96(11) stipulates that the minister responsible for local government may by law prescribe another 'basis for the assessment of rateable value of premises' – for a particular taxing authority or in general.

Advantages

Where land cannot be taxed for political or cultural reasons, buildings provide at least a viable option. In many cities in developing countries the value of buildings as a ratio of total value is considerable and with significant development, the tax base is relatively buoyant.

Disadvantages

In comparison to the determination of land values, the determination of values of buildings is much more complex, time-consuming and costly (McCluskey and Franzsen, 2005).

Split-rating systems – i.e. the separate valuation and taxation of land and improvements

This form of property tax is known by various names, including 'split-rate tax' (in the USA), 'differential rating' (South Africa) or 'composite rating' (Namibia and South Africa). Although phased out in South Africa in 2011, this form of property tax is still predominant in Namibia and Swaziland. In Namibia the significantly higher tax on unimproved land is used as a policy tool to stimulate the development of unimproved land.

Section 6 of the Rating Act, 1995, of Swaziland defines the tax base options as follows:

Method of rating
6. (1) a. Each rate shall be made, levied and assessed on immovable property on the basis of the valuation of the land and improvements thereon.
    b. The rates may be made, levied and assessed on the valuation of the land, the improvements, a combination thereof or the total valuation of the property.

Table 2.1 The 2010–11 tax rates for Piggs Peak Town Council, Swaziland

Residential properties – whether privately owned or government-owned	Tax rate
Vacant land	1%
Land which has been developed	0.80%
Improvements	0.50%
Commercial properties – whether privately owned or government-owned	
Vacant land	2.60%
Land which has been developed	1.50%
Improvements	1.50%

Information sourced from Piggs Peak Town Council (http://www.piggspeak.org.sz/thetown/rates/index.php).

c. *If the combination option is used, separate rates may be applied to the land and improvements components of the valuation.*

(2) The local authority shall obtain the approval of the Minister for the rating method determined under subsection (1) and thereafter, until the local authority determines otherwise with the approval of the Minister, all rates shall be made, levied and assessed accordingly.

(our emphasis)

Table 2.1 stipulates the 2010–11 tax rates for the Piggs Peak Town Council in Swaziland.

Advantages

Including both land and improvements in the tax base, the base is broader and more buoyant. Politically it should be more acceptable as valuable improvements are indeed captured and lower nominal tax rates can be applied (Bahl, 1998; McCluskey *et al.*, 2010).

Disadvantages

A significant disadvantage of a split-rate approach is the costly valuations required (Bahl and Wallace, 2010; Bourassa, 2009). Credible and defendable values must be determined for both the land component and the building component (Franzsen and McCluskey, 2005; Bourassa, 2009).

Capital improved value systems

The majority of countries levy some form of capital improved value system. However, systems vary rather significantly on how the capital value of taxable property must be assessed. In South Africa, municipalities levy property tax on 'market value'. Latin American countries levy property tax on capital value.

In Botswana (Franzsen, 2003) and the Philippines, land and buildings are valued separately. In Botswana the two separately determined values are then added and the tax calculated on the aggregate amount. In the Philippines, the assessment of land is based on market transactions while the assessment of buildings and other improvements is based on depreciated replacement cost. This approach is also used in most Latin American countries and is to some extent a solution to the scarcity of valuers. However, in some cities, for example in Bogotá, Colombia, the assessment process is changing to become more market-related.

Indonesia uses a simplified system of assessment for both land and buildings. Land is categorized into land value zones according to use and location, whereas buildings are classified into 40 different classes. Each class has a prescribed unit price per square metre. Therefore, individual properties are not separately valued, but rather assessed according to the prescribed land zone rate per m^2 and building class rate per m^2.

The principal valuation methods used for determining property tax assessments on all property types include the comparative, income (or expenditure and receipts) and cost (often depreciated replacement cost) methods – discussed below. These methods apply equally across the main property tax bases, whether these are annual rental value, capital value or unimproved value. The application of the methods has evolved to meet certain local needs and to reflect how the property market operates. The majority of property tax systems are based around the concept of market value and attempt to derive objective estimates of value based on market transaction evidence. However, where this evidence is scare or unreliable, jurisdictions have had recourse to cost-based approaches such as those used in metropolitan Manila, Dar es Salaam and several Latin American cities. The use of construction costs without any direct comparison to market values can lead to major problems with assessment levels; for example the average assessment level in Porto Alegre, Brazil was 30 per cent (De Cesare, 2002) and in Buenos Aires, Argentina, it was 35 per cent (Lafuente, 2009).

As discussed in more detail in Chapter 14, computer-assisted mass appraisal (CAMA) has become a fundamental tool to assist valuers, particularly during general revaluations. However, the development of such automated valuation processes relies extensively on relatively large quantities of transaction data. Data gathering, maintenance and analysis can be an impediment. Therefore, the application of such approaches has tended to focus on residential property and, to a much lesser extent, on commercial properties. The development of mass appraisal solutions for residential property is essential, given the relatively large number of those properties in comparison to commercial and industrial property.

Cities such as Cape Town, Hong Kong and Toledo, Ohio, have been successful in developing automated valuation systems for their residential properties, whereas some cities (Hong Kong, Toronto and Vancouver) have extended these systems to homogeneous office, retail and industrial properties as well.

The GIS in identifying the value influence of location is becoming imbedded within a number of jurisdictions. Cities such as Bogotá, Cape Town and Bangalore have been using GIS for property tax purposes. A more widespread application of GIS in terms of identifying parcels and supporting land titling projects may prove to be hugely beneficial for extending property tax base coverage. The use of GIS in the context of property taxation is discussed in more detail in Chapter 15. CAMA-based approaches and GIS are not yet widespread in developing countries, but there is clearly significant interest in developing such techniques. Within city jurisdictions commercial property typically tends to represent the most valuable taxable property and could potentially generate significant tax revenue. Given the uniqueness of some of these properties, and their high values, the valuation approaches normally adopted to determine values for these properties tend to be resource intensive.

Self declaration, in terms of returns giving information on the owner's property, is widely used as a means of updating the property inventory (Franzsen and McCluskey, 2008). This is the case in Hong Kong, Hungary, Malaysia, Philippines and many countries in Francophone Africa (e.g. Côte d'Ivoire, Rwanda and Niger). Indian cities, such as Ahmedabad, Bangalore, Chennai and Delhi, also use self declaration (even though it is referred to as self assessment (Rao, 2008)). Self declaration of transactions is also used in Manila, Philippines. True self assessment, however, is uncommon. Bogotá, in Colombia, has successfully used self assessment since 1993.

Advantages

A capital improved value approach fits well other property-related taxes such as property transfer and capital gains taxes (Bahl and Wallace, 2010). It provides a buoyant base and a good proxy for benefits received in terms of infrastructure (McCluskey *et al.*, 2010).

Disadvantages

The major disadvantages of a capital value approach are its dependence on accurate data which may be lacking in many countries (Bahl and Wallace, 2010) and the cost of implementation and maintenance of a system that requires relatively high levels of scarce skills (Franzsen and McCluskey, 2008).

Concept of market value

In terms of the concept of value, 'value is in the eye of the beholder'. In this regard, a seller often ascribes more value to the property offered for sale than a buyer would ascribe to it. In essence, therefore, value is a relative concept.

Thus the 'art and science' of valuation has seen a constant debate between what something is worth and what the market considers it to be worth. The concept of value, its definition and meaning, could be the basis for a book in its own right. In fact, to illustrate the point the following are just some of the early papers that have been written on the subject: Ross, 1970; Ratcliff, 1972; Wendt, 1974; Featherston, 1975; Smith, 1977; Marshall, 1978; Colwell, 1979; Albritton, 1980; Howcroft, 1980; Burton, 1982; Grissom, 1985; Horsley, 1992; Rothwell, 1994.

The value of a property is normally determined on the basis of market value or current use value. The interpretation of these two 'values' and their impact on the value of a property can have important consequences. Simply put, 'market value' must assume that all uses should be reflected in the value under the application of highest and best use, whereas, current use value represents that value in accordance with the current use of the property.

Assessors place a 'value' on property for the purposes of appraisal. The lexicon of value goes by many different names: 'full value', 'true value', 'market value', 'appraisal value', 'just value', 'fair cash value', 'actual value', 'fair and reasonable market value', 'full and fair value'. Many of these terms often relate to valuations for specific purposes, but the generic term of market value would appear to be the term that is most readily understood.

The concept of valuation is centred around the processes used to estimate, measure or predict a defined 'value'. Normally, this defined value is market value which for property tax purposes is generally defined by legislation. There has been considerable debate as to what is, or should be, the most appropriate wording for the definition of market value. Formal economic theory has given us a generally accepted generic definition of the term (Grissom, 1985; Shlaes, 1984):

> Market value is the highest price in terms of money which a property will bring in a competitive and open market under all conditions requisite to a fair sale, the buyer and seller each acting prudently and knowledgeably, and assuming the price is not affected by undue stimulus.

When land is assessed as an economic commodity, the basic laws of supply and demand dictate its monetary value. It is also clear that the concept of monetary value depends on market transactions taking place within a 'market' in which goods and services trade between buyers and sellers. In essence, the trading price is the price established in a competitive market at the intersection of supply and demand, that is the equilibrium or market clearing price. Implied in this definition are a number of assumptions including: a market exists at all times; persons entering the market do so voluntarily; all persons in the market are fully informed as to market conditions; market bids are based on estimates of the future use of the property. Equally, this state of market perfection does not always apply within the real estate market, which is often described as being one of the more imperfect of investment markets.

The concept of market value is somewhat hypothetical, in that it is derived from the market prices of other comparable properties. This does not necessarily mean that market value equals or *is* market price. However, if the sale price is consistent with the market criteria and other elements of comparison then the price can equal the market value. It is largely the inherent imperfections in the property market that create differences between market price and market value. Hence, market value is contingent on the specifics of a particular property in a particular location.

Sometimes value and price are the same, most particularly when there is no compulsion to buy or sell. Under other circumstances, there might be a wide difference between the market value of a property and the actual sale price. The appraiser must be careful to consider normal buyers' and sellers' attitudes for the type of property being appraised. The appraiser is estimating actual market value as opposed to theoretical value. The immobility of real estate makes it unique, and from a theoretical position no two parcels are exactly alike. The circumstances of one buyer and one seller may affect the sale price of a specific property, whereas the actions of many buyers and sellers of similar type properties determine the going rate for the sale or exchange of property on the open market.

It is important to distinguish between 'market value' and 'price'. A price obtained for a specific property under a specific transaction may or may not represent that property's market value: special considerations may have been present, such as a family relationship between the buyer and seller, or else the transaction may have been part of a larger set of transactions in which the parties had engaged. It is the task of the real estate appraiser/property valuer to judge whether a certain price obtained under a certain transaction is indicative of market value.

Valuations and prices do not have to equate, but it is important to accept that on average buyers and sellers should be using the same subset of information so that no significant bias results between values and prices. To consider this further, if we have an equilibrium market, where the supply and demand for property are in balance, then on average you would expect to see open market values equating to prices. But the reality is that the property market is not in equilibrium because of location scarcity. Prices will vary between potential buyers which reflect their relative strengths and particular interests (Brown and Matysiak, 2000).

It is a question of fact as to the current use of a property: it is either residential, industrial or recreational, and it has one value in terms of that current use. This is in many respects the value to the owner/occupier on the basis of the actual use being made of the property.

Examples of statutory definitions of 'value' for property tax

There are several examples of definitions of value in the legislation of various countries that demonstrate those key elements that the value must consider when determining 'value'.

'Capital improved value means the sum which land, if it were held for an estate in fee simple unencumbered by any lease, mortgage or other charge, might be expected to realize at the time of valuation if offered for sale on any reasonable terms and conditions which a genuine seller might in ordinary circumstances be expected to require.'

(Valuation for Land Act 1960, New South Wales, Australia)

'Capital value of land means the sum that the owner's estate or interest in the land, if unencumbered by any mortgage or other charge, might be expected to realize at the time of valuation if offered for sale on such reasonable terms and conditions as a bone fide seller might be expected to require.'

(Rating Valuations Act, 1998, New Zealand)

'Market value of a property is the amount the property would have realized if sold on the date of valuation in the open market by a willing seller to a willing buyer.'

(Local Government: Municipal Property Rates Act, 2004, South Africa)

In their standard on property tax policy, the International Association of Assessing Officers (2010), argues that to maximize fairness and understandability in an *ad valorem* property tax system, assessments should be based on the 'current market value' of property. They argue for this on the basis that only a system requiring current market value can capture value shifts across geographic areas and inherently account for the distribution of property-related wealth.

Highest and best use

There is little argument that the determination of highest and best use represents the basis on which market value should be calculated. Highest and best use is essentially an appraisal and zoning concept that evaluates all the possible, permissible and profitable uses of a property to determine the use that will provide the owner with the highest net return on investment in the property, consistent with existing neighbouring land uses (Eckert, 1990).

As a general definition 'highest and best use' constitutes (Appraisal Institute, 2010):

The reasonably probable and legal use of vacant land or an improved property, which is physically possible, appropriately supported, financially feasible, and that results in the highest value.

The valuation principle of highest and best use is based on the economic principle that investors and owners will generally seek the greatest return for capital invested in real estate. This means that they will choose the type and level of use that provides the greatest financial return for land. While this principle may seem simply common sense, highest and best use theory helps explain why some car-parking lots are still parking lots and others are being transformed into high-rise residential developments.

The highest and best use is the use that will render the maximum market value of a particular property. That use must be legally allowable, physically possible, have demand in the marketplace, and result in the maximum value for the property. For example, 'House X' in an area zoned for residential use may have a highest and best use as vacant and a highest and best use as improved that are both the same, i.e. a single family residence. A similar 'House Y' in an area zoned for commercial use may have a highest and best use as vacant as a commercial lot and highest and best use as improved as a residence. If the value of the commercial lot as vacant in respect of 'House Y' exceeds the value of that same house as a residence as improved plus demolition costs, the overall highest and best use of this property would be the 'as vacant value' of a commercial lot.

Current or existing use value

The alternative to using market value is to apply a value based on the current use of the property. This has the advantage of being much more objective and based on the pertinent fact of what the property is actually being used for at the valuation date. Current use would eliminate the potential intensification component from highest and best use. It is argued that current use is proactively environmentally friendly, recognizing the importance of conservation and sustainable land use. Current use is congruent with the approach that land should not be exploited beyond its sustainable capacity. It has the advantage that it is based on what the valuer/appraiser can see and is therefore more objective.

If we accept that most, or the majority, of property owners and investors wish to maximize their asset value, it is reasonable to expect that most properties will be used at highest and best use, that is the current use value will equal market value (based on highest and best use). However, there will be a few instances when the current use value and market value will deviate, due largely to the potential effect of planning and zoning possibilities.

Some countries and jurisdictions tend to use current use either as the basis for all property tax assessments or as the basis for giving preferential treatment for certain classes of property, such as agricultural land (USA), or land/buildings used for exempt or recreational purposes. In the UK, for example, rating assessments for commercial property are based on rental values, which are themselves based on the current use of the property. This particular approach takes the view that it is not proper to tax the occupier using the property for one use at a value higher given by a different use.

In some cases there may be a difference between the highest and best use and the current use caused by the imposition of statutory constraints or other zoning or preservation requirements. Often, in historic parts of towns and cities, buildings of architectural or historic interest have limited uses other than their existing use, but the site may well have a high value due to the location of the property. For example, churches and graveyards often occupy prominent and high value sites, but to value them at market value cannot necessarily be justified.

Property tax legislation can often make provision for certain classes of property where there is a clear difference between the current use value and the market value. These preferential valuations tend to apply predominantly to residential or agricultural properties. In Jamaica, statutory relief is granted in cases where the valuation takes into account a potential use of the land which is higher than its existing use, for example a dwelling located in a growing and expanding commercial area; agricultural land where possibly the potential for subdivision or alternative uses has been reflected; land occupied by approved organizations, such as sports clubs, where again the value of the land is enhanced due to its location and potential for development. In the USA all states use current use values for agricultural land (Youngman, 2005).

Traditional valuation methods

In general, the ultimate goal of an appraisal, whether for property tax or other purposes, is to provide an accurate estimate of the market value of the relevant real estate asset. The valuation process involves the combination of sound judgment, albeit often subjective, in conjunction with appropriate valuation methodologies to arrive at an accurate estimation of a property's value. However, an appraisal is at best an opinion of value, or an estimate that may or may not be 'accurate' given that it is very dependent on the availability of relevant data as well as the basic competence, integrity and judgment of the valuer.

Three approaches to market value

Traditionally there are three valuation methods for determining the market value of a property: the sales comparison approach, the cost approach and the income approach (Eckert, 1990). The appraiser will determine which of the methods is appropriate to the subject property under investigation. Properties that are typically purchased by investors (e.g. multi-storey buildings) will normally be valued using the income approach, while small retail or office properties will tend to be valued using the sales comparison approach. Single family residences and condominiums are most commonly valued with greatest weighting to the comparable sales approach. Properties that are rarely traded in the market, such as highly specialized industrial property, public utilities and network infrastructure are generally valued using the cost approach.

Sales comparison approach

As its name suggests, the comparable sales approach involves comparing the subject property against other similar properties that have recently sold. The economic principle underpinning this method is that of substitution which states that a prudent purchaser will not pay more to buy or rent a property than it will cost them to buy or rent a comparable substitute property (Jenkins, 2000). This approach lends itself well to the valuation of land, single family residences, condominiums and other types of property which exhibit a high degree of similarity, and for which a ready sales market exists.

The sales comparison approach looks at the price, or price per unit area, of similar properties being sold in the marketplace. Simply put, the sales of properties similar to the subject are analysed, and the sale prices adjusted to account for differences in the comparables to the subject to determine the fair market value of the subject. This approach is generally considered the most reliable, if good comparable sales exist.

The mechanics of the market comparison approach involve the use of relevant sales and market data in order to compare the property being appraised with other similar properties which have recently been sold. The sources used for determining value include actual sales prices, offers and rents and an analysis of economic factors affecting marketability. Because no two properties are ever identical, standard methods must be applied to gather data concerning comparable properties which are as similar to the subject as possible in regard to the following attributes: location; size (number of bedrooms and baths); age; property type; financing terms and general price range; and date of sale. Generally speaking the more good comparable data used, the more accurate the estimate of value. The approach is based on the assumption that property is worth what it will sell for in the absence of undue stress and if reasonable time is given to find a buyer. It is important that the appraiser investigate the sales to ensure that the sales are genuine open market transactions to ensure that there are no extenuating circumstances that may have affected the selling price. This is particularly important in those cases where there are few comparisons available.

To ensure proper comparisons between similar properties will ideally require an actual inspection. Inspections should determine, among other things, the condition of improvements at time of sale, the number and type of rooms, the plot size, aspect and topography and the sale price (if the sale was an arm's length or open market transaction). The known prices of the comparables are adjusted by adding or subtracting the amount which a given attribute or feature contributes to, or detracts from, the price of the comparable. For example, negative (downward) adjustments should be imposed to reflect those differences in terms of state of repair, date of sale, poor design. Conversely, positive adjustments should be made for the good design, special views and other features such as quality of materials, access and landscaping.

Some advantages of using the sales comparison approach include the following:

- It is the most easily understood method of valuation and the most widely used in practice.
- It is particularly applicable for appraisal purposes involving the sale of residential property, some types of commercial property and agricultural land.

Some disadvantages of the sales comparison approach include:

- finding sufficient similar properties which have recently sold
- adjusting attributes to make them comparable to the subject property – basically, the greater the amount of adjustment or number of adjustments, the less reliable the comparable can become
- the fact the older sales tend to become less reliable in a changing and volatile market
- difficulties in confirming transaction details to ensure that the sale is at arm's length
- rapidly changing economic conditions, periods of high inflation and high loan costs that can create an environment which makes subjective valuations difficult.

Cost approach

The cost approach establishes value based on the cost of producing or replacing an asset. The principle behind the technique is that the fair value of an asset should not exceed the cost of obtaining a substitute asset of comparable features and functionality. In other words, replacement cost is the greatest amount that a buyer would pay for a specific asset. The cost approach is sometimes called the summation approach and is largely based on the theory that the value of a property can be estimated by summing the land value and the depreciated value of any improvements made onto the land. It is the land value, plus the cost of reconstructing any improvements, less the depreciation on those improvements. The value of the improvements is sometimes abbreviated to RCNLD, an acronym for 'reproduction cost new less depreciation', or 'replacement cost new less deprecation'. There are two ways in which the valuer can assess cost. Reproduction cost is the cost of replicating the exact same improvements using the same or very similar materials based on today's costs. This is a replica in actual design and materials. In this method, the cost-as-new estimate is made as if looking at plans of an exact duplicate of the subject building. One of the main advantages of this approach is the greater accuracy of duplicating the building in actual design and materials. The main disadvantage is that advances in construction methods, materials and design make cost estimates of obsolete building construction very difficult as materials being no longer readily available creates difficulties in supply.

Replacement cost is the cost – at today's prices and using today's methods of construction – for an improvement having the same or equivalent usefulness as the subject property. The advantage of replacement cost new is the ready availability of accurate current costs, and a better understanding of modern building methods, design and materials. A major disadvantage relates to decisions made on the choice of current replacement materials and design for older construction. In practice, the replacement cost new tends to be the most frequently used cost approach base. Replacement cost is a more practical and relevant method of estimating cost as it eliminates non-essential or obsolete construction practices or materials. It also takes advantage of advancements in construction technology and processes.

Reproduction therefore refers to reproducing an exact replica, whereas replacement cost refers to the cost of building a house or other improvement which has the same utility, but using modern design, workmanship and materials. In most instances, when the cost approach is involved, the overall methodology used is a hybrid of the cost and market data approaches. For instance, while the cost to construct a building can be determined by adding the labour and materials costs together, land values and depreciation must be derived from an analysis of the market data. This approach is typically most reliable when used on newer structures, but the method tends to become less reliable as properties grow older.

As the cost approach has non-market-based components (costs), the approach may not be a good indicator of market value, even when new. This is most noticeable in respect of properties where the market demand is limited, such as hospitals and universities. The cost to produce the asset is not indicative of its market value, even when new. The accurate determination of obsolescence and depreciation (as the property ages) tends to be the most difficult aspect associated with the application of the cost approach.

Furthermore, there are situations where the subject property being valued is old and dated, or highly specialized or unique, where the cost method requires a significant degree of skill and judgment to account for the sometimes high levels of depreciation that may have to be applied. In this regard the possibility of error increases significantly as the age and specialization of the property increases. Of major importance to the accuracy of the cost approach is the availability of comparable land sales data to support the value of the land component of the relevant property. Therefore, many of the same limitations as discussed with reference to the comparable sales approach would also be relevant.

Income capitalization approach

The income capitalization approach, often simply called the income approach, is mostly used to value commercial and investment properties. This approach capitalizes an income stream into a present value. This can be done using revenue multipliers or single-year capitalization rates of the net operating income (NOI). The NOI is the gross potential income (GPI), less vacancy (= effective gross income), less operating expenses (but excluding debt service or depreciation charges applied by accountants).

Alternatively, multiple years of net operating income can be valued by a discounted cash flow analysis (DCF) model. The DCF model is widely used to value larger and more expensive income-producing properties, such as office buildings, hotels and retail malls. The DCF model measures market value by reference to a property's expected future cash flows generated from business operations. This typically involves a projection of income and expenses, the assignment of an end or terminal value at the end of the projection period and the determination of an appropriate discount rate that reflects the risk of associated with the cash flow projections. Typically a five- to ten-year projection period of cash flows is required, plus an estimated terminal value (which represents the value of the business enterprise beyond the projected period). This is then discounted to present value through the application of an appropriate discount rate that reflects the weighted average cost of capital for the business enterprise. The present value of the cash flows plus the terminal value represents the market value of the property.

However, the income approach has certain disadvantages. It is difficult to apply, as it requires a full financial model that forecasts future cash flows of the subject business. This generally is not a particularly easy task, as it requires the analysis of historic cash flows, the economic environment, and all other factors that are likely to have an impact on the cash flow of the subject property. A second disadvantage of the income approach is that during times of economic disasters, such as those that would affect tourist travel and hence hotel occupancy and hotel values, it becomes more difficult to estimate future cash flows.

Conclusions

An essential element of an *ad valorem* property tax is an active, formal and transparent property market. Transactions, whether these are rentals or sales, provide fundamental data for the purposes of determining assessments and providing evidence for defending assessed values before tribunals and courts. The availability of this type of data is an issue not only for developing countries and countries in transition, but even in some of the developed industrialized countries too.

The property market is the vehicle through which arm's length transactions are negotiated. What are transacted are interests in land – whether these are freehold interests, leases or licences. Once private rights are recognized and protected under the law, this security of tenure provides a key component for an effective land market. Part of this process involves the legal environment to ensure the proper legal recording of transfers, rentals, sales and so on. As a technical matter, private property requires a suitable legal, judicial and administrative apparatus. Objects of ownership must be established and recorded. Transfers of ownership must likewise be recorded. Such recording is necessary to help resolve disputes over ownership that may arise.

One of the benefits of a transparent and efficient land market is access to more reliable information about real property prices (Dale *et al.*, 2007). However, even with mature and efficient markets there are other factors which can affect the quality and indeed the reliability of the transactions that occur, for example high transfer taxes. Therefore, value based property taxes require, almost as a prerequisite, an active, transparent, secure, reliable market within which property interests can be traded and financed through the banking sector (Adair *et al.*, 2004).

A major issue in many countries with an *ad valorem* property tax is that valuation roll maintenance is neglected and not done in a comprehensive manner (Dornfest, 2010). Despite what the law may dictate, in many instances general revaluations are only undertaken infrequently (Franzsen, 2010). This is an issue in, for example, Brazil, Ghana, Malaysia and Uganda. In most instances the paucity of valuers and appropriate valuation skills are to blame, but in some cases political interference also plays a major role (e.g. Kenya and Malaysia).

In the end, the property tax must be capable of efficient and cost-effective administration. If it is based on annual or capital values, those values need to be based on openly negotiated market evidence. In addition, as property markets move in cycles, and properties change over time (e.g. through development, rezoning, amalgamation and subdivision), it is important that the administration is sufficiently equipped to undertake supplementary valuations to account for specific changes to individual properties and especially regular revaluations of the whole property tax base. Capital improved value approaches tend to have greater value volatility than annual value approaches. Therefore, there is a greater need for more frequent revaluations in respect of capital-based systems.

A key question in the context of some developing countries, where property markets are sometimes less than optimal or rather informal and where assessment skills may be lacking, is whether a value-based system is necessarily the best option. An outdated and/or incomplete system relying on discrete values may indeed be more inequitable than a pragmatic, crude alternative based on simple or adjusted areas, or on value bands. These alternative approaches are discussed in Chapter 13.

References

Adair, A., Allen, S., Berry, J. and McGreal, S. (2004) *The Development of Land and Property Markets in Central and Eastern Europe: Issues of Data*. London, RICS Foundation.

Albritton, H.D. (1980) A Critique of the Prevailing Definition of Market Value. *The Appraisal Journal*, April: 68–74.

Almy, R. (2001) *A Survey of Property Tax Systems in Europe*. Report prepared for the Slovenia Department of Taxes and Customs, Ljubljana, Ministry of Finance.

Amin, K. (2010) Property Tax System in Egypt. Paper presented at the *ATI/Lincoln Institute Workshop on Property Tax in Africa*, Stellenbosch, South Africa, December 4–5.

Appraisal Institute, (2010) *The Dictionary of Real Estate Appraisal*, 5th edition, Chicago, Il. Appraisal Institute.

Bahl, R.W. (1998) Land Taxes versus Property Taxes in Developing and Transition countries. In: Netzer, D. (ed.), *Land Value Taxation – Can it and will it work today?* Cambridge, MA: Lincoln Institute of Land Policy.

Bahl, R.W. (2009) *Property Tax Reform in Developing Countries*. Washington DC: USAID.

Bahl, R.W. and Wallace, S. (2010) A New Paradigm for Property Taxation in Developing Countries. In: Bahl, R., Martinez-Vazquez, J. and Youngman, J. (eds.), *Challenging the Conventional Wisdom on the Property Tax*, Cambridge, MA: Lincoln Institute of Land Policy.

Bahl, R.W. and Linn, J.F. (1992) *Urban Public Finance in Developing Countries*, UK: Oxford University Press.

Bahl, R., Martinez-Vazquez, J. and Youngman, J. (eds.), (2010) *Challenging the Conventional Wisdom on the Property Tax*, Cambridge, MA: Lincoln Institute of Land Policy.

Bell, M., Yuan, N. and Connolly, K. (2008) *A Compendium of Countries with an Area Based Property Tax*. Working Paper WP09KC1, Cambridge, MA: Lincoln Institute of Land Policy.

Bevc, I. (2000) Property Tax in the Republic of Slovenia. *Journal of Property Tax Assessment & Administration*, 5(4): 57–62.

Bird, R. and Slack, E. (eds.), (2004) *International Handbook of Land and Property Taxation*, Northampton, MA: Edward Elgar.

Bourassa, S.C. (2009) The U.S. Experience. In: Dye, R.F. and England R.W. (eds.), *Land Value Taxation*. Cambridge MA: Lincoln Institute of Land Policy, 11–25.

Bowman, J.H. and Bell, M.E. (2004) Split-rate Real Property Taxation: Property Tax Redistribution across Land Uses in Three Virginia Localities. National Tax Association Proceedings of the 97th Annual Conference, Washington DC: NTA,104–110.

Brown, G. and Matysiak, G.A. (2000) *Real Estate Investment: A Capital Market Approach*. London, UK, Financial Times Prentice Hall.

Burton, J.H. (1982) Early Contributions to Value Theory. In: Burton, J.H. (ed.), *Evolution of the Income Approach*, Chicago: American Institute of Real Estate Appraisers, 1–35.

CoM. (2011) City of Melbourne. (see http://www.melbourne.vic.gov.au/BuildingandPlanning/RatesAndValuations/Pages/RatesandValuations.aspx).

Colwell, P.F. (1979), A Statistically Orientated Definition of Market Value. *The Appraisal Journal*, January, 106–111.

Commission on Taxation (2009) *Report of the Commission on Taxation*. Dublin: Stationary Office.

Condon, S. (2011) Understanding land valuation. *Property Observer*. (see http://www.propertyobserver.com.au/residential/understanding-land-valuation/2011080851071).

Dale, P., Mahoney, R. & McLaren, R. (2007) *Land Markets – Why are They Required and How Will They Develop?* FIG Working Week (2007), (Hong Kong SAR, China).

De Cesare, C.M. (2002) Toward More Effective Property Tax Systems in Latin America. *Land Lines*, 14(1): 9–11.

DoE, (1991) *The New Tax for Local Government: A Consultation Paper*. London: Department of the Environment.

DoETR, (1998) *Modern Local Government: In Touch with the People*. London: Department of the Environment, Transport and the Regions.

Dornfest, A. (2010) In search of an optimal revaluation policy. In: Bahl, R., Martinez-Vazquez, J. and Youngman, J. (eds.), *Challenging the Conventional Wisdom on the Property Tax*, Cambridge, MA: Lincoln Institute of Land Policy, 75–107.

Eckert, J. (1990) *Property Appraisal and Assessment Administration*. Chicago: International Association of Assessing Officers.

Featherston, J.B. (1975) Historic Influences on Development of the Theory of Value. *The Appraisal Journal*, April, 3–20.

Franzsen, R.C.D. (2003) *Property Taxation within the Southern African Development Community (SADC): Current Status and Future Prospects of Land Value Taxation in Botswana, Lesotho, Namibia, South Africa and Swaziland*. Working Paper WP03RF1, Cambridge MA: Lincoln Institute of Land Policy.

Franzsen, R.C.D. (2005) Land Value Taxation in Western Australia. In: McCluskey, W.J. and Franzsen, R.C.D. (eds.), *Land Value Taxation: An Applied Approach* Aldershot, Ashgate, 191–226.

Franzsen, R.C.D. (2009) International Experience. In: Dye, R.F. and England R.W. (eds.), *Land Value Taxation*. Cambridge MA: Lincoln Institute of Land Policy, 27–47.

Franzsen, R.C.D. (2010) Commentary. In: Bahl, R., Martinez-Vazquez, J. and Youngman, J. (eds.), *Challenging the Conventional Wisdom on the Property Tax*, Cambridge, MA: Lincoln Institute of Land Policy, 108–117.

Franzsen, R.C.D. and McCluskey, W.J. (2005) *An Exploratory Overview of Property Taxation in the Commonwealth of Nations*. Working Paper WP05RF1, Cambridge MA: Lincoln Institute of Land Policy.

Franzsen, R.C.D. and McCluskey, W.J. (2008) The Feasibility of Site Value Taxation. In: Bahl, R., Martinez-Vazquez, J. and Youngman, J. (eds.), *Making the Property Tax Work: Experiences in Developing and Transitional Countries*, Cambridge, MA: Lincoln Institute of Land Policy, 268–306.

Grissom, T.V. (1985) Value Definition: Its Place in the Appraisal Process. *The Appraisal Journal*, April, 217–225.

Hassane, B. (2009) *Property Taxation in Francophone Africa: Case Study of Niger*. Working Paper WP09FAD1, Cambridge MA: Lincoln Institute of Land Policy.

Hills, J. and Sutherland, H. (1991) The Proposed Council Tax. *Fiscal Studies*, 12(4): 1–21.

Horsley, G.J. (1992) Market Value: The Sacred Cow. *Journal of Property Valuation and Investment*, 10: 694–700.

Howcroft, P.A. (1980) A Rational Expectations Approach to Concepts of Value. *The Appraisal Journal*, July, 82–92.

Jenkins, D. (2000) *Residential Valuation Theory and Practice*. Oxford: Chandos Publications.

Lafuente, M. (2009). *Public Management Reforms and Property Tax Revenue Improvements: Lessons from Buenos Aires*. Working Paper 0209. Washington DC: World Bank.

Malme, J.H. and Youngman, J.M. (eds.) (2001), *The Development of Property Taxation in Economies in Transition: Case Studies from Central and Eastern Europe*. Washington DC: World Bank Institute.

Marshall, R.D. (1978) Market Value: What Does it Mean in Real Estate Today. *The Real Estate Appraiser*, January, 31–34.

McCluskey, W.J. (ed.), (1991) *Comparative Property Tax Systems*. Aldershot, UK: Avebury Publishing Limited.

McCluskey, W.J. (1999) (ed.), *Comparative Property Tax Systems: An International Comparative Review*. Aldershot, UK: Avebury Publishing Limited.

McCluskey, W.J. (2005) Land Taxation: The Case of Jamaica. In: McCluskey, W.J. and Franzsen, R.C.D. (eds.), *Land Value Taxation: An Applied Approach* Aldershot: Ashgate, 19–63.

McCluskey, W.J., Almy, R. and Rohlickova, A. (1998) The Development of Property Taxation in the New Democracies of Central and Eastern Europe. *Journal of Property Management*, 16(3): 145–159.

McCluskey, W.J., Bell, M.E. and Lim, L.J. (2010) Rental Value versus Capital Value – Alternative Bases for the Property Tax. In: Bahl, R., Martinez-Vazquez, J. and Youngman, J. (eds.), *Challenging the Conventional Wisdom on the Property Tax*. Cambridge, MA: Lincoln Institute of Land Policy, 119–157.

McCluskey, W.J. and Bevc, I. (2007) Fiscal Decentralisation in the Republic of Slovenia: An Opportunity for the Property Tax. *Property Management*, 25(4) 400–419.

McCluskey W.J. and Franzsen, R.C.D. (2004) *The Basis of the Property Tax: A Case Study Analysis of New Zealand and South Africa*. Working Paper WP04WM1, Cambridge MA: Lincoln Institute of Land Policy.

McCluskey, W.J. and Franzsen, R.C.D. (2005) An Evaluation of the Property Tax In Tanzania: An Untapped Fiscal Resource or Administrative Headache. *Property Management*, 23(1): 43–69.

McCluskey, W.J. and Plimmer, F. (2007) The Potential for the Property Tax in the 2004 Accession Countries of Central and Eastern Europe. *RICS Research Paper Series*, London: Royal Institution of Chartered Surveyors.

Olima, W.H.A. (2005). Land Value Taxation in Kenya. In: McCluskey, W.J. and Franzsen, R.C.D. (eds.), *Land Value Taxation: An Applied Approach* Aldershot: Ashgate, 91–114.

Peteri, G. and Lados, M. (1999) Local Property Taxation in Hungary. In: McCluskey, W.J. (ed.), *Comparative Property Tax Systems: An International Comparative Review*, Aldershot, UK: Avebury Publishing Limited, 419–439.

Queensland Statutory Valuation Reform Review. (2010) Department of Environment and Resource Management. PriceWaterhouseCoopers.

Rao, V. and Ravindra, A. (2002) *Reforming the Property Tax System in India*. United Nations Development Program, New Delhi, India.

Rao, V. (2008) Is Area-Based Assessment an Alternative, an Intermediate Step or an Impediment to Value Based Taxation in India? In: Bahl, R., Martinez-Vazquez, J. and Youngman, J. (eds.), *Making the Property Tax Work: Experiences in Developing and Transitional Countries*, Cambridge, MA: Lincoln Institute of Land Policy, 241–267.

Ratcliff, R.U. (1972) Is There a New School of Appraisal Thought? *The Appraisal Journal*, October, 54–60.

Rochlickova, A. (1999) Property Taxation in the Czech Republic. In: W.J. McCluskey (ed), *Comparative Property Tax Systems: An International Comparative Review*, Aldershot, UK, Avebury Publishing Limited, 440–454.

Rosengard, J. (1998) *Property Tax Reform in Developing Countries*. Norwell, MA: Kluwer Academic Publishers.

Ross, T. (1970) Selling Price and Market Value. *The Appraisal Journal*, July, 49–53.

Rothwell, G. (1994) Valuation Methodology and Market Needs. *The Valuer and Land Economist*, February, 18–20.

Shlaes, J. (1984) The Market in Market Value. *The Appraisal Journal*, October, 494–518.

Smith, H.C. (1977) Value Concepts as a Source of Disparity among Appraisals. *The Appraisal Journal*, April, 61–67.

Szalai, A. and Tassonyi, A.T. (2004) Value Based Property Taxation: Options for Hungary. *Environment and Planning C: Government and Policy*, 22: 495–521.

Tayoh, B. (2009) *Property Taxation in Côte d'Ivoire*. Working Paper WP09FAC4, Cambridge, MA: Lincoln Institute of Land Policy.

Youngman, J.M. (2005) Taxing and Untaxing Land: Current Use Assessment of Farmland. *State Tax Notes*. September 5: 727–738.

Youngman, J.M. and Malme, J.H. (1994) *An International Survey of Taxes on Land and Buildings*. Amsterdam: Kluwer.

Wendt, P.F. (1974) What is Value. In: Wendt, P.F. (ed.) *Real Estate Appraisal: Review and Outlook*, Atlanta, University of Georgia Press, 1–15.

Zorn, K.C., Tesche, J. and Cornia, G. (2000) Diversifying Local Government Revenue in Bosnia-Herzegovina through an Area Based Property Tax. *Public Budgeting and Finance*, Winter, 63–86.

3

The Politics of the Property Tax
Enid Slack

Introduction

The property tax is an important tax for local governments in many countries around the world but it is rarely a politically popular tax. It has been criticized for being unfair because it is unrelated to ability to pay or to benefits received, unsuitable because it supports services that are unrelated to property and inadequate because it does not provide sufficient municipal revenues to meet expenditure needs. It has also been criticized for its effects on housing, land use and urban development. Notwithstanding these criticisms, the property tax can provide a significant source of revenue for local governments and is essential to local autonomy. The formulation of property tax policy thus has important consequences for the overall workings of municipal government.

Economics dictates that property taxes should be designed to meet a number of public finance principles such as equity and efficiency. The reality of how property taxes are implemented around the world, however, is often much different from what those principles would suggest. As one author notes, 'tax policy is the product of political decision making, with economic analysis playing only a minor supporting role' (Holcombe, 1998). Although the author is not referring specifically to the property tax, his comments apply as much or more to the property tax as to other taxes. Political pressure to maintain the tax

A Primer on Property Tax: Administration and Policy, First Edition.
Edited by William J. McCluskey, Gary C. Cornia and Lawrence C. Walters.
© 2013 Blackwell Publishing Ltd. Published 2013 by Blackwell Publishing Ltd.

burden at its current level or to develop policies that favour one group of taxpayers over another often overrides economics principles.

This chapter describes some of the property tax policy choices that are made where decisions have been based more on politics than on economic analysis. The first section sets out the unique features of the property tax that have an impact on the politics of the property tax. The second section sets out the economic principles for designing a property tax. The third illustrates the divergence between economics and politics using examples of various aspects of the structure of the property tax (such as the determination of the tax base and the setting of tax rates). The fourth section focuses on property tax revolts and the resulting limitations on property tax increases and other property tax relief measures. The fifth section discusses the politics of property tax reform. The sixth section contrasts the role of the property tax in achieving local autonomy with the reality of central control in many countries. The concluding section emphasizes the need to design property tax policies properly from an economics perspective while, at the same time, taking into account the need to be politically acceptable.

Unique characteristics of the property tax

There are several characteristics of the property tax that differentiate it from other taxes. These characteristics all have an impact on how the tax is implemented and explain, in part, why the politics and economics of the tax differ.

The property tax is a visible tax

The property tax is a very visible tax. Unlike the income tax, the property tax is not withheld at source. Unlike the sales tax, it is not paid in small amounts with each daily purchase. Instead, the property tax generally has to be paid directly by taxpayers in periodic lump sums (except in cases where the mortgage institution includes property taxes in monthly mortgage payments). This means that taxpayers often tend to be more aware of the property taxes they pay than they are of other taxes, and generally they will oppose tax increases. Moreover, the property tax finances services which are also very visible, such as roads, garbage collection and neighbourhood parks. Studies show that residents are more willing to pay for local services when they rate their government and service provision highly (Simonsen and Robbins, 2003).

Visibility is clearly desirable from a decision making perspective because it makes taxpayers aware of the costs of local public services. This awareness enhances accountability, which is obviously a good thing from both an economic (hard budget constraint) and political (democratic) perspective. It does not, however, make the property tax very popular. Visibility makes property taxes difficult to sell politically and even more difficult to increase or reform relative to other taxes. Indeed, the property tax is often regarded as the 'most hated' tax (Brunori, 2003). As will be shown, visibility and opposition to the property tax in general have important consequences for the formulation of tax policy.

The property tax is inelastic

The base of the property tax is relatively inelastic, meaning that it does not increase automatically over time. In the case of property taxes based on market value assessment, property values generally respond more slowly to annual changes in economic activity than do incomes. This inelasticity is exacerbated in many jurisdictions around the world because few of them update property values for taxation purposes on an annual basis. For property taxes based on the area of the property (the base used in many transition economies), the tax responds even more slowly to annual changes in income.

Inelasticity means that, in order to maintain property tax revenues in real terms (let alone to raise property tax revenues), it is necessary to increase the rate of the tax. As with visibility, inelasticity leads to greater accountability because taxing authorities have to increase the tax rate to increase tax revenues but it also leads, from a political perspective, to greater taxpayer resistance.

There is inherent arbitrariness in the determination of the tax base

Taxpayers also dislike the property tax because of the way in which it is administered, particularly when market value assessment is used as the base of the tax. Other taxes (such as income and sales taxes) are based on flows – income or sales. Although the tax base may sometimes be the source of argument between the taxpayer and the tax authority, there is, in principle, a measurable economic activity on the basis of which the tax is levied (Bird and Slack, 2004). Property taxes, on the other hand, are generally based on stocks – asset values. Unless the asset subject to tax is sold (in an arm's length transaction by a willing buyer to a willing seller) in the tax period, someone has to determine the value that serves as the basis on which to assess the tax.

Valuation is inherently and inevitably an arguable matter (Bird *et al.*, 2012). If there is a 'self assessment' system (as in Bogotá, Colombia, for example), owners are likely to under-value their property; if there is an 'official' (cadastral) assessment system, owners are likely to feel that their property is (at least relative to their neighbour's property) over-valued (Bird and Slack, 2004). In the end, someone has to determine the tax base for the property tax, in a way that is not true for any other significant tax. It is not surprising that the results are often perceived to be unfair and arbitrary. Taxpayers' perceptions around the fairness of the tax (and how it is implemented) have an impact on the extent to which local governments can raise the tax.

Property is immovable

The property tax is generally regarded as a good tax for local governments because property is immovable – it is unable to shift location in response to the tax, and it cannot be hidden. Thus, it is difficult to evade the tax. Although a change in property tax may be capitalized into property values in a particular community, and in the long run tax differentials may affect where people locate, these effects are of a smaller magnitude than those that would occur with income and sales taxes at the local level. This characteristic of the property tax makes it somewhat easier to levy and collect than other taxes.

Property taxes are related to benefits received from local government services

Property taxes are also well suited to local governments because of the connection between many of the services typically funded at the local level and the benefit to property values (Bird and Slack, 2004). Residential property taxes, in particular, are appropriate to fund local government expenditures because they are borne by local residents who use local services. To the extent that this is the case, local property finance of local services will promote efficient public decisions since taxpayers will support those measures for which the benefits exceed the taxes (Fischel, 2001). Both the benefits derived from local services (for example, roads, transit, schools) and the taxes used to finance these services are capitalized into property values. Since taxpayers are willing to pay more for better services and lower tax rates, either will translate into higher property values. Of course, this analysis is based on a number of assumptions such as that local governments do what voters want them to do and voters are free to move to other jurisdictions if they do not like the combination of services and tax rates. Moreover, others see the property tax as a tax on capital (see Zodrow, 2001, for the tax on capital approach).

Concluding comments on unique characteristics

Notwithstanding the strong case to be made for property taxes to finance local government services, the property tax only generates a significant portion of local government revenues in a few countries, mainly those in the OECD (Slack, 2010a). In most developing and transition countries, on the other hand, the property tax provides only a small, though not insignificant, share of the revenue available for local governments. Property tax revenues are low in these countries, in part because of the way the tax is administered: the coverage of the tax is not comprehensive, assessments are low, tax rates are low and collection rates are also often low. Property tax revenues are also low in many countries because it is politically difficult to increase tax rates on a visible tax.

Principles for designing the property tax

In designing a property tax (or any tax), economists set out a series of principles that should be applied:

- Equity based on benefits received: Where beneficiaries are identifiable and where the service is not primarily redistributive in nature, beneficiaries should pay for the service. Matching taxes to beneficiaries in this way can also reduce political opposition to the tax if people feel that they are getting something for their taxes.
- Equity based on ability to pay: Where beneficiaries are not identifiable or where the purpose of the programme is redistributive, the ability-to-pay principle can be applied. According to this principle, taxes are fair if their burden is distributed in accordance with some measure of the taxpayer's ability to pay taxes.
- Efficiency: Taxes represent a cost to taxpayers who respond to the tax by altering decisions such as where to live or work, how much to invest on improvements to their home, where to locate a business and other decisions. Efficiency dictates that these costs should be minimized.
- Accountability: Taxes should be designed in ways that are clear to taxpayers so that policymakers are accountable to taxpayers for the cost of government.
- Stability and predictability: Revenues should be stable and predictable over time.
- Easy to administer: The time and resources devoted to administering the tax should be minimized.

These principles, in many cases, overlap. For example, it is necessary to know how taxpayers respond to a tax (efficiency) to determine who bears the burden of the tax, and if it is fair (equity). Principles can also conflict. For example, a tax that is considered to be fair (equity) may require administrative procedures that make it too costly to administer. The remainder of this chapter provides examples of how these principles are applied (or not applied) to the property tax in the context of the political realities facing decision makers.

Characteristics of the property tax

The property tax is calculated by multiplying a tax rate (or series of tax rates) by the tax base. The following describes some of the choices that are made with respect to the tax base and tax rates and compares them with what economic principles would dictate.

Tax base

For a tax to be efficient and equitable, it is important that the tax base be as comprehensive as possible. In the case of the property tax, this means that the base should not exclude any properties, because exemptions narrow the tax base and thereby increase the taxes on the remaining taxpayers. It is inequitable when some property owners receive benefits from municipal services but do not have to pay for them, while others do have to pay for them. Differential costs also have implications for economic competition among businesses and between businesses and government. Finally, the proportion of tax-exempt properties tends to vary by municipality, thereby creating disproportionate tax burdens across communities.

In every country, however, some properties are exempt from property taxation. Many exemptions are mandatory under central government legislation; others are at local discretion. Exemptions may be based on ownership (such as government-owned property), on the use of the property (such as properties used for charitable purposes) or on the basis of the characteristics of the owner or occupier (such as age or disability).

Although there is great diversity in the use of exemptions, there are some properties that are exempt in most jurisdictions. For example, property owned and occupied by governments is generally exempt from property taxes (in some cases, payments in lieu of taxes are made). Other property types that are often exempt include colleges and universities, churches and cemeteries, public hospitals, charitable institutions, public roads, parks, schools, libraries, foreign embassies and property owned by international organizations.

Where there is the possibility that some properties will be exempt from property taxation, efforts will be expended on the part of taxpayers to try to change the provisions to exempt specific properties. Efforts will also be expended by those who oppose the exemption to try to maintain the status quo. Although the principles of equity and efficiency require a comprehensive property tax base, the political reality is that exemptions are likely to exist, at least for some types of properties because property taxpayers have an incentive to lobby to be excluded from paying the tax.

Tax rates

In many countries, local governments may, can and do levy a series of property tax rates that vary by property class (residential, commercial and industrial, for example). This system gives local governments the power to manage the distribution of the tax burden across various property classes within their jurisdiction, in addition to determining the size of the overall tax burden on taxpayers.

Variable tax rates can be justified in terms of equity and efficiency. On the basis of equity with respect to benefits received, it can be argued that the benefits from local public services are different for different property classes. Higher tax rates should be charged on those types of properties that use more services. As will be noted below, for example, residential properties tend to use more services than non-residential properties. On efficiency grounds, it has been argued that property taxes should be heavier on those components of the tax base that are least elastic in supply. Since business capital tends to be more mobile than residential capital, for example, efficiency arguments lead to the conclusion that business property should be taxed more lightly than residential property.

Notwithstanding the economic case for higher taxation of residential properties than non-residential properties, the reality of tax differentials is quite different. In almost every country, single-family owner-occupied residences are favoured (as are farm properties) over non-residential properties. These cases are discussed further below.

Property tax rates can also vary according to the services received. For example, in some jurisdictions, there is a general tax rate across the city and a special area rate or additional surcharge in those parts of the city that receive services only provided to them, for example garbage collection, street lighting, transit and so forth. Special area rates, which are earmarked for services in those locations, approximate to a benefit charge. Variable tax rates can also be used to distort decisions deliberately to achieve certain land use objectives. Since higher property taxes on buildings tend to slow development, and lower taxes speed up development, a municipal policy to tax land more than buildings would speed up development. Similarly, a municipal policy to develop some neighbourhoods instead of others would call for differential taxes in different locations.

Generally where variable tax rates are applied, properties are assessed at a uniform ratio (100 per cent or a lesser percentage) of market value. Another way to differentiate among property classes is through a classified assessment system. Under this system, classifications or types of property are differentiated according to ratios of assessed value but a uniform tax rate is applied. In terms of accountability, variable tax rates are more visible and easier to understand for taxpayers than a classified assessment system.

Residential properties

In most of the countries in which property taxes are levied, single-family owner-occupied residential properties are favoured over multi-unit dwellings and over commercial and industrial properties (Bird and Slack, 2004). Similarly, in most transition economies, enterprises tend to pay higher property taxes than individuals (Malme and Youngman, 2000).

Favourable treatment of single-family residential properties is achieved in three ways. First, where market value assessment is used, the system deliberately under-assesses single-family residential property compared with apartments and commercial and industrial property of comparable value. Second, many jurisdictions around the world have legislated lower tax rates on single-family residential property than on other types of property. Third, governments often provide property tax relief to residential property owners (and in some cases to tenants) in the form of tax credits, homeowner grants or tax deferrals (these are described further below). These measures are not generally made available to other types of properties.

Single-family owner-occupied residential properties are presumably favoured largely on political grounds: residential homeowners are much more likely to vote in local elections than are tenants, and the eligibility of business owners to vote is generally restricted. This favouritism occurs even though business owners are generally more mobile than residents and even though they generally use fewer services.

Farms

Farm properties are usually favoured in the property tax system as part of a more general policy of protecting farmland. A common way to favour farm properties is through assessment. Rather than assessing farms at their market value that reflects the highest and best use, farms are often assessed at their value in current use. This means that the value of a farm is determined by its selling price if it were to continue to be used as a farm. Alternative uses of the farm, or its speculative value, are not considered in the determination of value.

Value in current use for farmland is used in many Canadian jurisdictions and in New Zealand. In New Zealand, if the highest and best use exceeds current use, both values are recorded. The difference between the taxes as assessed on the two values may be postponed until the land is sold or no longer used for farming. In one Canadian jurisdiction (Ontario), tax rates on farmland pending development can be phased in over stages. The triggers for tax increases are: when the land is used solely for farm purposes but has been registered for subdivision and when the land is used solely for farm purposes but a building permit has been issued.

Other ways of favouring farm properties include providing exemptions for part or all of the farm property, lowering tax rates on farms or providing farm tax rebates. Full exemptions are given in Ireland and Cyprus, for example, whereas partial exemptions are provided in Jamaica and the Netherlands. Lower tax rates are applied in Ontario, Canada – the farm tax rate (and the rate for managed forests) is legislated to be 25 per cent of the residential tax rate.

Favourable treatment of agricultural land is usually designed to preserve it from conversion to urban use. It has been argued, however, that basing the property tax on value in current use is not sufficient to preserve farmland because the resulting tax differential is unlikely, given the generally low effective tax rates on land, to be large enough to compensate for the much higher prices that would be paid if the land were converted to urban use (Maurer and Paugam, 2000). Furthermore, favourable treatment of rural land can increase speculation at the urban fringe and hence end up increasing urban land prices. Nevertheless, farmers, like residential taxpayers, tend to have political clout, thereby enjoying favourable treatment under the property tax system in most countries.

Non-residential properties

Non-residential properties include a wide variety of property uses including commercial uses (such as offices, banks, retail outlets, restaurants, hotels), industrial uses (such as mines, manufacturing plants, shipyards) and special uses (such as pipelines and railway rights of way). Effective property tax rates (property taxes relative market value) are generally higher on non-residential properties than on residential properties.

The differential property tax treatment does not necessarily reflect the differential use of services by different property types, however. For example, users of non-residential property often provide their own garbage collection, security, and fire protection. Kitchen and Slack (1993) reviewed property taxes and municipal expenditures in eight municipalities in Ontario, Canada in 1990 and concluded that non-residential property taxes ranged from 28 to 51 per cent of total local property taxes but accounted for only 31 to 40 per cent of municipal expenditures. A US study (Oakland and Testa, 1995) estimated that the business-related share of state/local expenditures in the USA is less than the business-related share of state/local tax revenues. The ratio differed from state to state, however. The case can thus be made on benefit grounds for taxing non-residential properties at a lower rate than residential properties. This is rarely the case, however.

It has also been argued that property taxes should be heavier on those components of the tax base that are least responsive to a tax increase (least elastic in supply). Since businesses tend to be more mobile than homeowners (in other words, they are more responsive to tax changes), efficiency arguments lead to the conclusion that non-residential property should be taxed more lightly than residential property. In reality, however, lower rates are generally applied to residential properties.

From an economics perspective, the higher taxation of non-residential properties cannot be justified on the basis of equity (benefits received) or on efficiency grounds. Differentially higher taxation distorts land use decisions favouring residential use over commercial and industrial use (Maurer and Paugam, 2000).

Tax exporting

Property taxes on commercial and industrial properties – generally the most important part of the tax in developing countries, for example – can be shifted on to consumers and owners of capital who may not live in the taxing jurisdiction. To the extent that the product or service is exported outside the jurisdiction (this is known as tax exporting), consumers in other jurisdictions may bear part of the tax. Although non-residents who are commuters or visitors to the taxing jurisdiction use some services and therefore should pay some tax, there is a tendency to tax them more than the cost of those services.

Tax exporting is inequitable because the same benefits of local expenditures require different tax prices in different jurisdictions depending on the degree of exporting. It is inefficient because a jurisdiction that can export taxes can provide greater net benefits (expenditures minus taxes) and will be able to attract development. When an area exports its tax burdens, citizens will demand more services than they themselves are willing to pay for through their taxes. The result is an oversupply of public services. It is not accountable because those bearing the burden of the tax are not the same as those enjoying the benefits thus reducing democratic accountability.

Notwithstanding the efficiency arguments against tax exporting, 'politicians have a strong political bias toward exporting tax burdens (Brunori, 2003). Political leaders prefer to meet constituent service demands without incurring the risk of placing the burden of paying for those services on those constituents (Brunori, 2003). At the same time, this means that the public is ready to demand more and better services from their local governments if they do not have to pay for them. It may thus be necessary for the central government to set a ceiling rate to prevent excessive tax exporting (Bird and Slack, 2004).

Tax incentives

Although there is consensus in the academic literature that property taxes have a small but significant influence on business location (Bartik, 1991), there is no consensus that property tax incentives are an effective strategy to achieve economic growth. Tax incentives often lead to a deterioration of the tax base and are often accompanied by low levels of public services. Moreover, given the empirical evidence that taxes have a fairly small effect, a large tax incentive is needed to have an impact on firms' decisions. Lower taxes for specific firms mean higher taxes for all other taxpayers. Tax incentives are often wasted on firms that would have located there anyway. Tax incentives can lead to unfair competition among businesses and can lead to a situation where no major investments occur without them. Economists would argue that policymakers need to concern themselves more with issues of general tax policy (such as equity and efficiency) than with tax incentives.

The political rationale for tax incentives is that the benefits of claiming credit for job creation and investment outweigh all other considerations (Brunori, 2003). This rationale holds even if the incentives have a very small chance of producing the desired results. The reason that local policymakers engage in local tax competition is to attract and keep taxpayers who are believed to contribute more in local revenues than they consume in government services. 'Fiscal zoning', such as zoning for large residential lot sizes, is a way to bring in more affluent homeowners who are assumed to pay more in taxes than they use in services.

Property tax revolts, tax limitations and tax relief

Property tax revolts, whereby taxpayers attempt to restrict the amount of property taxes levied, are a political reality in some parts of the world. Generally, tax revolts have occurred in market value systems where rapid inflation of housing values has led to dramatic increases in property taxes. This type of volatility is particularly problematic for politicians because, as will be discussed further below, those taxpayers who face a significant tax increase 'revolt'. In response to taxpayer resistance to tax increases, some countries have implemented tax limitations. Tax (and expenditure) limitations are ubiquitous in the USA (Sexton and Sheffrin, 1995).

Tax limitations

The classic example of a property tax limitation arising from a tax revolt is Proposition 13, which was passed in California in 1978. Under Proposition 13, property tax rates cannot exceed 1 per cent of the property's market value, and valuations cannot grow by more than 2 per cent per year unless the property is sold (this provision is known as time-of-sale reassessment). Proposition 13 also required that state tax rate increases be approved by a two-thirds vote in the legislature and that local tax rate increases be approved by a referendum.

The objective of the Californian system is to provide certainty and stability for those taxpayers who stay in their homes, and it has been successful at achieving this goal. Property tax freezes of this nature, however, break the link between taxes and market values and, breaking this link results in several problems:

- Taxes are less uniform and more arbitrary.
- Equity is sacrificed because properties with similar market values are not paying the same taxes.
- There is no incentive to review one's assessment. If one of the reasons for the volatility has to do with assessment errors, these errors will never be corrected.
- It is very difficult to remove a freeze: 'once a freeze is imposed, the process of thawing may be too painful to bear' (Youngman, 1999).

Slack (2010b) simulated the impact on taxpayers if assessment capping had been introduced in 1980 in Ontario, Canada. She estimated the impact of a 5 per cent cap, a 10 per cent cap, and a cap based on the rate of inflation (all of which are imposed until the time of sale) on assessed values for residential properties across the province. The results, which are generally consistent with those found in the US literature, suggest that the change in assessed value arising from capping favours property owners with high incomes and high property values at the expense of owners with lower property values and lower incomes; seniors at the expense of young homeowners; owners of waterfront and recreational properties at the expense of owners of single-family homes and condominiums; and properties sold a long time ago at the expense of properties that sold more recently.

In short, tax limitations are largely inequitable and inefficient. As one author notes, certainty is 'purchased at a heavy price in tax equity' (Youngman, 1996). Moreover, once decision makers decide to implement a scheme that ensures certainty and stability, it is impossible to remove the limitations. Even in the face of subsequent huge state and local deficits in California, attributable at least in part to Proposition 13, political factors have made it impossible to revisit this issue.

Another example of a property tax system that was designed to achieve stability, and did so at the expense of equity, is the property system (known as the council tax or rates) in the UK. This system was introduced in the UK in 1993 following the repeal of the community charge (poll tax).

Under the UK system, there is no individual valuation. The market value as of 1 April 1991 (taking account of any significant change to the property between then and 1 April 1993) was determined for each residential property. Each property was assigned to one of eight value bands. Individual properties may be rebanded only under a few circumstances. If the local area changes for the worse, all homes in the area may be placed into a lower band. If a home is expanded, it will be rebanded only after it is sold; if a home decreases in value because part of it is demolished, it may be rebanded immediately. If the property increases in value because the occupier has carried out improvements, such as an extension, it will be rebanded but again not until it is sold.

Banding did not freeze residential property taxes in the UK but it did freeze assessments. However, since the council tax used an estimate of market value at a particular point in time (1 April 1991) and then froze assessments for the foreseeable future, it has had the same implications as any out-of-date assessment system: inequities have increased over time. Initially, there were to be frequent revaluations of property and amendments to banding ranges to keep the base up to date. There has been no revaluation of the council tax, however, since its introduction in 1993. The UK government announced a revaluation for 2007 (based on 2005 values), but due to political issues the revaluation was never implemented.

Tax relief

Most countries have implemented property tax relief measures to reduce the perceived burden on some taxpayers. Relief measures vary according to a number of factors: characteristics of the property (residential vs. non-residential), characteristics of the beneficiaries (e.g. owners vs. renters, income, age, etc.), and the extent to which these measures are permanent or transitory. Relief programmes include grants, exemptions, tax credits, deferrals and special relief schemes for poor taxpayers (reductions, cancellations or refunds of taxes). In some jurisdictions, more than one type of property tax relief is provided. For example, property tax credits may be combined with tax deferrals for the elderly. Reductions, cancellations or refunds may be needed for specific hardship cases, even where other relief schemes are used.

From a political perspective, property tax relief measures of different types have served, in many cases, to make the tax more palatable to the electorate (Oates, 2001). At the same time, however, many of these schemes have impaired the effectiveness of the system of local government finance. Limitations on property taxes in the USA have undermined the role of the property tax in encouraging efficient budgetary decisions (Oates, 2001). The result has been a decline in local property taxes and an increase in intergovernmental transfers. Another problem with property tax relief measures is the danger that transitional or remedial measures (such as phasing in tax increases) take on a life of their own and extend beyond the time required for the transition. Nevertheless, tax relief is politically popular even if economists think that many of the programmes are inefficient and inequitable.

Regardless of country, some of the most vocal opponents to property taxes and tax increases are seniors. In part, seniors oppose property tax increases because they are cash poor (even though they may be asset rich). In part, they simply may have more time to voice their opposition. Whatever the reason, they are a strong political force in their opposition to the tax and often receive special tax treatment.

One way to provide tax relief to seniors is through tax deferral schemes to address their cash flow problems. Property tax deferrals permit the property owner to defer some or all of his/her property taxes. The amount is recovered either by the local government or the central government. The outstanding amount becomes a lien against the property and is payable when the property is transferred. It is a deferral of taxes and not a tax rebate. In some cases, an interest charge (often below the market rate of interest) applies to the taxes deferred. It is not recommended that tax deferrals be expanded to include the non-elderly because the loans would be outstanding for a much longer period of time and it would be necessary to determine eligibility to receive a referral to ensure a reasonable number of beneficiaries.

Although the economic arguments for using tax deferral schemes are strong, they are not particularly popular among taxpayers and are thus not popular politically. The take-up rate in those places that offer them is extremely low '…largely owing to the strong attachment of the old to their homes and to their desire to leave them unencumbered for their heirs' (Bird and Slack, 1978). Tax deferrals provide another example where economics and politics diverge.

The politics of property tax reform

Several countries have implemented or tried to implement property tax reform. Case studies from six different countries (Canada, the UK, Hungary, Colombia, Indonesia and Kenya) are summarized in Bird and Slack (2004). These case studies show that, not surprisingly, the nature and extent of the reform has been different in different countries. Some countries have reformed the tax base (for example, updated the assessment system) while others have focused attention on the administration of the tax. The reasons for reform have also varied, and they range from simplifying the tax system, to increasing the revenue yield from the property tax, to removing inequities in the tax system.

Of all of the objectives for tax reform, removing inequities has proven to be the most elusive. This reason is that, no matter how economically desirable the long-run outcome of property tax reform may be in terms of the equity and efficiency of the tax, its transitional effects may be sufficiently undesirable in political terms to kill it. In short, there will always be winners and losers from tax reform: those who were relatively over-taxed before the reform was implemented will pay less tax; those who were relatively under-taxed before the reform will pay more tax.

The losers from a change in policy tend to be very vocal (even if they are the minority) because they value their losses more than the winners (even if they are the majority) value their gains. This problem is not unique to property taxes but it is particularly significant because of the visibility of the tax. With a visible tax such as the property tax, increasing the tax on some taxpayers (particularly when they are politically influential residential homeowners) is very hard to do. Furthermore, where the losses are concentrated and the gains are dispersed, as is often the case with tax reform, negatively affected interests will be motivated to spend time and resources in political action that can result in permanent, institutionalized groups (for example, office towers, hotels, seniors, waterfront properties) in opposition to reform.

Another problem with tax reform is that there is widespread suspicion that any change in tax policy is used by governments to raise the aggregate level of taxes so that the number of losers and the magnitude of the losses outweigh the number of gainers and the magnitude of the gains. In short, the public perception is that tax reform is not revenue neutral – a perception which, at least in the cases where the goal of reform is to increase revenues, is often correct.

If property tax reform is expected to result in major tax shifts within or among property classes, some form of phase-in mechanism is almost invariably politically necessary to cushion the impact. Failure to allow adequately for transitional problems and to cushion burden shifts is generally a fatal defect. The timing of phase-ins is often controversial because there is always a conflict between moving to a fairer system as quickly as possible and lessening the impact on those whose taxes would increase. One could argue, on the one hand, that existing inequities should be allowed to be perpetuated; on the other hand, it is not wise to create undue hardship by not phasing in tax changes.

Phase-ins are particularly needed where the reform has been delayed for a long time. The longer the reform is delayed, the bigger the shifts that are likely to occur and the more likely that reactions from those adversely affected will be strong. Phase-in schemes can dampen the tax shifts but they also reduce the fairness that the reform was trying to bring about. The case study from Ontario,

Canada (Bird *et al.*, 2012) shows how successive pieces of legislation were introduced to cap tax increases and claw back tax decreases for non-residential
properties. The result was to reintroduce those inequities in the property tax
system that necessitated the reform in the first place.

Case studies of property tax reform also suggest that sustained political will is
needed to ensure that property tax reform is implemented (see the examples of
Kenya and Indonesia in Bird and Slack, 2004). Reforms not only have to be politically acceptable and administratively feasible, they also have to be designed
properly from an economics perspective, however (Bird and Slack, 2004). Such
reform is seldom easy, usually difficult technically and often not too rewarding
in either revenue or political terms.

The property tax as a local tax

Local governments require autonomy over their fiscal affairs to carry out their
responsibilities. In theory, the property tax can provide this kind of autonomy.
To do so, however, local governments must have some political and legal control over the amount of revenue they can raise and spend – without undue
influence of higher levels of government. As Bird (1993) notes, 'local governments
should not only have access to those revenue sources that they are best equipped
to exploit – such as residential property taxes and user charges for public services
– but they should also be both encouraged and permitted to exploit these sources
without undue central supervision.'

A truly 'local' tax is one in which the local government determines the tax
base, sets the tax rates, collects the tax and keeps the revenues. Although a truly
local tax has all of these dimensions, the most important characteristic of a local
tax is the ability of the local government to set the tax rate. Only with tax rates
set locally (rather than by the central government) will there be local autonomy
and accountability for local expenditures and revenues:

> …if a city government feels that it requires more money to do what it is expected
> of it by its citizens, then it should be in a position to get that money from the people
> who will be the primary beneficiaries of the resulting expenditures and to whom
> they are ultimately accountable to at the ballot box – the citizens and voters of the
> city. (Kneebone and McKenzie, 2003)

Rate flexibility is essential if a tax is to be adequately responsive to local needs
and decisions, while remaining politically accountable. A case can be made for
central government assessment to ensure uniformity of the assessment base and
equity in the tax, however. Fair property taxes have to be based on assessments
that are uniform within each jurisdiction. Uniform assessment systems are easier to achieve where the assessment function is centralized. One study, for
example, found that the use of county rather than local assessors resulted in
more uniform residential assessments in US jurisdictions (Strauss and Sullivan,

1998). Furthermore, to the extent that there are economies of scale in the assessment function, these are more likely to be achieved at the central government level (Sjoquist and Walker, 1999).

In this way, the costs of local government are shared fairly across taxpayers. Furthermore, since the property assessment base is sometimes used as the measure of fiscal capacity for equalization grants from senior levels of government, the assessment base needs to be uniform across jurisdictions. When assessment is performed at the local level, there is an incentive to under-value properties to increase the equalization grant. Nevertheless, the assessment function is not always a central government function.

In reality, there are very few countries in which property taxes are truly local taxes. The trend in the USA, for example, has been towards 'less local taxing authority and much more centralization of state-local finances' (Brunori, 2003). Table 3.1 summarizes the extent of local discretion over determining the tax base and setting the tax rate for 25 countries around the world.

In most developing and transition countries, local property taxes are, in most respects, more 'central' than 'local' in nature. As Table 3.1 indicates, the property tax is largely a central tax in Latvia and Chile. Except for the Philippines, East Asian countries exhibit a low level of own-source revenue autonomy (Ebel and Taliercio, 2005). Rates are essentially set by the central government in countries such as Japan, Ukraine, Chile, Thailand and Tunisia. In some countries (Hungary, Colombia and the Philippines, for example), there is some local discretion within centrally set limits. Sometimes, there is complete local discretion such as in Argentina and Kenya.

Although not much has been written on the reasons for central control over what is generally considered to be a local tax, three explanations have been put forward for the lack of revenue autonomy at the local level in developing and transition economies. One explanation is that there has been confusion on the part of central and local government officials between revenue sharing and own-source revenue autonomy (Bird *et al.*, 1995). Revenue sharing means that the proceeds of the tax accrue in whole or in part to local governments but the central government sets the tax rates and assesses and collects the tax. Shared tax revenues can be distributed among local governments on the basis of where the revenues were collected or on the basis of a formula, for example on a per capita basis. Revenue sharing is similar to providing a transfer except that local government revenues are tied to the revenues of the central government. It is not the same as giving local governments their own authority to levy taxes. There is much more central control over revenue sharing than there is if local governments have their own taxing authority. In particular, the central government can arbitrarily change the amount of tax that it will share with local governments. An interesting example is provided by the province of Alberta, Canada. The provincial government agreed to share 5 cents per litre of fuel tax revenues with the two major cities in the province. Subsequently, it decided unilaterally to lower the rate to 4 cents per litre. After fierce lobbying on the part of the cities, 5 cents per litre was reinstated.

Table 3.1 Responsibility for tax base and discretion over tax rates

	Responsibility for assessment	Local discretion over tax rates
OECD:		
Australia	State government for central and local taxes	Yes for local tax; limits on annual increases in revenues
Canada	Generally provincial	Yes (restrictions apply in some provinces)
Germany	Local governments	Central base rates; locally determined leverage factors
Japan	Local governments based on a uniform national formula	Nationally set standard and maximum rates
UK	Central government	Residential tax only; tax ratios for bands set centrally
Central and Eastern Europe:		
Hungary	Local governments	Yes; within legal limits
Latvia	Central government	No, but local governments can grant relief
Poland	Local governments (using information in central registries)	Yes; subject to prescribed minimum and maximum rates
Russia	Central government	Yes, within narrow range set by senior governments
Ukraine	Central government – state tax administration	No
Latin America:		
Argentina	Provincial and local governments	Yes
Chile	National tax administration with local input	No
Colombia	Local governments	Yes, subject to central government limits
Mexico	State and local governments jointly	Yes
Nicaragua	National tax administration	No
Asia:		
China	Local tax office directly under the state council	No
India	Local authorities; some state assessment authorities	Yes, subject to state restrictions
Indonesia	Central tax department	No, but can change valuation deduction
Philippines	Provincial and local governments	Yes, subject to minimum and maximum rates
Thailand	Local governments	No
Africa:		
Guinea	Central government	No
Kenya	Local governments	Yes
South Africa	Local governments	Yes
Tanzania	Local authorities (funded by central government)	Yes
Tunisia	Urban municipalities within nationally set ranges	No

Source: Bird and Slack (2004). Reproduced by permission of Enid Slack.

A second explanation for the lack of revenue autonomy is that central authorities are simply reluctant to grant much fiscal autonomy to local governments (Ebel and Taliercio, 2005). This explanation suggests that central governments either do not trust local governments to exercise their taxing authority appropriately or they are afraid that allowing local governments to levy their own taxes will impinge on their own ability to levy property taxes or other taxes. Although there may be some cases where the central government should set limits on property tax rates (for example, to restrict their ability to export taxes to other jurisdictions), in reality the control seems to go well beyond this purpose.

A third explanation is that local governments have been reluctant to take advantage of the legal authority assigned to them (Ebel and Taliercio, 2005). One reason might be that, since individuals and businesses can easily move between local jurisdictions, a differential property tax rate could encourage individuals to move to those jurisdictions with lower tax rates. Although the resulting tax competition can create an environment in which municipalities become more efficient in their use of resources and more accountable to taxpayers, it can also result in harmful competition. The more likely reason, however, is that local government are unwilling to face the political fallout from levying taxes and would prefer to have the central government bear that responsibility even though the taxes are being used to deliver local services.

Conclusion

The review of property tax policies in different countries highlights the differences between what economic principles would dictate, on the one hand, and what policy choices are actually made, on the other. In short, economic analysis plays only a minor supporting role in tax policy decisions (Holcombe, 1998). Inadequate attention to economics principles in designing property tax policy results, in part, from the unique characteristics of the property tax. Its visibility, for example, means that taxpayers know what taxes they pay and are aware of annual changes in the tax. This visibility puts pressure on politicians to maintain the status quo in tax burdens from year to year, to favour certain properties over others, to provide tax relief whenever there is a tax increase and to undertake other measures that do not necessarily adhere to economics principles.

Policymakers would be wise to pay attention to economics principles to ensure that the property tax is both a fair and efficient tax, however. Responding to short-term political pressures at the expense of applying sound economics principles can result in an even less equitable and efficient tax in the long run and even greater taxpayer resistance. Given current interest in decentralization and the desire to increase property taxation for local governments in many countries around the world, it is important to ensure that the property tax system is not only politically acceptable and administratively feasible but also that it is designed properly from an economics perspective.

References

Bartik, T.J. (1991) *Who Benefits from State and Local Economic Development Policies?* Kalamazoo, MI: W.E. Upjohn Institute.

Bird, R. (1993) Threading the Fiscal Labyrinth: Some Issues in Fiscal Decentralization. *National Tax Journal*, 46(2): 207–27.

Bird, R.M., Ebel, R.D. and Wallich, C.I. (1995) *Decentralization of the Socialist State: Intergovernmental Finance in Transition Economies.* Washington, DC: World Bank.

Bird, R.M. and Slack, E. (1978) *Residential Property Tax Relief Measures in Ontario.* Toronto: University of Toronto Press for the Ontario Economic Council.

Bird, R.M. and Slack E. (2004) *International Handbook on Land and Property Taxation.* Cheltenham, UK: Edward Elgar Publishing Inc.

Bird, R.M., Slack, E. and Tassonyi, A. (2012) *A Tale of Two Taxes: Reforming the Property Tax in Ontario.* Cambridge, MA: Lincoln Institute of Land Policy.

Brunori, D. (2003) *Local Tax Policy: A Federalist Perspective.* Washington, DC: The Urban Institute Press.

Ebel, R.D. and Taliercio, R. (2005) Subnational Tax Policy and Administration in Developing Economies. *Tax Notes International, March* 7: 919–936.

Fischel, W.A. (2001) Homevoters, Municipal Corporate Governance, and the Benefit View of the Property Tax. *National Tax Journal*, 54(1): 157–173.

Holcombe, R.G. (1998) Tax Policy from a Public Choice Perspective. *National Tax Journal*, 51(2): 359–371.

Kitchen, H. and Slack, E. (1993) *Business Property Taxation.* Kingston: Queen's University, School of Policy Studies.

Kneebone, R.D. and McKenzie, K.J. (2003) Removing the Shackles: Some Modest, and Immodest, Proposals to Pay for Cities. In: Boothe, P. (ed), *Paying for Cities: The Search for Sustainable Municipal Revenues.* University of Alberta: Institute for Public Economics, Western Studies in Economic Policy No. 9: 43–77.

Malme, J.H. and Youngman, J.M. (2000) *The Development of Property Taxation in Economies in Transition. Case Studies from Central and Eastern Europe.* Washington, DC: World Bank.

Maurer, R. and Paugam, A. (2000) *Reform toward Ad Valorem Property Tax in Transition Economies: Fiscal and Land Use Benefits.* Land and Real Estate Initiative, Background Series 13, Washington DC: World Bank.

Oakland, W.H. and Testa, W.A. (1995) *Community Development-Fiscal Interactions: Theory and Evidence from the Michigan Area.* Working Paper 95-7. Chicago: Federal Reserve Bank of Chicago, Research Department.

Oates, W.E. (2001) Property Taxation and Local Government Finance: An Overview and Some Reflections. In: Oates, W.E. (ed), *Property Taxation and Local Government Finance.* Cambridge, MA: Lincoln Institute of Land Policy: 21–31.

Sexton, T.A. and Sheffrin, S.M. (1995) Five Lessons from Tax Revolts. *Proceedings of the National Tax Association*: 175–81.

Simonsen, B. and Robbins, M.D. (2003) Reasonableness, Satisfaction, and Willingness to Pay Property Taxes. *Urban Affairs Review*, 38 (6): 831–854.

Sjoquist, D.L. and Walker, M.B. (1999) Economies of Scale in Property Tax Assessment. *National Tax Journal.* 52(2): 207–220.

Slack, E. (2010a) The Property Tax in Theory and Practice. *IEB's World Report on Fiscal Federalism '10*, Barcelona: 24–33.

Slack, E. (2010b) Assessment Limits for Ontario: Could We Live with the Consequences? Paper prepared for the Association of Municipalities of Ontario, Canada.

Strauss, R.P. and Sullivan, S.R. (1998) The Political Economy of the Property Tax: Assessor Authority and Assessment Uniformity. *State Tax Notes*, 18: 327–338.

Youngman, J.M. (1996) Alternatives for Property Tax Revision and Reform. *State Tax Notes*, 11: 303–306.

Youngman, J.M. (1999) The Hardest Challenge for Value-Based Property Taxes: Part II. *State Tax Notes*, 16: 1393–1397.

Zodrow, G.R. (2001) The Property Tax as a Capital Tax: A Room with Three Views. *National Tax Journal*, 54(1): 139–156.

4

Administration of Local Taxes: An International Review of Practices and Issues for Enhancing Fiscal Autonomy[1]

John L. Mikesell

Introduction

Many countries have concentrated tax revenue, taxing authority and tax administration with the central government. However, there is a spreading sense that local governments are maturing (Bahl, 1999), that they no longer require central government guidance and control for them to make a positive contribution to provision and delivery of government services, that they can and should assume more responsibility for finance of services and that bringing decisions closer to the voters will improve government efficiency, effectiveness and responsiveness. An important element in the case for subnational revenue-raising responsibility is the idea that governments should face at least part of the political consequences of obtaining resources to provide services, in other words, that they should levy their own taxes to cover at least part of the cost of the services they are providing. Bahl and Bird (2008) argue the case for subnational taxes in developing countries as an element in fiscal decentralization, primarily because they are 'moving governance closer to the people' and that case extends at least as strongly to more developed nations.

As nations decentralize taxing authority and local governments have to finance a greater share of the cost of the services they provide, there are two significant lessons from international experience. First, taxes need not be administered by the government that levies them. Giving subnational governments

A Primer on Property Tax: Administration and Policy, First Edition.
Edited by William J. McCluskey, Gary C. Cornia and Lawrence C. Walters.
© 2013 Blackwell Publishing Ltd. Published 2013 by Blackwell Publishing Ltd.

meaningful authority to tax gives them power to adjust the size of their budgets and to establish how the tax burden from financing that budget will be distributed. Given the option, some subnational governments will choose to administer the taxes they levy and some subnational governments will levy taxes that others will administer. Both options can be feasible. Localization of decision making does imply that the governments should decide for themselves whether they will administer their own taxes. Choice of administration can be an element of fiscal autonomy.

Second, international experience makes clear that local and regional adminis-tration should not be automatically dismissed as technically impossible or unwarranted. Whether local and regional governments in fact administer the taxes that they levy depends on a mix of both technical and political considerations (Veehorn and Ahmad, 1997). The issues will be explored in greater depth later, but they may be summarized here. Local administration provides full scope for decentralization of revenue policy (how a tax is administrated is a practical element of policy itself) and exploits local familiarity with local business practices and institutions. Central administration permits any efficiency advantages of scale and technical expertise and permits a more balanced fight in disputes with powerful taxpayers. The actual administrative pattern should balance these advantages within existing national circumstances along with the practical issues of comparative administrative capacity across the tiers of government and with the political factors that shape decisions at all levels of government.

The choice of administrative system is not one to be taken lightly. Administration defines tax policy, as Tanzi and Pellechio (1995) point out, '... poor administration will change the way taxation affects the traditional objec-tives of government policy, namely, allocation of resources, redistribution of income, and stabilization.' No one style will be best in all operating environments and for all tax bases. Choosing an appropriate administrative system is integral to the choice of the tax system itself.

Countries that follow the path of revenue localization and assign taxing authority to tiers of government below the central level – regional and local – may choose various intergovernmental administrative assignments for tax collection. The possibilities may be arrayed into three groups: (1) a single central government agency that administers taxes levied by any level of government in the country, (2) a central government tax authority plus subnational tax autho-rities that operate independently of the central authority and of each other, (3) a tax authority operated by the central government and independent subna-tional authorities with considerable *shared and cooperative* operations of some administrative tasks. Independent subnational agencies that administer taxes levied by the central government is another possibility. For example, German lander and Swiss canton tax authorities administer major taxes for the central government, in the USA, where the state levies a real property tax, that tax is normally administered by local governments, and in Canada, where Quebec administers the national goods and services (value added) tax along with its provincial tax. This arrangement is, however, rare for revenue-productive taxes.

Unitary states tend to the first organizational format and federal states often use a mixture of formats. There are exceptions. For example, China is a unitary state with subnational tax administration operated by local governments. However, these lower administrators are heavily subordinated to the central State Administration of Taxes (SAT). Because taxes are shared upward, this central control is essential here because regional variations in administrative vigour and in interpretation could make the effective central tax rates vary across the local governments. There are reports that local governments can influence SAT to ensure that local revenue before collections accrue to the central government through their control of access to services such as water, power, housing and schools.

Not all taxes levied in a country necessarily follow the same administrative format – administration may be entirely independent for one tax, fully central for another, while there will be considerable cooperation for others. User charges and prices for goods and services sold by governments – electricity, housing, water, solid waste collection follow a different pattern: these systems are virtually always administered by the government providing the service.

Central administration

A single tax administration administers all taxes in many countries, including taxes levied by both national and local governments. Sometimes only the central government has taxing authority, in which case single administration is the only reasonable option. The uniformity argument is also strong when taxes have been adopted centrally for dedicated and shared distribution to regional or local government. It is also convenient when subnational governments may levy supplemental (or piggybacked) rates on a national base. Subnational taxes – taxes over which the subnational government exercises control at the margin – and taxes controlled by the central government that have been allocated to (i.e., shared with) subnational budgets are different. With shared taxes, the margin for tax policy remains centralized and an important factor for localization, accountability and prudence is gone. As Ebel and Yilmaz (2002) write 'Accountability at the margin is an important characteristic of a revenue system that fosters prudence in debt and expenditure management. It is impossible for a subnational government not to have control over revenue margins and still be fully accountable.' When the revenue choices are made by a different government, the subnational government is not accountable for the revenue side of fiscal operations.

When a tax is centrally administered, staff of the administrative unit are employed by the central government. There may be regional authorities along with the central authority, but these decentralized units are part of a single central administration. Central administration typically includes: (1) returns that encompass both the central tax and any subnational taxes, (2) a unified registration process for taxpayers, (3) taxpayer identification numbers that serve for all levels of government, (4) compatible and combined revenue and taxpayer accounting information systems, (5) unified delinquency control, audit strategy and audit programmes. The functions are somewhat different for property taxes. Here, the emphasis is on maintaining property records and developing a system of mass valuation of property parcels; the focus is not on encouraging voluntary compliance and, because the parcels are immobile, collection can proceed at a slower pace. The process has been particularly critical in countries in transition from plan to market.

Some national experiences

With centralized administration, the central administration – either centrally or through dependent regional branches – collects taxes levied by the central government, the revenue from which may finance central government services, may be distributed to regional or local governments through conditional or unconditional grant programmes or may be shared by formula with those lower governments and also collects any taxes that might be levied by subnational governments.

The National Tax Board plus regional tax authorities structure in Sweden offers an example of decentralization within a national system. The ten regional authorities (one for each county) are responsible for tax collection functions. Each tax authority has a county tax director and a governing council, but they are under the guidance of the National Tax Board. Within the National Tax Board is the Enforcement Service (KFM), itself organized with ten regional authorities (not coterminous with tax authority regions), assigned responsibility to confirm and collect debts. The KFM collects unpaid taxes for the tax authority, but its authority extends more broadly to other public claims (television licenses, parking fines etc., owed to central and local authorities) and to private claims (private judgments from general and administrative courts). The National Tax Board administers both organizations, issues directives on their implementation of the laws, and works to maintain uniformity of administration across the country. In the Swedish example, two regionally organized authorities administer tax collection, but both are subordinated to the single National Tax Board. Most central government tax systems, of course, do not have an entity like the KFM and more compact nations do not require regional authorities.

When there is a single, central administration, it would also collect any taxes levied by regional or local governments. Some countries do feature central administration of assigned regional or local taxes. The Russian Federation offers one example: the central Ministry of Taxation collects all taxes throughout the country, including those levied by legislative action of regional or local government, as well as shared taxes adopted by the Federation Duma for distribution to subnational governments. (The separate tax police was abolished in 2003.) Both subjects of the Federation and local units of self-government may levy taxes from an assigned list. Some taxes are piggybacked surcharges to a central tax (the enterprise profits tax has been such a tax), some may be levied by the

Federation Duma for support of subnational budgets (the individual income tax has been such a tax) and some are levied by action of the region (the retail sales tax was such a tax) or by localities, but the central Ministry administers all the taxes (Mikesell, 1999). Local land committees are responsible for calculation of cadastral (formula) valuation of land that provides the base for support of local governments, but the Ministry of Taxation is responsible for the overall operation of the system (Gerasimova *et al.* 2005).

In the early years of transition, there were continuing concerns in countries of the former Soviet Union about dual subordination in the central tax administration: while the tax inspectors were officially and organizationally part of the central government apparatus (the tax inspectorate within a ministry of finance or an independent ministry of taxation), the field staff had considerable loyalty to local authorities because those authorities provided them with office space, heat, supplies and other amenities, if not salaries or salary supplements, and it was common for regional authorities to have the right to approve appointments of regional administrators of the central tax authority. This created the great potential for administrative problems and abuses. In the transition period, not all tax payments were collected (and of those collected, not all were collected in live cash, as opposed to being collected in kind) and divided loyalties and closeness to the regional and local authorities meant that subnational budgets got favourable treatment in terms of what money could be extracted from taxpayers. Regional and local governments got cash; the central government got payment in kind and that payment could be valued at whatever amount the collection authority chose. While this problem from the early period of transition was extreme, it does illustrate a more general issue whenever administration of one government works for another: will effort be vigorous when the proceeds of that effort will go to another government? That is why clear performance expectations and standards are particularly necessary when shared administration is employed.

In several countries, a regional or local tax supplement accompanies (piggybacks) the tax levied by a higher level of government, using higher level administration for collection and enforcement. Examples of this arrangement include the following:

1. Localities in Nordic countries supplement the central tax with a piggybacked personal income tax administered by the central government. For example, the Swedish National Tax Board, previously discussed, administers local taxes based on the central personal income tax base. The proportional rates vary between municipalities, with the lowest rates in well-to-do suburbs of large cities and highest rates in the rural north and in municipalities suffering industrial decline. Similar income taxes apply in Denmark, Finland and Iceland.

2. Some local governments in the USA levy supplements to state individual income taxes. The state tax department administers the local taxes with its own tax. The same administrative structure – withholding, return processing,

revenue accounting, delinquency control, audit, enforcement – applies to both state and local taxes. The local tax is commonly satisfied through a single line on the larger state tax return. State administration makes it feasible to apply the tax to a broader measure of taxable income than that applied in locally administered payroll taxes but localities complain about slow distribution of revenue collections and about distribution of revenues to the proper locality. No state accepted the federal offer of free administration of their individual income taxes that was provided as part of the General Revenue Sharing programme in the 1970s – loss of autonomy in defining the state tax base was seen as an excessive price for the service.

3. Many local governments in the USA levy retail sales taxes that are supplements to the state tax. Although some localities administer their own sales taxes, more often the local taxes are a piggybacked supplement to the state tax, with state administration provided at low or no cost to the locality. Multi-branch merchants must segregate sales and collections according to taxing jurisdiction so that revenues may be distributed to the proper jurisdiction. The merchant's return will thus have as many lines as there are jurisdictions in which it makes taxable sales. However, the single state return with central administration is simpler for compliance than separate returns for many independent taxing administrations. The state authorities must undertake revenue accounting to separate payments between state and local amounts and among the several taxing localities and distribute collections on a timely basis.

4. Local governments in Switzerland levy supplements to canton individual income taxes. Each of the 26 Swiss cantons has its own tax system, and local governments are entitled to levy taxes to the extent authorized by the canton. The communal tax is levied as a percentage or multiple of the basic canton tax rate. A federal law requires cantons to harmonize their income tax concept and deductions with the federal base, but they may set the amount of deductions and their rate schedules. Each of the cantons has a separate administrative body for collection of its taxes. The communal tax is piggybacked on the canton tax, and federal tax is reported on the canton return. Thus, the canton is responsible for assessing and collecting federal, canton and communal income tax – centralization down from the canton but decentralized administration up to the federal level. In contrast to the case in many nations, subnational – canton and municipal – Swiss governments receive the bulk of income tax collections, not the federal government. And, again in contrast to most international experience, the income tax is a relatively modest revenue source for the federal level. But because the tax is collected across all cantons, it is important that the base and deductions be standardized in order that a uniform effective federal rate can be imposed on taxpayers without regard to their location.

5. The greatest array of regional taxes that are centrally administered occurs in Canada, where the national Canada Customs and Revenue Agency (CCRA) collects harmonized national value added and provincial sales, corporate

income and personal income taxes in some but not all provinces and not in the same way for all taxes. (Canada Customs and Revenue Agency and Department of Finance, 2000) For the harmonized sales tax and corporate income tax, the provinces or territories may select their rate but must use the national base (pure piggybacking). The goods and service tax base is broader than the traditional provincial retail sales tax, so movement to the harmonized tax system means base broadening. The 2011 referendum that took British Columbia out of the harmonized sales tax apparently was successful because of displeasure with the broader tax coverage. There is somewhat greater flexibility in choosing rates and preferences for the personal income tax than for the other taxes.

There are also non-piggybacked systems for central administration. Where it is permitted, local governments themselves can arrange for centralized administration. For many Ohio (USA) cities, a joint collection agency handles all aspects of enforcement and charges a fee to cover the cost of running the agency. Three regional entities around the state (Regional Income Tax Agency, Central Collection Agency and Columbus Income Tax Division) administer multiple taxes, providing a system in which a single return can cover a taxpayer's obligations to several jurisdictions, even though the base details may not be exactly the same for all. The agency collects a single payment for multiple-jurisdiction returns (taxes are employment based and a taxpayer may work in several jurisdictions) and provides the necessary division among cities. These taxes are coordinated with neither the Ohio state income tax, the federal income tax nor Ohio school district income taxes that the state administers on a piggyback basis. Municipalities can choose to levy the tax, can choose the rate that they levy and can choose whether to administer the tax themselves or to contract with a regional administration agency. This range of choices gives the municipalities great fiscal autonomy and, because the municipalities can opt in or out, requires that regional authorities pay great attention to the quality and cost of the service that it provides.

Local property taxes in many countries give local governments some choice of tax rate, but all parts of administration are performed by the national revenue agency. Sometimes, however, the localities do not choose the rate, but receive the proceeds of the centrally adopted and administered tax; these latter arrangements are properly considered origin-based transfers from a central tax, not local taxes.

Results from central administration

Evidence from international experience suggests the following specific conclusions about centralized administration:

1. A centralized administration improves the chances that any economies of scale will be realized. Smaller independent local administrations may obtain

the economies by contracting with larger entities or by combining operations with other administrations, but this is less certain to occur than if the administration is centralized. There are few tests for economies of scale in tax administration. In one study, Sjoquist and Walker (1999) found for property tax assessment in Georgia (USA) that a ten per cent in the volume of assessments results in an increase in total costs of approximately 3 per cent. However, Bell (1999) found from empirical analysis in the USA no evidence that larger jurisdictions produce more accurate valuations than smaller ones. Smaller units may achieve quality by contracting for outside expertise, thus negating any size advantage.

2. A centralized administration provides a single structure for dealing with all taxpayers throughout the country. That permits a single information system for tracking taxpayers and their economic activities and a single taxpayer identification number for all taxes. A single master file with all relevant data would provide a strong tool for enforcement and collection through matching across tax types. A single taxpayer identification number would assist enforcement and a single registration process into the information system would simplify taxpayer compliance.

3. A single centralized system improves the chances that taxpayers will receive consistent treatment by the tax authority, no matter where the entity or its taxable activities are located. Uniform treatment can improve the chances that administration will be seen as fair and that it will not be slanted to provide 'deals' to certain taxpayers. Because local administration is closer to the people, there is always the concern that the administration will play favourites and that confidential taxpayer information will be misused. A perception of balanced administration likely contributes to the probability of compliance with the tax.

4. A central organization can facilitate rotation of personnel, a critical component of internal control to reduce the potential for corruption. In a smaller administrative unit, there may simply be too few auditors of adequate skill relative to the number of complex assignments to maintain regular rotation for those assignments.

5. Central administration reduces the number of contacts between a taxpayer and the tax authorities and, because there are certain overhead costs that will be associated with collecting any tax, may reduce the cost of administration and compliance for the overall revenue system, central plus subnational. A single administrative authority eliminates the possibility that the taxpayer will be confused about what tax organization is responsible for answering questions, receiving filings, enforcement, etc., or that multiple audit visits will occur in a single audit cycle. When there are multiple administrative agencies involved, some payments, correspondence, appointments, etc., inevitably get misdirected by some taxpayers. None of this will happen if there is only one authority collecting taxes in the country.

6. The large administrative agencies that centralization produces may afford more qualified personnel, may be able to pay higher salaries (and thus reduce the attractiveness of corruption), may allow personnel to specialize to a degree not feasible with smaller administrative units and may have budgets that permit more sophisticated information technology. It is tempting to argue that higher pay will lead to better performance, a hypothesis generally untested. However, an investigation in one US state (Connecticut) by Bates and Santerre (1993) found no link between pay and performance in property tax collection, a somewhat narrow indicator. In small administrative agencies, staff may be required to handle all routine duties, thus losing both the gains from specialization and the internal control advantage of separation of duties.

7. A centralized, national tax administration can be better equipped, legally and in terms of resources, to deal with national and global business entities that might overwhelm subnational government agencies. Tannenwald (2001) observes that, in the USA, 'state and city tax departments are increasingly "outgunned" in attempting to enforce [the corporate income tax].' They simply lack the legal and accounting talent to keep up with the avoidance or evasion strategies of large business. This problem certainly must be even more acute in developing and transition countries.

8. A large, centralized national tax administration will be better able to deal with taxable activities that cross regional or local jurisdiction boundaries within the nation.

9. Central administration may permit adoption of more sophisticated structures of some taxes. For instances, it is easier for a local government to administer an income tax based on 'earned income' or payrolls than a broad tax on income from any source on the Haig–Simons concept; the former requires enforcement against employers in the jurisdiction, a far easier task than the broader reporting from entities outside the jurisdiction that the latter would almost certainly require. The payroll version of a local income tax, usually administered by a locality, typically means that jurisdictions in which the person works will collect the tax revenue, even though that may not be the jurisdiction in which the person lives and from which he demands local public services.

10. Central administration may facilitate transfers of revenues to mitigate horizontal fiscal disparity across subnational units of government. Revenue from taxes administered by subnational governments almost always stays with the government collecting the revenue, leaving great disparity between regions with high endowment of the tax base (e.g., natural resources, heavy industry, etc.) and those lacking such an endowment.

11. The separation between the lower and higher level taxes is not always clear to the taxpayer. In some US states, for instance, the local tax appears as a single line on the state vendor tax return, is fully subsumed in the state collection and enforcement process and is collected without differentiation on taxable transactions. In Canada, there is a single return for provincial and

federal income taxes, although a separate calculation of some detail is required for each. A single bill also normally applies with US property taxes, with a single collector distributing revenues to the overlapping jurisdictions that have levied taxes, making it harder for the taxpayer to know who to blame for the tax. These arrangements make the taxes more convenient, but blur political responsibility for the taxes being levied and collected. Also, the central administering unit almost always restricts the structure of any tax for which it offers administration (base definition and rate structure that may be applied), thereby limiting tax policy options available to the local government, as well as defining administrative policy (audit plans, collection policies, etc.) for the tax. These are policy choices effectively taken from the locality when its taxes are centrally administered.

Independent local administration

Independent subnational authority both to enact tax legislation (choose taxes, define bases and set rates) and to administer the taxes that have been enacted affords subnational units greater fiscal autonomy because the regional or local government controls both the design of the tax structure and how that structure will be applied. In many instances, these taxes administered independently for subnational authorities are not levied by the national government, so independent administration adds diversity to the overall revenue scheme of the country, in addition to providing fiscal autonomy. For instance, the state and local sales taxes in the USA affords major diversity away from income base dominance in the overall revenue system, and there is no federal tax upon which administration could be based.

Subnational governments need administrative capacity that is adequate for equitable and efficient collection of taxes for which they have assumed collections responsibility. Because administration itself is an element of revenue autonomy, the fact that centralized administration might be less costly for some taxes, might improve some facets of distributional equity, or might generate some additional revenue is not decisive evidence for dictating central administration. Leaving choice of administration to responsible subnational authorities is an element of autonomy and, as seen in the Canadian case, can lead to central administration of regional taxes or, in the case of the USA, to regional administration of local taxes, as well as to independent subnational administration. The choice should depend on the attractiveness (economic and political) of the options presented. Some taxes are less technically suitable for subnational administration than others and not all administrative functions for those that might be administered at lower tiers are efficiently performed by smaller governments. But where lower tier governments can otherwise become technically competent, subnational administration can be considered.

Particular attention should be devoted to the major broad-base taxes administered independently by subnational governments, especially individual income taxes and real property taxes. General retail sales taxes make a considerable contribution to subnational government finances in the USA and Canada. Cities in Nepal, India, and other countries in Asia and Africa have relied on the *octroi*, an easy, buoyant, and productive source of revenue. Jenkins *et al.* (2000) describe operation of the tax in Nepal:

> It was levied technically by using street barriers lowered and raised by tax inspectors. Together with the fact that this money was levied on out-of-town people and not on local constituents, the whole procedure reminded one of medieval robber-barons descending from their castles to collect 'fees' from traveling merchants, than of a tax fit for a modern government.

But it did provide a degree of revenue autonomy. There is even wider international experience with subnational administration of selective excises, fees, licenses, etc., but these sources typically have limited revenue potential, and subnational governments cannot rationally afford to devote substantial resources to their administration. Therefore, disappointing experience with minor sources ought not be taken to mean that independent administration is impossible, because it may mean that the governments do not see fit to waste their administrative resources on a tax with modest potential.

Some regional and local governments levy corporate income taxes, but there are difficult logical and technical problems in regard to allocation of corporate income among taxing jurisdictions, possibly unjustifiable compliance costs imposed on businesses by these taxes, and subnational governments are forever torn between rigorous enforcement to protect the tax base and giving favourable treatment to local businesses to encourage economic development. US states levy corporate income taxes that are similar to the comparable federal levy, but state and federal administrations are separate. Federal law provides ground rules that define when a state may tax income of a multi-state business (nexus) and for division of business income among states in which the business operates. However, the apportionment standards have become quite flexible through court rulings, and states use a number of different formulae, causing some corporations to be taxable on more than 100 per cent of their profits and others on considerably less. The system rejects any attempt at state-by-state accounting of profits earned by the corporation. Some Canadian provinces also administer such taxes, but most are in the scheme administered by CCRA. In contrast to the practice in the USA, Canada has a single, agreed apportionment formula for dividing corporate income among the provinces. Other subnational governments generally do not attempt broad corporate profits taxes, leaving such administration to the central level. The enterprise profits taxes that have been levied by subjects of the Russian Federation are administered by the national Ministry of Taxation.

Local administration may actually mean administration by contracted specialists. Contracts with private firms and other governments for technical parts of tax administration are common wherever local governments have responsibility for administration of real property taxes, but particularly in Canada, the USA and parts of Africa. These are true service contracts for delivery of particular services to the government, not the bidding off of right to collect taxes characteristic of the tax farming approach to privatizing administration (Stella, 1992). Until around the second decade of the twentieth century, US localities frequently contracted with 'tax ferrets' to locate unreported and untaxed properties, in exchange for a substantial share of the resulting tax revenue. Paying on the basis of amounts collected normally is not a satisfactory standard, inasmuch as a substantial sum will be collected in a mature voluntary compliance based system with essentially no administrative effort.

Frequently contracted functions include mapping, listing and valuation of parcels in real property taxation. In the USA, some states have experimented with contract auditors for sales and corporate income taxes, and both states and localities frequently contract with private firms on more difficult collection assignments, often paying on the basis of amount collected. Local governments in a few states, particularly Louisiana and Alabama, have contracted with private firms for administration of their retail sales taxes. There have been questions about the appropriate basis for compensation on these contracts and on some possible abuses of authority in collection. States also regularly use local law enforcement agencies or private collectors in pursuit of collections from difficult or dangerous taxpayers, often on a fee basis. Few accounts fall into this extreme collection system – these are accounts virtually given up as hopeless by the tax authorities, so any revenue at all is better than what the authorities would have otherwise collected.

Experience with local administration

Much of the experience with independent subnational administration, particularly of non-property taxes, comes from federations because they are more likely to offer some fiscal autonomy, including administrative autonomy, to lower tier governments.

1. In the USA '...tax policy and administration...are perhaps as decentralized as in any country in the world.' (Duncan and McLure, 1997). States have almost unlimited discretion as to the taxes they levy and, when levied, they will administer them by themselves. Local governments work under whatever system is allowed them by their states. Government finances in the USA are generally driven by the principle that the government wishing to deliver government services should be prepared to raise the necessary revenues and to administer the revenue system that has been selected to finance those services. With some few exceptions, including those piggybacked arrangements previously noted and some instances of intergovernmental cooperation to be discussed in the next section, tax authorities are independent operations. In general, both large and small subnational governments in the USA manage

independent tax collection duties, not perfectly and sometimes with quite notorious errors, but well enough that reports of these problems are news-worthy because of their rarity. While the technology and sophistication used by the US state and local governments likely far exceeds that available in developing and transition countries, it should be recalled that these taxes were initially administered with paper returns, file cards, pencils and adding machines. In particular, the sales tax was a product of the Great Depression of the 1930s. When real property tax revenues failed the states, the retail sales tax proved capable of generating revenue to continue state services and collection definitely used minimal technology.

2. Several Canadian provinces continue to administer their provincial retail sales taxes even as the Canada Customs and Revenue Agency administers the national goods and services (value added) tax. The Canadian experience clearly demonstrates the compatibility of a central value added tax and regional retail sales taxes, with a wide range of administration being feasible. As in the USA, the quality of provincial sales tax administration is regarded as high.

3. Australia provides another system of independent administration within a federation. Taxes are levied and collected at three levels of government, although a much greater share of subnational expenditure is financed by cen-tral grants, rather than taxes levied by these lower governments, than is the case in the USA and Canada. The states are effectively blocked by interpreta-tion of the national constitution or by grant stipulations from levying any general consumption or broad-based income taxes.

   The Australian Tax Office administers the broad-based goods and service (value added) tax, income taxes assessed on companies, trusts and indivi-duals, and a variety of lesser indirect taxes. Independent revenue departments in each state and territory administer taxes levied by these governments, the most significant being employer payroll taxes, land taxes and stamp duties. Municipalities levy and collect real estate taxes (rates). State government valuation offices or contract valuers, not offices of the municipalities them-selves, establish the taxable value for these municipal levies. The states establish the standards that must be used for these valuations. There is no provision for exchange of information across the levels of government.

4. Nigeria, another federation, provides a degree of subnational tax administra-tion. However, the results are less satisfactory than in the countries discussed before. The Federal Inland Revenue Services collects the national taxes, including shares going to federal, state, and local governments. The states collect their taxes, including what are called 'internally generated revenues' that have been adopted for them at the federal level (personal income taxes, stamp duties and capital gains tax) and some minor taxes that can be adopted by the state with their State Board of Internal Revenue. Local government revenue committees may administer minor sources levied locally, most market and trading licences (Akindele *et al.*, 2002). States have Joint State Revenue Committees that include the head of the state tax service and heads

of the local committees. There is a joint tax board that includes the head of the national revenue service and heads of the state services to deal with double taxation issues and to promote uniformity of the personal income taxes (IMF 2001). Subnational units frequently lack systems to track collections, master taxpayer lists and adequate staff. While they can track companies through the national VAT registrations, they have no identification number system for individuals. (Alm and Boex, 2002) The national government gives subnational governments little choice in regard to the basic structure of their taxes, even while permitting considerable administrative autonomy. The difference in tax effort across states thus reflects differences in administrative rigor rather than more transparent variation in tax base or rate. The experience reminds of the need to ensure administrative capacity or a means of obtaining it before allowing administrative autonomy.

5. In Brazil, another geographically large federation, central government, states and municipalities design, implement and collect their own taxes. Although the subnational governments have certain other taxing authority, the most interesting system of taxes in the country involves taxes on goods and services. The taxes are both broad and selective.

   a. Both central and state governments levy broad-based value added type taxes. The federal revenue service administers the federal VAT, the IPI (*Imposto sobre Produtos Insustrializados*). The tax is limited to delivery of industrial products at the producer level, defined to include importers of foreign products. Agricultural and mineral products are excluded, as are the retail and wholesale trade. Around 40 per cent of IPI revenue comes from three product groups: automobiles, tobacco products and beverages. And three-quarters of all collections come from three states: Minas Gerais, Rio de Janeiro and São Paolo.

   b. The states' VAT, the ICMS (*Imposto sobre operacoes relativas a Circulacao de Mercadorias e Servicos*), applies at all stages of the production – distribution chain, generally to goods but not to services (except interstate and intercity transportation and communication services) and is the most productive revenue source in Brazil. State tax authorities collect the tax, but the federal constitution requires states to transfer 25 per cent of their ICMS proceeds to their municipalities, partly on the basis of origin of collections and partly according to formulas enacted by each state legislature. The taxes operate as value added taxes, but provide no credit for capital goods. The individual states set the rate on intrastate trade within federally established floor and ceiling; there are multiple rates by type of product (the standard rate is 17 or 18 per cent, depending on the state; luxuries may be taxed at a higher rate and some staple food products may be taxed at a lower rate). However, a common federal rate applies to interstate sales. The interstate tax follows the origin principle: the importing state allows credit for tax paid to the state of origin. The normal interstate rate is 12 per cent, but on interstate trade from rich to poor state the rate is 7 per cent. The ICMS administrations establish fiscal frontier checkpoints – what amount to customs posts – to control inflows and outflows. Vehicles are stopped to identify the goods they carry. The information collected here is transmitted to assessing authorities to verify payment of tax on the transaction (Purohit, 1997). Of course, these check-points both interfere with the free flow of trade and create an opportunity for corruption. As Ebrill *et al.* (2001) summarize for the interstate trade: 'The exporting state receives revenue equal to the product of the inter-state rate and the value added there; the importing state collects the amount by which the tax collected on final sales at its own rate exceeds the amount retained by the exporting state.'

  c. There is no administrative integration from federal to state levels between IPI and ICMS, although ICMS registration is coordinated with federal income tax authorities. The IPI and ICMS use different legal norms and different bookkeeping. Even though the national tax code defines the main characteristics of ICMS, there are differences among the states in their taxes.

  d. The National Public Finance Council (*Conselho de Politica Fazendaria* or CONFAZ), a body consisting of all state secretaries of finance, acts to coordinate the interstate ICMS. The national government establishes the rate on interstate sales, but CONFAZ determines exemptions or reduc-tions in rates. Rate changes are infrequent because unanimous consent is required for changes, but there have been a number of exemptions approved. CONFAZ has not been successful in stopping tax wars between the states, fought through special tax preferences, one of the ideas behind its founding, but it has been working to develop a unified taxpayer master file that includes filer information from taxes at all levels as an aid to tax administration, and this would be a significant achievement.

  e. The final tier of indirect tax is the municipal ISS (*Imposto Sobre Servicos*), a tax on services. These taxes are on gross receipts of services in indus-trial, commercial and professional sectors. The taxes are levied and collected locally. Rates vary across municipalities from 0.5 to 10 per cent, within a maximum established by federal law. Yields are modest in com-parison to either IPI or ICMS.

6. The pattern in the Czech Republic, a unitary state in which the local govern-ment administers only minor taxes and fees, has much in common with many developing, transition and developed countries. The Czech Constitution establishes the principle that taxes can be imposed only on the basis of legal acts of the central parliament. Any local taxing authority must thus be regulated by central government legislation. Most taxes levied for local gov-ernment have been adopted by the national parliament and are collected by the central government tax authority (the General Financial and Tax Board). Most tax revenue received by municipalities in the Czech Republic comes from shared personal and corporate income taxes and a property tax allocated to them. Local governments may choose the property tax rate to be collected for them within boundaries established by the central parliament, but they

have no authority over the income tax rates or base. The income taxes are shared between central and local governments with the local share distributed according to origin of collections and population. The central General Financial and Tax Board under the Ministry of Finance administers these taxes through 223 local offices. These offices administer all major taxes in the Republic, including those accruing to both central and local governments.

a. The national parliament does, however, provide a small list of local fees and taxes, of limited revenue productivity, that municipalities may levy, although subject to centrally controlled rate limits: dog fees, resort and recreation fees on visitors, tax on use of public space, fees on entry tickets, fees on recreational units, motor vehicle entry fees and fees on gambling machines. Over 90 per cent of Czech municipalities levy at least one of the taxes; the most productive are those on the use of public space and gambling. These are administered by local government tax offices that are fully responsible for assessment, collection, enforcement, audit/inspection and first-level appeals. These local offices are entirely distinct from the local offices of the central tax administration. (Kubatova *et al.*, 2000).

b. This revenue assignment presents a facade of fiscal autonomy, including autonomous administration, but because the sources assigned have minimal revenue potential, the experience provides little evidence of the actual administrative capacity of local administrations. Rigorous administration has little revenue potential and the locality may rationally be less than vigorous in administration.

7. Hungary, another unitary state, places authority to tax and responsibility for administering taxes that have been levied at two levels: the central level and the local level. The former collect taxes levied by the central government, including both taxes that support services provided by the central government and taxes that are shared or otherwise distributed to support local government services. The local tax authorities administer taxes levied by the local governments. The central Tax and Financial Control Office, an independent authority of the national government, administers the income taxes, the value added tax and central excises through 19 offices operating around the country and four offices in Budapest. The local government tax offices administer the taxes levied by the local government; these offices are independent of local offices of the Tax and Financial Control Office and of each other. They have no contact save for information exchange.

a. When Hungary established a one-tier local government system in the Local Self-Government Law (1990), it created a system of local taxes to support a portion of the cost of the services to be provided by these governments. These local governments receive shares of certain centrally raised revenues (individual income tax, vehicle tax and rental fees for agricultural land) and receive state grants, but they also levy their own assigned taxes. The 1990 law provides the local tax options, and municipal governments choose which taxes they will adopt and what rates will apply.

b. Localities are permitted six types of taxes: (1) a local business tax based on net sales revenue of products or services sold, net of the cost of goods sold, the value of subcontractor's work and the cost of materials; (2) a communal tax on private individuals (a flat amount per dwelling); (3) a communal tax on businesses (tax based on number of employees); (4) a land tax (tax based on either area of plot or its market value); (5) a building tax (tax based on either useful surface area or market value); (6) a tourism tax (tax based on number of guest nights spent, charge per guest night or net floor space). The national law prescribes who will be subject to tax, how the bases will be defined and what the maximum rate will be. Local taxes generated 39.8 per cent of current local revenue in 1997, up from 15.5 per cent in 1991, when the options were new (Hogye *et al.*, 2000). The local business tax generates more than 80 per cent of local government tax revenue. A small number of taxpayers, sometimes only one, may pay half or more of total tax revenue in some jurisdictions. In these instances, the local government sometimes negotiates the payment with large taxpayers and sometimes those large taxpayers expect extraordinary rights to participate in decisions about how local revenue will be spent. When a business taxpayer operates permanently in more than one jurisdiction, the taxpayer determines the division of the base between jurisdictions.

c. The local tax offices perform the standard functions of tax administration: taxpayer registration, assessment and processing of declarations, receipt of payments, delinquency control and audit. To facilitate this work, local government tax offices use the same taxpayer identification numbers as do the central government tax offices, so a single identifier applies for all local taxes, although central and local files are not integrated. However, the local tax authority may request information from the central tax administration on taxpayers within its jurisdiction. Central authorities give local governments the software needed for computer-based taxpayer registration, thus allowing a uniform system of registration across the administrations (OECD, 2001). Local governments may not, however, access bank accounts to clear tax obligations, so the central offices have this collection advantage. Most localities appear to do no serious audit of tax returns.

d. The taxes allowed local governments in Hungary may not be high on the list of preferred alternatives for assignment to this tier of government. However, particularly in contrast to the experience with assignment of minor taxes to local government in the Czech Republic, the taxes in Hungary have made a considerable contribution to the finance of local government services and the local governments make a concerted effort to administer them. Serious options have brought a serious local administration and increased fiscal autonomy.

8. Estonia offers its localities authority to levy and administer a sales tax. The taxes are on the gross receipts of sales to final consumers and may not be

levied at a rate exceeding 1 per cent. Local officials verify taxpayer reports by checking reported gross receipts against VAT declaration of sales. They enforce the taxes by denying operating licences to businesses that have not paid the tax. Localities may choose to contract with the National Tax Board for collection of the tax. (Sootla *et al.*, 2000).

The special case of property taxes

Real property taxes are often cited as good candidates for independent subnational administration. Indeed, few fiscally significant taxes are more susceptible to local administration than the property tax. As McCluskey and Williams (1999) point out, real property 'is visible, immobile, and a clear indicator of one form of wealth. The property tax is thus difficult to avoid and if well administered can represent a non-distortionary and highly efficient fiscal tool.' It can take many forms, including taxes based on area, taxes based on market values, or, as Mikesell and Zorn (2008) point out, taxes informed by market values even where market data are scarce. However, except in a small number of countries, notably the USA and Canada (Almy, 2000), the tax has not been used to its full potential and is often levied, if at all, at the central level. This application significantly reduces the contribution that the tax could make to local fiscal autonomy, both in terms of giving local governments a tax whose rate they can control, and in terms of giving them a tax that could be locally administered. There are so few fiscally significant taxes that can be satisfactorily applied at the local level, it is unfortunate when they are assigned to a tier of government that has abundant other taxes at its disposal. When localities do administer the tax, they are responsible for maintaining property and ownership records, determining taxable property values, calculating and distributing property tax bills, managing receipt of payment and applying tax enforcement actions against non-payers (Eckert, 1990). As has been noted previously, the quality of their administration, particularly valuation of the tax base, is usually subject to evaluation by higher levels of government and those higher levels often provide training and technical assistance to local administration.

Why aren't locally administered local real property taxes a more significant subnational revenue source? The reasons are more political than economic. First, the difficulty and cost of administering an equitable property tax is exaggerated by those more familiar with income and consumption taxes than with property taxation. The property tax is based on stock values at a point in time, not on exchange-based flow values. As Bell and Bowman (1997) point out, '...the fact that most property does not sell in a market transaction each year means that the value is not observable.' This requires an assessment of the tax base, not an accounting exercise of gathering records for the tax period. And this assessment work is costly. However, there is virtually no compliance cost associated with the property tax, so the administrative cost is the total cost of collection;

there is no compliance expense required of the taxpayer – no recordkeeping, no forms, no calculations. Taxpayers in some countries, such as Sweden, Poland and the Slovak Republic, may be required to provide information to the tax authorities to assist their valuation work. Other countries require taxpayer valuation along with reporting. This is particularly common for countries in transition, where the break from government enterprise to private firm is underway or recently completed. Among developed countries, Turkey probably places greatest responsibility on the property owner, requiring reporting, valuation and calculation of tax. But neither Canada nor the USA find the reporting necessary.

The total collection cost for a typical real property tax (administration plus compliance) is not dramatically different from the total cost of collecting a sales or income tax when one recognizes both administrative and compliance costs in the cost of collection (Almy, 2001). The bias against the real property tax involves a miscalculation of the collection cost of the taxes, in particular the difference between the generally taxpayer-passive property tax versus the taxpayer-active income and consumption taxes. And the difficulty issue is exaggerated as well: in contrast with the focus of the private fee appraiser, the tax assessor is concerned less with the precise valuation of a single parcel than with producing a uniform standard for distribution of the property tax burden across parcels throughout the assessor's jurisdiction. As Dillinger (1991) explains

> ...it is important to distinguish tax valuation from the valuation governments undertake when they intend to purchase a property outright. In the latter case, a high standard of accuracy is required: the valuation must produce an *absolute* value in current market terms, as the amount changing hands will equal the entire value of the asset. Valuation for tax purposes, in contrast, requires only a determination of the *relative* value of properties at a common point in time. As it involves only an exchange equal to only a small percentage of the property's value, accuracy can be justifiably traded off in the interest of cost and administrative simplicity.

For that purpose, the techniques of mass assessment – simple, formula-based valuations driven by easily observable physical features of a property parcel with valuation coefficients based on a sample of market transactions – are well developed.

Valuation must be an estimating process and, thus, a market-based property tax absolutely requires a transparent and accessible appeals process in which errors (or worse) by the government tax assessor can be resolved. Administrative equity for the property tax demands an open and understandable appeals process, even more than it does for the income and consumption bases that rely on filings by taxpayers, employers and financial institutions. But a mass assessment system can produce a high degree of assessment uniformity at reasonable total collection cost.

As a practical matter, the property tax need not be market based. Some property taxes are flat taxes on the parcel with adjustment for size, location, use etc., and some property taxes are area based, either with or without adjustment for location, use and other factors. In Tanzania, the tax is limited to buildings (the government owns all land) and is based on the estimated reproduction cost of the structure (Kelly and Musunu, 2000). The alternatives sometimes have advantages. For example, a simple area based system affords a transparent measure for distribution of tax burden: those with more land or a larger structure pay a larger share of the property tax than do those with less. Zorn *et al.* (2000) propose such a scheme in Bosnia-Herzegovina because the area base 'reduces the contentiousness of what usually is the most controversial administrative question – the method used to value property.' In that environment, reducing contention was an important policy concern; the simplicity and transparency of the area base would have been a real advantage. Area based systems, as opposed to market value based systems, were common in countries in transition from Soviet-style systems 'because they satisfy a widely held belief that taxation decisions are official acts that must be satisfied by the proper authority, an approach at odds with a tax base drawn from market data...As a result, sometimes, the best way to introduce a value-based tax is to introduce market elements into the area based system.' (Malme and Youngman, 2001) An area based assessment scheme, with adjustment for location and type of property, is used in the Slovak Republic (Bryson and Cornia, 2000) Poland provides one particular example of an area based, municipally administered system (Bell and Regulska, 1992). In this instance, individuals and corporations have been required to present lists of their real estate to local officials as a part of the process, making property owners more actively involved in the taxing process than is usually the case for such taxes. McCluskey *et al.* (2002) suggest a British-style banded property tax in developing and transition environments; such assessments can be simple and inexpensive to administer, politically acceptable, transparent, equitable and revenue-productive even when market data are scarce and technology is limited.

Second, in many countries, the property tax has powerful political enemies. The tax strikes people with wealth accumulations quite directly, the real properties to be taxed are obvious to all, and the levy itself is visible. People with considerable property wealth usually have considerable political power and use that power to thwart taxes that aim directly at their holdings. They prefer taxes borne by others; preventing a real property tax provides them a way to duck a greater (and arguably fairer) share of the cost of government. As Burgess and Stern (1993) suggest, low utilization of property and land taxation 'reflects the success of the resistance of the rich and powerful to measures which harm their interests.'

Third, property owners have few avoidance options for the property tax. Because the tax is usually administered with few compliance requirements for property owners, the taxpayer has few alternatives for controlling liability that are within the law. And when valuation and calculation are done by a government agent, the taxpayer has scant opportunity to fiddle and finagle to reduce the amount of tax owed. There has been one notable exception. In some parts of the former Soviet Union, properties will not be added to the tax lists until structures are completed and registered with local authorities and, as a result, many properties are never quite finished although they are functional and occupied. Western countries avoid the problem by assessing on a percentage completed basis. Evading a real property tax requires active collusion with government officials, not concealment and accounting tricks; it cannot be done independently by the taxpayer, which is contrary to the case with the taxpayer-active taxes on income or consumption. Of course, the taxpayer may simply ignore the property tax that has been levied; in countries like India and the Philippines, as much of the tax as is collected often goes uncollected. And municipalities in the Slovak Republic have had difficulty collecting real estate taxes from insolvent businesses. But these failures to pay are evasion (outside the law), not avoidance (within the law), and even these tax payments can be guaranteed because if there is sufficient political will, the parcel of property itself is in the jurisdiction and can be claimed by the taxing government if payment is not made.

Another collection approach, the 'rate clearance certificate', from Kenya, relies on taxpayer initiative to clear outstanding liabilities and is effective when the property is transferred or when the property holder seeks a local business permit or some other local service is being requested. It has not proven particularly effective (Kelly, 2000). Publishing the names of delinquent property owners is also often done, but without much apparent impact. Tax sales (action against the property itself) do the trick; selling the parcel to recover taxes owed brings owners forward with payment in hand. However, tax sales are politically difficult, even in the most developed countries.

There are a good number of other international examples of independently administered local property taxes. Local governments in larger urban areas often are responsible for administration of their real property taxes, even when subnational governments are given no other significant fiscal autonomy. (Bahl and Linn, 1992) The Netherlands offers one example of a successful nationwide decentralization of property tax administration. Prior to 1992, the central government administered property taxes. Since then, administration of the property tax (*onroerende zaak belasting*) is a local responsibility. Municipalities maintain property records, assess properties (at market value) and collect the taxes. Municipalities are almost evenly divided between those using civil servants for assessment and those using contract assessment firms. Assessments are performed on a mass basis, and disputes on individual parcel valuations are taken to the courts for resolution. The National Valuation Board must approve local revaluation plans and makes ratio studies (studies of the ratio of assessed to current market value) to evaluate the uniformity of assessments done by a municipality, but it is not actively involved in administering the taxes. Tax rates vary from municipality to municipality, according to choices made by councils, and there are considerable differences in tax paid on comparable properties, depending on the location of the parcel in the country. (Sterks and de Kam, 1991)

Results from independent local administration

An important standard of modern public finance is the principle of subsidiarity, the idea that governmental actions should be taken at the lowest level of government, the level closest to the people, at which the desired objectives can be achieved. The principle, when applied to tax administration, suggests that independent regional and local tax administration ought not be dismissed, but should be considered as another alternative in the efficient, effective and responsive implementation of overall national tax policy. Casanegra de Jantscher (1990) maintains that in developing countries 'tax administration *is* tax policy'. The same certainly holds true in transition nations and, given variations in enforcement terms and conditions across a country, also applies to an important degree for tax policy in any nation. Therefore, if it is reasonable for regional and local governments to develop tax policy as an element of a programme for localization of government financing, then it is similarly reasonable to consider the degree to which independent regional and local administration may be economically and technically feasible. It certainly would be *politically* feasible and possibly politically desirable in a programme of increased fiscal responsiveness. This is particularly critical because the taxpayer's contact with the tax law – the representation of what tax policy is – is through its administrative apparatus. Hence, as far as the taxpayer is concerned, the representation of tax policy will be the tax administrators.

Regional and local governments, even within a single country, vary widely in terms of size, professionalism and economic development. This makes precise conclusions about independent tax administration difficult. However, general experience with independent regional and local tax administration suggests the following:

1. Familiarity with local conditions and easy adaptability to those local conditions can facilitate registration of taxpayers, collection and enforcement of many taxes. Indeed, when local governments have designed their own tax base and structures, local administration can be designed specifically for the tax in that application and policy and administration can be fully merged. Administration need not be a central one stretched to apply to the local structural peculiarities, administrative decisions can be made without dragging them through a centralized bureaucracy and, should enforcement be directed toward large taxpayers as an administrative strategy (Baer *et al.*, 2002), the selection will be based on large taxpayers within the local or regional tax system, not those large in national terms. One example: two growing communities in Colorado, Parker and Castle Rock, created a Joint Sales Tax Self-Collection programme in 2005, replacing state administration for their local retail sales taxes because they believed that state enforcement efforts were inadequate.
2. Local administration can apply taxes on economic activities that fall below the threshold of central government interest because local administrators

have familiarity with the local business environment from information generated through local licensing and regulatory processes and can generate revenue by bringing small enterprises into the tax system at relatively low cost. Bringing them into the subnational tax system may also assist central government revenue mobilization if there is information exchange between central and subnational administrations.

3. When administration of local taxes is separate, it is much easier for taxpayers to see which government is levying what taxes – and to hold the appropriate governments accountable. Transparency can be lost when a central authority administers the tax levied by a lower level of government. Taxpayers receiving a consolidated regional / local property tax bill or preparing a consolidated regional / local income tax return often cannot easily discern which government is levying which portion of the total tax bill. That reduces the degree to which fiscal autonomy improves accountability for budget choices that have been made. Independent administration usually exposes responsibility for the tax being levied.

4. Independent regional and local tax authorities can act as 'insulated chambers of experimentation' for tax administration. They can innovate new approaches and techniques, exploiting the nimbleness and creativity that often characterizes smaller organizations. For example, state revenue departments in the USA have been leaders in the application of new information technology, bar-coding and imaging to tax administration; the State Revenue Department of Western Australia markets its revenue collection information system widely; and Gujarat state in India has developed a computerized system for checking commercial vehicles to enforce the road tax at interstate check posts, which reduces clearance time from 30 to 2 minutes. US states have used posting of income and sales tax delinquent taxpayers on websites (names, addresses and amounts), cancellation of business licenses and suspension of driver's licences as more aggressive collection measures. Some subnational governments have greater flexibility and control over resources than others, some have more creative administrators than others and some have better environments for experimentation than others. That allows something like natural experiments in tax administration, a result that cannot easily happen within the confines of a single, centralized administration. Furthermore, the impact of confusion and mistakes if the experiment fails is localized and limited to the systems of the state or locality.

5. Independent administration can provide the taxing government quicker, and more certain control over its revenue. As Veehorn and Ahmad (1997) recognize, central administration means that 'local governments may perceive that they have very little control over receipts.' With independent administration, the government does not have to await distribution from the central administration because it has control over funds as soon as the taxpayer makes payment. Unfortunately, the central administration would typically not have quickness as an objective in dealing with another government's revenue. Also, independent local administration simplifies

revenue accounting: there is no dispute about the proper distribution of collections among taxing governments, a frequent point of contention when one government collects tax levied by another government. Slow and inaccurate payment has been a common complaint among localities in the USA whose sales or income tax is administered by the state government. Before the advent of electronic funds transfer, larger cities in the state of Texas would regularly fly to the state capital to receive payment of local sales tax collections so that the city could have faster use of the funds for short-term investment or payment of city obligations, rather than wait for the payment to be mailed. When the US states experience budget problems, one common approach is for them to delay scheduled payments (transfers or centrally collected local taxes) to their local governments. However, these complaints pale against the two year lags in shared personal income tax receipts received by localities in Hungary (Bird *et al.*, 1995). Delays are blamed on sorting returns when taxpayer residence differs from location of workplace or tax office. Such delays would work against any rate increases: there would be a long lag between when the taxpayer feels the higher tax and any public service benefits from the increase.

6. Subnational governments like the employment power that independent administration provides. Unfortunately, in some countries, labour intensity in tax collection and high collection cost is seen as a virtue. This is what Fjeldstad (2001) observed about local tax administration in Tanzania: 'for certain small taxes and charges the collection costs are the reason for the levy. In other words, the purpose is to create employment or at least an income-earning opportunity for someone who might otherwise be unemployed.' The influence is real, although not so blatant, in other countries.

7. Local governments may not be satisfied with the central standard of tax enforcement and local administration allows them to pursue a different enforcement policy. As Alm (1999) has observed, the output of revenue administration includes both government revenue and taxpayer equity, and subnational units may balance these two outputs differently from the central administration. In other words, local governments may have different views about the appropriate distribution of uncollected taxes; independent local administration allows enforcement policy to reflect these differences.

8. Independent administration would assure the regional or local government that their revenue interests were rigorously represented in disputes about the distribution of tax revenues from enterprises or individuals that might be taxable in multiple jurisdictions. The question of what jurisdiction is entitled to tax certain tax bases – the profit from business enterprise conducted in several jurisdictions or income for individuals with work assignments in several areas, for instance – is a thorny one if an effort is made to apportion the total in a manner that generally reflects portions of activity within the various taxing jurisdictions. Businesses and individuals tend to make legal interpretations that reduce their tax liability and some also evade tax owed. As a result, subnational governments may receive less revenue than they

believe to be owed them, even though the entity has paid all tax owed the central government. A central tax authority that administers both central and piggybacked subnational taxes is almost certainly going to be less concerned with getting the subnational tax apportionments right than would be independent subnational authorities. Furthermore, the subnational jurisdictions themselves may differ as to the appropriate distribution of the tax base. A single central administrative authority is not well-equipped to settle such disputes over regional interests. The case of each taxing jurisdiction could best be made by independent administrations, not by functionaries of the central administration.

9. Independent administration by the lower government that levies the tax provides assurance to the taxing government that full and appropriate diligence will be given the collection and enforcement of its taxes. When higher governments (and the employees of these governments) administer those taxes, there is the danger that administrators will give collection and enforcement of lower tier taxes less attention and lower priority than taxes levied by the higher tier. Allowing the collecting government to retain a portion of the lower tier tax it administers (paying a collection fee, in other words) may reduce the disincentive somewhat; such collection fees are, for instance, often provided when state governments in the USA collect local government sales taxes. However, if the fee is substantial, the reduced revenue to the local units may dampen the enthusiasm with which lower units pursue fiscal autonomy through enactment of their own taxes. Different sharing rates may create similar problems. In regard to India, Hemming *et al.* (1997) observe: 'The fact that the center retains different percentages of different taxes – with the rest being passed on to the states – may provide an incentive to concentrate the collection effort and resources of the central tax administration on those taxes...it retains in full or in higher percentage.'

10. Duplicate enforcement may provide a check against omissions when central and subnational administrations exchange information and may make corruption more difficult because two sets of enforcement officials must be paid off. As Radian (1980) observes, 'in countries where both central and local authorities collect taxes, there is higher extractive capability than in nations that rely solely on central administration.'

11. Burgess and Stern (1993) postulate that '[d]ifferences in the tradition of compliance probably explain as much of the worldwide pattern of taxation as do under-resourced or poorly organized tax administrations.' Countries differ widely in regard to their 'tax cultures' (Nerre, 2008) and policy and administration needs to fit the country. Local administration has a better chance of bringing the population into the system than would administration imposed on them from the distant national capital. Administration by local bodies, not by representatives of the central government, may help create a compliance tradition.

12. There is a competitive aspect to the case for independent administration. The argument made by McLure and Martinez (2000) for decentralization also

applies to tax administration: 'Just as competition in the marketplace protects consumers from the rapaciousness of business, so tax competition protects citizens from the rapaciousness of politicians and bureaucrats.' Tax authorities are popularly viewed as among the most rapacious of civil servants.

Economies of scale in tax administration appear to present an important barrier to independent administration. But that may not be controlling. Even if size of jurisdiction is relevant to achieving effective administration, many regions and municipalities have populations and economies larger than those of many independent nations; if the nations can successfully administer their own taxes, then surely economic and technical factors ought not preclude independent administration of taxes levied by those large regions and municipalities. The tax base of many national taxes – business income, value added, personal income – is frequently concentrated in larger urban areas. In those instances, the practical difference between national administration and local administration in those areas would not be great. Furthermore, smaller regions or municipalities can band together in administrative compacts for provision of any administrative services for which size might matter.

Share, joint and cooperative administration

When there are multiple tiers of generally independent tax administration, there are several possibilities for shared and cooperative administration both vertically and horizontally. Tax administration can employ division of tasks among central and subnational government, with lower units choosing tax base and rate and conducting certain function in administration while the central government 'co-administers' other functions. Kelly (2003) notes the importance of property tax 'co-administration' in Indonesia's decentralization programme: 'The key to success is to maintain the correct balance between central and local involvement in administration – not to make administration either a purely central or local government responsibility.' The core functions of tax administration – taxpayer registration and service, declaration or assessment, revenue and taxpayer accounting, delinquency control, audit, enforcement, and appeal or protest (Mikesell, 1998) – may, for a particular tax, be divided among tax authorities according to technical competencies, and some functions may be performed by more than one authority. They will be performed for each tax, but not necessarily by the government levying the tax and not necessarily all by the same government. Technologies may differ, but 'the functions themselves have been essentially constant since at least biblical times' (Baldwin, 1996).

The real property tax, while requiring considerable technical skill to obtain a uniform appraisal of property, applies to a base that is quite immobile and non-fugitive and whose value very much depends on local market conditions. In these circumstances, co-administration between central and local government can be an appropriate organization structure. A cooperative division of functions can combine local autonomy and familiarity with local conditions and central technical skills. But nations have not reached the same conclusion about the assignment of functions between central and local governments. This difference appears in the division in assignment of valuation and collection responsibilities across several nations (Dillinger, 1991; Almy, 2001; McCluskey and Williams, 1999):

Central Valuation, Central Collection: France, Pakistan, Indonesia, Sweden, Jordan, Albania, Armenia, Czech Republic, Georgia, Latvia, Russia, Portugal, Cyprus, Estonia, Jamaica, Singapore. Municipalities in Estonia perform some duties in administration of the property tax, but the central government has the dominant role in assessment and collection.

Central Valuation, Local Collection: United Kingdom, Kenya (except largest cities), Germany, Columbia, Austria, Turkey, Denmark, New Zealand.

Local Valuation, Central Collection: Tunisia, Slovenia. The Russian land tax previously mentioned, with valuation by local land committees and the remainder of administration done by the national Ministry of Taxation, might be considered an example of this arrangement. However, the cadastral valuation system the land committee must use is closely controlled from the national level.

Local Valuation, Local Collection: Brazil, India, Japan, Mexico (sometimes state), Kenya (largest cities), Philippines, Hungary, Romania, Slovak Republic, Greece, Italy, Netherlands, Switzerland (cantons), United States. In the USA, it is not unusual for local law enforcement officials to serve as collection agents for both local and state tax administrations when dealing with particularly difficult taxpayers.

Denmark illustrates one intergovernmental division of functions, where revenue from three kinds of property tax is assigned to subnational governments: a land tax on all plots of land; a service tax on buildings used for administration, commerce and manufacturing; and a property value tax on owner-occupied dwellings and summerhouses. The central government has main responsibility for valuation of immovable property. Central government appoints 224 valuation committees of three members with secretarial assistance from the municipality. The basic information for valuation and collection is stored in computerized registers. The Central Customs and Tax Administration, part of the national Ministry of Taxation, maintains a register of sales prices, and the municipalities maintain a valuation and collection register with: (1) description of the land parcels from the national survey and land register, and (2) a building and dwelling register with the description of buildings and dwelling units. The Central Customs and Tax Administration carries out the central coordination of valuation and gives instructions to the valuation committees. A property tax office in each municipality collects the municipal and county share of the land tax and service tax. The computer-generated annual property tax bill, divided into instalments as determined by the municipality, also includes municipal charges on the property (for roads, sewerage, district heating, street lighting, water etc.) Payment can be made in cash at the municipal office, by the postal giro system or through the bank automatic payment system. Central government collects the property value tax via withholding in combination with the individual income tax.

Although independent administration is the rule for tax administration in the USA, there are some prominent exceptions. Cooperative administration is frequently used for administration of property tax on certain complex properties (industrial property, telecommunications, transportation, etc.): a state agency handles these complex assessments while local governments administer the remainder of the tax, including assessment of less complex properties. Local governments do administer, along with their own tax, the property taxes that a few state governments continue to levy. The states and the federal Internal Revenue Service do exchange information on both individual and corporate income taxes, and states have both formal and informal information exchange with each other.

Tax administration in Canada provides other examples of joint administration. As earlier noted, tax administration for provincial and territorial taxes mixes centralized and independent administration for individual and corporate income and sales taxes. The pattern for the major local tax – the property tax – is, however, one of cooperative administration between the regional and local governments. Arrangements for local government finances in Canada are left to the individual provinces and territories, not the federal government. Property taxes yield virtually all the tax revenue collected by local governments in Canada (98 per cent) and localities collect 80 per cent of all property taxes levied. As a share of GDP, these property taxes are among the highest in the world. That makes good quality assessment particularly important. Local governments establish their own property tax rates and manage collection of taxes they have levied, but the province or territory establishes the basic structure and requirements for the local taxes, establishes the policy for valuation of property parcels and is responsible for ensuring that assessment is done according to the assessment standard that reflects provincial tax policy. Thus, overall administration of the property tax combines centralized and independent administration of the collection functions. For uniformity, valuation is centralized while the other functions are handled by the local government levying the tax.

The provinces use four different organizational structures to ensure uniform assessments. Most also are organized to provide the efficiency advantages of large scale operation:

1. Crown corporations: British Columbia (BC Assessment), New Brunswick (Service New Brunswick), Newfoundland and Labrador (Municipal Assessment Agency) and Saskatchewan (Saskatchewan Assessment Management Agency) have set up government corporations to do property assessments for local governments in the province. The corporations are owned by provincial government with representation of the localities on their governing boards.

2. Non-profit corporation: Ontario (Municipal Property Assessment Corporation, MPAC) has established a non-profit corporation owned by municipalities in the province to administer provincial assessment policies. MPAC has a head office with most of its staff located in 36 field offices across the province. Property owners may appeal MPAC assessments to an independent Assessment Review Board, whose decisions are final and binding.
3. Provincial Tax Assessment Departments: Manitoba, Nova Scotia, Prince Edward Island and the territories administer assessment through traditional government agencies.
4. Provincial Assessment Supervision: Alberta Assessment Services, an agency of provincial government, establishes assessment standards, provides technical support and maintains quality control for assessments. The municipalities do the actual assessment using appointed assessors, however, according to the promulgated standards.

The corporations provide other services to local governments, but property assessment is the principal service that they offer. The focus of each arrangement is to improve the uniformity of assessment of the tax base across the province or territory; without such uniformity, an equitable application of the property tax is impossible. The taxing locality can then levy and collect the tax applied to the base that has been assessed according to the regionally uniform assessment standard.

Land tax administration in Estonia presents a somewhat different approach to cooperative administration. Estonia, the first country of the former Soviet Union to adopt a market value based land tax (1993), introduced the tax as an element of broader reforms toward fiscal decentralization and privatization. The tax yields only around 6.5 per cent of local government revenue, with shares slightly higher in rural areas than in urban areas. Local councils annually set the tax rate within limits set by the central governments on the capital value of the land without buildings, timber, plants or structures. Since 1996, land tax collections have been local revenue. However, to encourage quicker privatization of municipal land, from the start of 2000, the municipalities receive only the tax on private land; the tax on land under public leases goes to the central government. Administration involves both central and local governments. The National Land Board, part of the Ministry of Environment, estimates value while the National Tax Board, part of the Ministry of Finance, collects the tax. Municipalities collect information on property transactions and submit the data to the National Land Board and provide the National Tax Board with information necessary to maintain its Land Tax Register. At the conclusion of the valuation process, local officials calculate the taxable value of each land parcel. The National Tax Board administers tax billing and collections through its local offices. Taxes are collected in three instalments through commercial banks. Unpaid taxes become liens against the property and the National Tax Board may seek sale of property for non-payment of tax. Administrative costs from both levels of government is estimated to be roughly 5 per cent of collections.

Programmes that centralize valuation but leave other elements of property tax administration to lower levels are found in several countries. For example, Malawi taxes property on a ratings basis; assessment is on a quinquennial cycle with local property valuation on the basis of information from the central government Ministry of Lands, and the local authorities set the rates and handle collection (Kelley *et al.*, 2001). In Turkey, the national Ministry of Finance estimates property values, with a considerable requirement for self assessment, while the municipalities collect the taxes they have levied on that property. That mix of functional responsibilities meets the needs of many countries seeking to localize revenue authority and administration while wishing to maintain a broad uniformity of standard for application of the property tax.

Finally, Mexico presents a special case of cooperative administration. In general, the central government administers federal taxes and all states have signed agreements whereby they trade the exercise of most of their taxing authority for a share of federal revenues. However, state governments sign agreements (*convenios de colaboracion administrative*) with the federal government, which allows them to audit and otherwise verify compliance with federal laws in exchange for a significant portion of additional federal revenues they locate. That gives them revenue based on their particular knowledge of local economic activities about which the central administration might not be aware. In the USA, some states administering local sales taxes provide the local governments periodic lists of their local sales tax payers so that the locality can check for omissions and request state enforcement action.

Shared administration allows independence while permitting administrative specialization. It provides many of the advantages that fully centralized administration might afford, while permitting considerable autonomy and advantages of small, local operations. When the decision to cooperate and share is made voluntarily by the subnational government, there can be no argument that such relationships interfere with fiscal autonomy. If performance by the central authorities falls below the standard expected by the subnational government, the subnational government can terminate the relationship. When shared administration is required, however, it is more difficult for the relationship to remain satisfactory. Higher tier governments are not in the habit of offering performance guarantees to lower tier governments and, when there are many subnational units whose taxes are being administered, producing such guarantees for each of them would be difficult.

For property tax valuation, the guarantee would be in terms of achieving the legally intended assessment ratio or level of assessment (the ratio of the value determined for tax purposes [the assessed value] to the legally targeted value [often current market value]) and of achieving a target level of disparity of assessment ratios to assure that the tax is distributed across properties in the way that the law intends. Valuation is the most difficult stage in property tax systems, and achieving an appropriate degree of assessment ratio uniformity is critical for the levy of an equitable and productive tax. In the USA, a number of states conduct this uniformity testing of the assessment work done by local jurisdictions to ensure that these governments – either themselves or the contractors they have hired to perform the work – are doing an adequate job of valuation. The Canadian corporations that provide property tax valuation services to localities regularly report their uniformity and level of assessment statistics as a measure of the quality of the work they have done.

For taxes other than the real property tax, the guarantee would need to be in terms of certain activities associated with administering the tax (taxpayer satisfaction with and accuracy of assistance provided by taxpayer service centres, audit coverage rate, delinquency rate, closure of account receivables, speed and accuracy of return processing and payment deposit). Calculating noncompliance rates and their distribution across types of taxpayers – the most appropriate indicators of quality of tax administration for taxes placing considerable compliance responsibilities on taxpayers – is generally not feasible for subnational units. Meeting revenue targets or forecasts, although a tempting standard, would not be reasonable, in light of the difficulty of making accurate revenue forecasts: Is the revenue target missed because of poor tax collection or because of an inaccurate revenue forecast? Is the revenue target being exceeded because of unexpectedly successful tax administration or because of an unexpectedly robust economy driving revenue collections? Kahn *et al.* (2001) find a Brazilian programme to provide monetary compensation to tax collectors based on individual and group performance in finding and collecting taxes from evaders to have had a great impact on collection of fines. The bonus or reward (*Retribuicao Adicional Variavel*) was created in 1989 in the federal tax system.

Conclusion

The decision to decentralize administration of local taxes frequently involves, as Dillinger (1991) describes, 'a tradeoff between indifference and incompetence.' When the central government receives no revenue from administration of a tax, that tax is likely to receive less attention than is given taxes yielding revenue for the central government. But the local government may have lower capacity to administer its taxes than does the central government, in terms of qualified personnel, technology and ability to stand up to large businesses. Hence the tradeoff: the central government is capable but less interested in local collections and the local government is keenly interested by less capable.

That is the basic dilemma in providing subnational governments new authority for their own tax administration: regional or local governments are unlikely to have the full capacity to administer their own taxes if they have never actually done it before, and central governments are reluctant to permit self-administration without demonstrated administrative capacity. Therefore, when considering whether subnational governments would be capable of self-administration, the question should be the extent to which they could become capable of the tasks, not whether they are currently prepared to do the work. It certainly means that training and technical assistance should accompany any major decentralization of administrative authority. In sum, incompetence can be remedied, but indifference is permanent.

A basic problem in providing subnational governments with greater fiscal autonomy in developing and transition nations is that both the tax bases and taxing authority granted them are often inherently weak – the bases are narrow and have modest yield prospects, the taxes have modest buoyancy, the taxes are difficult to collect and the localities frequently have constrained enforcement powers. Modest bases are a problem when the taxes continue to be centrally administered and even more of a problem when the small bases are to be locally administered. In these instances, local authorities do not find it reasonable to devote considerable resources to the enforcement of these taxes. Passively accepting whatever revenue happens to come in is usually the most reasonable approach. Granting tax authority for an array of minor taxes not only obscures the actual tax burden, thus violating the transparency requirement, it also makes low quality administration more likely. It is a mistake to decentralize by granting subnational governments the authority to administer a great list of minor taxes. Permitting a single meaningful revenue source is much more valuable than permitting a long list of minor sources.

Assignment of reasonable taxing powers helps give a government control over its fiscal destiny. It allows the government, acting for its citizens, choice over its level of spending and how that spending will be financed from segments of its economy. That is an important element for fiscal autonomy. From the revenue side of the public economy, fiscal autonomy (and responsibility) is greatest when the subnational government chooses what taxes it will levy, defines the bases it will use, sets the rate and preference structure for those bases and administers the taxes that have been adopted. While surcharges on central tax bases can give a considerable degree of fiscal autonomy without some of the problems that full autonomy can create, subnational governments may not agree, if given the choice, that the autonomy thus given is adequate. In particular, they may be concerned that a government not receiving the revenue from a tax that it administers is likely to feel less urgency in collection of, or reform of, that tax than are those using the revenue to finance their operations. They may feel that administration in practice is inextricably intertwined with tax policy and that, without having choice over administrative decisions, they lack appropriate fiscal autonomy.

International experience demonstrates that regional and local governments can administer the taxes they levy, given political will and operational support. Capacity can be developed in a tax authority. Horizontal and vertical cooperation and exchange of information can improve administration and simplify compliance. Issues beyond capacity development, technical assistance and information exchange include: (1) coordination of registration for national and subnational taxes to ease business development and to facilitate information exchange for administration; (2) use of a single taxpayer identification number to the greatest extent possible; (3) exchange of audit and other compliance data to the fullest extent permitted by law; (4) locating taxpayer services offices together to the greatest possible extent; (5) coordinating payment mechanisms for central and subnational taxes. Cooperation does often entail some reduction in administrative autonomy, however. When cooperation is optional, its practice certainly proves of benefit to all cooperating administrative units.

Note

1   This chapter is largely based on a paper by Mikesell, J. *'Developing Options for the Administration of Local Taxes: An International Review'* published in Public Budgeting & Finance, Spring 2007 (a Wiley-Blackwell journal).

References

Akindele, S. T., Olaopa, O.R. and Obiyan, A.S. (2002) Fiscal Federalism and Local Government Finance in Nigeria: An Examination of Revenue Rights and Fiscal Jurisdictions. *International Review of Administrative Sciences*, December: 557–577.

Alm, J. (1999) Tax Compliance and Administration. In: Hildreth, W.B. and Richardson, J.A. (eds.), *Handbook on Taxation*. New York: Marcel Dekker.

Alm, J. and Boex, J. (2002) An Overview of Intergovernmental Fiscal Relations and Subnational Public Finance in Nigeria. International Studies Program Working Paper 02 – 1, Atlanta: Georgia State University.

Almy, R. (2000) Property Tax Policies and Administrative Practices in Canada and the USA: Executive Summary. *Assessors Journal*, July/August: 41–57.

Almy, R. (2001) *A Survey of Property Tax Systems in Europe*. Report prepared for Department of Taxes and Customs, Ministry of Finance, Republic of Slovenia.

Baer, K., Benon, O.P. and Toro, J.A,R. (2002) *Improving Large Taxpayer Compliance: A Review of Country Experience*. IMF Occasional Paper 215, Washington DC: International Monetary Fund.

Bahl, R.W. (1999) Fiscal Decentralization as Development Policy. *Public Budgeting & Finance*, IXX: 59–75.

Bahl, R.W. and Bird, R. (2008) Subnational Taxes in Developing Countries. *Public Budgeting & Finance*, XXVIII: 1–25.

Bahl, R.W. and Linn, J.F. (1992) *Urban Public Finance in Developing Countries*. Washington DC: World Bank.

Baldwin, J. (1996) Evolving Taxpayer Information Systems. *State Tax Notes*, 10: 1105–1114.

Bates, L.J. and Santerre, R.E. (1993) Property Tax Collector Performance and Pay. *National Tax Journal*, XLVI: 23–31.

Bell, M.E. (1999) An Optimal Property Tax: Concepts and Practices. Washington DC: Economic Development Institute, World Bank.

Bell, M. and Bowman, J.H. (1997) Local Property Taxation in South Africa: Current Performance and Challenges for the Post-Apartheid Era. *Public Budgeting & Finance*, XVII: 71–87.

Bell, M. and Regulska, J. (1992) Centralization versus Decentralization: The Case of Financing Autonomous Local Governments in Poland. In: Pestieau, P. (ed.), *Public Finance in a World of Transition, Proceedings of the 47th Congress of the International Institute of Public Finance / Institut International de Finances Publiques.* The Hague, Netherlands and Koenigstein, Germany: Foundation Journal Public Finance: 187–201.

Bird, R.M., Wallich, C. and Peteri, G. (1995) Financing Local Government in Hungary. In: Bird, R.M., Ebel, R. and Wallich, C. (eds.), *Decentralization of the Socialist State.* Washington DC: World Bank.

Bryson, P. and Cornia, G.C. (2000) Fiscal Decentralization and the Property Tax. In *Fiscal Decentralization Initiative for Central and Eastern Europe* [http://lgi.osi.hu/publica tions_datasheet.php?id=65]. Washington DC: Local Government and Public Service Reform Initiative: 1–17.

Burgess, R. and Stern, N. (1993) Taxation and Development. *Journal of Economic Literature*, XXI: 762–830.

Canada Customs and Revenue Agency and Department of Finance (2000) *Federal Administration of Provincial Taxes, New Directions.* Ottawa: Department of Finance.

Casanegra de Jantscher, M. (1990) Administering the VAT. In: Shoup, G.C. and Sicat, G. (ed.) *Value Added Taxation in Developing Countries.* Washington DC: World Bank: 40–52.

Dillinger, W. (1991) *Urban Property Tax Reform.* Washington DC: World Bank.

Duncan, H.T. and McLure, C.E. Jr. (1997) Tax Administration in the US of America: A Decentralized System. *Bulletin of International Fiscal Documentation*, 51, February: 74–85.

Ebel, R. and Yilmaz, S.(2002) *On the Measurement and Impact of Fiscal Decentralization.* Washington DC: World Bank.

Ebrill, L., Keen, M., Bodin, J-P. and Summers, V. (2001) *The Modern VAT.* Washington DC: International Monetary Fund.

Eckert, J.K. (ed.) (1990) *Property Appraisal and Assessment Administration.* Chicago, Illinois: International Association of Assessing Officers.

Fjeldstad, O-H. (2001) *Fiscal Decentralisation in Tanzania: For better or for worse?*, CMI Working Paper 10 Bergen, Norway: Chr. Michelsen Institute.

Gerasimova, V., Vladimirova, S., Krupa, O., Mikesell, J. and Zorn, C. (2005) Land Value Taxation for Russian Local Governments: Evidence from Saratov Oblast. *Proceeding of the 98th Annual Conference on Taxation of the National Tax Association.* Washington DC: National Tax Association.

Hemming, R., Mates, N. and Potter, B. (1997) India. In: Ter-Minassian, T. (ed.), *Fiscal Federalism in Theory and Practice.* Washington DC: International Monetary Fund: 527–539.

Hogye, M., Jenei, G., Kiraly, L., Varga, E., Deak, D., Velkei, C., Lendvai S. and Suveges A. (2000) Local and Regional Tax Administration in Hungary. In: Hogye, M. (ed.), *Local and Regional Tax Administration in Transition Countries.* Budapest: Local Government and Public Service Reform Initiative, Open Society Institute: 213–288.

IMF (2001) *Nigeria: Selected Issues and Statistical Appendix.* IMF Country Report No. 01/132. Washington DC: International Monetary Fund.

Jenkins, G.P., Kelly, R. and Khadka R. (2000) *Central–Local Fiscal Relations in Low-Income Countries: The Case of Nepal.* Economic Reform II Discussion Paper No. 69. Cambridge, MA: Harvard Institute for International Development.

Kahn, C.M., Emilson, C.M., Silva, C.D. and Ziliak, J.P. (2001) Performance-Based Wages in Tax Collection: The Brazilian Tax Collection Reform and Its Effects, *The Economic Journal*; CXI (January 2001); 188–205.

Kelly, R. (2000) Designing a Property Tax Reform Strategy for SubSaharan Africa: An Analytical Framework Applied to Kenya. *Public Budgeting & Finance*, XX: 36–52.

Kelly, R. (2003) *Property Taxation in* Indonesia: Challenges from Decentralization. Working Paper WP03RK1.Cambridge, MA: Lincoln Institute of Land Policy.

Kelly, R., Montes, M., Maseya, E., Nkankha, K. and Tombere, K. (2001) *Improving Revenue Mobilization in Malawi: Study on Business Licensing and Property Rights*. Lilongwe, Malawi: Government of Malawi and United Nations Capital Development Fund, United Nations Development Programme.

Kelly, R. and Musunu, Z. (2000) Implementing Property Tax Reform in Tanzania. Working Paper WP00RK1 Cambridge, MA: Lincoln Institute of Land Policy.

Kubatova, K., Vancurova, A., Hamernikova, B. and Ochrana, F. (2000) Local and Regional Tax Administration in the Czech Republic. In: Hogye, M. (ed.), *Local and Regional Tax Administration in Transition Countries*. Budapest: Local Government and Public Service Reform Initiative Open Society Institute: 81–140.

Malme, J.H. and Youngman, J.M. (2001) Introduction. In: Malme, J.H. and Youngman, J.M. (eds.) *The Development of Property Taxation in Economies in Transition, Case Studies from Central and Eastern Europe*. Washington DC: The World Bank: 1–10.

McCluskey, W.J. and Williams, B. (1999) Introduction: A Comparative Evaluation. In: McCluskey, W.J. (ed.) *Property Tax: An International Comparative Review*, Brookfield, Vermont: Ashgate Publishing: 1–31.

McCluskey, W.J., Plimmer, F.A.S. and Connellan, O.P. (2002) Property Tax Banding: A Solution for Developing Countries. *Assessment Journal*, March/April: 37–47.

McLure, C. and Martinez-Vazquez, J. (2000) *The Assignment of Revenues and Expenditures in Intergovernmental Fiscal Relations*. Paper for the Intergovernmental Relations and Local Financial Management, World Bank Institute, Washington DC: World Bank.

Mikesell, J.L. (1999) Decentralizing Government Finances in the Russian Federation: Regional Sales and Imputed Income Taxes. *Proceedings of the Ninety-Second Annual Conference of the National Tax Association*: 15–21.

Mikesell, J.L. (1998) Tax Administration: The Link Between Tax Law and Tax Collections. In: Thompson, F. and Green, M.T. (eds.), *Handbook of Public Finance*, New York, Marcel Dekker: 173–198.

Mikesell, J.L. and Zorn, C.K. (2008) Data Challenges in Implementing a Market Value Property Tax: Market and Market-Informed Valuation in Russia, Ukraine, and the Baltic States. In: Bahl, R., Martinez-Vazquez, J. and Youngman, J.M. (eds.), *Making the Property Tax Work, Experiences in Developing and Transitional Countries*. Cambridge, MA: Lincoln Institute for Land Policy: 183–206.

Nerre, B. (2008) Tax Culture: A Basic Concept for Tax Politics. *Economic Analysis & Policy*, 38, March: 153–167.

OECD (2001) *Fiscal Design Across Levels of Government, Year 2000 Survey, Country Report: Czech Republic*. Paris: Organisation for Economic Co-operation and Development.

Purohit, M.C. (1997) Value Added Tax in a Federal Structure: A Case Study of Brazil. *Economic and Political Weekly*, XXXII: 357–361.

Radian, A. (1980) *Resource Mobilization in Poor Countries, Implementing Tax Policies*. New Brunswick, New Jersey: Transaction.

Sjoquist, D.L. and Walker, M.B. (1999) Economies of Scale in Property Tax Assessment. *National Tax Journal*, LII: 207–220.

Sootla, G., Kasemets, K. and Kunnapuu, S. (2000) Local and Regional Tax Administration in Estonia. In: Hogye, M. (ed.), *Local and Regional Tax Administration in Transition Countries*. Budapest: Local Government and Public Service Reform Initiative Open Society Institute: 141–212.

Stella, P. (1992) Tax Farming – A Radical Solution for Developing Country Tax Problems? Working Paper WP/92/70. Washington DC: International Monetary Fund.

Sterks, C.G.M. and de Kam, C.A. (1991) Decentralizing Taxation in the Netherlands. In: Prud'homme, R. (ed.), *Public Finance with Several Levels of Government / Les finance publiques avec plusieurs niveaux de gouvernement*. The Hague, Netherlands and Koenigstein, Germany: Foundation Journal Public Finance.

Tannenwald, R. (2001) Are State and Local Revenue Systems Becoming Obsolete? *New England Economic Review*, 4: 27–43.

Tanzi, V. and Pellechio, A. (1995) The Reform of Tax Administration. Working Paper 95/22. Washington DC: International Monetary Fund.

Veehorn, C. and Ahmad, E. (1997) Tax Administration. In: Ter-Minassian, T. (ed.), *Fiscal Federalism in Theory and Practice*. Washington DC: International Monetary Fund: 108–134.

Zorn, C.K., Tesche, J. and Cornia, G. (2000) Diversifying Local Government Revenue in Bosnia-Herzegovina through an Area-Based Property Tax. *Public Budgeting & Finance*, XX: 63–86.

5

Establishing a Tax Rate

Kurt Zorn

Introduction

Determination of a tax rate is an integral and critical component of any tax system, whether the tax is based on consumption, income or wealth. The property tax is no exception. How the rate applied to the defined property base is established can have a significant effect on the property tax's ability to mobilize revenues, its fairness, the costs associated with administering the tax and its economic effects.

Generally there are many steps involved in the administration of a property tax system. These steps include: establishing laws and statutes which provide general guidance regarding what property should be subject to taxation, how it should be valued and how it should be taxed; developing rules and regulations for the administration of the tax; discovering property; preparing an inventory of property; estimating the value of property; determining the taxable value of the property; establishing a tax rate; and calculating the property tax bill (Brown and Hepworth, 2002). While there is an extensive academic and practitioner literature about property taxation and property tax administration, one aspect that tends to receive less attention is how property tax rates are established.

The literature does devote considerable attention to how the property tax base is determined and how that base is valued. Of course, determination and valuation of the tax base is essential to arriving at a levy in any tax system. However,

A Primer on Property Tax: Administration and Policy, First Edition.
Edited by William J. McCluskey, Gary C. Cornia and Lawrence C. Walters.
© 2013 Blackwell Publishing Ltd. Published 2013 by Blackwell Publishing Ltd.

equally important to the determination of the tax levy is the tax rate applied to the tax base. This is certainly true with the property tax where the property tax base and the property tax rate are inextricably intertwined when determining a property tax levy. If there is a desired amount of revenue that needs to be raised from the property tax, it is simple to see that a large property tax base results in a low tax rate. Conversely, if the tax base is relatively small, the property tax rate must be high to achieve the targeted tax levy.

The purpose of this chapter is to provide a detailed look into considerations that lie behind the establishment of a property tax rate. Included in these considerations is the fact that the way property tax rates are established can have an effect on revenue mobilization, fairness, economic neutrality and transparency.

What level of government should set the property tax rate?

There is a rich literature that deals with the issue of fiscal decentralization and the principles behind both expenditure and revenue assignments in a decentralized system. See, for example, Bahl and Linn (1992); Bird (2000); Bird and Vaillaincourt (1999); Ebel and Yilmaz (2002); Martinez-Vazquez (2001); and McLure (1998). It is generally agreed that governmental functions that involve maintaining a growing and stable economy along with ensuring national security should be the province of the central government. Similarly, policies and programmes intended to redistribute income should be the responsibility of higher, rather than lower, levels of government in order to ensure fairness.

On the other hand, the correspondence principle, which argues that expenditure assignment should be correlated with the level of government that best matches the area where the recipients of the benefits from these goods and services reside, suggests that the vast majority of government goods and services should be provided at the subnational level and, more explicitly, the local level of government. A final concept that tends to reinforce the notion of a subnational emphasis on expenditure assignment is the principle of subsidiarity. Under this principle, the delivery of goods and services should be assigned to the lowest level of government that can efficiently provide them.

Subsidiarity recognizes that tastes and preferences for publicly provided goods and services tend to vary widely, making decentralization of their provision desirable to the extent reasonable. Therefore, at least conceptually, it makes sense to deliver the vast majority of public services at the subnational level where local officials, who are more in touch with the preferences of the citizenry, decide what to provide, how to provide it and for whom to provide these goods and services.

If subnational governments are going to be expected to participate in the delivery of publicly provided goods and services, they must have the ability to finance them. Fiscal decentralization, which is predicated on the correspondence and subsidiarity principles and which argues that local policymakers should be granted an appropriate amount of fiscal autonomy with regard to expenditures, suggests that there should be a similar degree of autonomy on the revenue side of the equation. The logical financing sources for subnational governments most likely will consist of revenues they mobilize themselves along with transfers from higher levels of government. And taxation is an important component of any plan for local revenue mobilization.

Determining exactly what taxes subnational governments should have access to can be a challenge. The benefits of local fiscal autonomy and more direct accountability have to be weighed against the costs, such as loss of central control over the fiscal matters of subnational governments. Granting greater autonomy to local officials also may have its drawbacks. Because officials are directly accountable for a set of revenue sources, they may be reluctant to fully utilize them due to a fear of political backlash. This, in turn, may result in officials at the subnational level making inefficient use of the revenue sources available to them, resulting in a deterioration of the quality and quantity of goods and services they are able to provide. In addition, with increased autonomy, subnational governments may try to levy taxes on tax bases for which they have little or no accountability. Ideally, subnational governments' access to tax bases should be limited to those that correlate with jurisdictional boundaries.

The literature does provide guidance with regard to proper revenue assignment, specifically in the case of taxes. When considering what taxes should be under the purview of subnational governments, Bahl argues that central governments should consider four criteria (Bahl, 2001). First, the revenue adequacy of the taxes should be considered. Specifically, a determination must be made regarding how much of the expenditure responsibility it has assigned to subnational governments should be covered by taxes. Second, the taxes assigned to local governments should correspond to expenditures. 'Local governments should not have access to taxes where there is potential to export a significant part of the burden to persons who live outside the expenditure benefit zone.' Third, it is important that subnational governments be assigned taxes they can administer efficiently, effectively and equitably. Fourth, local governments should have some discretion in setting the tax rate. Without an opportunity to adjust the tax rate, the local government lacks the ability to adjust the relative price of locally provided goods and services. An important feature of fiscal decentralization is the enhancement of transparency regarding the link between expenditures and revenues. If the tax rate is centrally determined, accountability is compromised because it is no longer clear what influence, if any, local officials have over rate setting.

Others reinforce the notion that tax rate setting is an important component of any subnational tax structure. Bird (2000) argues that a completely subnational tax possesses four characteristics: it is assessed by the subnational government; the tax is collected by the subnational government; revenues accrue to the subnational government; and the subnational government sets the tax rate. There are, of course, many situations where the central and subnational governments share the aforementioned responsibilities with regard to a particular tax. However, '...the most critical aspect of subnational taxing power is who is politically responsible for setting the tax *rate*' (Bird, 2000). Without the ability to set the tax rate, subnational governments lack the ability to significantly affect the level and composition of their revenues. Therefore, autonomy and accountability are compromised. However, this ability to set rates does not have to be complete. If subnational governments are allowed to set rates within a range determined by the central government, they are afforded at least a degree of autonomy and will be at least partially accountable for the rates set.

Property taxes are often mentioned whenever subnational taxes are being discussed. Depending on how they are designed and administered they have the potential for satisfying the four criteria posited by Bahl (2001) and the conditions outlined by Bird (2000). Malme and Youngman (2001) argue that property taxes have the potential to be an important component of a well-functioning intergovernmental fiscal system. And, as noted above, in order for the property tax to be an effective and responsive tool in local fiscal policymaking it is important that local governments have considerable say in setting the tax rate.

Setting the property tax rate

On the surface, the relationship among the tax rate, the tax base, and the amount of tax revenues (tax levy) raised from the property tax is straightforward:

$$L = rNTB \qquad (5.1)$$

where

L = the property tax levy
r = the property tax rate
NTB = the net property tax base. (The net property tax base is defined as the base to which the property tax rate is applied. A discussion of how the net base varies from the gross property tax base is provided later.)

The amount of the tax levy is directly related to both the size of the property base subject to the tax and the level of the tax rate. Tax revenues will increase under a number of scenarios including when the rate and base both increase, when the tax rate experiences a larger percentage increase than the tax base decreases or the tax rate decreases less percentage-wise than the tax base increases or when the tax base increases but the tax rate remains unchanged or vice versa. However, as those familiar with the property tax will tell you, the relationship among the rate, base, and levy is not as simple as it first appears.

Determining the tax base

The first step in structuring a property tax is determining what types of property will be subject to the tax. Often the choices include land, structures on the land and personal (movable) property.

Once the property subject to taxation has been identified, a basis for valuing that property must be chosen. Generally one of three different approaches is used – the capital value approach, the rental value approach or the area based approach. The capital approach values property at its market value, based on its highest and best use as identified in an arm's length transaction. The rental approach bases the property's value on the open market rental value for its current use. The area based approach uses the physical size of the property, usually per square metre, as the basis for valuation of property. A variation on this approach is a unit basis of valuation where the tax is based on each physical unit without reference to area or size. The end result, regardless of the valuation method chosen, is the gross property tax base (GTB).

The size of the GTB will depend on how effectively the valuation is performed. Some approaches are fairly uncomplicated, such as the area based approach, requiring no particular level of sophistication in order to arrive at an accurate valuation of the tax base. On the other hand, the rental and capital value approaches are more data intensive, and accurate valuation demands more expertise on the part of administrators. Because valuation is relatively easy using an area based approach, it is not uncommon to find this approach in use in developing and transitional countries. Rental and capital value approaches to valuation tend to be more prevalent in developed countries and in those countries that possess a longer history of reliance on the property tax.

Ideally the GTB would form the basis for property taxation but in reality that generally is not the case. The GTB is often reduced either by passive or active administrative actions. The former refers to situations where valuation approaches are not applied properly, resulting in a divergence between what constitutes the true size of the base (GTB) and the base subject to the tax (NTB). The more complicated the valuation process, such as those that occur under the rental and capital value approaches, the higher the probability that passive administrative actions will impact the tax base. In reality, there is the possibility that some actors in the process may use the more complex rental or capital valuation processes as 'cover' for very deliberate moves to manipulate a divergence between net value and gross value. For example, assessors in the USA sometimes purposely under-value real property, causing its assessed value to differ from its market value (capital value).

The GTB may also be reduced through active administrative actions. When valuing property, a conscious decision may be made to treat various types of property differently. One approach may be to use different valuation algorithms for different types of property, which result in variations in value across property types. For example, residential land parcels may be valued on the basis of comparative sales, while agricultural land is valued based on soil productivity.

Another approach is to use a common valuation method and then adjust the value subject to taxation depending on what classification category the property fits. This second approach can be demonstrated algebraically (see Equation 5.2);

$$NTB_i = z_iGTB_i \qquad (5.2)$$

where

NTB_i = the net property tax base for property in property class i
GTB_i = the gross property tax base for property in property class i
z_i = the percentage of gross value of the tax base that is subject to taxation

An example of this divergence between the gross and net tax base is the rather common phenomenon of classifying property types in the USA. Usually for political reasons, a decision is made to treat residential (R) and commercial/industrial (C/I) real property differently. Often the rationale, even if it is not explicitly stated, is that it is politically advantageous to provide a 'tax break' for residential property owners relative to business property owners. By doing this, politicians may be viewed in a more favourable light by the bulk of their constituency, residential homeowners, and receive more favourable consideration during elections.

So, for example, under a capital valuation approach, the market value of a parcel of residential real property and of a parcel of commercial real property may have equal gross values (GTB_R and $GTB_{C/I}$) of $200,000. But the value of the net property tax bases (NTB_R and $NTB_{C/I}$) will vary if the jurisdiction has chosen to treat property differently based on its class. In this example, assume that the jurisdiction has determined that commercial and industrial property should be valued at its full gross value ($z_{C/I} = 1.0$) and residential property should only have half of its gross value subject to taxation ($z_R = 0.5$). Therefore, the NTB subject to taxation will vary between these two parcels ($200,000 for the commercial parcel and $100,000 for the residential parcel) despite the fact that they both have the same gross property value.

A second way that active administrative actions may cause a divergence between the GTB and the NTB is through the application of exemptions and deductions. Of course, more than one approach may be employed simultaneously. For example, property may be classified and also eligible for deductions and exemptions.

This difference can be shown algebraically by the following (see Equation 5.3):

$$NTB_p = GTB_p - X_p - D_p \qquad (5.3)$$

where

NTB_p = the net property tax base for parcel p
GTB_p = the gross property tax base for parcel p
X_p = exemptions for parcel p
D_p = deductions for parcel p.

Commonly used exemptions include properties used for religious, educational and charitable purposes. In addition, property tax abatements, which are popular in the USA, may exempt all or a portion of business-related real and personal property. The application of deductions tends to vary widely and is commonly based on characteristics such as the age or income of the property owner, how the property is used, etc.

Types of tax rates

Once the net property tax base (NTB) has been determined, the focus shifts to what tax rate should be applied to the subject property. Two general types of property tax rates exist – flat rates and progressive rates. Generally flat rates are more predominant than progressive rates.

In its most fundamental form, a flat property tax rate is a single rate uniformly applied to the entire NTB in a political jurisdiction (see Equation 5.1). The advantages associated with using a flat tax rate for property taxation include uniformity, simplicity, transparency and predictability of revenue. One rate is easy for the taxpayer to comprehend, and tax officials will find its application to be uncomplicated. Also, if the value of the property subject to taxation is known, simple multiplication provides information on how much revenue the property tax will generate.

Despite the apparent simplicity of using a flat rate for property taxation, things can get complicated rather quickly. This arises when multiple flat rates are employed. One way multiple flat rates may be employed is when there are overlapping jurisdictions that rely on the property tax as a source of revenue. While each separate jurisdiction applies a single flat rate to property within its political boundaries, an individual property parcel within these jurisdictions' boundaries will be subject to multiple flat rates. This can be seen algebraically as:

$$L_p = \sum_{j=1}^{J} r_j NTB_p \tag{5.4}$$

where

j = jurisdiction j
r_j = the flat tax rate for jurisdiction j
p = parcel p
J = total number of jurisdictions that have parcel p as part of their NTB

The result of the application of these multiple rates is that the property tax may no longer be uniform. Two identical properties with the same valuation may face different tax bills due to their different physical locations. For example, if two identical parcels are located a few hundred metres apart in a municipality, and parcel A is located in a special service district (such as water conservation district) and parcel B is not located in the special district, parcel A will be subject to both the municipal property tax rate and the water conservation property tax rate while parcel B will only be subject to the municipality's tax rate. Just because the total tax rate is not uniform does not imply that the difference in rates is unfair. It is possible that parcels in the special service district are receiving benefits consistent with the property taxes paid.

In addition, the property owner will no longer perceive the property tax system to be simple, easily understandable or predictable. Instead of only having to keep track of a single jurisdiction's tax rate setting process, the property owner must monitor and understand the rate setting processes employed by a number of jurisdictions. And, until all of the jurisdictions have completed their rate setting and the subsequent tax billing, the parcel owner will not know what his or her total property liability will be.

Another way multiple flat rates may occur is when a single jurisdiction chooses to apply varying rates to different classes of property, resulting in multiple flat rates within the jurisdiction as:

$$L_i = \sum_{i=1}^{I} r_i NTB_i$$

(5.5)

where

i = property class i
r_i = the tax rate for property class i
I = the total number of property classes in the jurisdiction.

The classification may be based on use of the property, location of the property or on ownership of the property. If the use, location or ownership of the property is being used as a proxy for value of the parcel, these multiple flat rates are similar in their effect to progressive property tax rates.

Once again, uniformity is sacrificed because property receives differential treatment based on its characteristics. In addition, simplicity and transparency are adversely affected because the taxpayer and tax officials must know which properties fall in which categories and the tax rates that apply to the particular types of property.

Finally, it is possible for there to be a set of multiple flat rates applied to a single parcel due to a combination of overlapping jurisdictions and different tax rates applied by those jurisdictions based on the classification of property.

Unlike flat tax rates, which treat property within a particular jurisdiction or property classification uniformly, progressive property tax rates increase as the value of the NTB increases. Factors that may influence the value of land or both land and structures include the parcel's location, use, land fertility, condition of structure, age of structure, amenities etc.

The obvious advantage of this approach to structuring property tax rates is the ability to generate a more robust stream of revenue compared to applying a single flat rate to the jurisdiction's NTB. In addition, this approach to rate setting increases the equity of the property tax because it correlates the tax levy with the property owner's ability to pay based on the property's value. On the other hand, a progressive property tax rate structure is more difficult to administer and less transparent to property owners.

The most common progressive rate structure applies larger tax rates as NTB increases. For example, the first $50,000 of NTB may be subject to a rate of 1 per cent; property valued from $50,001 to $100,000 may be taxed at 1.5 per cent; and property with an NTB over $100,000 may be subject to a tax rate of 2 per cent. Normally these progressive tax rates are applied as average tax rates on the entire NTB and not as marginal tax rates on the increments of value in each bracket.

Different progressive rates can be applied to dissimilar classes of property and it is also possible for overlapping jurisdictions to levy different rates on property with different values. In these cases, simplicity and transparency clearly are compromised.

Determining the tax rate

Tax rates generally are established by either official determination or by the residual method. The former approach is often associated with a culture where '...taxation decisions are [considered to be] official acts and therefore must be ratified by the proper authority...' (Malme and Youngman, 2001). The formal process of determining rates and ensuring that the appropriate decision making bodies have provided their stamp of approval become the primary concern, with revenue mobilization being a secondary concern. One advantage of this approach is that determination of the rate or schedule of rates is relatively simple even though the politics surrounding the establishment of rates may be complex.

Another approach to determining the property tax rate first ascertains how much revenue needs to be raised by the property tax and then sets the rate at the level necessary to raise the requisite revenue. This approach to rate setting often is referred to as the residual method. Under this approach, the jurisdiction determines what its expenditure needs are and projects the revenues it expects to realize from non-property tax sources, with the difference between these two amounts representing the amount of revenue that must be raised from the property tax. The amount to be raised, the property tax levy (L_j), is divided into the net property tax base (NTB_j), to arrive at the property tax rate (r_j).

$$r_j = \frac{L_j}{NTB_j} \tag{5.6}$$

and

$$L_j = E_j - NPR_j \tag{5.7}$$

where

E_j = expenditures in jurisdiction j
NPR_j = non-property tax revenues in jurisdiction j

Clearly the primary consideration behind the residual method is revenue mobilization. This focus comes at the expense of simplicity and transparency because of the need to know what budgeted expenditures are, what revenues are expected from other sources and what the size the NTB is. None of these pieces of information are necessary under the official determination approach.

Who sets the rate?

If the property tax is part of an overall effort toward fiscal decentralization, conceptually decision makers at the subnational level should possess autonomy and have accountability with regard to the tax. This autonomy should extend to rate setting, in the form of either complete control or partial control over tax rates.

In reality the level of government possessing responsibility for setting tax rates varies among countries. At one extreme, the central government retains complete control over rate setting for property taxes and generally relies on an official determination approach when setting rates. This approach is more likely to be found in developing and transitional economies because of the increased likelihood that cultural values designate property tax rate setting as an official act and the fact that there is not an existing infrastructure at the subnational level of government to administer the property tax effectively and efficiently. In a similar vein, it is not uncommon, in developing and transitional countries, to find property tax systems that use an area based valuation approach because these systems are easier to understand and to administer (Malme and Youngman, 2001).

At the other extreme, local governments possess complete control over their tax rates with no involvement of higher levels of government. Quite often in these situations the residual approach serves as the basis for determining the tax rate. However, the majority of situations fall somewhere in between these two extremes.

Central governments may choose to limit subnational governments' discretion over property tax rates using one of three control mechanisms. First, the central government may set statutory limits on property tax rates. This may consist of a ceiling on the statutory (or legal) rates or a specification of a range in which tax rates must fall. In other words, the r_j in Equation 5.6 is subject to an upper limit or both an upper and lower limit. Second, the central government may impose a limit on the property tax levy (L_j) which indirectly constrains the ability of the local government to set property tax rates. For example, if the increase in the tax levy is limited to 5 per cent and the NTB_j increases by 3 per cent, the maximum amount the local government can increase its tax rate (r_j) is approximately 2 per cent. Similarly, if NTB_j increased by 10 per cent, the local government would be required to cut its tax rate by approximately 5 per cent. Third, a limit on the increase in expenditures at the local level can indirectly affect the local government's ability to set property tax rates. This occurs because E_j in Equation 5.7 is constrained, meaning that the amount of revenue that needs to be raised through the property tax (L_j) is reduced, *ceteris paribus*. Therefore, a smaller levy is required from the net property tax base, resulting in a lower property tax rate.

Rate setting in practice

As demonstrated above, there are many considerations that go into setting a property tax rate. Not surprisingly there exists a wide variation in how property taxes are set and by whom they are set. What follows is a few country examples that help to demonstrate different approaches that are used to set tax rates. In addition, a summary table provides an overview of different rate setting characteristics in a number of countries.

The Czech Republic is an example of a country where the central government officially determines property tax rates. An area based valuation standard is used and multiple flat rates are applied. These tax rates vary with building use and location. As can be seen in Table 5.1, the area of a building in square metres serves as the base for the tax (NTB) and it is multiplied by the tax rate determined for the type of use the building is subjected to.

The value is then adjusted for location, using the following coefficients (Table 5.2):

Table 5.1 Property tax rates in Czech Republic, per m²

Residential buildings	CZK 1
Weekend and recreation buildings	CZK 3
Isolated garages	CZK 4
Buildings used for agricultural production, forestry or water enterprises	CZK 1
Industrial and energy property	CZK 5
Other buildings used for business purposes	CZK 10
Any other buildings or construction not mentioned above	CZK 3

Rates are increased by CZK 0.75 per m² for each additional floor, if the building consists of more than one floor
Information sourced from the Confederation Fiscale Europeenne (http://www.cfe-eutax.org/taxation/real-estate-tax/czech-republic, accessed 19 March 2012).

Table 5.2 Location coefficients, Czech Republic

1.0	In municipalities having up to 1,000 inhabitants
1.4	In municipalities having 1,001–6,000 inhabitants
1.6	In municipalities having 6,001–10,000 inhabitants
2.0	In municipalities having 10,001–25,000 inhabitants
2.5	In municipalities having 25,001–50,000 inhabitants
3.5	In municipalities with more than 50,000 inhabitants
4.5	In Prague

Information sourced from the Confederation Fiscale Europeenne (http://www.cfe-eutax.org/taxation/real-estate-tax/czech-republic, accessed 19 March 2012).

Table 5.3   Personal property tax rates, Russian Federation

Value	Maximum rate
Up to 300,000 rubles	0.1 per cent
300–500,000 rubles	0.1–0.3 per cent
Above 500,000 rubles	0.3–2.0 per cent

Source: Mikesell et al., (2006)

Table 5.4   Property rate schedule adopted by parliament, $J

Property value	Tax rate
Less than 200,000	600
200,001–1,000,000	600+0.3% of the amount over 200,000
1,000,001–2,500,000	3,000+0.5% of the amount over 1,000,000
2,500,000–more	10,500+1.75% of the amount over 2,500,000

Source: Sjoquist (2005). Reproduced by permission of David Sjoquist.

In Russia, the personal property (real estate) tax is centrally administered, but local authorities have some discretion over tax rates. This tax is levied on owners of residential houses, apartments, summer houses, garages and other buildings throughout the Russian Federation. Flat tax rates are set by local authorities, who can determine what criteria to use, such as type of property, use or value, when arriving at NTB. However, the tax rates are subject to ceilings established by the central government (Table 5.3).

Under this system it is possible for local authorities to construct a number of different rate scenarios. One possibility is a flat rate of 0.1 per cent (or less) applied to all personal property in the jurisdiction. On the other hand, it is possible to apply a series of progressive tax rates that vary as the value of personal property increases. Also, a combination of rates, based on value and use, is possible under the parameters set by the central government.

A number of countries, such as Jamaica, Chile, Pakistan, Cyprus and the Philippines, have experience levying property tax rates that vary with property values (Sjoquist, 2005). Although Jamaica now uses a flat property tax rate, in the recent past a schedule of progressive property tax rates, established by the central government, were levied on the value of unimproved land. However, these rates were effectively limited by a cap on maximum property tax liabilities (levies).

The examples provided above, regarding the structure of property tax rates used in the Czech Republic, Russian Federation and Jamaica, provide a glimpse at the variety of structures and practices present in the world. An overview of tax rate setting characteristics compiled by Bird and Slack (2005) further underscores the variety when it comes to property tax rate setting. As can be seen from Table 5.5, there is substantial variation in the amount of local discretion

Table 5.5 Characteristics of tax rate setting, selected countries

	Different tax by property class	Local discretion over tax rates
OECD:		
Australia	Yes	Yes for local tax; limits on annual increase in revenues.
Canada	Yes	Yes (restrictions apply in some provinces)
Germany	Yes	Central base rates; locally determined leverage factors
Japan	No; assessment differentiation	Nationally set standard and maximum rates
UK	Two separate taxes	Residential tax only; tax ratios for bands set centrally
Central & eastern Europe:		
Hungary	Yes	Yes, within legal limits
Latvia	No	No, but local governments can grant relief
Poland	Yes	Yes, subject to prescribed minimum and maximum rates
Russia	Yes	Yes, within narrow range set by senior governments
Ukraine	No	No
Latin America:		
Argentina	Yes	Yes
Chile	No	No
Colombia	Yes	Yes, subject to central government limits
Mexico	Yes	Yes
Nicaragua	No	No
Asia:		
China	No	No
India	Yes	Yes, subject to state restrictions
Indonesia	No	No, but can change valuation deduction
Philippines	No, assessment differentiation	Yes, subject to minimum and maximum rates
Thailand	Yes	No
Africa:		
Guinea	Yes	No
Kenya	Yes, but rarely differentiated	Yes
South Africa	No, relief mechanisms used	Yes
Tanzania	Yes	Yes
Tunisia	No	No

Source: Bird and Slack (2005). Reproduced by permission of Enid Slack.

afforded local authorities and whether distinctions are made among different classes of property when setting tax rates.

Conclusions

There are many things that need to be considered when administering a property tax. Attention tends to be focused on the definition of the tax base, determining the value of the tax base and collecting revenue. An aspect of property tax administration that is integral, but often underappreciated, is deciding how to establish the property tax rate.

A large number of considerations go into the setting of a tax rate – how to define the tax base, what type of rate to use, whether the primary focus is on revenue mobilization and who should set the rate. Depending on the choices made, property tax rate setting can be a fairly simple procedure or can be quite complex. In turn these choices can have a significant effect on the fairness, economic neutrality, transparency and revenue productivity of the property tax system.

References

Bahl, R. and Linn, J.F. (1992) *Urban Public Finance in Developing Countries*. New York: Oxford University Press.

Bahl, R. (2001) *Fiscal Decentralization, Revenue Assignment, and the Case for the Property Tax in South Africa*. Working Paper 01–7, Georgia State University: Andrew Young School of Policy Studies, International Studies Program.

Bird, R.M. (2000) *Intergovernmental Fiscal Relations: Universal Principals, Local Applications*. Working Paper 00-2, Georgia State University: Andrew Young School of Policy Studies, International Studies Program.

Bird, R.M. and Vaillaincourt, F. (eds.), (1999) *Fiscal Decentralization in Developing Countries*. Cambridge: Cambridge University Press.

Bird, R.M. and Slack, E. (2005) *Land and Property Taxation in 25 Countries: A Comparative Review*. CESifo DICE Report, 3 (http: //www.cesifo-group.de/portal/pls/portal/docs/ 1/1193436.PDF, accessed 9/28/2011).

Brown, P.K. and Hepworth, M.A. (2002) *A Study of European Land Tax Systems*. Working Paper WP02PB1: Cambridge, MA: Lincoln Institute of Land Policy.

Ebel, R.D. and Yilmaz, S. (2002) *Concept of Fiscal Decentralization and Worldwide Overview*. Working Paper, No. 30346, Washington DC: World Bank Institute.

Malme, J. and Youngman, J.M. (eds.) (2001) *The Development of Property Taxation in Economies in Transition: Case Studies from Central and Eastern Europe*. Washington DC: World Bank.

Martinez-Vazquez, J. (2001) *Intergovernmental Fiscal Relations and the Assignment of Expenditure Responsibilities*. Working Paper, Georgia State University, Andrew Young School of Policy Studies.

McLure, C. (1998) The Revenue Assignment Problem: Ends, Means, and Constraints. *Journal of Public Budgeting, Accounting and Financial Management* 9(4): 652–683.

Mikesell, J.L., Zorn, C.K., Gerasimova, V., Vladimirova, S. and Krupa, O. (2006) *Land Value Taxation for Local Government Finance in the Russian Federation: A Case Study of Saratov Oblast.* Working Paper WP06KZ1: Cambridge, MA: Lincoln Institute of Land Policy.

Sjoquist, D.L. (2005) *The Land Value Tax in Jamaica: An Analysis and Options for Reform.* Working Paper 05–11, Georgia State University, Andrew Young School of Policy Studies, International Studies Program.

6

Property Tax Collection and Enforcement

Roy Kelly

Introduction

The ultimate objective of property taxation is to mobilize government revenue as efficiently and equitably as possible to pay for public services. Property taxation policy and administration must therefore be successfully designed and implemented to mobilize the appropriate level of public revenue, while ensuring fairness and minimizing administrative, compliance and efficiency costs.

Governments throughout the world are undertaking property tax reforms to improve revenue yield, taxation efficiency and/or taxpayer equity. Property tax revenue yields can be improved by implementing policy changes to broaden the property tax base definition and to introduce changes in tax collection and enforcement incentives, sanctions and penalties, among others. Property tax efficiency can be enhanced by introducing policy changes to minimize exemptions to ensure a broader property tax base, by defining the tax base to include land only or by introducing a two rate property tax rate system, which taxes land higher than improvements and/or by establishing higher tax rates on vacant, undeveloped land, among others. Property tax equity can be improved by introducing policy changes on definitions of tax liability, tax rate structures and/or tax relief measures to ensure horizontal and vertical equity, based on the benefit or ability to pay principles.

A Primer on Property Tax: Administration and Policy, First Edition.
Edited by William J. McCluskey, Gary C. Cornia and Lawrence C. Walters.
© 2013 Blackwell Publishing Ltd. Published 2013 by Blackwell Publishing Ltd.

Although distinct policies can be adopted which fine tune the property tax policy framework, the ultimate impact of these policy choices on revenue yield, efficiency and equity depends on the quality of property tax administration. Ultimately, unless property tax revenues are effectively collected, all other intended policy objectives will not be achieved. Governments must ensure that all property is captured on the tax rolls, that property is valued close to market value, that tax liability is assessed and levied accurately, that a dispute resolution mechanism is in place and that the tax revenues are actually collected. Each of these important administrative actions is necessary in order to realize property tax revenues and any intended efficiency and equity objectives.

Strategically speaking, collection and enforcement are the most important components of the property tax system. The property tax is primarily a fiscal instrument designed to provide government revenue, although the property tax can also be used to improve efficiency (e.g. through using vacant land taxes or betterment taxes) and/or improve equity (e.g. through taxing real estate capital). These objectives can only be obtained, however, if the property tax is uniformly and effectively collected and enforced. That is, the various property tax objectives (i.e. revenue, efficiency and equity) in law cannot be realized unless the revenue is actually collected and enforced.

If raising revenue is the primary objective for property taxation, it is clear that identification and valuation of the tax base, important as these may be, are only supportive activities. They are not the ultimate purpose for a tax system. Therefore, a property tax agency should not view itself as a mapping agency or a valuation agency. Maps, property information and property valuations are intermediate outputs needed to achieve the final output of revenue collection. Property tax agencies must always view themselves as essentially tax collection agencies.

This chapter focuses on the ever important role of the property tax collection process. The first section briefly presents a conceptual revenue model to illustrate the importance of tax administration, especially the critical role of tax collection. The next section briefly explores reasons for low property tax revenue collection and identifies possible government interventions to improve property tax revenue mobilization. The third section focuses on the key steps of the property tax collection process; determining tax liability, assessing the tax liability, billing and notifying the taxpayer, receiving and accounting for the tax revenues and enforcing against noncompliance, while the final section concludes with some summary thoughts.

Policy and administrative determinants of property tax revenues

Successful property taxation systems depend on a combination of appropriate policy and administrative variables. Governments must choose among policy options related to tax base definitions, exemptions, valuation standards, tax rate structures, collection and enforcement provisions and dispute resolution mechanisms. Simultaneously governments must establish tax administration systems which can maintain fiscal cadastre records, generate accurate property valuations, calculate tax liability assessments, bill and collect revenues, enforce against noncompliance, handle objections and appeals and provide taxpayer service.

As the following conceptual model indicates, the level of tax revenues depends on both tax policy choices and administrative efficiency (Linn, 1980; Kelly, 2000, 2004). Total tax revenue is a function of two variables related to policy choices, namely tax base definition and tax rate, and three variables linked to administrative choices, measured through the coverage ratio (CVR), valuation ratio (VR), and collection ratio (CLR).

$$\text{Tax revenue} = [\text{Tax base} \times \text{tax rate}] \quad \times \quad [\text{CVR} \times \text{VR} \times \text{CLR}]$$

(Policy-related variables)   *(Administration-related variables)*

(6.1)

Definition of model variables

The **tax base** variable is defined in government policy in terms of what is and is not to be taxed.

The **tax rate** variable is defined as the statutory tax rate.

The **coverage ratio** (CVR) variable is defined as the amount of taxable property captured in the fiscal cadastre, divided by the total taxable property in a jurisdiction, measuring the accuracy and completeness of the property tax roll information.

The **valuation ratio** (VR) variable is defined as the property value as recorded on the valuation roll divided by the real market value of properties on the tax roll. This measures the accuracy of the overall property valuation level (i.e. what percentage of market value is being captured through the valuation process). Property valuation is to allocate the relative tax burdens of properties, not necessarily the absolute tax burden per property. The absolute tax burden is determined largely through the tax rate structure.

The **collection ratio** (CLR) variable is defined as tax revenue collected over total tax liability billed for that year. This collection ratio measures the collection efficiency on both current liability and tax arrears. The revenue collection ratio measures the tax revenues collected over the total amount collectable. The ratio should not measure the amount collected over the tax amount budgeted or targeted to be collected. In addition, it is important to note that the revenue collection ratio can be subdivided into three subratios measuring the quality of tax liability assessment, the collection on current tax liabilities and the enforcement efficiency in collecting outstanding tax liabilities.

Although tax policy decisions on the base and rates determine the 'potential' revenue yield and/or the impacts on efficiency and equity, the realization of

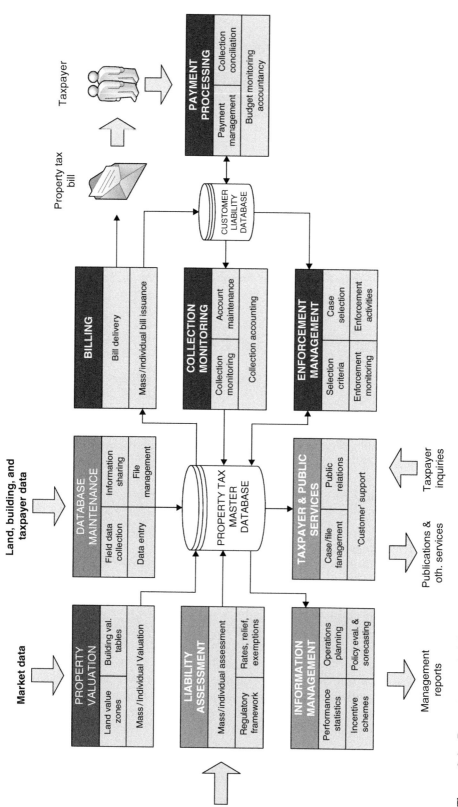

Figure 6.1 Property tax administration management system components

those revenue and policy objectives depends on the quality of administration, which will determine the extent to which the tax base is captured in the fiscal cadastre (i.e. coverage ratio), the absolute accuracy of the property valuations (i.e. valuation ratio) and the extent to which levied taxes are collected (i.e. collection ratio). These coverage, valuation and collection ratios are the critical administrative variables that determine the effective tax rates and tax burden for each property, thus determining the total revenue yield, economic efficiency and equity.

As Figure 6.1 illustrates, property tax administration involves an integrated set of activities related to: (1) creation and maintenance of the property database, (2) determination of the property valuation and assessment, (3) tax notification and billing, (4) tax collection, (5) enforcement against noncompliance and (6) dispute resolution and taxpayer service. As Table 6.1 indicates, each of these six major functions of property tax administration is linked to one or more of the administrative ratios. Tax policy and administration reforms are undertaken to improve these various ratios.

The first two administrative activities focus on creating the property assessment roll, by collecting and managing information on taxpayer and property characteristics and determining the property valuation and assessment for taxation purposes. This combination of information on the taxpayer (subject) and the taxable property (object) produces the property valuation assessment roll, which serves as the basis for levying, billing, collecting and enforcing the tax liability. Essentially these coverage and valuation-related administration activities generate the intermediate output of the valuation assessment roll upon which the tax collection function depends for mobilizing the revenues.

As important as the coverage and valuation ratios are, it is ultimately the performance of the actual revenue collection ratio that generates the revenue yield and influences taxpayer behavioural changes, which determine the final efficiency and equity impacts of the property tax system. In short, it is the successful act of tax collection which ultimately determines the impact of any statutory tax policy.

The conceptual revenue model illustrates the combined impact on revenue yield from tax administration reforms related to coverage, valuation or collection. The property tax in Indonesia, for example, is estimated to have a coverage ratio of about 80 per cent, a valuation ratio of about 60 per cent and a collection ratio of about 80 per cent. If administrative reforms were introduced which could improve each ratio by 10 percentage points, that is, up to a coverage ratio of 90 per cent, a valuation of 70 per cent and a collection ratio of 90 per cent, property tax revenues could be improved by 48 per cent overall, without any policy changes to the actual tax rate or tax base (Kelly, 2004). This improvement estimate is calculated as the change between the existing administrative efficiency of the coverage ratio (0.8)×valuation ratio (0.6)×collection ratio (0.80)=0.38 and the efficiency of the improved administrative ratios of 0.9×0.7×0.9=0.57. The percentage change from 0.38 to 0.57 is 48 per cent.

Table 6.1 Property tax administration functions and administrative ratios

Property tax function	Objective	Action	Critical administrative ratio
Tax base identification	To determine what will be taxed	Identify the tax base (land, building and/or machinery and equipment) Identify the exemptions from the tax base	Coverage ratio
Tax base valuation	To determine how the tax burden will be distributed among the taxpayers	'Weight' the tax base (either by area, other characteristics or value) Influence the distribution of the tax burden among the taxpayers	Valuation ratio
Tax liability assessment	To determine how much tax will be levied To determine how the tax burden will be distributed among the taxpayers	Determine the overall tax level Influence tax burden distribution among taxpayers through varying effective tax rates	Collection/ enforcement ratio Tax rate (policy variable)
Tax collection	To collect the tax	Issue and deliver the tax bills Collect the tax	Collection/ enforcement ratio
Tax enforcement	To determine how much revenue will be collected though enforcement	Enforce against noncompliance (sanctions and penalties)	Collection/ enforcement ratio
Tax (and valuation) appeals resolution	To ensure that the tax is equitably administered	Resolve disputes concerning the property information, valuation or tax assessment	Linked to coverage and valuation ratio and to the tax rate
Taxpayer service	To provide service to the taxpayer	Taxpayer education Taxpayer service	Linked to collection ratio (i.e. good taxpayer service will encourage higher collection ratio)

Source: *Kelly (2000)*

The conceptual revenue model emphasizes the importance of implementing property tax related administrative reforms linked to improving coverage, valuation and collection. The challenge for property tax reformers is being able to identify the most appropriate reform strategy to correctly identify the major administrative constraints and to design appropriate interventions and strategically sequence those actions to develop the necessary synergy for sustained reform momentum.

In the USA and other OECD countries, since the cadastral information systems and the tax collection systems tend to function well, the administrative reform priority tends to focus narrowly on improving the valuation ratio. The major opportunity for improving property taxes within these environments is to develop a cost-effective, accurate estimation of market values for each property on the tax roll. Thus, the appropriate reform strategy may be to place primary focus on improving the valuation ratio, placing a secondary emphasis on updating and refining property information and revenue collection systems.

By contrast, however, in most non-OECD countries, property valuation is not the major administrative constraint. Rather, these countries face major obstacles in creating a complete listing of properties for a fiscal cadastre and more importantly, in billing, collecting and enforcing payment of the property tax liabilities. In contrast to most OECD countries with coverage and collection rates both close to 100 per cent, most developing and transitional countries have coverage ratios estimated to be 40–60 per cent and collection ratios estimated to be 30–60 per cent (Youngman and Malme, 1994, 2002; Kelly *et al.*, 2001; Bird and Slack, 2004).

Property tax reforms in these countries do not have the luxury of focusing solely on property valuation and the fiscal cadastre but rather must place first priority on establishing an accountable and efficient tax collection system and, perhaps most importantly, on mobilizing the necessary political will to collect and enforce the property tax. Many countries do not have a culture of paying taxes, and this creates unique challenges in instituting successful tax collection. However, in the absence of a credible tax collection system, investing in major improvements in property tax coverage and valuations will make little difference in improving revenue yield, efficiency and/or equity.

Unfortunately many property tax reforms in developing and transitional countries have been designed and implemented as narrowly focused property valuation reforms rather than as comprehensive property tax administration reforms. These reforms have typically placed priority on increasing property valuation accuracy (largely through introducing new valuation techniques or by contracting private sector valuers), and through improving the tax base coverage (largely through creating GIS-based tax maps), for example, Philippines in late 1980s (Dillinger, 1991; Kelly, 1995) and Tanzania in mid-late 1990s (Kelly and Musunu, 2000; McCluskey *et al.*, 2003).

This 'valuation-pushed' implementation strategy typically produces new property valuation systems and property values, maps, improved property information and, often, linkages with computer-assisted valuation and geographic information systems (see Box 6.1). The emphasis is on the intermediate outputs of maps and property values, focusing on the coverage and valuation ratios, rather than on the final output of revenue generation, which depends on the collection ratio. This valuation-pushed strategy assumes that short-term and long-term revenue can be increased by improving the quality of the property

---

Box 6.1   Contrasting reform implementation strategies

Collection-led strategy	Valuation-pushed strategy
Expected activities:	**Expected activities:**
collection systems	valuation systems
delinquency lists	property revaluation
enforcement against noncompliance	property information collection
objections and appeals	mapping
property information	computer-assisted valuation (CAV)
valuation systems	geographic information system (GIS)
	objections and appeals
Sequence of outputs:	**Sequence of outputs:**
improve tax collection	revise property valuation systems
potential for enforcement	new maps (often digitized)
improve equity through enforcement	update information and values
update property information	computerize CAV and GIS Systems
improve property valuations	improve collections
Reform priority sequence:	**Reform priority sequence:**
collection, coverage, valuation ratio	valuation, coverage ratio
Examples:	**Examples:**
Chile, Indonesia (late 1980s)	Philippines, Tanzania, Uganda
Quezon City (Philippines) 2002	
Appropriate reform environment:	**Appropriate reform environment:**
developing/transitional countries	OECD countries

---

valuations and property information. Revenue collection and enforcement improvements are often neglected or relegated to secondary importance.

In contrast to the traditional valuation-pushed approach to property tax reform, however, more countries have recognized the need to follow a more 'collection-led' implementation strategy (e.g. Chile and Indonesia in the mid to late 1980s (Kelly, 1993, 2004; Rosengard, 1998); Quezon City, the Philippines, since the early 2000s (Ignacio, 2005), where first priority is placed on improving the revenue collection and enforcement component (collection ratio), while simultaneously building on improvements to property information and valuations (coverage and valuation ratio, respectively) (see Box 6.1).

The collection-led strategy recognizes that improved property valuation and property information accuracy, in the absence of improved property tax collection, will not maximize the short- and long-term revenue yield, efficiency and/ or equity. That is, unless revenue collection and enforcement are strengthened, taxpayers facing improved (and potentially higher) property valuations will still be able to continue avoiding paying the revised tax liability, thus rendering any hypothetical revenue or equity gains ineffective.

The collection-led strategy focuses on improving the revenue collection system, ensuring a combination of accurate and prompt billing, establishing multiple convenient payment points, including the use of banks and post offices, allowing payment in instalments, introducing payment incentives and taking timely and strict enforcement follow-up against delinquent accounts and non compliance. This collection-led approach assumes that strict collection and enforcement, with improved taxpayer service, can generate immediate improvements in revenues, encourage voluntary compliance and create subsequent pressure for improving the quality of property information and valuations, which can again further improve revenues, equity and efficiency.

Property tax reforms throughout the world are increasingly taking a more balanced, comprehensive approach, recognizing the ever-important role of improved property tax collection. The challenge in designing a successful collection-led strategy is to understand the inherent obstacles for improving overall revenue collection, identify creative solutions to overcome these constraints and implement the right package of incentives, sanctions and penalties which will be effective within each unique legal, institutional and social environment.

Common reasons for low rates of collection and enforcement

Property tax collection and enforcement can be a major problem for governments throughout the world. While property tax collection ratios in OECD countries tend to be close to 100 per cent, collection rates in developing countries range from between 30 to 60 per cent (Youngman and Malme, 1994, 2002; Bird and Slack, 2004). Property tax collection figures are not systematically available for developing countries. The 30–60 per cent average collection rate is estimated from various case studies on countries from Asia, Latin America and Africa. Some case studies even put the collection rate lower: for example, Dillinger (1991) states that the collection rate in Ibadan, Nigeria was only 9 per cent while a separate World Bank (1986) study states that property tax delinquencies in the West African countries of Senegal, Nigeria, Ivory Coast and Liberia averaged about 50 per cent but were sometimes as low as 10 per cent in the 1980s. In Albania in 1994 and 1995, the property tax collection rate was only 15 per cent and 25 per cent respectively, due to taxpayer resistance and the poor state of the economy (Almy, 2001). In contrast, the property tax collection ratio for urban and rural areas in Indonesia was about 50–60 per cent up to the 1990, improving to close to 79 per cent in 1994 with the introduction of the 'payment point system' (Kelly, 1993).

The key to improving property tax collection is to understand the various reasons for low collections and taxpayer noncompliance, identify possible options for government intervention and then develop the human and systems capacity, and to garner the political will to implement improved collection and enforcement.

Table 6.2   How to improve tax collection performance

Possible reasons for low collection rate	Possible solutions
Citizens have no faith in how the government will spend the collected revenue. They feel that collected revenues will be misused, and therefore refuse to, or are reluctant to, pay.	Develop a credible budget. Improve government budgeting, revenue and expenditure decisions and financial management systems. Improve public relations between the government and the taxpayers. Correct misinformation about expenditures decisions. Publicize the budget details and summary on results and outputs. Use participatory planning and budgeting techniques. Introduce citizen report cards and other third-party monitoring and evaluation systems.
Citizens have no faith in the ultimate equity of the property tax system. Outdated property information, unequal property valuations, 'mis-assessment', mismanaged collections, unsystematic enforcement, and lack of fair appeals procedures create mistrust.	Improve property tax policy and administration. Re-examine policies related to tax base definitions, exemptions, rates, deductions and assessment ratios, incentives, sanctions and penalties and appeals. Administration improvements may need to focus on property information, valuation, assessment, collection, enforcement and appeals. Introduce a two-stage dispute resolution (appeals) process to minimize compliance and administration costs and ensure greater perception of taxpayer equity. Use effective public relations (taxpayer service) to inform taxpayers on overall equity of the property tax structure.
Citizens are willing to pay but the property tax payment is lumpy and highly visible, generating difficulties and/or resistance to pay.	Enable taxpayers to pay in instalments (e.g. quarterly rather than in a single payment). To reduce visibility (and possible political resistance) enable taxpayers to pay property tax automatically through their mortgage companies or through automatic bank payment systems (North America, Singapore).
Citizens are willing but do not pay because of poor tax administration. Tax bills are late or never delivered because of inadequate bill distribution systems, payment system are not understood, too complicated or payment points are inconveniently located. Compliance costs for payment are very high in relation to the amount of the tax or the possible penalty for noncompliance.	Improve tax administration. Use computers to calculate and issue tax assessment notices, change the legal concept of notification, institute a more effective bill delivery system, use barcoding with addresses and improve the taxpayer education programme. Simplify tax payment procedures to reduce compliance costs by establishing convenient payment options.

Table 6.2   (*cont'd*)

Possible reasons for low collection rate	Possible solutions
People do pay but the tax revenue collected may be mishandled and incorrectly managed. This is especially a problem in cash-based societies.	Transfer 'teller function' to the banking system; install a carefully designed payment control system. Introduce alternative payment options such as payment through automatic payment from bank accounts (North America), credit card (North America, Singapore), using neighbours to collect property tax (Paraguay).
People do not pay because they know the government ultimately will not enforce the tax obligation. There is a lack of enforcement measures (e.g. incentives, sanctions or penalties) and/ or there is a lack of political will to use the available enforcement measures. Often taxpayers will use the court system to effectively forestall any attempt at enforcement.	Ensure that the payment control system generates a prompt and accurate delinquency list to enable enforcement, re-evaluate the incentives, sanctions and penalty structure and mobilize political will to enforce. Effectively develop and utilize non-court options for encouraging compliance. Mobilize political will. Require taxpayers to pay tax liability prior to court appeals.
People do not pay because there is a lack of tax payment mentality. Some cultural/political systems have a recent history of free services from the government and thus do not understand the rationale for taxation in general. In rural areas, customary land tenure systems make it difficult to enforce through seizure and auction of property.	Civic education to explain role of public sector in providing services and the link to payment for services through user charges, fees and property taxation. Taxpayer education programme to explain the importance of property taxation in financing public services. Carefully evaluate the cultural/political norms and implement creative alternative means to stimulate compliance.

As summarized in Table 6.2, the appropriate response to improved property tax collections depends on the exact nature of the collection problem, and must be tailored to the specific social, legal and institutional environment unique to each country. Let us identify some of the major reasons why citizens may not voluntarily pay their property taxes, and then identify possible options for government interventions to help overcome each specific constraint:

Problem: Citizens have no faith in how the government will spend the collected revenue. They suspect that collected revenues will be misused and therefore refuse to or are reluctant to pay.

Possible response: Develop a credible budget. Improve government budgeting, revenue and expenditure decisions and financial management systems. Improve public relations between the government and the taxpayers. Correct misinformation about expenditures decisions. Publicize budget details and summaries on service delivery outputs. Use participatory planning and budgeting techniques. Introduce citizen report cards and other third-party monitoring and evaluation systems.

Problem: Citizens have little faith in the ultimate equity of the property tax system. Outdated property information, unequal property valuations, 'mis-assessment', mismanaged collections, unsystematic enforcement and lack of fair appeals procedures have created mistrust.

Possible response: Improve property tax policy and administration. Re-examine policies related to tax base definitions, exemptions, rates, deductions and assessment ratios, incentives, sanctions and penalties and appeals.

Improve administration to enhance quality of property information, valuation, assessment, collection, enforcement and appeals. Introduce a two-stage dispute resolution (appeals) process to minimize compliance and administration costs and ensure greater perception of taxpayer equity. Use effective public relations (taxpayer service) to inform taxpayers about overall equity of the property tax structure.

Problem: Citizens have difficulty paying the property tax or be reluctant to pay the tax because it is too lumpy and highly visible.

Possible response: Enable taxpayers to pay in instalments (e.g. quarterly rather than in a single payment). Reduce visibility (and possible political resistance) by enabling taxpayers to pay property tax automatically through their mortgage companies or through automatic bank payment systems (e.g. North America, Singapore).

Problem: Citizens are willing to pay, but do not pay, because of poor tax administration. Tax bills are late or never delivered because of inadequate bill distribution systems or because payment systems are not well understood or too complicated. Payment points are inconveniently located and individual compliance costs for payment are very high in relation to the amount of the tax or the possible penalty for noncompliance.

Possible response: Improve tax administration. Use computers to calculate and issue tax notices, change the legal concept of notification, institute a more effective bill delivery system, use barcoding with addresses and improve and expand taxpayer education programmes. Simplify tax payment procedures to reduce compliance costs, by establishing convenient payment options.

Problem: Citizens do pay the property tax, but the tax revenue collected may be mishandled and not properly recorded in the accounts. This can especially be a problem in cash-based societies and in more remote rural areas.

Possible response: Transfer 'teller function' to the banking system; install a carefully designed payment control system. Rotate tax collectors. Where possible, require daily deposits of tax collections. Introduce alternative payment options such as payment through automatic payment from bank accounts (North America), credit card (North America, Singapore), using neighbours to collect property tax (Paraguay) (USAID, undated) and linking property tax payments to payment of other premise-based services like electricity or water, among others.

Problem: Citizens do not pay because they are confident that ultimately, the government will not enforce the tax obligation. There is a lack of enforcement measures (e.g. incentives, sanctions or penalties) and/or there is a lack of political will to use the available enforcement measures. Taxpayers may use the court system to effectively forestall any attempt at enforcement.

Possible response: Ensure that the payment control system generates a prompt and accurate delinquency list to enable enforcement, re-evaluate the incentives, sanctions and penalty structure and mobilize political will to enforce. Effectively develop and utilize non-court options for encouraging compliance (e.g. publishing names of delinquent taxpayers in newspapers (e.g. East Africa). Use system of requiring tax payment certificates and imposing tax liens. Require taxpayers to pay tax liability prior to court appeals. Enforce seizure of properties and auctions to recover outstanding tax liabilities.

Problem: Citizens do not pay due to lack of established tax payment mentality. Some cultural/political systems have a recent history of free services from the government and thus citizens may not understand the rationale for taxation in general (e.g. transitional countries). In some countries, customary land tenure systems make it difficult to apply the concept of individual tax payments and to enforce through seizure and auction of property (e.g. Africa).

Possible response: Introduce civic education programmes to explain the role of the public sector in providing services and the importance of property taxation in financing public services. Carefully evaluate the cultural/political norms and implement creative alternatives means to stimulate compliance.

To properly design and implement the appropriate government response to citizen reluctance to pay the property tax, taxing jurisdictions must first understand the underlying constraints to improved property tax revenue mobilization. Policy and administrative changes must then be designed and implemented within the sequence of administrative activities related to property tax collection. The following section outlines the key steps needed for any effective property tax collection system.

Designing an effective property tax collection system

The property tax collection process involves three basic sets of activities. First, the tax liability must be assessed for each property, determining correct legal liability, applying proper tax rates, deductions and credits and notifying taxpayers of their tax liabilities. Second, the tax payments must be received and properly accounted. Third, taxpayer compliance must be enforced. And throughout this entire process, taxpayers must be provided with timely and complete information through a 'taxpayer service' to encourage compliance, minimize compliance costs, improve tax administration efficiency and ensure equity.

Assessing the tax liability

Using information contained on the property valuation roll, the tax department must correctly assess the tax liability for individual taxpayers. This tax assessment process involves determining the legal liability, applying the proper tax rates, deductions and credits in order to calculate the tax liability and then billing the taxpayer for the correct tax amount.

Determining legal tax liability

Tax liability must be clearly defined in order to properly levy the property tax and enforce against noncompliance. Although there is often a conceptual distinction made between an *in personam* and an *in rem* definition of tax liability, ultimately all taxes fall on a taxpayer, in the sense that an individual, not the property, will ultimately pay the tax liability. The concepts of *in rem* and *in personam* are subject to considerable confusion and debate. There is general agreement that the legal liability of an *in rem* system rests with the property while the *in personam* system rests with the taxable person, however defined. In practice, however, tax systems identify a taxpayer (person) even under *in rem* systems, because ultimately taxes are paid by a person not a property. In fact, the conceptual distinction rarely affects actual property tax administration since laws typically define the tax object as the property and the tax subject as the taxpayer responsible for paying the tax.

Thus, in practice, to better facilitate tax administration, tax legislation usually defines tax liability very broadly, dealing separately with any specific liability and enforcement issues raised by the conceptual differences between *in personam* and *in rem* systems (Youngman, 1996).

Under a broad definition, property tax liability can be defined as falling on the owner, occupant and/or beneficiary of the property, as determined by the tax department. This broad definition used in Indonesia (Kelly, 1993) is similar to that used in California (Cal. Rev. & Tax. Code §405) where tax liability falls on any person 'owning, claiming, possessing or controlling' an interest in the property on the lien date or in the Canadian Indian Act, §83(1)(a), which defines tax liability as falling on persons 'occupying, possessing or using' the property (quoted in Youngman, 1996).

Under this broad definition, the tax liability can fall on several persons simultaneously, making all parties 'jointly and severally liable' for the tax. Using this broad definition of the taxpayer, and holding the taxpayers jointly and severally liable, facilitates the tax administration process, especially in countries with incomplete legal cadastres, and where legal ownership is unclear. The tax administration can pursue the owner, occupant and/or any identified beneficiary of the property, greatly facilitating the tax collection and enforcement process.

Levying the tax liability

Based on the established policies and legal regulations, the tax department must apply the appropriate set of tax rates and tax relief instruments (e.g. credits and deductions) to determine the tax roll. The tax rate is either predetermined in national or state level legislation or must be set by the local council within the established national or state level guidelines. Similarly, tax relief amounts are usually set in national or state level legislation with or without local discretion. Typically the tax relief measures include both those applicable to the property itself (e.g. based on such factors as land use, size and/or location) and/or those applicable to the taxpayer, however defined (e.g. based on such factors as taxpayer age, veteran status and income group).

The taxing jurisdiction must properly apply those tax rates and tax relief measures against the information on the taxpayer as well as information on the property as contained in the valuation roll. A tax roll is then issued by the taxing jurisdiction which would include the relevant legal information on the taxpayer name and address, the property location and value and the calculated tax liability amount ready for preparation of the tax bills. Levying the tax through issuing the tax roll legally establishes a legal tax lien on a particular property, which can only be cancelled through payment of the proper tax amount.

Notifying tax liability/tax billing

Based on information contained on the tax roll, the tax department will prepare and mail the tax bills, notifying property owners/occupants of their tax liability. The billing/tax notification process involves determining whom to notify, what information should be included in the notification and how the tax bill notification should be delivered to the taxpayer (see Box 6.2). Tax legislation must clearly define the legal definition of notification to ensure fair and efficient tax administration. In addition to tax bill notification, tax departments are usually required to notify individual taxpayers of changes in property valuations, assessment of specific penalties and intent to proceed to enforcement against noncompliance, among others.

Who is to be notified?

The tax bill notification should be sent to the property address in care of the designated taxpayer, if known. If the name of the taxpayer is not known, the tax bill should be addressed to 'owner and/or current resident'. Under a system of special request, the tax bill could be sent to a different mailing address. In some cases, tax bills can be sent to a third party, such as a mortgage company, which has been determined responsible for paying the tax liability.

Ideally, separate tax bills should be issued for each individual parcel. If a taxpayer has more than one parcel, that taxpayer would receive more than one tax bill. A simple system of one tax bill for one individual property facilitates the accounting and better enables effective enforcement. However, under special circumstances, it may be justifiable to issue one tax bill for several properties. For example, it would be more cost effective to send a single bill to

---

Box 6.2   Example legal definition of notification (*excerpt from Government of Kenya 'The Rating Act' Ca.267, 1972*)

Section 26

(1) Except where otherwise provided by this Act, any notice required... shall be published by advertisement once in the Gazette and in one or more newspapers circulating in the municipality.

(2) Any notice... may be sent or served either –

    (a) by delivering it to the person to... whom it is to be sent or served; or

    (b) by leaving it at the usual or last known place of abode or business of that person, or, in the case of a company, at its registered office; or

    (c) by ordinary or registered post; or

    (d) by delivering it to some person on the premises..., or, if there is no person on the premises..., then by fixing it... to some conspicuous part of the rateable property; or

    (e) by any method which may be prescribed:

provided that, if the rating authority, ..., has reason to believe that such notice has not been received by the person..., it may advertise, in the manner provided in subsection (1), the general purport of such notice, ..., and thereupon the notice... shall be deemed to have been received by that person, and the advertisement may refer to one or more notices, ... and to one or more rateable owners.

(3) Any notice, demand or other document by this Act...may be addressed by the description 'owner' or 'occupier' of the premises..., without further name or description.

4. When any notice, demand or other document required... for the purposes of this Act has been sent by ordinary or registered post, delivery or service thereof shall, ..., be deemed to have been effected at the time at which a letter would be delivered in the ordinary course of the post.

---

a taxpayer owning multiple properties, if these are low value properties. Under special circumstances in some countries, a special category for multiple property taxpayers can be established where a single bill can be sent to a settlement/rural village, allowing the village chief to collect taxes from non-registered plots. In rural societies, especially those with no parcel-based information, it may be necessary to send one tax liability notice to the village chief for collection from the villagers. This system had been used in rural Indonesia since the 1600s, where the village head in essence becomes the 'tax assessor' in practice, allocating the relative tax burden among the villagers based on such criteria as relative property size, property value or even non-property-based criteria.

Some tax systems allow public notification rather than individual notification. For example: some Canadian Provinces issue a public notice rather than sending out individual tax bills; Grenada posts the tax liabilities in public places rather than trying to identify the correct addresses for bill delivery; and tax bills in

Costa Rica are deposited at the central bank, the municipal treasuries and the city council for taxpayers to claim, and no individual notification is made to property owners (Garzon, 1989).

What is to be included in the tax bill notification?

The tax bill notification should include sufficient information to fully inform the taxpayer of the specific tax liability amount, with supporting data on the property and the procedures for paying the taxes. A tax bill typically should include such information as:

1. name and address of taxpayer
2. parcel address
3. property identification number
4. parcel description (land and building area, land and building classification)
5. property valuation (broken into its components of land and building)
6. tax liability due
7. tax payment due date
8. payment location
9. information concerning legal requirements (dates, penalties, and procedures for appeal, etc).

   To improve taxpayer service and reduce compliance and administrative costs, many taxing jurisdictions take advantage of the tax bill notification process to provide additional information to taxpayers on the role of the property tax, its importance in funding public services, the appeals/dispute resolution process and a contact address/telephone number for further information. In many countries, this information is also provided through various channels including community group meetings, television, radio, newspapers, movie theatre advertisements, posters and leaflets. In modern tax systems using ICT, taxpayers can also access their billing and tax liability information through the Internet.

   Most modern property tax systems rely on computerization to manage property tax information, produce the valuation and tax rolls and handle the tax billing process. However, in many developing countries, these administrative tasks continue to be handled on a manual basis. Under a manual system, each piece of taxpayer- or property-related information requires increased administrative costs and time. Thus, general information on payment procedures and location are usually preprinted on the tax bill form while individual taxpayer and tax property information which must be manually transcribed is kept to a minimum (i.e. name, address, and amount owed).

   Given the information-intensive nature of property tax administration, including the tax billing process, all property tax reforms now typically include a major computerization component to increase the efficiency and equity of property tax administration. These computer-assisted property tax administration management systems should be linked to the broader computer-assisted budgeting and financial management systems.

How is the tax bill notification delivered?

Tax bills are delivered in a wide variety of ways (e.g. postal system or hand delivered by the tax officials, local government officials or private delivery service). The principle is to develop a system which minimizes administration and compliance costs.

The tax bill delivery method is influenced by the legal definition of 'notification' and the specific circumstances within the country. Mail is usually preferred in cases where addresses are clear. In the USA, using mailing barcodes has reduced the number of wrong address returns in the USA (see Connecticut Task Force report at http://www.ct.gov/opm/cwp/view.asp?a=2984%26q=383178).

Because of the various problems related to use of the postal system in some countries, however, the tax department often must rely on its staff or local government officials to hand deliver the tax bills. Other options can include the hiring of off-duty postal workers, electricity bill readers, farm extension workers to deliver the tax bills, or using neighbourhood networks or other people who have frequent contact with taxpayers. Although perhaps expensive, special private couriers can also be used.

If the postal system is not utilized, it is important to develop an incentive system which will encourage the delivery of the tax bills. For example, in countries where the property tax accrues to a higher level local government, lower level officials (e.g. village level officials) are often reluctant to deliver tax bills or assist in the revenue collection process because they receive neither institutional nor personal benefits from the property tax. Furthermore, these

---

Box 6.3   Tax bill delivery in Indonesia

Tax bill delivery is a major problem in Indonesia, especially in rural areas. In practice, the postal system is only effective for properties with clear addresses (namely commercial, industrial and high value residential), largely in urban areas. Even when the postal system is used, there is a high return rate of undelivered tax bills. Taxpayers are reluctant to accept delivery of the tax bills.

Because of the postal system problems, tax bills are generally hand delivered through the government network. The government tax office will invite the highest value taxpayers to a seminar during which a senior government official will explain the importance of the property tax and compliance as a social responsibility. Tax bills will be handed out personally to these taxpayers. Lower value bills are then given to the local government administrative apparatus for delivery to the taxpayers. The individual delivering the tax bills is compensated per tax bill delivered.

local government officials often are not given transport money or daily allowances to cover even the marginal costs of bill delivery activity. Given low salaries and other alternatives for compensation, these lower level local government officials can be reluctant to exert sufficient effort to ensure delivery of tax bills.

All tax systems should stipulate that failure to receive the actual physical tax bill does not exempt the taxpayer from his tax liabilities and related penalties. The taxpayer is legally responsible for paying the taxes on time; the legal tax liability is not dependent on receiving the tax bill (see Box 6.3).

Payment and receipt of tax payments

Upon receipt of the tax bill notification, the taxpayer is responsible for paying the property tax amount, while the tax department is responsible for receiving the tax payment, accounting for the payment receipts, maintaining the integrity of the funds collected and generating an accurate and timely delinquency list for subsequent enforcement purposes. The payment and accounting procedures should be simple and as painless as possible, in order to minimize taxpayer compliance costs while simultaneously allowing the tax department to minimize its own administrative costs.

The key is to minimize both administrative and compliance costs. Unlike major national taxes such as VAT, retail sales taxes and income taxes, the property tax is a very administration-intensive tax, where the tax department is responsible for identifying, valuing, assessing, billing, collecting and enforcement. The taxpayer's personal involvement with the property tax process is largely through the act of tax payment. Thus, to encourage voluntary compliance, the tax payment process should be structured to minimize the time and effort required for individual taxpayers to meet their tax obligations.

Most modern property tax systems provide taxpayers with a variety of methods in which to pay their property taxes. For example, taxpayers are given the option to make payments by sending a cheque, using computer-based banking, automated tellers at financial institutions, telephone banking, pre-authorized checking, credit cards or by paying in cash or cheque at convenient locations, such as the local government finance department, regional tax payment centres ('*collecturia*' in Latin America), post offices or financial institutions. The more places designated, the easier it is for the taxpayer to pay, but potentially, the harder it is for the tax administration to keep track of payments unless the system is computerized, linking the various payment points with the tax department.

To encourage ease of compliance, property tax systems generally allow taxpayers to pay in instalments over a period of time, with various incentives tailored to reduce both the administrative and compliance costs. Taxpayers must have sufficient time to mobilize the funds necessary to pay the property tax. Since the property tax liability is lumpy, the taxpayer may require some effort to gather the necessary payment. The key is to provide enough time for the taxpayer to mobilize the necessary funds, but not enough time for the tax-payer to forget the notification.

In general, most countries provide at least 30 days from the time of notification (Singapore, Kenya, Barbados and USA). Senegal provides three months, while Indonesia and Ecuador provide six months. The Land and Building Tax Law (1986) in Indonesia stipulated that tax due dates were determined to be six month after receipt of the tax bills. The intent was to force the tax department to deliver tax bills, inform citizens of their tax liabilities and improve taxpayer service. The impact was to make multiple tax due dates within a single taxing jurisdiction, increasing the administrative costs of ensuring signed receipts for each tax bill and enabling taxpayers to avoid tax payment by refusing to sign for the tax bill, thus never establishing a tax lien (legal liability) on the property. This was changed in 1988 under the 'collection led strategy', (Kelly, 1993). Specific tax payment due dates are normally defined in legislation.

Most tax jurisdictions allow for property tax payment in instalments and accept partial payments. The principle is to reduce the visibility and size of the annual property tax bill and minimize compliance and administration costs, while balancing the cash flow needs of the local government and the taxpayer.

Many tax jurisdictions have introduced automatic payments through the banking system, where taxpayers can sign up to have their property tax paid automatically in 6–12 equal instalments throughout the year through the bank (e.g. Canada, Singapore). Taxpayers of properties which have mortgages nor-mally pay their property taxes through their mortgage companies, which can reduce the risks to mortgage companies, securing their asset collateral.

Tax bills are lumpy, and therefore, for cash flow reasons, taxpayers prefer to spread payment over time. Although administrative and compliance costs can increase with the number of instalments, governments prefer to receive funds early and/or periodically for their own cash flow reasons. In addition, high rates of inflation can diminish the real value of tax revenue over time, unless the tax liabilities are indexed for inflation.

The following examples illustrate the varied experience in structuring instal-ment payments. In the USA and Canada, most taxing jurisdictions provide for two payment instalments, some provide for four instalments while a few provide for a variable number of instalments (Almy, 2000). In Canada, monthly instal-ments are allowed, if linked to automatic payments through the banking system. In Chile, taxes are paid in four equal instalments, indexed for inflation every six months. In Indonesia, rural and urban property taxes must be paid in one instal-ment, unless special arrangements are made with the tax department. In Jamaica, property taxes must be paid in a single payment unless tax liability exceeds J$5.00; landowners may then elect to pay on a bi-annual or quarterly basis. In Nuevo Leon, Mexico, property taxes for the minimum tax bill of M$18,000 are paid in one instalment, while higher value tax bills can be paid in six bi-monthly instalments. However, a discount is available if payment is made in one lump sum. In most transitional countries in Europe, taxpayers have the option of payment in 1–4 instalments; but in Armenia, taxpayers can make any number of payments as long as the tax is paid in full by 31 December each year (Almy, 2001).

Along with general improvements in establishing transparent and accountable governance, public financial management, and property tax policy and administration, tax departments often provide specific incentives to encourage increased taxpayer compliance. Tax departments can provide both positive incentives to *encourage voluntary tax compliance* by reducing compliance costs and/or providing discounts for timely payments, as well as providing negative incentives to *discourage tax noncompliance* by imposing a system of sanctions and/or penalties. Options for negative incentives are discussed further under the section on enforcement. On the positive side, tax departments can encourage voluntary compliance through providing improved tax payment services, thus reducing the compliance costs for taxpayers and/or through providing a discount for prompt and complete tax payment.

Many countries will provide a discount for early payment of the property tax to encourage high voluntary compliance. Early tax payment can reduce the need for governments to borrow funds short-term for cash flow reasons and, even with a discount, can result in a higher 'real' value of tax receipts for the government, especially in countries with high rates of inflation.

The level of discount necessary to induce taxpayers to switch to early payment depends on the opportunity cost of the funds. Assuming a perfect capital market, the taxpayer will voluntarily pay their property taxes early if the discount is at least equal to the rate of return being foregone through early payment. For most residential taxpayers, this would be equal to their interest rate received from their savings account.

The following examples illustrate the varied experience in providing discounts to induce early payment: In Mexico City, taxpayers can reduce their bills up to 22 per cent if payment is made early, and covers the whole year rather than being paid in four equal instalments. In Ecuador, property taxes are due anytime after 1 January, a maximum discount of 10 per cent is provided if the tax is paid within 15 days. This 10 per cent discount decreases by one percentage point each 15 days, up to six months. After six months, a 10 per cent annual penalty is assessed. The rating law in Kenya provides the option to provide a reduction of up to 5 per cent of the tax liability for early payment. In Barbados, there is a 10 per cent discount if the tax is paid within 30 days and a 5 per cent reduction if the tax is paid within 60 days (Garzon, 1989). Quezon City (Philippines) provides a 20 per cent discount if the total property tax is paid as a one-time annual payment and a 10 per cent payment if you pay your quarterly payments on time.

Enforcing against noncompliance

Despite good public incentives for compliance, there are always those taxpayers who fail to comply with their legal tax obligations. Thus, in addition to the positive incentives for compliance, all property tax systems must be able to apply a series of negative incentives, such as penalties for late payments, application of interest payments on outstanding liabilities, sanctions such as the withholding of services for non-payment, and ultimately the penalty of property seizure and auction to recover outstanding tax liabilities.

Tax enforcement is needed to deter noncompliance and fraudulent conduct by taxpayers. Large amounts of delinquent accounts can be attributed to poor administration, lack of an effective penalty structure and/or lack of political will. To combat delinquency, the tax administration must produce and maintain a delinquency list, issue demand notices and administer a series of sanctions and penalties, including the ultimate act of property seizure and auction to recover the outstanding taxes and penalties.

Delinquency list and delinquency notification

Effective enforcement begins with the production of a delinquency list. This delinquency list must be produced and maintained in a timely manner to enable the tax administration to effectively enforce the tax. The delinquency list is derived from the accounts maintained during the receiving and accounting steps of the collection process.

Immediately following the tax payment due date, some tax laws require that a demand notice be sent to the delinquent taxpayer (Indonesia). This demand note informs the taxpayer of his delinquency and provides information on the amount due, the payment procedures and the consequences for noncompliance. This notice is to inform the delinquent taxpayer that the tax department is aware of the delinquent account and firmly intends to collect the delinquent tax. Following the initial demand notice, the tax department usually sends a variety of follow-up notices regarding the imposition of specific sanctions or penalties, depending on the requirements of the law.

In other tax systems (North America), the original tax bill serves as the demand notice, allowing the tax department to commence recovery of delinquent accounts immediately, with no subsequent action. Although not required by law, the tax department typically will send reminder notices to encourage voluntary compliance.

Sanctions and penalties

In cases of noncompliance, tax administration can apply either sanctions and/or penalties. These should be applied in a timely manner in accordance with the law to improve the credibility in the integrity of the tax system. The principle is to make non-payment increasingly expensive to the taxpayer. The tax administration system must make it cheaper for the taxpayer to comply than to remain in delinquency.

Sanctions

Sanctions are negative incentives designed to encourage taxpayer compliance. Sanctions are designed to deny a service to the taxpayer (or property) in cases of noncompliance. For example, taxpayers can be required to have a tax clearance certificate which can be effective in implementing sanctions. The only shortcoming is that taxpayers in many countries are often forced to experience inordinate delays and inconvenience due to the inability of the tax administration to perform the necessary checks to issue the required tax clearance certificate within a reasonable time. Taxpayers can also be required to show a tax payment receipt in order to receive a government-provided service such as a passport, birth certificate, pension, automobile licence, business licence, or a government loan (e.g. Kenya and Brazil) and/or for all property-related services (e.g. loans, building permits, development licences, utilities). In countries where property is legally registered, it is also possible to use tax liens (caveats or encumbrances) on the title to enforce the sanction. The effectiveness of the sanctions depends on the ability to cross-reference the services with the tax records. Cross-referencing services with property tax can be quite difficult in the absence of unique taxpayer and property tax identification numbers. In countries without a complete legal registration system, tax departments find it nearly impossible to link property taxpayers (subjects) to specific properties (objects).

Tax clearance certificates and tax liens are very effective ways to apply sanctions. The two approaches should be used concurrently; they are not mutually exclusive. Tax clearance certificates are a passive way for the government to apply sanctions. That is, the government waits until the taxpayer requires a tax clearance certificate for a specific property-related (or perhaps a person-related) service. Tax liens, on the other hand, require that the government take a more proactive role by applying a tax lien to the property title.

Tax clearance certificates and tax liens are not mutually exclusive. In some cases a tax lien can be more effective than a tax clearance certificate. For example, in the case of loans, most countries only require a tax clearance certificate if the loan is for the specific property. But a tax certificate is not required if the property is to be used as collateral for a business loan.

Legal systems must specify the precedence of liens. In most countries, the property tax lien is superior to all other private rights and liens (e.g. housing mortgages, business loans or personal loans), regardless of whether they were acquired before or after the lien for property taxes, and regardless of the claimant. In some countries, federal tax liens are superior to local government tax liens, while in other countries the date of the tax lien will determine the order of precedence. This means that in the case of property foreclosure (i.e. sale), the proceeds from the sale of a property will first pay the government tax debt. All remaining monies will be used to settle other outstanding debt obligations, with the residual amounts (if remaining) returning to the property owner.

Penalties: interest and fines

In addition to sanctions, the tax department must be able to apply a variety of effective penalties. Penalties must be available to deal with both civil and criminal offences. Property tax delinquency is usually considered a civil offence punishable by monetary penalty (e.g. fines and interest). Fraudulent conduct and wilful evasion are considered criminal offences punishable by fines and imprisonment.

Two important principles should be followed in establishing an enforcement system: fairness and efficiency. The fairness principle seeks to minimize the burdens placed on delinquent taxpayers who are experiencing temporary financial distress, yet also takes into consideration the diminished level of services (resulting from delinquencies) to other citizens who pay their property taxes on time. Fairness also dictates that the taxpayer should be protected against unscrupulous tax officials. The efficiency principle gauges the ability of a system to collect a large portion of overdue property estate taxes after they become delinquent, with minimal collection costs and market-behaviour distortions (Herber and Pawlik, 1987).

Penalties for non-payment of property taxes should be structured to make it increasingly expensive for the taxpayer to remain in noncompliance. It is important to remember that the purpose of the penalty structure is not just successful collection of the revenue per se, but perhaps even more importantly the encouragement of voluntary compliance generally.

The structure of the penalty usually involves a combination of unit or percentage fines, interest and ultimately seizure and sale of the property. The fines and interest should be structured carefully. It is important to synchronize them with other taxes to minimize administrative and compliance costs. Often the fines and penalties within a country are mandated by a separate tax enforcement law applied to all taxes (e.g. VAT, income and property) (e.g. Indonesia). In other countries, the individual tax laws (e.g. property, VAT and income tax) have separate provisions (e.g. Kenya). It is critical to ensure that the interest rate for late payment is consistent across all taxes. There is no reason why the interest rate for late payment on the property tax should be less than those used for other central taxes (e.g. VAT and income taxes).

Interest and fines are distinctly separate instruments. Interest on outstanding tax liability is charged mainly to discourage taxpayers from delaying payment to secure an interest-free loan from the government. Therefore, to discourage this form of delay tactic, it is important to automatically charge an effective interest rate which is higher than the commercial nominal interest rate. Interest rates set at exactly the market interest rate do not actually penalize late payments but do allow the government to maintain the real value of the tax liability.

If set sufficiently higher than market rates, the interest rate does include a penalty element (i.e. the difference between the market interest rate and the government interest rate). Unfortunately, the interest rate used by most governments tends to be less than the market interest rate, thus actually providing a subsidized loan to the delinquent taxpayer (e.g. Kenya up until 2000 only charged 1 per cent a month when the market interest rate was closer to 3 per cent per month). In addition, including the penalty element in the interest rate obscures the distinction between interest and fine for both the taxpayer and the tax administration. For these reasons, countries tend to have a penalty structure which contains both an automatic interest charge and an explicit fine (e.g. late payment charge).

Most taxing jurisdictions apply a one-time penalty for late payment, along with an interest charge for each additional month past the deadline. For example, a taxing jurisdiction may apply a 10–15 per cent one-time charge for any delinquent account, along with a 3 per cent penalty per month after the tax due date.

The following examples illustrate the varied experience in structuring penalties and interest payments. In Brazil, each city may vary, but most apply a 20 per cent one time penalty for the first month and then 1 per cent additional each month. The penalty rates are applied after adjustments by a price index for inflationary effects. In Peru, the penalty for paying after the deadline is a 10 per cent surcharge per month, or for a fraction of a month, on the amount of the tax due. In Indonesia, late payments are subject to a penalty of 2 per cent per month up to 24months. In Costa Rica, they apply 2 per cent per month up to a maximum of 60 per cent. In Kenya, the interest rate for late payment is now 3 per cent per month. In Barbados, there is a one-time 5 per cent late fee, plus 1 per cent per month. In all of the above examples, the rate of interest varies, depending on the country's nominal interest rate. The general rule should be to peg the interest rate to the prime interest rate plus 1–2 percentage points.

Penalties: seizure and auction

Ultimately the tax department must have the right to seize and auction delinquent properties. If seizure and auction is not permitted or exercised, all previously imposed interest and fines are rendered ineffective. That is, taxpayers will remain indifferent to the imposition of interest and fines if ultimately the amounts are irrecoverable through non-enforcement.

The law must be explicit regarding the procedures for seizure and auction of properties. As previously stated, the procedures must be fair and efficient. Clear deadlines must be established for the various steps: demand notice, warning letters, periods to respond to each demand, tax lien release period, final warning notice, judgment, release period and sale/auction.

To enforce the interest and fines, the tax department should have the option to place a tax lien on the property where there is a legal land registry system. Tax liens are sometimes called tax encumbrances, caveats or a charge against the title of the property. Tax liens are only effective when the property is legally registered, the titling office is securely administered and the court systems are established to enforce liens. The tax lien can then be recovered through a process of foreclosure (as stipulated in the country's law). If a legal land registry system does not exist, the tax department should have the option to directly seize and auction the property, in line with sufficient legal safeguards, in order to ultimately enforce the tax liability.

In the USA, a tax lien is established upon levying the property tax. In other countries, the government must take explicit action to legally establish a tax lien on the property in default. In these countries, about 30–60 days prior to establishing a property lien, a notice of intent to lien is sent to the delinquent taxpayer. If the delinquent taxes are not paid, a lien is filed with the land registry.

Procedurally the tax department should be required to follow legally mandated notification requirements. These notification requirements could include the publication of the delinquency list in a major paper. Publishing names of delinquent taxpayers is common in Anglophone Africa (e.g. Malawi, Kenya, Uganda, Zambia and Tanzania). In addition to 'shaming' delinquent taxpayers to pay their taxes, the publishing serves as the 'legal notification' to enable the tax department to commence enforcement proceedings to recover the outstanding debt. This would have the effect of encouraging tax compliance in order to avoid a potential 'loss of face'. In countries where auction is not politically or legally possible, the potential loss of face through public exposure may provide sufficient incentive for tax payment.

In the USA, there are two basic types of auction: regular auction and over-the-counter sale (Herber and Pawlik, 1987; Alexander, 2000). The regular auction process allows the government to sell the tax lien (a portion of the property value) just like a second mortgage on the property. Investors are allowed to buy the tax lien, with a guaranteed interest rate. In the event that the interest payments are not received, the investor can foreclose on the property and assume ownership.

In contrast, the over-the-counter sale allows the tax jurisdiction to auction off the whole property (100 per cent). This is a 'do or die' situation; investors like it but the taxpayer may get short-shifted and the taxing jurisdiction may find this option politically unacceptable. In the over-the-counter sale, the taxing jurisdiction usually allows the property to remain delinquent for some time prior to the final auctioning process (e.g. 3–5 years).

To be most successful, regular auctions require a legal cadastre, a legal system which permits tax lien enforcement, a pool of investors willing to invest in real estate delinquent taxes and a legal system to protect the rights of the taxpayers in cases of procedural error. In the absence of a legal cadastre, governments must either resort to the over-the-counter sale or develop an alternative. An over-the-counter sale is politically difficult in any country and largely explains why seizure and auction are often not enforced.

As an alternative, many countries allow the seizure and sale of movable property – similar to the sale of tax liens in that the seizure and auction only covers the amount of the tax liability rather than the entire property. In many cases the delinquent property tax amount may be too little to justify seizing and selling the entire property asset, especially given the implied political costs. Thus, tax legislation often allows the seizure and auction of movable property (if clearly identifiable and able to be linked to the property owner, occupant and/or beneficiary) in order to provide flexibility in enforcement. In cases of low levels of tax delinquencies, it may be politically and administratively easier to seize and auction air conditioners, machinery and equipment, or inventory rather than seizing and auctioning the entire property itself. Other options can include placing an attachment on individual bank accounts, rents, wages and/or payments from the government (e.g. social security benefits or income tax refunds).

What is the international experience with immovable property seizure and auction? In North America property tax systems have established a 'credible threat' for enforcement by systematically pursuing property seizure and auction. Knowing that the government will ultimately seize and auction property to collect outstanding debt usually encourages delinquent tax accounts to be settled before the need to commence the actual seizure and auction process. Collection rates in North America therefore are close to 100 per cent of outstanding tax liabilities.

In non-OECD countries, on the other hand, property seizure and auction is very rare. Land ownership and land rights can be very sensitive social and political issues, making it difficult to garner the political will to undertake the final enforcement step of seizure and auction. Selling of land for debt recovery within countries with customary land tenure systems is virtually impossible, and outside of the industrialized countries, there are few countries which have been able to seize and auction for noncompliance. Two notable exceptions were Chile and Indonesia. In Chile, from 1985–1990, about 50 properties were seized with about 10 properties being auctioned for noncompliance. Accompanied by an effective public relations campaign, the collection efficiency in Chile went from about 65 to over 80 per cent during that time. Prior to 1985, seizure and auction had not occurred for about 20 years (Rosengard, 1998).

Indonesia, which also followed a collection-led property tax reform strategy in the late 1980s, undertook their first property tax seizure in October 1991, which was the first seizure for noncompliance since independence in 1945. Indonesia effectively utilized publicity of this event as part of their public relations campaign to generate increased voluntary compliance (Kelly, 1993).

Quezon City in the Philippines adopted a 'collection-led' approach in 2001, shifted from a system of tax amnesties to using property auctions to deal with noncompliance. Combined with taxpayer service initiatives and early payment incentives, these property auctions increased property tax compliance. The National Tax Research Center (NTRC), the research arm of the Department of Finance, estimates that the auctions may have encouraged up to 52 per cent of delinquent property owners to settle their tax obligations (Ignacio, 2005).

Ultimately the rationale for property seizure and auction is not solely to recover the outstanding taxes on the specific property. Rather it is to send a strong warning signal to other taxpayers to encourage tax compliance. All enforcement activities should be accompanied by a massive public relations campaign, with the more publicity the better.

Summary thoughts

Governments throughout the world are undertaking important policy and administrative reforms to improve property tax revenue yield, equity and efficiency. In order to succeed, these reforms must focus comprehensively on improving tax base coverage, property valuations, collection, enforcement and taxpayer service. Property tax policies can only be realized through a system of effective tax administration.

Ultimately, property tax must be collected if the reforms are going to achieve their revenue, equity and efficiency objectives. Although comprehensive tax maps and accurate valuations provide important intermediate outputs needed for the final output of revenue collection, the top priority for property tax administration must be property tax collection. A comprehensive reform analysis, design and implementation which follow a 'collection-led' implementation strategy is critical for these property tax initiatives to succeed.

Property tax revenue collection is a challenge in many countries. Although the tax collection ratio may be close to 100 per cent in many OECD countries, in most other countries, the revenue collection ratio ranges between 30 and 60 per cent. These low collection levels can be attributed to such factors as lack of political will, inappropriate policies, poor administration and lack of taxpayer education and service, among others. Improving property tax collections will require countries to place priority on mobilizing strong political will, while adopting innovative, targeted policy and administrative interventions.

Policy and administrative interventions to improve tax collection must be designed and implemented within the three key steps of the collection process: assessing tax liability assessment and billing, receiving and accounting for tax payments and enforcing against noncompliance. The key to success is to keep the policy, administrative systems and procedures sufficiently simple and effective in order to minimize compliance and administrative costs, while maximizing revenue, equity and efficiency.

All property tax systems prefer to rely on voluntary taxpayer compliance, minimizing the need to take enforcement action against delinquencies. Voluntary compliance depends on ensuring that taxpayers have a clear understanding of civic responsibility, the link between taxation and public services and the role of property taxation in mobilizing public funds. It is also helpful for taxpayers to have a basic understanding of property tax policy as applied to an individual, and the property tax administration process and procedures. Therefore effective civic and taxpayer education programmes, with proactive taxpayer service are essential for promoting voluntary compliance.

Property tax systems must include incentives to encourage voluntary compliance and to discourage noncompliance. The taxpayer's main interaction with the property tax is through the tax collection process, where they receive a tax bill notification and either voluntarily pay the tax or become subject to subsequent enforcement procedures. Establishing a proper set of incentives, along with strong political will to apply the incentives, will encourage improved property tax payments.

The key to increasing voluntary compliance is to reduce the compliance costs by providing improved taxpayer service in the form of information, as well as easy-to-pay options such as through using cheques, credit cards, automatic bank payments and/or convenient payment points in cash-based societies. In addition, taxpayers must be provided with clear payment due dates along with adequate time within which to pay. Taxpayers should also be provided with options to pay in instalments and perhaps receive discounts for early or timely payments.

Taxpayers also respond well to incentives which discourage noncompliance. These negative incentives can include the threat of and/or application of lump sum penalties and interest penalties for late payments, tax liens, sale of tax certificates, attachments on wages and bank accounts and/or seizure of movable and/or immovable property. In addition to collecting the outstanding tax delinquencies, these negative incentives can be used effectively to encourage greater voluntary compliance and discourage noncompliance. International experience confirms that taxpayers do respond well to these forms of positive and negative incentives.

In addition to reducing the compliance costs faced by taxpayers, the tax department must minimize administration costs by keeping the tax collection system simple, efficient and fair. Using information from the property valuation roll, the tax department must establish the tax liability, produce and deliver the bills, collect and properly account for tax payments, take action against noncompliance while consistently providing taxpayer service. Streamlining the administration system and procedures, while establishing a system of personal and institutional incentives and making effective use of ICT, tax departments can maximize revenue collections while minimizing the administrative costs and simultaneously reducing the compliance costs to the taxpayer.

Since the primary mission of the tax department is to mobilize property tax revenues, effectively designing and implementing tax collection policies and administrative systems and procedures is a core requirement for improved, sustainable property tax administration. The challenge in developing effective property tax reforms is to avoid being distracted by the intermediate outputs of tax maps and property valuations and to stay focused on the ultimate objective of the property tax system, that is, collecting property tax revenues in a fair and efficient manner.

References

Alexander, F.S. (2000) Tax Liens, Tax Sales and Due Process. *Indiana Law Journal*, 75(3): 748–807.

Almy, R. (2000) *Property Tax Policies and Administrative Practices in Canada and the USA: Executive Summary. Assessment Journal*, July/August: 41–57.

Almy, R. (2001) *A Survey of Property Tax Systems in Europe.* Report prepared for the Slovenia Department of Taxes and Customs, Ljubljana, Ministry of Finance.

Bird, R. and Slack, E. (eds.), (2004) *International Handbook of Land and Property Taxation.* Northhampton, MA: Edward Elgar.

Dillinger, W. (1991) *Urban Property Tax Reform: Guidelines and Recommendations.* Washington DC: World Bank.

Garzon, H. (1989) *The Property Tax Systems Applied in Selected Latin American and Caribbean Nations.* Occasional Paper No. 131, Metropolitan Studies Program, Maxwell School of Citizenship and Public Affairs, Syracuse University.

Government of Kenya (1972) The Rating Act (CA 267).

Herber, B. and Pawlik, P. (1987) *Delinquent Real Estate Taxes: A Major New Revenue Source of State and Local Governments.* Unpublished manuscript, University of Arizona, Tucson.

Ignacio, C.H. (2005) Innovating Tax Administration Measures: Quezon City. In: Amatong, J.D. (ed.), *Local Government Fiscal and Financial Management: Best Practices*, Manila, Department of Finance), 70–87.

Kelly, R. (1993) Property Tax Reform in Indonesia: Applying a Collection-Led Strategy. *Bulletin of Indonesian Economic Studies*, 29(1): 1–21.

Kelly, (1995) Property Tax Reform in Southeast Asia: A Comparative Analysis of Indonesia, the Philippines and Thailand. *Journal of Property Tax Assessment & Administration*, 1(1): 60–81.

Kelly, R. (2000) Designing a Property Tax Reform for SubSaharan Africa: An Analytical Framework applied to Kenya. *Public Budgeting & Finance*, 20(4): 36–51.

Kelly, R. (2004) Property Taxation in Indonesia: Emerging Challenges from Decentralization. *Asia Pacific Journal of Public Administration*, 26 (1): 71–90.

Kelly, R., Montes, M., Maseya, E., Nkandkha, K. and Tombere, K. (2001) *Improving Revenue Mobilization in Malawi: Study on Business Licensing and Property Rates.* Final Report, Report submitted to Decentralization Secretariat, Ministry of Local Government, Government of Malawi and UNCDF.

Kelly, R. and Musunu, Z. (2000) Implementing Property Tax Reform in Tanzania. *Journal of Property Tax Assessment & Administration*, 5(1): 5–25.

Kelly, R. and Sugana, R. (2007) *Improving Revenue Mobilization in Cambodia: Strategy for Developing a Modern Land & Building Tax.* Unpublished report submitted to Department of Taxation and UNDP Cambodia.

Linn, J.F. (1980) Property Taxation in Bogota, Colombia: An Analysis of Poor Revenue Performance. *Public Finance Quarterly*, 8(4): 457–476.

McCluskey, W.J., Franzsen, R.C.D., Johnstone, T and Johnstone, D. (2003) *Property Tax Reform: the Experience of Tanzania.* London: Royal Institution of Chartered Surveyors.

USAID, (undated) Success Story: An innovative strategy helps town increase tax revenue, improve parks. Neighbors Help Collect Taxes. http://www.usaid.gov/stories/paraguay/ss_pg_neighbor.html

Rosengard, J. (1998) *Property Tax Reform in Developing Countries*. Norwell, MA: Kluwer Academic Publishers.

World Bank (1986) *Urban Taxation in West Africa. EDI Training Materials Course Note 785/013*. World Bank Report No. 4754-WAP, Washington DC: World Bank.

Youngman, J.M. and Malme, J. (1994) *An International Survey of Taxes on Land and Buildings*. Amsterdam: Kluwer.

Youngman, J. (1996) Tax on Land and Buildings. In: Thuronyi, V. (ed.), *Tax Law Design and Drafting*, Volume 1, Washington DC: International Monetary Fund.

Youngman, J.M. and Malme, J. (eds.), (2002) *The Development of Property Taxation in Economies of Transition: Case Studies from Central and Eastern Europe*. Washington DC: World Bank.

7

The Tax Everyone Loves to Hate: Principles of Property Tax Reform

Jay K. Rosengard

Introduction

Almost every country has some type of annual tax on land and buildings, for reasons that have been well documented elsewhere – for example, see Rosengard (1998); Bahl and Martinez-Vazquez (2007); and Fisher (2009) – but can be summarized as follows:

- It is often the main source of local government discretionary revenue, and thus an essential component of fiscal decentralization that supports local autonomy and complements intergovernmental fiscal transfers. For a series of papers analysing property tax trends and their implications for local autonomy in the context of America's fiscal federalism, see Bell *et al.* (2010).
- It is economically efficient because it is hard to avoid and easily enforceable.
- It is perceived as socially equitable because it is roughly progressive, loosely correlated with local government benefits, a relatively good proxy for a tax on multi-year income and a way to enable the public sector to derive a share of private sector windfall gains from appreciation of real estate values largely due to public investments in previously unserviced land.

A Primer on Property Tax: Administration and Policy, First Edition.
Edited by William J. McCluskey, Gary C. Cornia and Lawrence C. Walters.
© 2013 Blackwell Publishing Ltd. Published 2013 by Blackwell Publishing Ltd.

Although ubiquitous, the property tax is also universally despised, again for reasons that have been well documented elsewhere but can be summarized as follows:

- While the high number of statutory taxpayers creates a large tax base – a good thing in theory – it can be a political and administrative nightmare in practice.
- While the tax's high visibility is good for government transparency and accountability, heightened taxpayer awareness also tends to intensify taxpayer resistance.
- While computer-assisted mass appraisal and other applications of appropriate technology increase administrative efficiency and effectiveness, property valuation nevertheless still has a contentious subjective component.
- While the tax is seen as fair in general, there is no direct relationship between tax liability and ability to pay the tax, which leaves some taxpayers 'asset rich but cash poor'.
- While the tax supports local government autonomy, it can also worsen regional disparities in wealth, as the 'rich get richer and the poor get poorer'.
- While citizens might accept the tax in principle, there is still widespread resentment in some countries to enforcement proceedings, sometimes seen as a threat to the sanctity of the home.

The dilemma is real and profound: most countries have a property tax, but few of their citizens like the tax. The property tax is the tax everyone loves to hate. Countries can seldom live with the tax as initially designed, yet neither can they live without the tax at all.

Thus, this chapter focuses on the reform of an existing system of property taxation rather than on the creation of an optimal property tax. Leaders seldom have the opportunity to design a property tax with a blank slate. There is usually already some sort of system of taxing land and buildings, with a variety of established special interests and a political, social and historical context. The challenge is to make an existing property tax less taxing.

Attempts to enhance the property tax's strengths and mitigate its weaknesses are numerous and widespread. This is true for both high-income and emerging economies. Unfortunately, most of these efforts have been unsuccessful – see Bahl *et al.* (2010) for a comprehensive review of these failures.

The remainder of this chapter provides guidance on property tax reform by addressing the most frequent mistakes and highlighting common elements of success: the primary rationale for reform; fundamental principles of reform; strategic choices for reform; policy pitfalls of reform; and lessons learned from reform initiatives.

Primary rationale for reform

The four primary rationales for initiating property tax reform are to improve fiscal performance, social equity, economic efficiency or administrative cost-effectiveness – see Muellbauer (2005) for both a general review and a specific application of these objectives to the reform of property taxation in the UK after the 2004 Barker Review.

The main strategic shortcoming of reform efforts is either failure to articulate clearly the rationale for reform, or to have unprioritized, contradictory objectives. Low revenue yield is the most common reason for property tax reform in emerging economies, so revenue enhancement is most often the principal objective of reform – see Bahl and Martinez-Vazquez (2008) for international comparisons of property tax revenue and Rosengard *et al.*, (2007) for an example of the potential for increased property tax revenue in Vietnam (Ho Chi Minh City) and China (Shanghai).

Property tax reform can also be revenue neutral if social, economic or administrative considerations are more important, which is usually the case in high-income countries. However, reform cannot be designed to reduce tax revenue in any country and survive. This is not the same as limiting the rate of tax revenue increase, as was the case in the California Proposition 13 'tax revolt' of 1978 and the replications it inspired throughout the USA.

Just as with other types of tax reform, revenue shortfalls doom property tax reform, given that there is no fiscal compensation for the financial and political capital expended in reform efforts – revenue losses and political costs outweigh social, economic or administrative benefits.

Horizontal and vertical inequities are another common reason for property tax reform, so the reform might be redistributive in nature as opposed to being distributionally neutral. The objective is to treat 'equals equally' (horizontal equity) and 'unequals unequally' (vertical equity), so that those with the same property values have the same tax liabilities and those with higher value property pay more than those with lower value property. Although this might appear to be a simple and straightforward proposition, 'equity' means many things to many people. As US Senator Russell Long remarked, a tax loophole is 'something that benefits the other guy. If it benefits you, it is tax reform.'

Another inequity that might be addressed is the perceived unfairness of property tax liabilities that rise at a much higher rate than income growth. This is often the case, particularly in high-income countries, during property bubbles such as the real estate booms accompanied by unmitigated property tax increases during the 1970s in California and Massachusetts that culminated in their respective Proposition 13 and Proposition 2½ tax revolts. Proposition 13 (People's initiative to limit property taxation) was a California ballot initiative that, after its passage in 1978, became Article 13A of the Constitution of the State of California. It capped the property tax at 1 per cent of assessed market value, rolled back property values to their 1975 assessment, restricted annual increases in assessed value to an inflation factor not to exceed 2 per cent per year and prohibited reassessment of a new base year value except upon completion of new construction or change in ownership. For analysis of the fiscal impact of Proposition 13, see Chapman (1998); Hoene (2004); Wasi and White (2005); and Citrin (2009). See Martin (2009) for a description of how the Proposition 13 'fever' spread, and Haveman and Sexton (2008) for an analysis of the impact of property tax assessment limits over the past three decades.

Proposition 2½ (Mass. Gen. Laws Ch. 59 §21C) was a Commonwealth of Massachusetts initiative petition inspired by California's Proposition 13 that, after its passage in 1980 (effective in 1982), capped the total annual property tax revenue that a municipality could raise at 2.5 per cent of the assessed value of all taxable property in the municipality, and limited the annual increase of property tax revenue to 2.5 per cent (excluding the amount attributable to taxes from new real estate).

However, given the weaknesses of the property tax summarized earlier, there is often a gap between perceived and actual fairness. This gap is widened by difficulty in determining economic as opposed to statutory incidence – there is no consensus on who bears the ultimate economic burden of the property tax in either high-income or low-income countries; see Sennoga *et al.*, (2008) for a review of the ongoing debate over property tax incidence and economic impact.

Inefficiencies in resource allocation is a third reason for property tax reform, so the reform might be interventionist in nature to address tax-induced distortions in behaviour rather than economically neutral. The objective is to minimize the impact of property taxation on the production and consumption decisions of households and firms, for example by ensuring that investment decisions are not determined by destructive property tax competition between local jurisdictions and that property tax policies leave consumers indifferent when deciding whether to buy or rent a home.

Revenue can be increased by changing the tax design (i.e. enlarging the tax base and/or increasing the tax rate) or improving tax administration (i.e. upgrading tax rolls, revaluing property and/or strengthening billing, collection and enforcement procedures). Thus, administrative weaknesses are the last major reason for property tax reform, where there is a mismatch between tax complexity, taxpayer sophistication, economic structure and administrative capacity. The objective is to reduce administrative costs while improving administrative speed, accuracy, service and integrity.

Although much tax policy is actually made in implementation, administrative reform is often neglected, leading to the frequent unintended negative consequences of conceptually sound but poorly executed property tax laws and regulations – something might look good on paper, but simply cannot be credibly implemented as designed. Tools to improve administrative cost-effectiveness include simplification, rationalization, standardization and automation of property taxation.

Fundamental principles of reform

There are four fundamental principles of property tax reform that should be heeded regardless of the primary rationale for reform:

- simple in practice trumps optimal in theory
- revenue generation trumps social engineering
- economics of taxation trumps political mathematics
- behavioural change trumps paper tigers.

For examples of both the application and neglect of these principles, see the four case studies (Jamaica, Philippines, Chile and Indonesia) in Rosengard (1998).

Simple vs. optimal

While the theory of optimal taxation is attractive, it is nonetheless a theory, and theories are usually not achievable in practice without considerable adaptation to real-world constraints. For example, the distribution of property in emerging economies is highly skewed, with a relatively small number of properties comprising the bulk of property value. It therefore makes little sense to spend a significant amount of resources on property discovery, valuation and assessment for most properties, especially if the effective tax rate is very low. Instead, a combination of self-reporting and simplified computer-assisted mass appraisal for most properties, coupled with individual valuations for expensive real estate, should be able to capture 90 per cent of value most of the time, and what is missed is not worth calculating or collecting – this is much more cost-effective than trying to capture all value all of the time. In short, it is better to be approximately right than precisely wrong.

Revenue vs. non-revenue

The primary purpose of the property tax is to generate revenue. It is a very poor tool for non-revenue objectives such as guiding allocative decisions like attracting investment, achieving social goals like combating property speculation or recovering capital costs like those incurred in large-scale infrastructure investment. It is also an ineffective means of achieving income redistribution through highly progressive tax schedules. While these are all important policy objectives, there are policy tools better suited to achieving these objectives. Instead, the property tax should focus on maximizing revenue at minimum financial, economic, political and social cost. In the words of Louis XIV's Controller-General of Finance, Jean-Baptiste Colbert, 'The art of taxation consists in so plucking the goose as to obtain the largest amount of feathers with the least possible amount of hissing.'

Economics vs. politics

In the short term, economic and political cost–benefit calculations about property taxation might diverge, but in the long term they converge. It might be politically tempting to grant many special favours to powerful constituencies through tax exemptions, exclusions, deductions and credits, but these tax expenditures eventually leave local government with two unattractive alternatives: either receive less property tax revenue and make corresponding budget cuts, or increase tax rates on the remaining smaller tax base to generate an equivalent amount of money. The first alternative is seldom a popular political move, while the latter usually leads to increased tax evasion, economic distortions (deadweight loss) and corruption. A maxim of the economics of taxation is a large tax base and a low tax rate, which is also the only tenable long-term political strategy: not only is it economically efficient, but it also avoids many of the political, social and administrative problems of a small tax base and high tax rate.

Behaviour vs. fiat

Property tax reform is fundamentally about instilling behavioural change in both taxpayers and tax administrators. It is much more cost-effective if people comply voluntarily with tax laws and regulations rather than comply only when compelled to by enforcement measures. The key is to construct positive and negative incentives for property tax stakeholders that create a system of convergent self-interests, so that what is good for the individual is also good for society – the rational action from the perspective of a taxpayer or tax administrator is also the socially desired action. Many countries pass commendable property tax reform legislation, but are then surprised when very little changes in practice. Policymakers believed that these laws were self-enforcing by fiat, despite personal or institutional incentives that dictated otherwise.

Strategic choices in reform

There are four key strategic considerations entailed in designing and implementing property tax reform:

- defining the tax base
- determining the tax rate
- evaluating administrative options
- mitigating transitional pains.

The first two considerations are principal design parameters, while the latter two considerations are fundamental implementation parameters. See Bahl and Martinez-Vazquez (2007) for a stylized simulation that illustrates the importance of these strategic considerations in formulating reforms to increase property tax revenue, and Bell and Bowman (2002) for the application of these strategic considerations to property taxation in South Africa.

Design parameters: defining the tax base and determining the tax rate

As depicted in Figure 7.1, the two variables that set the ceiling for potential property tax revenue are the tax base (what you tax) and the tax rate (how much you tax).

The property tax base is determined by taxable wealth (value) and the number of properties (quantity), that is, how much of the value of how many properties may be taxed.

This, in turn, is a function of assessed value as a share of unadjusted current market value (valuation accuracy, as well as assessment ratio and other valuation adjustments) for each taxable property, together with the degree of inclusiveness in defining taxable properties.

Thus, reform of property tax design essentially is a question of broadening the tax base by first expanding the types of property classified as taxable (reducing exemptions and exclusions) and second striving to tax as much value of these properties as possible (mandating frequent revaluations or indexing between valuations, increasing the assessment ratio and reducing deductions, credits and deferrals).

Other than simplification of tax rate structures or reduction of tax rates, which are complementary and mutually reinforcing, there is much less latitude for reform of property tax rates. Worldwide empirical observations indicate a proclivity for relatively low (around 1 per cent of market capital value for residential property), flat (proportional), and uniform (usually not more than two classes, residential and non-residential) property tax rates, due to economic,

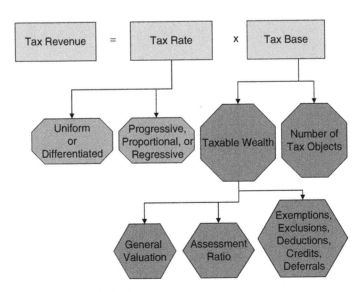

Figure 7.1   Property tax principal design parameters

political, and administrative considerations: economists note the social welfare losses associated with high tax rates (deadweight loss increases as the square of the tax rate); politicians fear the repercussions of taxing real estate at too high a rate (see the first section above); and tax administrators wish to maximize voluntary compliance by minimizing the perceived gains of evading high tax rates (not worth cheating).

The main exception to this maxim of a broad-base, low-rate property tax is land value taxation, which either imposes a higher tax rate on land than on improvements or does not tax improvements at all but instead taxes only the land value at an even higher rate to make up the revenue loss. While there is no consensus on the economic efficiency and social equity impact of this approach, more than 30 countries have adopted land value taxation for administrative and political expediency – see Dye and England (2010) for a concise review of the theory and practice of land valuation taxation. A more extreme version of land value taxation, a single tax on land replacing all taxes on labour, business and trade, is championed by George (1879) in his seminal work *Progress and Poverty*.

Implementation parameters: evaluating administrative options and mitigating transitional pains

Although the statutory property tax base and rate set the ceiling for *potential* property tax revenue, *actual* property tax revenue is also a function of tax administrative efficiency and effectiveness in executing the tax design at every stage of implementation, including:

- property identification, valuation and assessment
- tax billing and collection
- enforcement for non-complying taxpayers.

Much tax policy is actually made in tax administration, that is, in the translation of tax laws and regulations into field realities. Thus, there is considerable scope for reforming the property tax by upgrading tax administration. Examples include:

- enhancing the completeness and accuracy of the property tax roll through better property identification, valuation and assessment practices
- improving the collection ratio (the ratio of tax collected to tax assessed) by strengthening tax billing, collection and enforcement practices.

While most property tax reforms in emerging economies begin with a focus on improving the quality of the property tax roll, commonly known as the 'data-led' approach, these usually end in failure because they are front-loaded with many financial and political costs while benefits are perpetually delayed future

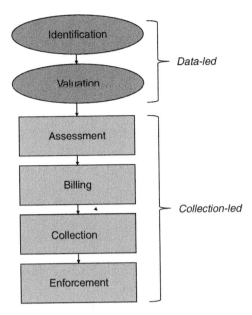

Figure 7.2 Data-led and collection-led approaches to property tax reform

promises. A notable exception to this approach was tried in Indonesia in the mid 1980s, where the emphasis was first on generating revenue and building credibility, dubbed the 'collection-led' approach, while gradually improving data quality. These two approaches are contrasted in Figure 7.2.

A key component of improved collections was facilitation of voluntary compliance, coupled with projection of a credible enforcement threat. This was achieved through a combination of improved taxpayer service, including use of the banking system for tax payments (dubbed the 'payment point system'), together with escalating sanctions that culminated in the seizure and liquidation of land and buildings to settle unpaid tax liabilities. This final enforcement measure was only politically and administratively feasible because of the government's policy of deliberately pursuing the tax object (real estate) rather than the tax subject (taxpayer), so it could avoid the sensitive and often problematic issue of identifying ownership of taxed land and buildings. More than two decades later, the reformed property tax system in Indonesia is still performing quite well, although it now faces many new challenges in the context of Indonesia's comprehensive decentralization programme. See Kelly (1993) for a more detailed description of Indonesia's collection-led strategy and Rosengard (1998) for a case-study-based comparison of the data-led and collection-led approaches. Kelly (2004) provides an update of Indonesia's property tax reform in the context of the country's decentralization programme.

There are also special challenges in property tax reform where there is no well-developed real estate market, either because: (1) the country is transitioning from a planned economy to a market-based economy such as in central and eastern Europe, China and Vietnam, a phenomenon detailed in Malme and Youngman (2001); or (2) land is communally owned, as in rural South Africa, a predicament examined in Bell and Bowman (2006).

The implementation challenges are especially acute in very poor but rapidly urbanizing nations (i.e. much of sub-Saharan Africa), where the need for property tax reform is also critical due to the importance of fiscal decentralization initiatives. See Franzsen and Youngman (2009) for an overview of the state of property taxation in Africa, and McCluskey *et al.*, (2003) for a detailed examination of the challenges of property tax reform in Africa through the lens of a case study of Tanzania's experience with property taxation.

Finally, property tax reform will upset the status quo to which key stakeholders have already adapted. Thus, a special implementation consideration is mitigation of short-term disruptive effects created as a by-product of the transition to a new long-term equilibrium.

For example, if reformers pursue a collection-led approach to property tax reform, short-term inequities will probably arise as those already on the existing tax roll are compelled to meet their tax obligations, while those with omitted or grossly under-valued property will not yet be paying their fair share of tax liabilities. This makes a compelling argument for keeping the effective tax rate low until the tax roll is relatively comprehensive and accurate. However, there is indeed nothing more permanent than something temporary, and transitional adjustments often become permanent. This has been the case in Indonesia. During the property tax reform of the 1980s, the finance minister refused to use his authority to increase the assessment ratio above 20 per cent (under the property tax law, the finance minister could set the assessment ratio from 20 to 100 per cent) until the tax roll was deemed to be relatively complete and accurate, even though this would have been the easiest way to increase revenue quickly. However, although the property tax roll was vastly improved roughly two decades ago, shortly after the collection system was up and running, the assessment ratio is still at 20 per cent today for most property (it has been increased to 40 per cent for very high value property). At a 0.5 per cent nominal tax rate, this leaves Indonesia with an effective property tax rate of 0.1 per cent for most land and buildings, one of the lowest in the world.

Another type of short-term adjustment pain is the 'sticker shock' of greatly increased property tax liabilities after property revaluation. This can be mitigated by reducing the tax rate during a transitional period so tax liabilities go up incrementally, especially during a real estate bubble. During periods of market stability, this can be mitigated by more frequent revaluations and by indexing property values between revaluations. Keeping increased property tax liabilities more in line with income growth by reducing tax rates might have tempered some of the anger that generated the Property 13 tax revolt (and its spinoffs) described earlier; a good example of indexing between valuations is described in the Chile case study in Rosengard (1998).

Policy pitfalls of reform

There are three key dimensions of policy pitfalls in designing and implementing property tax reform: political, technical and tactical. Many of the policy pitfalls discussed in this section are not restricted to property tax reform and can be applied to tax reform in general. See Gillis (1989) and Boskin (1990) for more detailed discussions and case study illustrations of these pitfalls.

The primary political challenge is that any property tax reform inevitably creates winners and losers, both within the tax administration and among the general public. Moreover, internal and external special interests tend to be organized and proactive, while the majority of tax employees and taxpayers are diffuse and reactive.

Internally, this problem is most acute when corrupt employees who feel threatened by reforms can easily sabotage the reform through delayed, slow or incorrect administration: the reform suffers death by administration. Externally, this difficulty is most pronounced when the reform is targeted at relatively wealthy property owners: the reform is murdered by the rich and powerful.

If the problem is primarily political, so is the solution. Without the visible and sustained support of political leaders, the reform is probably doomed before it is launched: the reform is stillborn.

However, even with strong political support, a reform can fail due to technical shortcomings. The most prevalent of these are: firstly, poor or incomplete information on the present situation, often leading to inaccurate tax forecasting of the likely impact of the reform and thus unintended consequences; and second, insufficient financial and human resources, contributing to inadequate administrative capacity for effective implementation of the reform. Considerable attention to the behavioural and administrative dimensions of property tax reform is essential for success – design change in an implementation vacuum is a potent recipe for failure.

These technical shortcomings are exacerbated for emerging and transitional economies by inappropriate recommendations from donors and consultants. These advisors often try to replicate tax systems with which they are most familiar without understanding the specific context of the country they are attempting to assist. Moreover, procurement of source-country advisors and equipment is commonly linked to financial assistance, regardless of their appropriateness. Host countries should assess the full costs and benefits of external assistance before agreeing to this assistance.

The third policy pitfall is tactical, revolving around the timing and sequencing of property tax reform.

Tax reform in general has been most successful when it has been least needed. This applies to revenue-enhancing property tax reform as well because it allows tax administrators to develop their systems and information bases with very low transitional tax rates. It also facilitates a learning period for taxpayers to familiarize themselves with the new system, thus enhancing longer-term understanding of, and voluntary compliance with, the property tax.

There are two approaches to the sequencing of property tax reform: 'big bang' reform of everything, everywhere at the same time; and 'asymmetrical' reform characterized by phased implementation.

The former usually takes place in politically driven reform, where proponents are afraid of losing support with a more incremental approach but have not thought through potential implementation problems, particularly the behavioural response of affected taxpayers. Consequently, hurried reforms are often failed reforms. The US property tax revolts described earlier and Indonesia's recent decision to assign the property tax to local government are examples of this approach. This was done through a new law on local taxes and charges, passed in 2009 (*Undang-Undang Republik Indonesia Nomor 28 Tahun 2009 Tentang Pajak Daerah Dan Retribusi Daerah*).

The latter commonly takes place in technically driven reform, where proponents need to develop a political constituency by demonstrating success; they can also use this time to test and revise their approach, concentrate scarce resources on the highest return targets and conduct a mass communications campaign to build public awareness and understanding. Indonesia's property tax reform of the 1980s is a good example of this approach.

Conclusion

While there is no fixed formula for successful property tax reform that applies to all jurisdictions in all countries at all times, there are nevertheless common challenges and general lessons from past attempts to improve property taxation around the world. This chapter summarizes the fundamental principles, strategic choices and policy pitfalls of initiatives that have been undertaken in a wide variety of environments to improve fiscal, social, economic or administrative performance of property taxes.

But no matter how well a property tax is designed and implemented, it will probably remain the tax everyone loves to hate. Thus, the challenge is to strike a balance between two conflicting sentiments.

The first sentiment is well-articulated by former US President James Madison: 'The power of taxing people and their property is essential to the very existence of government.' The second sentiment is reflected in this rueful observation by the political philosopher and statesman Edmund Burke: 'To tax and to please, no more than to love and to be wise, is not given to men.' A third quote, this one from the 18th century Prussian king, Frederick the Great, succinctly sums up the dilemma and offers an antidote: 'No government can exist without taxation. The money must necessarily be levied on the people; and the grand art consists of levying so as not to oppress.'

References

Bahl, R. and Martinez-Vazquez, J. (2007) *The Property Tax in Developing Countries: Current Practice and Prospects.* Working Paper WP07RB1, Cambridge, MA: Lincoln Institute of Land Policy.

Bahl, R. and Martinez-Vazquez, J. (2008). The Determinants of Revenue Performance. In: Bahl, R., Martinez-Vazquez, J. and Youngman, J.M. (eds.), *Making the Property Tax Work: Experiences in Developing and Transitional Countries.* Cambridge, MA: Lincoln Institute of Land Policy, 35–57.

Bahl, R., Martinez-Vazquez, J. and Youngman, J.M. (eds.), (2010) *Challenging the Conventional Wisdom of the Property Tax.* Cambridge, MA: Lincoln Institute of Land Policy.

Bell, M.E. and Bowman, J.H. (2006) *Implementing a Property Tax Where There Is No Real Estate Market: The Case of Commonly Owned Land in Rural South Africa.* Cambridge, MA: Lincoln Institute of Land Policy.

Bell, M.E. and Bowman, J.H. (eds.), (2002) *Property Taxes in South Africa: Challenges in the Post-Apartheid Era.* Cambridge, MA: Lincoln Institute of Land Policy.

Bell, M.E., Brunori, D. and Youngman, J. (eds.), (2010) *The Property Tax and Local Autonomy.* Cambridge, MA: Lincoln Institute of Land Policy.

Boskin, M.J. and McLure, C.E. Jr. (eds.), (1990) *World Tax Reform: Case Studies of Developed and Developing Countries.* San Francisco: ICS Press.

Chapman, J.I. (1998) *Proposition 13: Some Unintended Consequences.* Occasional Paper, San Francisco, CA: Public Policy Institute of California.

Citrin, J. (2009) Proposition 13 and the Transformation of California Government. *The California Journal of Politics & Policy* 1(1): 1–9.

Dye, R.F. and England, R.W. (2010) *Assessing the Theory and Practice of Land Value Taxation.* Policy Focus Report, Cambridge, MA: Lincoln Institute of Land Policy.

Fisher, R.C. (2009) What Policymakers Should Know About Property Taxes. *Land Lines,* January, 8–14.

Franzsen, R.C.D. and Youngman, J.M. (2009) Mapping Property Taxes in Africa. *Land Lines,* July, 8–13.

George, H. (1879: 2001) *Progress and Poverty: An Inquiry into the Cause of Industrial Depressions and of Increase of Want with Increase of Wealth.* New York City: Robert Schalkenbach Foundation.

Gillis, M. (ed.), (1989) *Tax Reform in Developing Countries.* Durham, NC: Duke University Press.

Haveman, M. and Sexton, T.A. (2008) *Property Tax Assessment Limits: Lessons from Thirty Years of Experience.* Policy Focus Report, Cambridge, MA: Lincoln Institute of Land Policy.

Hoene, C. (2004) Fiscal Structure and the Post-Proposition 13 Fiscal Regime in California's Cities. *Public Budgeting & Finance* 24(4): 51–72.

Kelly, R. (1993) Property Tax Reform in Indonesia: Applying a Collection-Led Implementation Strategy. *Bulletin of Indonesian Economic Studies* 29(1): 85–104.

Kelly, R. (2004) Property Tax Reform in Indonesia: Emerging Challenges from Decentralization. *The Asia Pacific Journal of Public Administration* 26(1): 71–90.

Malme, J.H. and Youngman, J.M. (eds.), (2001) *The Development of Property Taxation in Economies in Transition: Case Studies from Central and Eastern Europe.* WBI Learning Resources Series. Washington DC: World Bank.

Martin, I.W. (2009) Proposition 13 Fever: How California's Tax Limitation Spread. *The California Journal of Politics & Policy* 1(1): 1–17.

McCluskey, W.J., Franzsen, R.C.D., Johnstone, T. and Johnstone, D. (2003) *Property Tax Reform: The Experience of Tanzania*. London: RICS Foundation.

Muellbauer, J. (2005) Property Taxation and the Economy After the Barker Review. *The Economic Journal*, C99–C117.

Rosengard, J.K. (1998) *Property Tax Reform in Developing Countries*. Norwell, MA: Kluwer Academic Publishers.

Rosengard, J.K., Van, B., Du, T.H., Tin, V.P., Xu, F. and Pasha, M. (2007) *Paying for Urban Infrastructure and Services: A Comparative Study of Municipal Finance in Ho Chi Minh City, Shanghai and Jakarta*. Hanoi: United Nations Development Programme.

Sennoga, E.B., Sjoquist, D.L. and Wallace, S. (2008) Incidence and Economic Impacts of Property Taxes in Developing and Transitional Countries. In: Bahl, R., Martinez-Vazquez, J. and Youngman, J.M. (eds.), *Making the Property Tax Work: Experiences in Developing and Transitional Countries*. Cambridge, MA: Lincoln Institute of Land Policy, 63–102.

Wasi, N. and White, M.J. (2005) *Property Tax Limitations and Mobility: The Lock-In Effect of California's Proposition 13*. Working Paper 11108, Cambridge, MA: National Bureau of Economic Research.

8

Legal Issues in Property Tax Administration

Frances Plimmer

Introduction

'Tax' can be defined as:

> A compulsory, but authorized, contribution, usually of a pecuniary kind, made by the general body of subjects or citizens to a sovereign, government or municipal authority. A tax must be authorized for a public purpose and be enforceable at law, and the obligation to pay it must be imposed compulsorily on a group of persons or organizations. However, it need bear little relation to the benefit received by any payer of the tax. (Abbott, 2008).

In summary, therefore, a tax is:

- a compulsory levy
- imposed by an organ of government
- raising funds for public expenditure
- with no quid pro quo expectation.

Taxation is one of several ways that a government can raise revenue for public purposes, user fees being an increasingly popular additional method. However, taxes and user fees should be distinguished. Taxation applies broadly to a great

A Primer on Property Tax: Administration and Policy, First Edition.
Edited by William J. McCluskey, Gary C. Cornia and Lawrence C. Walters.
© 2013 Blackwell Publishing Ltd. Published 2013 by Blackwell Publishing Ltd.

number of people, circumstances or events and need not provide any benefit to an individual taxpayer; user fees can be distinguished from taxes because they do provide benefits, although in their form they may well appear to be a kind of taxation.

This potential for confusion has resulted in the expectation of 'benefit' from a tax (the so called 'benefit principle'), with the corollary that without receipt of any benefit, there should be no liability to pay the tax. This contradicts the very principles of a tax, which, as stated above, is 'a compulsory levy ... with no "quid pro quo" expectation'.

It could, of course, be argued that all revenue from taxation is spent on public purposes, so all citizens (whether or not taxpayers) benefit from the services which are provided by government and government agencies. Thus, education, defence, health, justice, for example, are all services paid for out of taxation and from which we all benefit. However, there may be no immediately apparent advantage to an individual taxpayer who has no children to benefit from the education, who lives in a country which is not threatened by hostile forces, who enjoys good health and a crime-free existence.

Taxation can also be used as an instrument to redistribute wealth, by ensuring that the 'rich' (however these individuals are defined) subsidize the 'poor'. Within the context of a property tax, the 'rich' are normally associated with higher value properties, and the 'poor' with lower values. This principle justifies taxing the 'rich' at higher levels or merely ensuring that they pay more tax, when compared with the 'poor'. This principle also underpins the 'ability to pay' argument, often used against property-based taxes.

This chapter is subdivided into several sections. Section 2 examines a number of broad issues around tax policy; section 3 focuses on property taxation and aspects around property ownership; section 4 looks at key issues around fairness and equity while section 5 draws a number of conclusions.

Tax policy

As well as raising revenue, tax policy can also be used to achieve behavioural change and, it is well recognized that the full implications of any changes must be carefully considered in advance: 'taxation affects the decision-making process of business, households and individuals, reaching into all aspects of life and the economy.' (Treasury Committee, 2011)

Indeed, even when behavioural changes are not an objective of changes in the taxation system, they can be an unanticipated outcome, thus causing additional problems for the taxpayers involved, the taxing authorities and the politicians. The implications of this are discussed further below.

As Almy *et al.*, (2008) say:

> while constitutions lay out the framework for taxation, authorize it, and perhaps
> establish some fundamental principles...constitutional guidance tends to be broad

and general. Legislatures provide statutes to create specific provisions for systems of taxation. Statutes can be more detailed or less detailed depending on the degree of discretion to be granted to the administrative agencies that implement statutory provisions.

Where there is only a framework imposed by statutes, additional regulation may be necessary to interpret or provide additional guidance. The final sources of interpretation are the courts. Thus, the legislation governing any particular tax may comprise statutes (central government or state legislation), regulations (made by one or more regulating authority) and case law (judicial interpretation of either statutes, regulations or both). Such a system (although widely recognized) places the taxing powers or the interpretation of a parliament's intention and in the hands of non-elected officials. The extent to which it is desirable to have legislation made at a subdemocratic level is debatable.

For the purposes of this chapter, the term 'legislation' is interpreted to include any and all of the above law-making powers, as appropriate for an individual country, unless the context specifies differently. Also, all of these are considered as law-making bodies (central or national government; minister, government departments or agencies, lower tiers of government and the judiciary), because their powers, responsibilities or the actions imposed on them to amend, implement or interpret the law on which a nation's taxation is based.

Principles of statutory tax policy

Tax legislation is developed over time, and reflects the historical (and therefore the economic and societal) development of a jurisdiction. As Wales is quoted as saying (Treasury Committee, 2011) in relation to the UK: 'The UK tax system, as it stands today, reflects the economic, social and legal history of our country. If legislators were to start afresh, it would be constructed somewhat differently. Society changes and the economy changes.'

This means that any changes to an existing taxation system are likely to be piecemeal alterations which result in high levels of complexity and confusion and in difficulties of interpretation, inconsistencies, in some cases, major economic and social problems. There tends, of course, to be something of a time lag here, in that problems precede solutions and, where problems are resolved or are no longer of consequence, the legislative solutions may remain. Current legislation may not always be relevant to existing issues.

It is, of course, possible to identify some basic principles which should be achieved by legislation to underpin any tax system, including the following:

Fairness

While it may not be possible to define 'fairness', given its complex and inherently subjective nature, a system which is widely judged to be 'unfair' is likely to lead to social resentment which could result in increased incidences of avoidance, evasion and ultimately in a loss of legitimacy. Distributional objectives, rates of tax (flat or progressive), welfare provisions and fundamental principles are all subject to perceptions of 'fairness'. There is also a political dimension:

> A tax system which is felt to be fundamentally unfair will quickly lose political support. However, judgments about the fairness of policy details are politically contested and a major way in which parties distinguish themselves from one another. This can obscure the fact that there is a significant amount of consensus on fairness. The differences are often a matter of degree and emphasis. (Treasury Committee, 2011)

Perceptions of fairness can be improved by the extent to which taxpayers are involved in the taxation process, either through the ballot box or through more direct consultation. Thus, according to Sheffrin, (2010), 'procedures or processes that are perceived to be fair are those in which individuals affected by the decisions have a voice in the process.' This can also be achieved through 'Local control of property tax rates, with decisions made by local governing boards...'

Fairness can also be achieved (at least in part) by high degrees of certainty, stability and practicability. These include:

- reducing tax avoidance
- confidence that taxation legislation will be interpreted and applied consistently
- a predictable year-on-year tax burden
- clarity of information so that less time and money is spent by taxpayers in finding out how the legislation affects them, leading to...
- a reduction in the number of disputes and appeals, leading to a more efficient system in terms of cost and time on both sides.

When levels of taxation are high, avoidance becomes of greater significance to taxpayers, and when taxation policy is complex, tax avoidance becomes increasingly sophisticated and takes up more resources (expertise, time and money), which could be better spent improving economic opportunities and growth.

Barriers to certainty include complexity, ambiguity and inconsistency in the tax system, out-of-date and archaic laws and a lack of clarity in the language used in the legislation. The statutory authority should not produce a taxing instrument which then has to be interpreted, clarified and/or expanded upon by ministerial or judicial statements and decisions. Legal certainty should be enshrined in the original legislation and subsequent clarification kept to a minimum. Existing legislation should be reviewed periodically to ensure that it achieves these goals.

Similarly, a higher degree of stability and predictability year on year, for both taxpayers and taxing authorities should be an important goal of tax policy. Taxpayer certainty is achieved when tax policy is clearly targeted. Both taxpayers and taxing authorities need a degree of certainty as to tax paid/revenue in the future, for budgeting purposes. Sudden and unexpected changes in tax policy and in levels of taxes paid damage business – both public and private. Instead, taxing authorities and taxpayers should be able to plan and invest with confidence.

Tax neutrality

A tax neutral system is one in which taxation does not distort choices or behaviour. A non-neutral system results in incentives for taxpayers to change their behaviour which may or may not be intentional. Taxation policy may be used as a behavioural device. There is an argument which says that such a purpose is not appropriate for a property tax, but there are instances where a property tax has been used to alter behaviour, for example, to discourage those who leave property vacant, by increasing their tax burden. Of course, it is the unintentional outcomes which cause the most problems, and where such unintentional outcomes include a reduction in economic efficiency by, for example, distorting price signals, losses may be incurred by both consumers and producers.

Economic growth

It is generally accepted that tax policies should support economic growth. However, there may be complex tradeoffs, involving tax revenues being used to purchase goods and services (e.g. education) which increase economic growth. Nevertheless, there is a perception that economic growth should not be the major consideration of a property tax:

> Tax is not an option within a developed economy; it is an integral part of it. A developed economic is always a mixed economy; the state and private sector do, without exception, interact in such economies to create an environment in which personal, social and societal goals are met. …economic growth is an element in achieving these goals, but it is not the sole way in which they are achieved. (Treasury Committee, 2011)

It is also recognized (ibid.) that: 'The tax system is often a blunt and indirect tool, and, additionally, using the tax system in this way inevitably increases complexity.'

The Treasury Committee's report (ibid., para. 31) opines that: 'if tax policy is used to support wider … objectives it should be judged as representing the best value for money with respect to alternatives such as regulation or spending.'

Thus, using a tax system to support other policy goals, risks unexpected behavioural changes and could put in jeopardy revenue flows. The Treasury Committee (2011) recommends that such uses of the tax system are reviewed regularly.

Competitiveness

This does not merely reflect the rates at which taxes are levied. It also means that stability and certainty in tax liability must be achieved, distortions minimized and businesses encouraged to have the confidence to invest and expand, within both a global and a local economy.

Property taxation

A property tax is a tax imposed on the value, 'deemed value or against the income arising from property ... ' (Abbott, 2008) or some surrogate of 'value', and may be recognized by different terminology (e.g. rate, real estate tax), but also conforms to the definition above.

Invariably, therefore, property taxes (like other taxes) are imposed by legislation enacted by national or central government. In some jurisdictions, it may be that all aspects of the tax are enshrined in the enacting legislation; in others, national or central government legislation may establish the main principles, leaving the details to be imposed by subsequent regulatory processes introduced by a lesser power, such as a minister, government department or agency, or lower tier(s) of government.

Basically, and notwithstanding the political and administrative dimensions, a state or nation is defined geographically, with recognized physical topographic borders. Thus, spatially, the land defines the state and is therefore hugely important in the political, social, cultural and economic identity of the state. It represents also a fundamental human need – we need shelter (land and buildings) for our physical survival; economic and social activities have a spatial dimension. Doing without land is simply not an option. Land is, therefore, the fundamental source of the wealth of a nation.

However, within national legislation, how we as individuals or a community or a nation fulfil that need for land and buildings normally involves a degree of choice, in terms of ownership and occupation patterns and the development of the various bundles of rights which can be attached to ownership and occupation. These are essential to regulate our relationships with other landowners and users and with public authorities. Such regulations are also necessary to achieve an orderly community with infrastructure, essential services, as well as the opportunities for economic and social activities which create wealth. Together with historical influences, these combine to provide a nation and its citizens with our cultural and national identity, and all of this stems from the land.

Thus, from the letter and implementation of the law of the land flows the whole gamut of what it means to be the government and a citizen and inhabitant of a country. Land is an essential, visible, valuable, state-controlled (and often state-owned) commodity. Indeed, it might be said that as a physical representation, the land is the state. The right to derive a share in the economic benefits of the output of its land by imposing a tax on those who produce those benefits is therefore a fundamental part of what it means to be the ruler or government of a country.

As Almy *et al.*, (2008) express it:

> Essentially property is a cultural concept having to do with legal relationships among people about the things that can be possessed. Without laws to define property and governments to protect property rights, property does not exist. The concept of privately owned real property was – and remains – alien in some primitive societies, particularly nomadic ones; land was communally or tribally held.

The evidence of the state taxing its citizens based on their property rights dates back many thousands of years – the earliest tax records date from about six thousand years BC. Found in Iraq, these clay tablets from the former city state of Lagash, are evidence of the 'bala', meaning rotation, in which the taxation of different districts of the state was undertaken on a monthly basis so that the process of taxing the entire country was broken down into more manageable components. Today we would call this a rolling programme of taxation.

There is similar evidence throughout the ancient world, including Babylon, China, Egypt and Persia. Taxes were imposed on the land and the produce of the land, initially in the form of agricultural and similarly natural products of the land (e.g. minerals) and more recently in the form of its monetary value, that is, either the rental or capital value or some other value proxy reflected in its ownership.

For property (or real estate) taxes, the subject matter (i.e. what is normally taxed) is a legal interest or the right to occupation, or more specifically the value (or some proxy of the value) of land, land and buildings, or buildings alone, and is likely to reflect the evolution of the legal and cultural concepts of ownership within the jurisdiction where the tax is being imposed. This is important to understand, not only when it comes to identifying the tax base, but also to reflect the fact that the tax needs to be socially acceptable (or 'fair') to the tax-paying (and wider) community. The enacting legislation should reflect these, if the system is to operate effectively and efficiently, or even to operate at all.

Thus, the legal definition of taxable 'property' also changes as the social and cultural expectations, norms and values of different countries evolve. This is an important point. Taxation is part of the often unwritten contract between state and subjects – the state will provide a range of public services, and subjects will pay for these through taxes if, and only if, the system of taxation (in all its aspects) is generally accepted as 'fair'. 'Fair' is, of course, a subjective concept and likely to change depending on personal, social and economic circumstances, but also with cultural norms and values. While it may be impossible to define 'fair' (as discussed above), characteristics of 'unfairness' may be more easily identified. It is worth remembering that civil wars have resulted from what have been considered to be unfair systems of taxation.

Defining 'property' as the basis for taxation

In order to impose a tax on property, there must be a legal definition of 'property' which identifies what is and what is not the subject of taxation. Without this, it is not possible to provide any kind of assessment on the bundle of rights in land and/or buildings which are liable to tax.

Over time, for example, British law has removed from the statutory definition of taxable 'property' (and therefore from taxation), stock in trade and other personal items, as well as agricultural land and buildings. In the UK, and other jurisdictions, legislation has introduced a reduced burden of tax for what may be called socially deserving occupiers, such as those on low income, the elderly, and places of religious worship. Such changes reflect ever-evolving socially and politically desirable objectives, and it is expected that tax policy will achieve this outcome.

As Youngman (1994) points out:

> 'As the concept of property as a social and political phenomenon changes, the process of valuing and taxing that property must change as a result.' ...

and it is with legislative changes that such amendments are made.

Similarly, legislation defines the nature of the 'value' on which tax is to be paid, whether it is the value to an occupier (England, Scotland and Wales); or to an owner (e.g. domestic property in Northern Ireland); or the actual purchase price of the current owner (e.g. California, under Proposition 13). It is well recognized that the most appropriate basis of property taxation is one which reflects the prevailing form of land tenure, partly to ensure a suitable supply of market-based transactional data for assessment purposes, but also to achieve a high degree of taxpayer comprehension of the assessment, acceptability and therefore the level of tax paid.

Private property rights

Where there are no private rights of property ownership and the state owns all land, the logic of property taxation (in terms of the taxpayer benefiting from the value of land) breaks down, unless individuals or communities are awarded some other rights based on the land which can be subject to tax, for example the right to crops.

It is normally the case, therefore, that the taxation of property reflects some tangible benefit or potential benefit of the real estate to produce 'value' for the taxpayer, who can reasonably (in economic and social terms) be taxed in relation to that benefit. Thus, an owner or an occupier is taxed on the basis of the 'value' to that owner / occupier, often by way of some estimate or surrogate of the rental or capital value.

It is therefore necessary for the legislation to recognize and define private property rights and the nature of taxable property within its jurisdiction, to enforce such responsibilities and obligations between it citizens and also between government bodies and its citizens. This legitimizes property rights, protects them and secures for the individual property owners security of tenure and enjoyment of the bundle of rights and responsibilities attached to the land which they hold. This is important for a range of purposes, including the trading of such rights, their use as collateral in an orderly society, as well as paving the way for these rights to become the object of property taxation.

This does not prevent governments from imposing regulations involving the use of land, for example, through planning regimes, which of course affect its use and therefore both its market and taxable values.

Legal and extra-legal markets: squatter populations

In some locations, including megacities, where there are informal settlements, there are residential and commercial developments for which there is no official authorization and to which none (or very few) of the occupiers have any recognized legal property rights. In most developing countries over 70% of the land is outside the system of land registration (Lemmen, 2010).

In countries in central and eastern Europe, a prerequisite for the introduction of a property tax was the development of a land register (or cadastre), linked to a record of land ownership and market transactions (McCluskey and Plimmer, 2007). Indeed, these were considered to be a major goal in the achievement of the decentralization of power for the newly created democracies, part of which included the establishment of a property tax system to raise revenue for the provision of local services.

In such circumstances, the development of a property taxation can become one of the links in the land administration process which provides occupiers with a degree of security of tenure, land and other property rights, cadastral and financial services and a functioning land market as a means to improve their quality of life and provide longer-term economic prospects.

Informal settlements are, almost by definition, outside the law. Their existence, their right to exist and their access to services and infrastructure may depend on the tolerance (or apathy) of the authorities. The extent to which they are understood, mapped, planned and accepted within the law varies; however, where such properties are subject to any form of taxation, they tend to acquire a degree of legitimacy, as do the rights of their occupiers or owners to be there.

There is clearly an argument for imposing a property tax on such residents, particularly if they have any benefit at all from public services. The British taxation system has never been concerned primarily with the nature of property ownership as a basis for property taxation. Historically, occupation (defined, in part, as the physical presence of an individual on the land) is sufficient to result in tax liability – even where occupation is illegal. The payment of taxation in this case does not confer any degree of legitimacy on the occupiers. While such occupiers benefit from services provided, the taxation system leaves the issue of legal rights to those who choose to claim them back by ousting the 'squatters' from the land.

However, without an understanding of what developments or structures exist physically on the land and without the personal information of who occupies those structures and for what reason, a property tax system cannot be seen to be effective, efficient or in any real sense 'fair'.

One solution to the range of problems which result from informal settlements is to actively encourage economic opportunities within such locations, and this means recognizing the rights to land and buildings of their 'occupiers'. In this way, occupiers are able to improve their economic and physical circumstances with confidence and are able to use such rights for a range of purposes, including collateral for financial loans, and authorities acquire a degree of authority in levying taxation on the property owners/occupiers.

Other implications of ownership

Property taxation is generally perceived to be an obligation on those citizens who have a degree of real estate wealth to pay towards the public services which their society enjoys and often from which their property benefits. However, in order to develop a functioning property tax system, there needs to be developed registers of:

- land parcels
- surveyed land and buildings/improvements
- taxpayers and (normally) their ownership rights
- assessments for tax purposes.

All of these may also be used for other purposes – they may even be developed for other purposes in some jurisdictions, with their use within a property tax regime apparently subsidiary to their main purpose. Increasingly such data is linked to geographic information systems (GIS), which brings a whole range of benefits and, in some communities, such e-government enjoys support from the population in terms of ensuring that the data available is accurate and up to date.

Clearly with modern technology, there is the potential for a range of databases to be linked, for example cadastres, GIS, tax registers, property data and increased integration, with open public access increases the transparency of any linked in property tax.

Scope of the tax

The legislation underpinning property (or indeed any other form of) taxation, must identify and adequately define:

- the object(s) to be taxed
- the tax base (i.e. the definition of 'value' on which the tax is to be paid)
- those individuals who are liable to be taxed (i.e. the taxpayers)
- any exemptions and reliefs from tax liability
- the process of assessment, although not necessarily the methodology of assessment
- the authority and qualifications of those responsible for assessment
- the means of collection and enforcement.

As stated by the IAAO (2010):

'the things to be valued (and taxed) must be clearly defined in legislation.'

Legislation may also define the purposes for which the revenue may be spent as well as those purposes for which such revenue may not be spent. The responsibilities of the spending authorities, limitations and any requirement to consult or otherwise gain approval of the taxpayers may also be defined in legislation.

The scope of the tax i.e. what is and what is not to be taxed, should be contained in state or primary legislation and should not be left to regulation or judicial interpretation, because the issue of taxation is so fundamental to the rights and responsibilities of citizens.

The legislations should specify the scope of the tax in terms of what is taxed (e.g. land, land and buildings or improvements to land); the forms that 'land' might take – clarifying whether it includes additional rights, such as to minerals, advertising, air space (becoming increasingly relevant with WiFi technology). The extent of any taxable personal property (e.g. stock in trade) that is included, should also be established, particularly if the tax assessment is based on the profitability of running a business (going concern). The clarity of such detail will ensure that there is certainty in the scope of the tax, which will make the tax administration more comprehensible and therefore easier and cheaper.

Identification of the taxpayer

It is important that legislation identifies clearly and unequivocally who is responsible or liable for the payment of the tax to the tax collecting authority. Such an individual will be the person to whom the tax demand is sent and from whom payment is required.

Such individuals need to be defined in relation to the real estate on which the tax is levied – either as owner or occupier or in some other capacity. Where ownership patterns are complex or where there are likely to be a number of 'owners' with different rights to the property, legislation may specify a hierarchy of ownership, with tax collectors working down through the hierarchy to identify the individual liable for the tax payment. This occurs, for example, in Britain, in identifying the taxpayer for the residential council tax.

In some countries, ownership records are not (or have not historically been) publicly available. Again, the UK is an example of this. In order to avoid dispute and (what would have been regarded as) an unwarranted intrusion into the privacy of individuals resulting in delay and additional expense, legislation for non-domestic taxation identifies the taxpayer as the 'occupier', and there is case law to interpret what exactly this term means for taxation purposes (see above). From the taxing authorities' point of view, it is the prompt receipt of revenue which is most important, so the identification of an 'occupier' as being liable for the tax payment is an acceptable solution. It is then for the 'occupier' to make arrangements with others who are legally or morally responsible to pay or to contribute to the tax bill (i.e. bear the burden) accordingly.

Thus, the person liable for the tax payment may not necessarily bear the burden of the tax, and this is an important distinction when discussing property taxes.

For example, where it is administratively difficult (and therefore expensive) for the tax collecting authority to send tax demands and require payment from individuals who would otherwise be taxpayers, legislation may allow another to be substituted as the taxpayer. In such a case, the individual liable to pay the tax, collects the money due to the tax authority and transmits it, effectively on their behalf.

For example, in the UK, in the case of caravan sites which accommodate leisure vans which are often unoccupied for part of the year, it would be hard for the tax collecting authority to send out tax demands to those owners-occupiers of the individual vans and expect payment, because these individuals are often absent and may change frequently. It is far easier (and therefore cheaper) for the tax collecting authority to require the site owner to pay the tax both for the site and for the individual vans on that site. The site owner is then reimbursed by the individual van owners who pay their share of the tax in the form of additional rent.

Uniformity/equity/fairness/treatment of taxpayers

The characteristics of uniformity, equity and 'fairness' are basic expectations of a property tax and its implementation.

Uniformity

According to the IAAO (2010), uniformity implies proportional taxation and can be defined in relation to ability to pay. It can also be defined as proportional to value and can be reflected in both the rate of tax imposed and the assessment ratios (i.e. the percentage of assessed value to appraised value). These are achieved in part by accurate, uniform valuations (ibid.) but also by the imposition of a rate of tax which is not regressive in its effect.

Thus, uniformity requires clearly defined and achieved standards of value – usually an *ad valorem* or open market value system which, according to the IAAO (2010):

> provides the fairest, most objective basis for an ad valorem tax. Revenue needs may change annually. So may property values. Some properties will increase in value while others decline. A uniform relationship between property value and property taxes can be maintained only if current market value is the basis of assessment.

Uniformity also implies that everyone is treated the same way within the law and that implies that all taxable objects (real estate) are identified and assessed, and their taxpayers subject to the same demands for tax payment and everyone else in that situation.

Uniformity has additional benefits for the taxing authorities. Thus:

> A policy of uniformity also can have buoyancy benefit. When effective tax rates are uniform, governments can more easily identify a publicly acceptable rate of tax. When effective tax rates are not uniform, which occurs when valuations are out of date, governments take their rate-setting cues from relatively over-valued taxpayers. As a result, they decide upon a general rate of tax that is lower than the rate the under-valued would accept. Consequently, less revenue can be raised than when valuations are uniform. (IAAO, 2010)

Uniformity is recognized (ibid.) as a criterion against which to evaluate a particular property tax system.

Equity

Equity is generally understood to be:

> 'Administration according to the rules of fairness and natural justice and not solely by the application of a universal set of rules...Equity is the soul of a civilized legal system and is intended to mitigate the rigors of the body of law encased in books and statutes.' (Abbott, 2008).

According to the IAAO (2010) in terms of property taxation:

> 'equity is achieved through enforcement, which ensures that assessments and, ultimately, taxes are distributed as equitably as possible under the law. Whether this distribution is perceived as fair is a separate issue...'

Merely including real estate into the tax system of a jurisdiction can be seen as providing an element of equity because real estate then becomes one of several bases on which taxation is imposed – thus ensuring that a larger spread of tax liability based on wealth is achieved.

Equity in property tax is generally discussed in terms of horizontal and vertical equity. Horizontal equity means that all taxpayers in similar circumstances (particularly with regard to their taxable real estate) pay the same amount of tax. Thus, close neighbours who own and occupy substantially similar properties should pay the same level of property tax. Vertical equity means that taxpayers in different circumstances pay different levels of tax. Thus, those with lower value properties (implying that they are also on low incomes) should pay less tax and should also be paying a lower proportion of their disposal income in tax, than those with higher value real estate.

Neither progressive nor regressive tax systems achieve vertical equity. However, while there may be other political and social reasons for a progressive tax system, there are few convincing arguments for a regressive tax regime.

Fairness

'Fairness' is an entirely subjective concept, and therefore, without criteria by which to judge, it might be said to be meaningless. Within property taxation, 'fairness' can be interpreted broadly within the perceptions, cultural and norms and values of any given society. This means that 'fairness' as a concept cannot be applied universally, but it should be possible for a government to establish from its citizens what they will and will not accept or tolerate within a tax system and establish some criteria for 'fairness' for its own property taxation purposes accordingly.

For example, Sheffrin (2010, 251) discusses issues of fairness and reports that the opportunity of the taxpayers to influence their level of tax is, in the USA, considered an important aspect of fairness. Thus, the use of acquisition value as a basis of taxation is recognized as 'fair' because it is a value wholly chosen by the purchaser/owner as the basis on which future taxes will be paid, even though this means that there is no attempt at all to achieve any level of horizontal equity between taxpayers owning similar properties (ibid., 253).

He also discusses the potential for a banded system of property taxation which he describes as '[limiting] taxpayer uncertainty on a year-to-year basis; [allowing] local variation in property tax rates to provide voter voice and differential taxation; and [having] a non-linear structure in which taxes are levied based on where properties are placed in discrete intervals or bands. It can provide a better link between tax payments and services, particularly at the higher end of the distribution.' (Sheffrin, 2010; McCluskey et al., 2002).

As discussed above, it may be more useful to discuss perceptions of 'unfairness'.

Investigating 'fairness' further, if it is accepted that a fundamental requirement of taxation is that all taxpayers in the same situation should be treated the same way within the law, then this becomes an inherent expectation within the legal provisions and of administrators in their implementation of the taxation liability.

'Fairness' may also include exempting those who have no money to pay or to encourage and support what might be recognized as deserving sectors of the community. As indicated elsewhere, there are very good practical arguments for such exemptions, and those with greater disposable wealth may accept paying more tax and therefore find such an exemption 'fair', particularly if their society has a tradition of welfare provision.

'Fairness' is also in part a question of public relations and taxpayer education. Perceptions of individual 'unfairness' may be based on erroneous information or simply a misunderstanding. Ensuring that public information is clear, available and comprehensive, and allowing individuals the chance to comment and ask specific questions on such matters, can go a long way to altering individual and society perceptions of 'fairness'. This device can also be used to inform governments of shifts of opinion, so that they can debate issues of 'fairness' and discuss how legislation might be amended to reflect a greater degree of public acceptance. It is, of course, well recognized that: 'As society and the economy change, the tax system should change to reflect them.' Treasury Committee (2011) This ensures the continued social approval (or at least acceptability) of a property tax and avoids the worst of public hostility to what they perceive as an 'unfair' system.

Exemptions and reliefs

Just as the obligation to pay tax must be enshrined in legislation, the provision of exemptions from that obligation or relief from full payment must also be contained in primary legislation – they cannot be inferred. Exemptions and reliefs may be specified within the legislation, or the legislative body which spends and/or collects the tax may have discretionary powers to impose and remove such exemptions/reliefs.

Exemptions and reliefs should be targeted at those sectors of the community which the community recognizes as needing the economic support of a reduced or removed tax obligation. Thus cases of financial hardship – either of an individual or a property sector – may be introduced. Similarly, exemptions and reliefs can be used as a device to encourage economic, environmental or social activities at the local level which are either seen by government as socially beneficial or which obviate the need for government to spend its funds to provide similar services.

Where individual taxpayers enjoy relief from full tax payment, then other taxpayers must pay more to compensate for this loss of revenue. Exemptions and reliefs may therefore be politically and/or socially contentious, particularly if they are not regularly reviewed and updated to reflect current social norms. Exemptions and reliefs should therefore reflect the cultural and societal views of 'fairness' within the jurisdiction.

In any event, issues of equity between taxpayers and non-taxpayers should be observed, that is taxpayers should be aware of and accept the reasons why they must pay more tax to allow for the exemptions and/or reliefs to be applied to others. These concessions should be made available to groups of individuals or property types, not to individuals, and should be administered even-handily. It is extremely dangerous if such concessions are made on the grounds of political favouritism or to specific individuals who could otherwise afford to pay. It brings the tax system, and the politicians involved, into disrepute and potentially leads to social unrest.

Exemptions and reliefs may be of historical origin, with the reasons for their introduction no longer relevant, or they may be time-specific – reviewed by the legislature at periodic intervals. Certainly, their removal tends to cause dissatisfaction from the sector of the community which benefited from the advantage, and the more time during which the exemption has been enjoyed, the stronger the political challenge to its removal.

To avoid such challenges, the IAAO (2010) recommend 'sunset provisions'.

> Once granted...exemptions tend to become entrenched and thought of as rights related to property ownership. Unless specific inequities related to a previous established exemption are discovered, legislative review of existing exemptions is unlikely without sunset provisions. Such provisions specify a date in the future after which the exemption will cease to exist. Although there may still be a need for the exemption, the expiration provision make the exemption more visible and presents an opportunity for future legislatures to review and recertify each exemption.

Exemptions and/or reliefs can be applied to the object of the tax (i.e. the land and/or buildings); the taxpayer; the tax base on which the tax is assessed; or the amount of money due. They can recognize the practicalities of tax collection – there is no point in taxing individuals who have no money – or encourage economic, environmental and social objectives, or reflect the concerns (culture) of the community. Thus it is usual for the following to be exempt taxation or subject to a form of tax relief:

- places of worship
- land and buildings owned by central government
- individuals on low income.

Some jurisdictions offer a small percentage reduction in tax paid for prompt payment. Again, the opportunity for tax collecting authorities to be able to offer such a concession must be enshrined in legislation.

Appeals/procedural issues

Almost invariably, the obligation to pay property tax is accompanied by the right to object, either to the level of tax paid, the circumstances which give rise to tax liability, or some other relevant aspect of the tax. Such rights must be enshrined in legislation – again, they cannot be inferred. Thus, legislation must specify:

- the right to object or appeal
- the grounds on which such an objection/appeal can be made
- who can make such an objection/appeal
- the timescale within which such an objection/appeal is permitted
- other administrative details, such as on whom the objection/appeal should be served; who will hear the appeal; rights to appeal their decision.

The legislation can be used to ensure a wide rights of objection/appeal. For example, anyone – not necessarily a tax payer – can object/appeal against any aspect of the taxation provisions of any real estate at any time; or only an individual taxpayer can object/appeal against the taxable value of real estate for which that individual is liable, within a specified time period.

Limiting such rights may be designed to reduce costs or to allow the assessors time to deal with appeals within a given time period so that they are then able to focus their attention on some other aspect of their work, such as a revaluation. It can also encourage dialogue in advance of an appeal between representatives of taxpayers (either as individuals or as groups) and the assessors, to ensure that the assessments are both understood and potentially even agreed in advance of becoming imposed by law.

However, it is important that the society's expectations of justice or 'fairness' (however that is interpreted) – often recognized as principles of natural justice (e.g. both parties have a right to be heard) in respect of the procedure imposed – are respected within the appeal process.

Collection and enforcement

Collection and enforcement of tax payment, both in terms of process and those individuals who undertake the work, must be legally authorized. A tax system should be cost effective and the costs of compliance and collection kept to a minimum. Costs of administration are those incurred not only by government (and its agents), but also those of compliance incurred by the taxpayers and their advisers. Any analysis of, and reform to, tax policy should include consideration of such public and private administration and enforcement costs as an integral part.

Again, the methods adopted in enforcing payment also need to meet the expectations and cultural values of the taxpayers and wider community affected.

For example, in the UK, it is traditional that the non-payment of tax is enforced by means of 'distress', a method of debt recovery which involves the taking and selling of the goods of the debtor to cover both the debt and the costs involved. There is legislation to cover such a method of debt collection (which may also be used for non-payment of rent). However, distress has been abolished in various jurisdictions (including some states in Australia and the USA). According to Abbott (2008):

> '[distress] may also be considered a contravention of the European Convention on Human Rights, which requires a "fair and public hearing" when determining a person's civil rights.'

This demonstrates the need for tax administration to evolve to reflect the cultural and societal norms and values of the community which is subject to taxation, and expects its legislators to respond to their opinions and requirements in the drafting and enactment of tax legislation.

Conclusions

Taxation is first and foremost an obligation enshrined in law and, as it is a creation of law, all aspects of the tax must be contained in legislation – they cannot be inferred. Legislation may be made at national, state, local, judicial or ministerial levels. Nevertheless, both the fundamentals and the details of the taxation provisions need to be articulated in clear, modern and unambiguous terms and be regularly and frequently reviewed to ensure that they remain 'fit for purpose'.

Thus, the legislation must achieve and continue to achieve a range of outcomes, including meeting the needs, expectations, norms and values of its citizens, as well as specifying clearly and unequivocally a range of definitions, responsibilities, administrative procedures and processes.

Additional desirable outcomes include: 'fairness' (or perhaps, a better expression is the absence of unfairness); support of economic growth and competition; provision of certainty, both as to interpretation and liability; legal clarity; being the subject of proper legislative and democratic scrutiny; being simple, comprehensible and clear in its objectives; being targeted; achieving economic and social stability; liability to pay being simple to calculate, cheap and convenient to collect from the taxpayers' perspective; and the whole system being coherent.

Given the variety of countries around the world where property taxation is imposed, it is not surprising that different systems are imposed in different ways in different jurisdictions. They reflect to a greater or lesser extent the historical development as well as the current needs for revenue and local administrative requirements in each jurisdiction. In reviewing, interpreting, criticizing and evaluating such systems, the fundamental characteristics (the culture, tradition, expectations, norms and values) of the citizens should be recognized in the tax law, its implementation and its wider relationship between the various tiers of governments, property-related agencies and its citizens' property and wider civil rights, if it is to work effectively and efficiently. Indeed, it could be argued that where property taxes are subject to widespread criticisms by the taxpayers, governments have failed to keep up to date with the evolution of these cultural issues in the legal and practical implementation of the tax.

Paying tax is a fundamental responsibility of citizens who expect to enjoy government services, but where the nature of the tax or its mode of imposition causes major criticism, there is a very real risk of civil unrest and there are examples from history – from different countries – where widespread disapproval of a property tax has caused governments major political and financial problems (e.g. California's Proposition 13; Britain's poll tax revolts).

Taxation therefore is a very visible demonstration of the (written or unwritten) contract between the state and the citizens of the country. The state expects and requires taxes to be paid to fund its operations; the citizens expect and require that such a tax should be imposed in such a way that it reflects their concept of 'fairness', which is generally undefined, and includes how the tax yield is spent. This is particularly important in relation to a property tax which tends to fund public services at a local level, because services on which the tax's output is spent tends to be highly visible to the taxpayers.

When a property tax works well, no-one pays much attention to it, but when it goes wrong, for whatever reason, social discontent is easily (and often swiftly) manifested to the local representatives responsible (or apparently responsible). Getting it right and continuing to get it right must therefore be a fundamental goal of government, and the starting point for this is the body of legislation which imposes the tax.

References

Abbott, D. (2008) *Encyclopedia of Real Estate Terms*. Delta, London: Alpha Publishing.

Almy, R., Dornfest, A. and Kenyon, D. (2008) *Fundamentals of Tax Policy*. Chicago: International Association of Assessing Officers.

IAAO (2010) *Standard on Property Tax Policy*. Kansas, Il: International Association of Assessing Officers.

Lemmen, C. (2010) *The Social Tenure Domain Model. A Pro-poor Land Tool*. International Federation of Surveyors (FIG). Global Land Tool Network (GLTN); United Nations Human Settlements Programme (UN-Habitat). Copenhagen. Available at: *http: //www. fig.net/pub/figpub/pub52/figpub52.htm*. [Accessed 11 November 2011]

McCluskey, W.J., Plimmer, F.A.S. and Connellan, O.P. (2002) Property Tax Banding: A Solution for Developing Countries. *Assessment Journal*. (March/April): 37–47.

McCluskey, W.J. and Plimmer, F. (2007) *The Importance of the Property Tax in the New Accession Countries of Central and Eastern Europe*. RICS Research Paper Series. London, UK, The Royal Institution of Chartered Surveyors, 7(17).

Sheffrin, S.M., (2010) Fairness and Market Value Property Taxation. In: Bahl, R., Martinez-Vazquez, J. and Youngman, J. (eds.), *Challenging the Conventional Wisdom on the Property Tax*. Cambridge MA: Lincoln Institute of Land Policy: 241–262.

Treasury Committee (2011) Principles of Tax Policy. Available at: http: //www.publica tions.parliament.uk/pa/cm201011/cmselect/cmtreasy/753/75301.htm [Accessed 7 June 2011]

Youngman, J.M. (1994) *Legal Issues in Property Valuation and Taxation: Cases and Materials*. Chicago: International Association of Assessing Officers.

9

Tax Criteria: The Design and Policy Advantages of a Property Tax

Gary C. Cornia

Introduction

This chapter describes and illustrates the various criteria that are employed to guide tax policy and tax administration. The aim is to provide policymakers with a set of guidelines they can use to evaluate the tax schemes they confront. The guidelines or principles used here are described in most public finance texts (Gruber, 2005). In keeping with the theme of the book the issues are addressed from the perspective of local policymakers.

Taxes, tax systems and other revenue producing devices (fees and charges) have the potential to change the behaviour of individuals and organizations. Clearly, if taxes can change individual and organizational behaviour, then in aggregate they may also change entire economies. The question is: what is the direction of the change to an economy? The changes that are caused by taxes may be positive. However the public and the media generally view the behavioural outcomes triggered by taxes as negative. Illustrations of the negative effects of taxes are easily developed. A tax, for example, may raise the price of a good or service and the increased price may cause a decline in its consumption. This outcome would be especially likely if the tax was only imposed on a limited number of goods or services (Spilker *et al.*, 2011). The consumer would obviously have the option to purchase fewer of the taxed goods and more of the non-taxed items. The rational consumer would likely reduce the purchase of the taxed

A Primer on Property Tax: Administration and Policy, First Edition.
Edited by William J. McCluskey, Gary C. Cornia and Lawrence C. Walters.
© 2013 Blackwell Publishing Ltd. Published 2013 by Blackwell Publishing Ltd.

goods. Over time, we would reasonably expect that the reduction in purchases would reduce the demand for the taxed good, the number of workers who are employed to produce the taxed goods and eventually the reduction of the profits of the owners of the business producing the goods. Eventually, production of the taxed good would decline, and invested capital would be reallocated to more profitable activities.

Because of the potential behavioural and economic implications of taxes, the conceptual intent, implementation and long-term administration of taxes demand a policy design that is sympathetic to the market. As a starting point for tax design, policymakers are well advised to identify tax schemes that do the least to change the relative prices of goods and services because the resulting tax will minimize the economic disruptions. Tax schemes that minimize distortions are described as neutral. Finding a neutral tax is never an easy task. Few absolute rules exist that can be followed to meet this challenge. For example, there is disagreement or at least discussions over what kind of economic distortion we should worry about. Box 9.1 offers a brief review of how economists, politicians and even consumers differ in their views of what is important and should be considered when measuring the economic distortions associated with taxes.

Several general guidelines exist for finding a neutral tax scheme. First, as noted, governments should apply any tax broadly. A narrow tax base creates distortions. Second, if a tax is not broadly applied, it should be imposed on goods or services that are not very responsive to price increases. These are products

---

Box 9.1   How economists and individuals consider the distortions created by taxes

'Any tax has two effects, which economists call the income and the substitution effects. The income effect of a tax is the change in the choices made by the taxpayer because payment of the tax has reduced the taxpayer's real income. The substitution effect arises because the very existence of the tax changes the relative prices of the taxed goods, and therefore gives an incentive to taxpayers to substitute non-taxed goods for taxed goods. The income effect does not give rise to any efficient problems; it simply implies that resources are transferred from taxpayers to the government, and we hope that government will do something useful with the money. But, the change in the behavior from the substitution effect causes an economic distortion that does not benefit anyone. That is, when the higher price of a taxed good causes me to substitute to a different non-taxed good purely because of the distorted price than I am worse off and the government gets no revenue. This is the source of the loss of economic efficiency from taxation, because people are worse off than they were previously, and by a larger amount than the tax collections themselves. This phenomenon is sometimes called a deadweight loss. People hate taxes because of income effects, but economists hate taxes because of substitution effects.'

Nechyba (2002)

that consumers will purchase with little consideration for the price. This may be because the price is so low or the good is in such demand that the consumer will purchase regardless of the price. Finally, tax schemes need to be careful about excessive rates. High tax rates are always a challenge to neutrality (Fisher, 2006).

Part of the problem in designing taxes is that commonly held views about taxes may be wrong or the observed outcomes counterintuitive. Individuals might expect an increase in the personal income tax to cause people to work less because after the income tax is increased individuals would receive less economic return for their work effort. Verifying this assumption has proven difficult. This is partially because it is difficult to find accurate data to examine the effect of an income tax on behaviour. But when such data is found there is some evidence that higher income taxes may cause individuals to work more, not less – a somewhat counterintuitive outcome (Anderson, 2003).

Does the fact that taxes may distort behaviour suggest that taxes should not be imposed? The answer to that question is straightforward: a categorical no! No matter how distasteful taxes may seem, most citizens and societies recognize the important contribution to the quality of life that government – funded by taxes – can provide. Consider how ineffective or unappealing a country, region or local area would be without judicial courts, property rights, rules to prevent corruption, basic public infrastructure, education, recreation and public safety. These are the goods and services that are almost always funded by taxes and provided by governments. However, the distortions that may be created by tax systems make it apparent that policymakers must exercise caution in the design and the implementation of taxes and fees. Undoubtedly it is in the interest of everyone in a society that the taxes that are used are designed to minimize the level of distortion created in an economy. The first recommended goal of our analysis is that taxes are needed, but governments should adopt taxes that are as neutral or non-intrusive as possible.

Independent and autonomous revenues

An fundamental assumption of the evolution from a developing or a transitional economy into a market economy is that if the decentralization of government accompanies the political changes the process of economic maturity will move more rapidly and be accompanied by an increase in the welfare of citizens. There are multiple reasons for this assumption as well as some empirical support.

A common argument for decentralization is that local governments are more inclined to provide the services that citizens demand, and provide them in the quantities they want. Why do analysts believe this happens? The proximity of citizens to local government suggests that citizens will be predisposed to participate in public dialogue about government services because they feel their comments and demands will have an impact. Second, because local governments are closer to the people, they are more likely to listen and respond to the wishes of local citizens. Local governments can avoid 'one-size-fits-all' in the provision of services. The outcome is quite different when services are provided by the central government – central services are almost always provided uniformly across the country, creating too much of a good or a service in some regions – where the demand is low – and too little in regions where the demand is high. Since the pioneering work of Tiebout (1956), it is standard to assert that the decentralization of government facilitates a system of competing local governments that are attempting to appeal to citizens by providing a specific mix of public services and taxes. But, decentralizing service delivery is only one of the steps that are required when developing responsive governments. The ability to respond to the demands of citizens also depends on having access to, and control of, the required fiscal resources.

A fundamental conjecture of the proponents of decentralization is that access to a source of revenue that is independent of others' control is essential if there is a desire for responsive local governments. Failure to meet the condition of an independent revenue source will eventually result in local governments being funded by revenue sources that they can neither control nor readily alter. If the determination of the tax base and the tax rate is entirely in the domain of officials in the central government then local citizens will correctly sense that they have less influence over the level of taxes they are required to pay and thus less commitment to be involved with government decisions. When revenue comes from a provincial or central government it almost always comes with negative implications. At a minimum, officials in the central government are less inclined to respect local demands (Oates, 1993).

Often there are few incentives for local governments to use the 'outside' funds carefully. Top-down funding creates a process that separates spending decisions from taxing and revenue decisions. When grants of revenue arrive from the central government local officials feel very little of either political pain or responsibility that is generally associated with raising funds.

A common outcome of central funding is that the centre eventually requires that the revenue allocations are equal or close to equal on a per capita basis between all units of local governments. Rich or poor communities receive the same amount of revenue from the centre – regardless of actual need. And after they receive the funds they have few options on how they may use the funds. For example, even though a local community may collectively desire more spending on education than on public safety the centre may decree that the funds will be used for police and fire. Local public administrators may be unhappy with such an outcome, but there is little they can do because funding from a higher level of government gives the contributing government considerable, often overwhelming, fiscal influence and this naturally translates to political and administrative influence. When the centre constrains how the funds can be used, it reduces the sovereignty of the local government and also constrains the ability to meet the wishes of its citizens.

Revenues that are controlled by a local government – or taxes where the local government can develop and implement policy about the base and rate of a tax and its administration – elicit a different pattern of behaviour. Local citizens are likely to be more engaged – voting, attending public gatherings, contacting local officials – in the political process because they can directly observe and sense the consequences of the fiscal actions taken by their local elected officials. Citizens can feel or anticipate the implications of high taxes or low taxes and respond when and as they see fit. Local funds also allow local officials to spend *their* money without substantial interference or oversight from the central government. If a local government concludes that the citizens desire more fire protection and less community recreation, the local officials – because the outcome is funded by revenues they have raised – will have latitude in making and implementing the decisions to reach these goals (World Bank, 2000).

We believe it is reasonable to assume that the demands for public services differ substantially between the citizens of different local governments. If local governments have the ability to raise their own revenue and use the revenue in a manner that provides goods and services that the majority demand we believe such outcomes reinforce local governments because by being more responsive to the demands of their citizens local governments increase their political currency. In the long run the increased political support and scrutiny strengthens local governments (Oates, 1972).

The second criterion for sound tax policy is as follows: subnational governments require a local revenue source that allows local autonomy in tax design and tax policy implementation.

Adequate and stable revenue

In the final analysis a tax system must provide sufficient revenue so that the goods and services demanded by citizens from local governments can be provided. Having adequate revenue is obvious but it is often downplayed by elected officials. In spite of the need for revenue, political leaders easily become uncomfortable with a tax system that produces growing or even consistent levels of revenue. At issue is the challenge of justifying to the taxpayers and the voters the revenue flowing into the public coffers.

Nevertheless, public officials should avoid becoming either overly apologetic or defensive because of adequate tax revenues – adequate tax revenues allows officials to provide fundamental local public services. After the political rhetoric and public criticism is over – it is clear that the market does not and will not provide many of the services produced by government and not having access to these goods and services would diminish the quality of life for many individuals and families (Hillman 2003). Having inadequate government services has long-term negative implications. For example, failure to have access to basic government goods and services would likely undermine the ability of transitional and developing counties to attract and retain foreign investment. Foreign investment will flow to regions with adequate infrastructure, safe living conditions and a reliable and trained workforce. Inadequate annual revenue suggests that local governments may end up making policy tradeoffs that may become dysfunctional over time. An adequate and stable source of revenue is an important criterion of basic tax design.

Hedging the revenue bets

Insuring sufficient revenue to operate a local government requires more than a single source of tax revenue. For example, if possible, a careful farmer cultivates multiple kinds of crops, hopeful that when the market price of one crop declines the other prices will remain high. Crop diversity also protects from weather-related risk. The same principle is important in tax policy. Because different taxes can be unpredictable over time it stands to reason that having more than one source of revenue will protect local governments from service interruptions. In practice this generally implies that a revenue system that is designed with an eye on – or an appreciation of – the uncertainty of future economic trends will be comprised of different types of taxes including taxes on wealth, income and economic transactions. Such a system will contribute to stability in annual revenues (Nelson and Cornia, 2010).

Having sufficient revenue available creates a climate where public employees can pursue their occupations confident that they will be compensated fairly and can make public employment a viable career. In addition, groups or individuals who sell products and services to local governments are also confident that they will be paid for their services and products. Likewise, capital markets that lend funds to the public sector are comfortable that they will be repaid in a timely manner. Sufficient revenue also means that citizens can expect to receive a consistent level of public services. A stable revenue stream protects local governments from having to increase and decrease tax rates to meet the variations in revenue. Unstable tax rates can interrupt business planning and undermine the attractiveness of a community for investment. Such an outcome creates a tax system that is distorting. The fourth general tax design criterion that follows from this discussion is that local tax systems are more stable if they collect and receive revenue from multiple tax bases.

How broad is the tax base?

Public officials can choose from a number of tax bases, but generally their choices are limited to taxes that are linked to wealth or property, transactions or sales, and personal and business income (Musgrave and Musgrave, 1976). In addition to deciding on the tax base, tax design also requires decisions on how extensively the base will be taxed. In other words, will the tax base be broad or narrow? Consider this question in the context of a transaction tax and specifically a retail sales tax. Policymakers may conclude that it is good policy to narrow the sales tax base and to exclude expenditure on essentials such as food and clothing from the sales tax base. This decision may be driven by concern over the economic burden that a sales tax on essentials creates for poor individuals and families. At first glance, removing essential items from the sales tax may appear as a reasonable policy. This decision, however, needs to be considered in the context of the implications of revenue stability. Removing the sales tax on food may result in the tax being more heavily imposed on goods and services that, unlike food, are very sensitive to economic cycles. The result is a less stable flow of revenue.

In order to understand the implications of creating or changing a tax we suggest that the analysis start by considering the following relationship:

$$\text{tax revenue} = \text{tax rate} \times \text{tax base} \qquad (9.1)$$

When insufficient taxes are being collected, a natural and common response of administrators and politicians is to think that the problem is occurring because the tax rate is too low. But the basic problem may not be the tax rate but the definition of the tax base. A tax base that excludes sizable portions of the base is frequently the root cause of the lacklustre performance of a tax.

This part of the analysis is easy; the hard part is deciding what to include in the base. Part of the problem is political; many interest groups work with elected officials to have exemptions to the base granted for the economic factors or interests they represent. The pressure from such groups to narrow the tax base can be overwhelming. A tax base can become narrow as the makeup of an economy matures and changes. As an illustration, a transaction tax that includes goods in the base but exempts services may have been reasonable 20 or 30 years ago. Today as economies become more and more based on services, the exemption of services from the tax base is more difficult to justify. It will always be useful to consider changes in the economy and how they have altered the tax base. The point is this: The answer to insufficient revenues may have much more to do with a narrow tax base than the tax rate. Only after an analysis of the tax base is it prudent policy to consider the role of the tax rate in determining the adequacy of the revenue from a tax (Mikesell, 2011).

Consistent revenue flow is associated with a tax base that is relatively immune to cyclical changes in the economy or not influenced by economic cycles. An example of a tax that is influenced by economic cycles is a tax that is based on the net earnings of businesses. It is obvious that most business taxes are heavily influenced by the net revenues of a business. It is equally obvious that during periods of sustained economic growth the revenues and the profits of the business usually increase and, in time, tax revenues from business will also increase. However, just the opposite happens to business income in periods of slow or negative economic growth. During a slowdown the amount of profits and eventually the amount of taxable revenue declines. There is substantial policy danger in such a situation. While all tax bases are not equal, other things being equal a narrow tax base is more buoyant than a broadly defined tax base. So adopting a 'stable' tax also suggests avoiding the temptation to narrow the tax base through exclusions to the base.

We believe the fifth important criterion of tax design is to keep the base as broad as possible. When the tax base is broad, the result is lower rates. This criterion may do more to avoid tax distortions than any other single tax principle.

Financial support for infrastructure

We have suggested that a stable stream of tax revenue contributes to the uniform and certain day-to-day functioning of local governments. There is at least one additional reason why a stable revenue stream is important to local government. Central, regional and local governments in emerging and developing countries confront a backlog of infrastructure needs. Capital investment in ports, roads, mass transit, water systems, schools, airports, healthcare and higher education are illustrations of infrastructure that frequently needs to be built or upgraded in order for a local government to compete in the global economy. Even without regard for global issues, such infrastructure contributes to the improvement in the net welfare of a community.

Because building or rehabilitating infrastructure requires a commitment of substantial funds it implies that the most feasible method to finance the construction of a facility is to seek funds from an international 'donor' or a financial institution. While the practice of seeking funds in the capital markets is relatively new for emerging economies, borrowing for infrastructure is the common method used to fund facilities in established market economies. Financial institutions will lend funds when there is evidence that the principal and interest associated with the loan will be repaid in a timely and scheduled manner. However, without evidence that the tax system can produce stable revenue to retire the debt that is incurred, governments will find it difficult and perhaps impossible to borrow funds under affordable conditions. This outcome is especially serious for local governments. A local government with a revenue source that reflects a history of stable and timely tax collections will have a much better chance of securing funds for infrastructure. When there are questions about the certainty of repayment, financial institutions may either reject the loan or if they are willing to loan funds they will require a higher interest payment to compensate for the risk of non-payment (World Bank, 2001).

The need to provide affordable infrastructure for current, as well as future citizens, suggests an additional criterion: a stable revenue stream that will continue into the future.

Capturing the increased value resulting from public infrastructure

Investing in public infrastructure that enhances the environment or livability of a community should, in the normal functioning of an economy, also eventually increase the trade and industrial activity occurring in a community. Examples of such outcomes from investing in infrastructure are easy to find: airports, roads, water systems and public markets all contribute to the economic wellbeing of a community.

If a tax system helps to fund and provide infrastructure, then a reasonable expectation would be for the tax system to capture a portion of the incremental economic benefit associated with the infrastructure. One justification for this argument is that by capturing a portion of the increased value that the infrastructure creates, the public investment can help to finance the repayment of the debt that was incurred to fund the project. Among all of the taxes available at the local level the property tax has the highest potential to capture part of the value created by an investment in infrastructure. If, for example, the construction of a mass transit system results in an increase of the value of existing residential dwellings and commercial buildings, then a properly administered property tax system would account for the increased value of the properties, and there would be a corresponding increase in the property tax payment. In this way the value created by the new investment is partially captured by the property tax. The additional revenue could help pay for the long-term debt associated with the project (Cornia *et al.*, 2009).

Another example of a tax that may capture part of the increased economic activity associated with infrastructure is a retail sales tax. Again, consider what a new or improved transit system might add to the economic value of a community. If the economic activity associated with the investment in the mass transit also increases taxable market or sales transactions then a sales tax could indirectly capture a portion of the increased value associated with the investment in the infrastructure. In other words, more sales with commercial activity will be reflected in an increase in revenue from the sales tax.

Immobile base

In addition to concerns about the structural stability of revenue sources local officials also need to be concerned with the potential that taxpayers may have to avoid the tax by shifting their economic choices to a non-taxed activity or to a non-taxing jurisdiction. These are both examples of the substitution effect described in Box 9.2. Whenever there is both the opportunity and the ability to avoid a tax by shifting economic activity, it is essentially impossible to restore revenue once taxpayers realize that it makes economic sense to avoid the tax. When taxpayers shift purchases or income, it obviously causes revenues to decline and the decline triggers a response to potentially increase rates in order to at least maintain the previous level of revenue – but of course increasing the tax rates provides an even stronger set of incentives to avoid the tax. Box 9.2 describes the consequences of imposing a tax on a mobile base.

Solutions exist that can partially resolve the revenue losses when economic activity is shifted from the higher tax area to the lower tax area. However, in

---

Box 9.2   Consequence of imposing a tax on a mobile tax base

Economists Robert Inman and Andrew Haughwout examined the growth of jobs in the city of Philadelphia in the USA to the growth of jobs in the its surrounding suburbs and found that the center city was losing jobs while the outer cities were gaining jobs. Using a basic econometric model and controlling for a variety of factors he concluded a primary cause of this outcome was because Philadelphia has chosen to impose a wage tax on labor – while the suburbs had decided to not impose the wage tax. That is, the city created a reason for a mobile tax base – labour – to flee to the suburbs. This is not an isolated case. The county surrounding Portland, Oregon just voted to do follow a similar policy – tax labour at a higher rate in the city relative to the surrounding communities Haughwout and Inman, 2001

---

most cases over time the solution creates a reduction in the autonomy of local government. For example, local governments could agree to a policy to have the centre or provincial governments administer and even collect the tax and share the collected revenue. By collecting the tax from a larger geographic area, the ability to avoid the tax is reduced. Here the outcome is also likely to be less than optimal because the centre is collecting a tax, but it does not fully benefit from the tax and thus has modest incentive to collect the tax with administrative enthusiasm. This is clearly the case for taxes that require substantial administrative effort to collect and remit. The point is basic: local governments work best when they impose their taxes on an immobile base, otherwise the incentives to avoid the tax will undermine the long-run stability of the tax. This suggests an important criterion: locally imposed taxes should be placed on an immobile base.

Benefit tax

An advantage of a private firm is that the owners receive signals from the market on the success or failure of their service or products. If they are returning an economic profit the signal is to continue the operations, perhaps even expand the operation, and if they are losing money the signals are also clear: change practices or go out of business. But there is more to a market than just information about a firm's profits or losses. When a good or service is sold in a market there is also an implicit process that requires that the price of the item is no greater and perhaps less than the perceived benefits from the item. Such outcomes, where benefits exceed or equal costs, create efficient exchanges. It is the classic intersection of the supply and demand curves or the market equilibrium recited in basic economic courses.

The goods and services provided by governments generally do not benefit from similar market exchanges or market prices to validate either their success or efficiency. Elected officials and appointed officials cannot examine any direct financial data from an operation and conclusively determine if the service or good should be continued or curtailed. Public officials are left to using non-market – often political – information to decide how much of a good or service to provide. This makes the management of public organizations more difficult than private firms. Fortunately, there are certain tax bases that can approximate the market because there is a relationship between the amount of tax paid and the public benefit received. At the local level the property tax is a reasonable example of such a tax base. This outcome occurs when the property tax is related to the level of local public services (Zodrow, 2001).

Public officials are wisely advised to employ taxes that display at least a modest relationship between the taxes paid and the services consumed. If such a relationship is established it fosters efficiency in the delivery and consumption of public goods and services and provides feedback to public officials and administrators on the relationship between taxes and services.

Ability to pay taxes

It is routine for elected policymakers and the designers of tax schemes to at least implicitly consider the economic ability of taxpayers to meet the financial obligation imposed by a tax or series of taxes. Understanding the tax burden on certain income groups can add important insights to the measure. For example, a tax on tobacco products may fall more heavily on poorer individuals and families than it does on richer groups because the poor generally spend a larger portion of their income on tobacco than the well-to-do. In order to make such an analysis about the sales tax on tobacco requires knowledge of spending patterns that reflect income class. In the case of tobacco and alcohol spending, this would be straightforward, but making the distinction between the tax burdens on income groups when a broad tax is considered is usually a difficult undertaking. One common problem is that the economic burden of the tax is often different from the taxes' legal burden. For example, a transaction tax is legally imposed on the seller but the actual or economic burden of the tax is likely passed forward to the buyer of the taxed good or service (Haughout and Inman, 2001).

Public finance economists, by employing a number of assumptions, are able to posit the expected incidence of a tax. A tax is considered *regressive* if it collects a larger percentage of poor individuals' or families' income compared to rich individuals or families. Conversely, if a tax collects a greater percentage of the rich's income than the poor person's income it is labelled *progressive*. A *proportional* tax system is one that takes the same percentage of income from all income groups.

Deciding which tax or overall tax system is appropriate – regressive, progressive or proportional – often cannot be based solely on the criteria used by economists. The decisions are almost always influenced by both personal and political values. Naturally, the introduction of non-economic values into the deliberation complicates the analysis, but they also facilitate decisions to be made. For example, few individuals or groups would argue with the notion that a well-to-do person – other things being equal – is better prepared to pay taxes than a relatively poor person. The rich simply have a greater *ability to pay*.

The difficult part of the issue is deciding how much different the taxes on the well-to-do can or should be relative to the poorer individuals. Can the rich comfortably pay a higher portion of their income than the poor by a factor of three or four, or should the difference be much smaller? The danger is that if the rich pay too large a share of their income they lose the incentive to work as many hours or as hard and eventually the overall economy will be hurt or what incentives are created to encourage them to avoid the tax. This is an example of a question where political values may be more helpful in resolving the disagreements.

Ease of compliance

Taxes almost always impose a burden on taxpayers beyond the direct fiscal effects. A significant contributor to this additional burden comes from a taxpayer having to collect the tax, record and keep track of the tax revenues, and the cost of remitting the tax revenues to the public agency. The burden of meeting the requirements of the tax process that falls on a taxpayer is called the cost of compliance. Some compliance costs are easy to understand and even estimate. For example, the individual income tax compliance burden includes the often significant cost of the preparation and filing of the tax forms. These costs can be measured by direct observation or the use of questionnaires. Measuring the compliance cost of other taxes is more difficult. For many taxes while the immediate burden of the tax is on the taxpayer – the initial payment comes out of their pocket – the compliance cost is placed on a business concern. The VAT and retail sales taxes are examples. In the case of a few taxes the compliance burden is relatively light, but with many taxes the compliance burden imposed on the tax can be heavy if the process is not carefully designed and implemented.

The VAT is an example of a tax where compliance requires that business firms collect and maintain detailed information on many aspects of the cost of doing business. The result is a tax with relatively high compliance costs. Other taxes with high compliance costs are direct business taxes, such as a tax based on business income or production. There are ways for tax designers to minimize the cost of tax compliance. The filing of tax forms should be uniform between governments, and the design of the tax forms should also try to make the process as simple as possible and thus minimize the amount of data that is require to be collected and reported (Pearlman, 1998).

Good tax design also suggests that taxpayers should not be concerned that the compliance with the tax will result in the disclosure of private financial or personal matters or, in the case of business, offer strategic information to competing firms.

Ease and cost of administration

In addition to the cost of compliance, politicians and policy designers must consider the administrative cost – or the government's costs – of collecting a tax. Some tax processes may be so difficult to administer that the amount of revenue collected relative to the cost of administration makes the tax not worth the effort to collect. For instance, a market-based property tax imposed in a developing country or region that does not have reliable information on the legal ownership or occupancy of the property or a current or accurate legal description of the property or reliable market information would be costly to administer. In such a situation it might be *possible* to collect the tax, but the administrative burden and cost makes the use of this version of the tax unrealistic.

There are various administrative steps that require careful consideration when designing a tax. The first requirement is the ability of the administrators to discover the economic activities that are part of the tax base and also identify who is the responsible taxpayer. For many taxes and tax schemes this is not a difficult step to accomplish, but in many emerging countries this step is complex for almost all taxes. For example, discovery is difficult if there is no existing social culture of tax compliance. It is also difficult when the needed legal documents and legal processes are not current. The administration of a tax requires that an administrative body has access to financial, accounting and appraisal skills needed to place a taxable value on the economic activity.

A list of the issues that tax administrators should consider when estimating their ability to facilitate the collection of a tax is given in Table 9.1.

Transparent taxes

There is a prevailing inclination for elected officials to prefer to finance government with taxes whose burden is less obvious or less direct to the taxpayer. The reason for this preference is understandable. Direct taxes create political issues for politicians while indirect taxes create far fewer political challenges. These reactions foster the design, creation and ongoing policy drift towards taxes or tax processes that are less visible to the taxpayers. The VAT is an illustration of a tax that is to some extent indirect; this is especially true if the consumer of the purchased good or service is not notified via the sales receipt of the amount of the VAT when a purchase is made. Many excise taxes are also less visible to the taxpayer. Either the taxpayer is not directly notified of the tax or it is imposed in such small amounts that taxpayers ignore the tax. Taxes collected at one level of government and shared or funnelled to a different level of government also have the characteristics of indirect taxes.

A reasonable question with respect to indirect taxis is if they minimize raising political challenges, should their use be avoided? We think there are several

Table 9.1 Administrative considerations for taxes

Administrative steps	Details of steps	Challenges
Discovery of taxable activity	Taxable actions (tax base) must be observed and recoverable records kept	Finding and recording evidence of taxable activity
Valuing taxable activity	Placing an economic or financial value on the taxable activity	Can range from relative ease of valuation to extreme challenges such as business income and property
Computation of tax	Calculating the value of the tax: base $\times$ rate $=$ value	
Billing and remittance	Bill the individual/group responsible for the payment of the tax; remit tax	Extreme burden on record maintenance for governments
Appeal	Provide administrative and legal process to challenge tax	Keeping the process Transparent
Audit	Provide a process to audit the taxable activity of taxpayers	Resources and access
Enforcement	Establish legal steps to enforce the reporting of tax data and enforce payment	Established legal system and political support for enforcement activities

Source: Compiled by author

important reasons to avoid relying too heavily on indirect taxes. A non-transparent tax system offers opportunities to either institute or allow procedures to develop that can be used to promote noncompliance by taxpayers who have curried favour with the tax administration office or senior elected officials. Any system that adds to the potential for corruption in an emerging economy should be avoided.

Of course, the effect on the income of the citizens of a direct tax and an indirect tax could easily be identical. However, we expect the behaviour of the taxpayer and the elected official to be quite different between the direct and the indirect tax. The visible nature of a direct tax places more political pressure on the elected officials and forces caution imposing a tax and caution if they attempt to alter the rates or base of the existing tax. Direct taxes also encourage citizens to engage in the political processes, and in doing so they likely impose some fiscal restraint on governments. There will be less fiscal restraint associated with indirect taxes. Elected officials who can avoid responsibility for the tax will be more inclined to alter or increase the tax rates associated with indirect taxes because they can do so without suffering direct political repercussions. Indirect taxes also reduce the likelihood that citizens will be politically active or engaged (Murray, 1997).

It is understandable that elected officials and public managers will prefer indirect taxes to direct taxes. It is also clear that creating a culture of citizen involvement in government will be more successful if taxes are transparent.

Political acceptability

Closely tied to tax transparency is the political acceptability of a tax or tax scheme. The most efficient and effective tax system will not succeed if there is no political or social acceptance of the tax. Of course, any tax system that imposes the rule of law to extract resources from citizens will always have problems with political acceptability, but, removing the rule of law will not work. Politicians understand that processes relying only on voluntary compliance will eventually fail. The result is that elected officials must use compulsion to get citizens to contribute to government, and such systems generate political opposition.

There are, however, steps that public officials can follow to minimize the political opposition to tax system. It is clear that policymakers must be sensitive to the rate of taxation. There is no magic number on what the rate of taxation should be but it seems good policy to not allow the rates of a specific government to exceed by a significant range the tax rates of surrounding local governments or providences. The same can be said about tax bases. Local governments that have tax bases that are quite different from the tax bases of surrounding communities can expect opposition or noncompliance from its citizens. Taxpayer opposition to a tax can overwhelm the tax if the requirements of compliance are confusing, time consuming or expensive. In a similar vein, taxpayers, especially business owners, will oppose taxes that are not consistent over a period of time. Finally, local governments need to be more active in explaining to taxpayers and citizens what they get from the taxes they pay, in terms of the benefits from government-provided goods and services (O'Flaherty, 2005).

Subnational tax systems and horizontal inequity

Local government can be funded by transferring revenue from the centre or even a regional government to the local level. However, as noted in the introduction of this chapter, such an approach is not without risk. Among the risks is the danger that local governments will not carefully use funds from the centre because there are no direct political costs associated with funds which the local governments are not responsible for raising. Local officials may be inclined to spend funds on services or goods for which the benefit associated with the service is less than the cost of providing the service. Naturally making the determination of the benefits and cost of a service is very difficult. But it is almost impossible to expect such an outcome when public officials do not have to worry about the political cost of raising revenue. In such situations the tendency is to overspend.

Returning to the standard argument that local governments should bear a substantial portion of the political, administrative and fiscal responsibility of raising taxes the following reservation about decentralization is observed. Fiscal decentralization is likely to succeed when there are few financially challenged local governments – and this outcome is unlikely. We are unaware of any country where there is not substantial differentiation between the fiscal resources of local governments. The difference may be a result of uneven proximity to deposits of natural resources, access to transportation, commercial markets or tourist attractions. Regardless of the reasons for the fiscal differences the result is that the 'rich' local governments are able to fund basic services and poor local governments find it difficult without increasing tax rates. The poor local governments, if left totally to their own resources, will not be able to provide some of the services that citizens in richer communities take for granted. The resulting inequity in delivered services can be resolved if the central or regional government shares some of its funding. Financial processes could be put in place that account for the needs of the local government, perhaps giving a larger per capita amount of revenue to governments with greater needs, like poorer local governments.

But it is important that the shared funding does not overwhelm the fiscal effort of the local governments. Grants to local governments should not become so large that the poorest local governments are exempted from exerting at least some fiscal effort. Even with a system of grants local governments will be more responsive and responsible if decisions to spend are accompanied by a related need for own source revenue. Conversely, the richest local governments should be able to fund basic services without support from the centre or regional government. Meeting these conditions offers hope of achieving fiscal accountability and fiscal responsibility for local officials (Oates, 2008).

The relative advantages of the property tax

If we assume that local governments have the power to implement a property tax, an income tax or a general sales tax, a logical step is determining which of the tax bases a local government should rely on for its revenues. We offer general observations about the relative strengths and shortcomings of each tax base now. We assume that all taxes in our comparison are administered at the local level and that other local governments also have the option to make similar choices.

Advantages of the property tax

In this section we discuss the specific advantages associated with a property tax. In keeping with the rest of the chapter these advantages are given from the perspective of local governments and are intended to highlight how a property tax would benefit local governments.

Large and dynamic tax base

A standard assertion of tax policy is that a broad based tax (i.e. a tax base that does not exempt large portions of the tax base from taxation) is an important step to avoiding a tax that creates economic distortion. Distortions are created when participants in the base that is taxed try to shift to the non-taxable part of the tax base. They can do this by changing location, consumption patterns or trying to legally change their status to the exempt part of the base. A non-distorting outcome is also more likely if the rates associated with the tax are kept as low as possible, and a broad base facilitates having a low rate.

Among all of the taxes available to local governments the property tax is the one that offers the best opportunity to have a base broad enough that it can affect virtually every individual and business firm within a community. This includes homeowners, renters, commercial and industrial property and building owners, vacant land and agricultural land.

It is also a tax base that reflects the economic activity within a community. When the local economy is growing, the market value of the property tax base will echo the increased economic activity. However, we note that the tax base, or the assessed value, will not imitate the increased value unless a public assessor has the resources (staff and revenue) and the political will to appraise the property at its current value. Assuming that the assessor is willing and able to value property by following the market, the result is a tax base that grows with the economy. It is also a tax that can decline as the economy declines but often does so at a slower rate than the overall economy. From the perspective of local elected officials, who should seek a steady stream of revenue and avoid borrowing funds to balance the budget, this type of tax base is ideal.

Local control and administration

The property tax does allow for local administration of the tax. This includes the processes of maintaining records of ownership, determining the base and determining the taxable value of the base. However, there are several cautions. With respect to the determination of the base and valuing the base we believe that the centre must take a role in legally defining what is in the base and what the accepted value of the base should be. This suggests that the base should be as broad as possible and the value should reflect what the property would sell or trade for in a market transaction. Without legal (definitional) leadership from the centre there is a concern that some local officials will offer legal and extra legal exemptions to certain types of property or property owners. We believe that this is a situation where some aspects of local tax policy must be managed or controlled by the centre. But, aside from definitional leadership, local governments are very capable of day-to-day administration including discovery, valuation, billing and collecting (Bryson and Cornia, 2003).

The local control of the administrative process is a critical step in making the property tax a truly *local tax* and with that distinction there follows the advantages of a tax system that encourages political participation by citizens. It also contributes to government officials who are responsive to the demands of the citizens in the community.

Fewer issues with tax competition and tax harmonization

A steady challenge in emerging and developing countries, as well as developed countries, is the constant pressure by business firms to gain a competitive advantage by avoiding some of the costs of doing business. At one time or another virtually all domestic business firms, farmers or foreign investors try to minimize the cost of their taxes by seeking to have their economic activities granted an exemption from the tax base. If an outright exemption is not agreed to, they will then request to have the taxable value of the base reduced. When all else fails, they will likely ask to be taxed at a reduced rate. The arguments that are made for receiving an exemption or reduction are generally based on the rationale that if a firm or industry faces a lower tax burden it will be inclined to invest more capital and hire more employees. In other words, the rate of economic development in a community will increase. When such exemptions are granted it becomes an input subsidy but as such it does not guarantee that it will provide a sufficient incentive to actually increase the economic strength of the government granting the exemption (Netzer, 2002).

The ease with which tax exemptions are granted varies by tax. Exemptions from taxes based on business income appear to be somewhat easy to gain via accounting processes or legislative design. Transaction based taxes also appear to be susceptible to manipulation, either through record keeping, the sourcing of the sale or direct legislative action.

The result of such actions is the possibility of reducing the tax base without a corresponding increase in economic activity. The ultimate result is that the remaining tax base is so narrow it no longer produces sufficient revenue to meet the revenue needs of local government without resorting to uncomfortably high rates on the remaining tax base.

With adequate and clear policy guidance from the centre the property tax is quite difficult to avoid having to comply with. Consequently, the distortions associated with tax avoidance are lower with the property tax. Unlike the income and sales taxes, where transactions can be sourced to less obvious locations, the property tax base has a physical presence and is thus difficult to obscure. It is also a transparent tax. Public records on valuation and payment make avoidance of the property tax more visible and because it funds local services the relationship between the taxes collected and the services provided make it more difficult to avoid by business firms without suffering some political backlash.

Correspondence between taxes and services

A potential advantage of the property tax is that it is used to fund services that are consumed by local citizens. If there is a perceivable relationship between the level and type of public services available for local citizens and the amount of taxes paid there is an expectation that citizens will be more inclined to voice their support of different levels of services and different levels of taxes.

Disadvantages of the property tax

We have offered a favourable view of the property tax, a view that implies that the problems with the property tax are manageable. Of course, such a view should be tempered by economic and political reality. There are many advantages with the property tax but there are more than a few serious disadvantages. Many of the disadvantages are political in nature, but regardless of the source of the disadvantage they must be included in property tax design considerations. Some of these have already been noted in the previous sections of this chapter.

Exemptions erode the base

We noted earlier that there is always strong political pressure to exempt certain classes and types of property from the property tax base. Many of the exemptions are associated with non-profit organizations, charitable organizations, churches, educational activities and the property of other governments. These exemptions may be justified by the services that such activities provide to citizens, but the erosion to the tax base is often substantial. The size of the exemption is especially noticeable in larger cities where such functions are concentrated. Although data is often hard to acquire the percentage of exempt property in a mid to large sized city may exceed 50 per cent of the property tax base. Naturally, the result is pressure for an increase in the tax rate on existing property and property owners.

Visible tax with annual payments

While the compliance costs associated with the tax property are often modest the property tax does require in most situations that taxpayers make annual payments. The size of the annual payments can easily create political unrest with the property tax. For example, in the USA the property tax has been limited in virtually every state. The result is a reduction in local autonomy but this issue has not been of sufficient concern to reduce the move to limit the tax.

Requires good land and building records

In order for a property tax to succeed it needs to be supported by cadastral records that report either the owner or the occupier of the property, the size and quality of the property and the size and quality of the improvements to the property. In many developing and transitional countries such records do not exist or when they do exist they only exist for limited areas of a city or region. Acquiring and maintaining the land records does require a sizable investment in both capital and human resources. It also requires the development of a legal system to support the collection and updating of the land records. Without a foundation of land records the property tax will not succeed in the long run.

Conclusion

Designing, implementing and administering a tax system is never easy. There are always countless reasons why an individual or firm does not want to pay taxes of any kind. However, there are equally important reasons why individuals and firms benefit from the services provided by taxes. The lists are easy to compile, and start with roads, schools and public safety.

The challenge is to find taxes that create few economic distortions and yet produce sufficient revenue to fund government. We have identified a series of principles that should be used to guide local tax design decisions. We believe that the property tax, while far from perfect, is the clear winner as the tax of choice for local government finance.

References

Anderson, J.E. (2003) *Public Finance: Principles and Policy*. Boston: Houghton Mifflin.

Bryson, P. and Cornia, G. (2003) Moral Hazard in Property Tax Administration: A Comparative Analysis of the Czech and Slovak Republics. *Comparative Economic Studies*, 45(1): 44–62.

Cornia, G., Chapman, J., Facer, R. and Walters, L. (2009) Alternative Models for Financing Transportation: A Case Study of Land Taxation in Utah. *Public Works Management Policy*, 13(3): 202–214.

Fisher, R.C. (2006) *State and Local Public Finance*. 3rd ed. South-Western College Publishing, Mason, Ohio.

Gruber, J. (2005) *Public Finance and Public Policy*. 2nd ed. New York: Worth Publishers.

Haughout, A. and Inman, R.P. (2001) Fiscal Policies in Open Cities with Firms and Households. *Regional Science and Urban Economics*, 31, April: 147–80.

Hillman, A.L. (2003) *Public Finance and Public Policy: Responsibilities and Limitations of Government*. 2nd ed. Cambridge: Cambridge University Press.

Mikesell, J. (2011) *Fiscal Administration*. 8th ed. Boston: Wadsworth Publishing.

Murray, M.N. (1997) Would Tax Evasion and Tax Avoidance Undermine a National Retail Sales Tax? *National Tax Journal*, 50: 167–82.

Musgrave, R.A. and Musgrave, P.B. (1976) *Public Finance in Theory and Practice.* New York: McGraw Hill Book Company.

Nechyba, T.J. (2002) *Land Lines*, 14(1): 2–3.

Nelson, R. and Cornia, G. (2010) State Tax Revenue Growth and Volatility. *Regional Economic Development.* St Louis Federal Reserve, 6(1): 23–58.

Netzer, D. (2002) Local Government Finance and the Economics of Property-Tax Exemption. In: Brody, E. (ed.), *Property-Tax Exemption for Charities: Mapping the Battlefield.* Washington, DC: The Urban Institute Press, 47–80.

Oates, W.E. (1993) Fiscal Decentralization and Economic Development. *National Tax Journal*, 46: 237–43.

Oates, W.E. (1972) *Fiscal Federalism.* New York: Harcourt Brace Jovanovich.

Oates, W.E. (2008) On the Evolution of Fiscal Federalism: Theory and Institutions. *National Tax Journal*, 61: 313–334.

O'Flaherty, B. (2005) *City Economics.* Boston: Harvard University Press.

Pearlman, R.A. (1998) Fresh from the River Styx: the Achilles' Heels of Tax Reform Proposals. *National Tax Journal*, 51: 569–78.

Spilker, B Ayers, B., Robinson, J., Outslay, E., Worsham, R., Barrick, J. and Weaver, C., (2011) *Taxation of Individuals and Business Entities.* 2nd ed. New York: McGrawHill/ Irwin.

Tiebout, C.M. (1956) A Pure Theory of Local Expenditures. *Journal of Political Economy*, 64, October: 416–24.

World Bank. (2001) *Developing Government Bond Markets: A Handbook.* Washington DC: World Bank.

World Bank. (2000) *Entering the 21st Century: World Development Report 1999/2000.* Oxford: Oxford University Press.

Zodrow, G. (2001) The Property Tax as a Capital Tax: A Room with Three Views. *National Tax Journal* 54(1): 139–56.

10

Estimating Property Tax Revenue Potential

Lawrence C. Walters

Introduction

Changes in tax policy inevitably raise questions of fiscal impact. Whether the issue is creating a new tax on land and constructed improvements, reforming the current property tax system or merely fine tuning existing real estate tax practices, sooner or later the question of net revenue effect must be confronted. This is especially the case if there is no viable property tax in place. Decision makers must weigh the political costs of implementing a new tax, and generally will insist on some estimate of expected revenues and often the expected incidence of the proposed tax before making a final decision. Revenue potential is also very useful in assessing the effectiveness of property tax administration as actual revenue is compared to estimates of potential.

This chapter addresses the question of assessing the property tax revenue potential. In the discussion which follows several concepts from the public finance literature on both capacity and effort are reviewed. The strengths and weaknesses of these approaches in the context of a property tax are discussed. Next, a fairly general approach to assessing property tax capacity is developed with cases drawn from OECD member countries and the USA. Finally, a summary of approaches is offered that assumes only minimal data at a more local level.

A Primer on Property Tax: Administration and Policy, First Edition.
Edited by William J. McCluskey, Gary C. Cornia and Lawrence C. Walters.
© 2013 Blackwell Publishing Ltd. Published 2013 by Blackwell Publishing Ltd.

Table 10.1: General government total tax revenue and property taxes as a percentage of GDP

Country Group	Countries include	Taxes on property (% of GDP)			Total taxes (% of GDP)			Taxes on property as % of total taxes		
		Minimum	Mean	Maximum	Minimum	Mean	Maximum	Minimum	Mean	Maximum
Advanced economies										
	Australia, Austria, Belgium, Canada, PR China: Hong Kong, Cyprus, Denmark, Finland, France, Germany, Greece, Iceland, Ireland, Israel, Italy, Japan, Luxembourg, Malta, Netherlands, New Zealand, Norway, Portugal, San Marino, Singapore, Slovenia, Spain, Sweden, Switzerland, United Kingdom, United States	0.30	1.93	4.55	12.72	28.28	57.63	1.65	7.28	22.01
Emerging and developing economies:										
Africa	Rep. of Congo, Lesotho, Mauritius, Morocco, South Africa, Swaziland	0.30	1.02	1.70	6.74	27.66	58.34	1.13	4.53	7.88
Developing Asia	Bhutan, PR China: Macao, Maldives, Thailand, Vietnam	0.04	0.33	0.82	10.73	18.97	24.82	0.37	1.52	3.30
Central and eastern Europe	Bosnia and Herzegovina, Bulgaria, Croatia, Czech Republic, Estonia, Hungary, Latvia, Lithuania, Poland, Romania, Slovak Republic	0.23	0.63	1.50	17.26	22.68	26.68	1.06	2.75	5.74
CIS and Mongolia	Armenia, Belarus, Georgia, Kazakhstan, Moldova, Ukraine	0.24	0.63	1.58	16.37	23.34	35.63	1.06	2.53	4.43
Middle East	Egypt, IR of Iran, Kuwait	0.04	0.19	0.30	0.09	7.75	15.64	1.53	16.65	44.44
Western hemisphere	St Kitts and Nevis, St Vincent and the Grenadines, Argentina, Barbados, Bolivia, Chile, Costa Rica, Honduras, Jamaica, Paraguay, Peru	0.20	1.25	3.00	12.27	21.14	31.57	0.33	5.51	13.50
Totals for emerging and developing economies		0.04	0.78	3.00	0.09	21.57	58.34	0.37	4.54	44.44
Overall average		0.04	1.26	4.55	0.09	24.37	58.34	0.37	5.68	44.44

Adapted from Table W4 in the IMF Government Finance Yearbook (IMF 2008), with calculations by the author. Data is for most recent year available, generally 2005 to 2007. See source for specific countries.

Fiscal capacity and fiscal effort

It is important to recognize at the outset that the question of revenue potential is really a question of income and political will. To take only a minor liberty with a well-worn concept in public finance, land, buildings and equipment do not pay taxes. Only people pay taxes. Thus, the revenue potential from the property tax is a function of aggregate income, the share of that income extracted through other taxes and the willingness of government decision makers to employ the ownership (or use) of land and immovable improvements as a mechanism for allocating part of the overall tax burden.

From this perspective, it is helpful to understand how much of national income is collected through property taxes around the world. Table 10.1 reports property tax collections for selected countries. In advanced economies, taxes on property vary from less than 1 per cent of gross domestic product (GDP) in Austria to over 4 per cent of GDP in the UK and France, with an average rate for the listed countries of just under 2.0 per cent of GDP. Given that total collections for all types of taxes in these countries average close to 30 per cent of GDP, it can be seen that the property tax is typically a relatively small tax, averaging just 7.3 per cent of total taxes. However, it should also be noted that in some countries, the property tax exceeds 16 per cent of total taxes, and is an even more significant revenue source for local governments. In the USA, for example, the property tax represents over 27 per cent of local government general revenues and nearly 73 per cent of local government taxes.

In developing countries, tax rates in general tend to be lower than in advanced economies, and the property tax is no exception. The average property tax collection rate among the developing countries listed in Table 10.1 is about 0.78 per cent of GDP, or less than half the rate in advanced economies, and rates below 0.5 per cent of GDP are not uncommon. Within this set of countries, the property tax represents about 4.5 per cent of total taxes.

Thus, it would appear that a reasonable target range for the property tax is 1–2 per cent of GDP. Higher rates are feasible, but they will in all likelihood require somewhat lower rates for other taxes. Collection rates below 1 per cent of GDP suggest that there is an opportunity to enhance revenues through a strengthening of the property tax. Rates in excess of 3 per cent of GDP are found in some countries, but such rates will require very efficient and effective local tax administration.

Of course, in many countries the property tax is not a national tax, but is administered, collected and retained at a subnational level. Thus the revenue potential or fiscal capacity question is often considered at a more local level. The theory and practice of more local estimates is discussed in the penultimate section.

Fiscal capacity

Revenue potential is a function of fiscal capacity, generally defined as the size of the tax base relative to similar measures in other jurisdictions. Typically fiscal capacity is measured by calculating the average tax rate for a set of jurisdictions, then estimating the revenue collected at the average tax rate. If the expected revenue at the average rate is higher in jurisdiction A than in jurisdiction B, then A is said to have greater capacity than B. For recent examples of approaches that measure relative capacity based on an average rate applied to a known (or knowable) base, see Kincaid (1989); Hy *et al.* (1993); Tannenwald and Cowan (1997); Chernick (1998); Tannenwald (2002); Bucovetsky and Smart (2006). An alternative approach to measuring fiscal capacity is simply to consider the incomes of a given jurisdiction compared to other areas. Approaches that measure capacity based on income or some variation of income include Chernick (1998); Compson (2003); Rodgers (2005). This concept of 'income is the base' is the intuition behind comparisons such as those shown in Table 10.1 and widely reported elsewhere. The preceding section began by noting that the overall tax burden as a percentage of income is an important indicator. Nonetheless, income indicators such as GDP are somewhat problematic when considering the revenue potential of the property tax. A large portion of GDP is employee compensation, most of which translates into personal consumption expenditures. Personal income, also frequently used as a measure of the base, suffers from a similar shortcoming. It is difficult to see how personal consumption is a reasonable indicator of real estate value.

Consequently, neither of these capacity approaches is very satisfactory when applied to the property tax. The average rate approach assumes that the base is known. Often it is precisely the estimation of the base that is at the heart of revenue estimates for the property tax. One of the unique features of an annual property tax is that the taxable value of most properties must be estimated since most properties are not involved in market transactions in any given year. In the aggregate, then, estimating revenue potential or fiscal capacity for the property tax using an average rate approach is circular. While methods based on income are insightful, most measures of personal or household income are not tied to the income derived from land and permanent improvements. To lay a foundation for an alternative approach to measuring revenue potential and property tax capacity, it is helpful to consider how professionals estimate the value of real property.

Estimating aggregate property value

Estimating the value of a given property generally involves applying at least one of three different approaches to value: the cost approach, the comparable sales approach or the income approach (Appraisal Institute, 2001). The cost approach estimates value as the cost of replacing the land and improvements, less any relevant estimates of obsolescence and depreciation. The comparable sales approach estimates value by comparing a property to other similar properties which have sold in the recent past. It is this approach which provides the foundation for the Case–Shiller index, the Davis–Heathcote/Lincoln Institute index (Davis and Heathcote, 2007) and for the Sirmans–Slade indices (Sirmans and

Slade, 2011). These are well thought out and carefully constructed indices, but they are country-specific and focus largely on residential properties where there are rich databases of comparable sales.

What has not been as carefully explored is the possibility of using the third approach to value: the income approach. In this approach, market value is defined as the discounted present value of the free cash flow (CF) that is generated by a property. Free cash flow is an accounting concept representing the cash flow available for distribution to all securities holders, including both equity and debt. It is defined in equation 10.1 as follows:

$$CF = EBIT(1 - r) + Dep - \Delta WC - CE \qquad (10.1)$$

Where

EBIT = Earnings before interest deductions and taxes
Dep = Depreciation
WC = Working capital
CE = Capital expenditures
r = income tax rate

At the aggregate level, the system of national accounts kept by nearly all countries employs very similar concepts as part of the calculation of GDP. The concepts of interest are outlined, for example, in the US National Income and Product Accounts (NIPA), which employ a very similar concept known as the gross operating surplus (GOS). The US Bureau of Economic Affairs defines GOS as follows:

> Net operating surplus, which is a profits-like measure that shows the incomes earned by private enterprises from current production. It is calculated by deducting the costs of compensation of employees, taxes on production and imports less subsidies, and consumption of fixed capital from value added, but before taking account of financing costs (such as net interest) and other payments (such as business current transfer payments). Net operating surplus plus consumption of fixed capital is equal to gross operating surplus. (www.bea.gov/glossary)

Similarly, OECD National Accounts defines GOS as:

> Gross operating surplus is the surplus generated by operating activities after the labour factor input has been recompensed. It can be calculated from the value added at factor cost less the personnel costs. It is the balance available to the unit which allows it to recompense the providers of own funds and debt, to pay taxes and eventually to finance all or a part of its investment. (stats.oecd.org/glossary)

Thus, GOS differs from free cash flow in the treatment of income taxes (included in free cash flow, but not in GOS), changes in working capital and the treatment

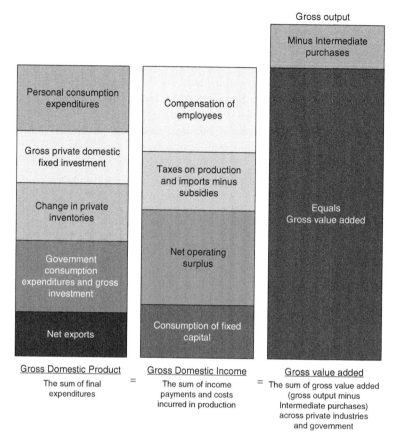

Figure 10.1:   Relationship between GOS and GDP concepts
Source: Fox et al. *(2010) and US Bureau of Economic Analysis*

of capital expenditures and depreciation. Figure 10.1 provides a graphic definition of net and gross operating surplus and compares the concept to other terms
used in US NIPA accounting. In the figure it can be seen that the familiar GDP
metric is equivalent to adding GOS, taxes on production and imports (less subsidies) and employee compensation. What this suggests is that GDP less employee
compensation is a pre-tax 'profits-like measure' not unlike the basis of the income
approach as applied in the unit method to estimating the 'going concern' value
of large utilities, railroads and other enterprises.

   In the unit method to value, real property is considered an essential part of the
ongoing operations of an enterprise (Appraisal Institute, 2001). The determination
of value begins therefore with valuing the entire enterprise as a going concern.
While arriving at the value of real property requires a number of adjustments for
intangible value, tangible personal property etc., the basis of value in the income
approach as employed in the unit method is the free cash flow generated by the
enterprise. The argument made here is that GOS can be seen in a similar light,
as the cash flow generated by a jurisdiction viewed as a going concern. Thus

GOS can be used to estimate fiscal capacity and to compare that capacity across jurisdictions. Of course, in the income approach, the cash flow over a period of time is discounted to obtain a net present value. However, if the object is to simply compare capacity across jurisdictions, it is not necessary to discount a time series, since common assumptions about time and discount rate would apply to all the values identified. To see how the approach can be used, the next section develops a GOS-based measure of property tax capacity for a selection of OECD countries.

Property tax capacity and effort in the OECD

The financial data used for OECD countries in this example all come from *OECD.StatExtracts* (stats.oecd.org). GOS (plus taxes on production and imports less subsidies) is estimated by subtracting employee compensation from GDP for each country (see Figure 10.1). Because the selected OECD countries vary greatly in overall size, total GOS is divided by land area to yield a measure of income (other than employee compensation) per unit of land area (km^2) for the years shown in Table 10.2. Table 10.3 presents the same information in a standardized form by dividing GOS/km^2 for each country by the overall average of the 26 countries included in this analysis. Thus, a value 1.0 in Table 10.3 would indicate that the country's GOS/km^2 is equal to the 26-country average. Table 10.3 also orders the countries by their 2008 rank based on this ratio.

Table 10.3 indicates that three of the smallest countries in Europe (Luxembourg, the Netherlands and Belgium) appear to have the highest property tax capacity, while much larger countries like Canada and Australia have the lowest apparent capacity. This is not surprising since property values per unit of land area tend to be much higher in developed urban areas. Canada and Australia pull the overall country average down quite substantially because of their substantial tracts of largely undeveloped land area. This issue will be treated in more detail in the next section. More interesting in Table 10.3 is the comparison of countries of approximately the same geographic size. Denmark, the Netherlands and Switzerland, for example, are all roughly the same size, yet the Netherlands far outstrips the other two countries in property tax capacity. The GOS per km^2 in the Netherlands in 2008 was nearly four times that of Denmark and nearly 2½ times that in Switzerland. Another interesting comparison is between Austria and the Czech Republic, again two countries of roughly the same size. Rather surprisingly, the Czech Republic appears to have somewhat higher property tax capacity (3.81 times the country average) than does Austria at 3.53 times the country average.

These differences in fiscal capacity have a noticeable impact on the property tax effort of these countries. Table 10.4 reports the total property tax receipts as a percentage of GOS. Overall, the average for these 26 countries has been fairly stable at about 5.6 per cent of GOS for the period covered by the table. However, the variation between countries is quite substantial.

Table 10.2:   Gross operating surplus per km² (US dollars, current prices, PPPs)

Country	1995	2000	2005	2008
Australia	18,161	24,933	36,304	47,183
Austria	1,038,129	1,373,733	1,638,141	1,850,804
Belgium	3,767,930	4,580,029	5,665,845	6,388,766
Canada	29,415	38,180	49,949	57,073
Czech Republic	1,058,023	1,231,135	1,632,862	1,998,912
Denmark	1,151,330	1,512,692	1,789,730	1,937,581
Finland	146,946	211,869	251,590	296,744
France	1,030,519	1,344,627	1,591,038	1,812,219
Germany	2,553,753	2,996,087	3,697,364	4,131,508
Greece	666,792	864,123	1,167,256	1,435,527
Hungary	623,190	844,499	1,099,264	1,284,832
Ireland	399,509	781,674	1,151,100	1,266,364
Italy	2,454,046	3,019,113	3,338,116	3,780,986
Japan	3,534,267	4,092,685	5,137,504	5,889,929
Korea	1,900,591	2,932,438	4,002,988	5,268,876
Luxembourg	3,988,493	6,132,073	8,650,609	11,920,457
Netherlands	3,128,135	4,888,614	6,239,039	7,336,412
Norway	163,801	291,434	400,565	528,705
Poland	452,532	650,186	939,580	1,169,371
Portugal	749,137	997,337	1,276,416	1,446,160
Slovak Republic	607,557	773,333	1,138,792	1,580,302
Spain	645,324	906,384	1,276,677	1,562,695
Sweden	234,838	289,100	348,423	398,301
Switzerland	1,680,571	2,057,360	2,317,517	3,031,458
United Kingdom	1,715,863	2,290,906	3,160,822	3,566,605
United States	338,473	438,538	616,649	707,076
Overall Average	268,827	344,287	452,619	524,308

Information sourced from OECD, with calculations by the author.

Table 10.5 reports the standardized property tax effort for each country as the ratio of property tax collected (per km²) to the 26-country average. If Table 10.4 is reporting what are essentially property tax rates, Table 10.5 reports standardized rates in relation to the 26-country average. Thus, the value of 165.5 per cent for the UK in 1995 indicates that effective property tax rates in the UK in 1995 were 65.5 per cent higher than the 26-country average that year. And again it is perhaps most interesting to compare the effort of similar countries. In Table 10.3, Spain, Portugal and Greece, while differing in overall size, exhibit essentially

Table 10.3:   Property tax capacity: GOS/km^2 divided by OECD (sample) average GOS/km^2

Country	1995	2000	2005	2008	2008 Rank
Luxembourg	14.84	17.81	19.11	22.74	1
Netherlands	11.64	14.20	13.78	13.99	2
Belgium	14.02	13.30	12.52	12.19	3
Japan	13.15	11.89	11.35	11.23	4
Korea	7.07	8.52	8.84	10.05	5
Germany	9.50	8.70	8.17	7.88	6
Italy	9.13	8.77	7.38	7.21	7
United Kingdom	6.38	6.65	6.98	6.80	8
Switzerland	6.25	5.98	5.12	5.78	9
Czech Republic	3.94	3.58	3.61	3.81	10
Denmark	4.28	4.39	3.95	3.70	11
Austria	3.86	3.99	3.62	3.53	12
France	3.83	3.91	3.52	3.46	13
Slovak Republic	2.26	2.25	2.52	3.01	14
Spain	2.40	2.63	2.82	2.98	15
Portugal	2.79	2.90	2.82	2.76	16
Greece	2.48	2.51	2.58	2.74	17
Hungary	2.32	2.45	2.43	2.45	18
Ireland	1.49	2.27	2.54	2.42	19
Poland	1.68	1.89	2.08	2.23	20
United States	1.26	1.27	1.36	1.35	21
Norway	0.61	0.85	0.88	1.01	22
Sweden	0.87	0.84	0.77	0.76	23
Finland	0.55	0.62	0.56	0.57	24
Canada	0.11	0.11	0.11	0.11	25
Australia	0.07	0.07	0.08	0.09	26

Information sourced from OECD, with calculations by the author.

similar property tax capacity. Table 10.5 indicates that the tax effort exhibited in Greece and Portugal is similar and substantially below the 26-country average. Spain on the other hand was slightly above the average level of effort in 2008 and appears to have experienced a substantial increase in effort over the 1995 to 2008 period covered by the table.

These tax effort calculations have significant revenue implications. If Greece for example, were to increase its property tax effort to the 26-country average, the additional revenue would be approximately US$6 billion per year. While this would not solve all of Greece's financial difficulties, it would help. It is also worth noting that the total tax burden in Greece would still be below the 28 per cent

Table 10.4: Property taxes as a percentage of GOS (US dollars, current prices, PPPs)

Country	1995	2000	2005	2008
Australia	6.9%	7.2%	6.4%	6.1%
Austria	1.3%	1.2%	1.1%	1.2%
Belgium	2.9%	3.8%	4.1%	4.4%
Canada	8.6%	7.8%	7.6%	7.8%
Czech Republic	0.8%	0.8%	0.7%	0.7%
Denmark	4.1%	3.8%	4.4%	4.5%
Finland	2.0%	2.1%	2.3%	2.1%
France	5.2%	5.5%	6.3%	6.4%
Germany	2.1%	1.7%	1.7%	1.7%
Greece	2.1%	3.7%	2.4%	2.3%
Hungary	0.8%	1.1%	1.4%	1.4%
Ireland	3.4%	3.4%	4.7%	5.9%
Italy	3.7%	3.1%	3.3%	3.5%
Japan	6.9%	6.0%	5.3%	5.0%
Korea	8.9%	7.7%	7.8%	8.4%
Luxembourg	4.0%	6.1%	4.6%	4.5%
Netherlands	4.4%	4.9%	4.5%	4.0%
Norway	2.2%	1.7%	1.9%	2.0%
Poland	2.1%	2.3%	2.4%	2.3%
Portugal	1.8%	2.2%	2.2%	2.3%
Slovak Republic	0%	1.0%	0.8%	0.7%
Spain	3.4%	4.1%	5.7%	5.9%
Sweden	2.3%	3.3%	2.7%	2.7%
Switzerland	6.1%	7.5%	6.5%	6.2%
United Kingdom	9.3%	11.6%	11.0%	11.3%
United States	6.8%	6.8%	6.3%	6.4%
OECD total	5.6%	5.6%	5.5%	5.6%

Information sourced from OECD, with calculations by the author.

average for advanced economies. It should be observed that as part of their broader reform effort in 2011, Greece did pass legislation increasing the property tax and changing the method of collection.

Adjusting for undeveloped land

As noted in the discussion of Table 10.3, including total land area in the calculation of capacity is potentially distorting if the jurisdictions involved have

Table 10.5: Property tax effort: Property tax/GOS divided by OECD (sample) average property tax/GOS

Country	1995	2000	2005	2008	2008 Rank
United Kingdom	165.5%	205.0%	199.1%	203.6%	1
Korea	157.1%	136.9%	141.7%	151.7%	2
Canada	152.4%	137.8%	137.7%	140.0%	3
United States	120.8%	121.3%	114.3%	114.1%	4
France	92.8%	96.9%	113.3%	114.0%	5
Switzerland	108.8%	132.3%	116.9%	111.4%	6
Australia	121.9%	127.9%	114.9%	109.6%	7
Ireland	59.6%	60.8%	85.8%	106.7%	8
Spain	60.6%	73.0%	102.2%	105.4%	9
Japan	122.1%	105.5%	95.5%	89.4%	10
Denmark	72.8%	67.0%	79.8%	81.1%	11
Luxembourg	71.1%	108.3%	82.3%	80.1%	12
Belgium	51.6%	67.4%	74.5%	78.5%	13
Netherlands	78.2%	85.9%	81.3%	72.3%	14
Italy	65.1%	55.6%	60.5%	62.8%	15
Sweden	41.6%	59.0%	48.7%	48.6%	16
Greece	36.9%	65.8%	42.6%	41.7%	17
Portugal	31.7%	38.9%	40.0%	41.1%	18
Poland	36.9%	40.6%	42.7%	40.7%	19
Finland	34.7%	37.8%	41.1%	37.9%	20
Norway	39.5%	29.9%	34.0%	35.0%	21
Germany	36.8%	30.0%	30.4%	30.9%	22
Hungary	14.4%	18.6%	25.7%	24.8%	23
Austria	23.5%	20.6%	20.4%	21.4%	24
Czech Republic	14.6%	14.0%	12.8%	12.8%	25
Slovak Republic	0.0%	17.2%	14.1%	12.3%	26

Information sourced from OECD, with calculations by the author.

substantial areas of undeveloped land, as is the case in Australia, Canada and the USA. In such cases, a better approach is to focus on the developed land. To see this more clearly, this section discusses the US case in greater detail.

The USA has a total land area of over 9.1 million km^2, but less than five per cent of that land area is developed. About 40 per cent of US land area is actively devoted to agriculture, and approximately 30 per cent is owned by the federal government. The balance is divided between tribal areas held by indigenous groups, state-owned land and land which is privately owned but largely idle. In western states particularly the percentage of federally-owned (and therefore tax exempt) land can be very high. Nevada is the extreme example with over 90 per cent

Table 10.6: US state property tax capacity using total and developed land area*

State	Based on total land			Based on developed land only		
	1997	2002	2007	1997	2002	2007
Alabama	0.77	0.79	0.78	0.45	0.44	0.43
Arizona	0.50	0.55	0.60	1.07	1.05	1.06
Arkansas	0.53	0.49	0.47	0.47	0.44	0.43
California	3.08	3.16	3.32	2.32	2.49	2.64
Colorado	0.55	0.63	0.61	0.94	1.08	1.03
Connecticut	12.65	11.92	12.37	1.66	1.67	1.79
Delaware	10.59	10.53	11.28	2.51	2.41	2.47
District of Columbia	197.93	227.90	244.90	10.53	14.71	16.00
Florida	2.92	3.18	3.41	0.93	1.02	1.04
Georgia	1.80	1.89	1.72	0.73	0.76	0.67
Idaho	0.14	0.15	0.17	0.39	0.45	0.50
Illinois	3.18	2.92	2.80	1.49	1.48	1.45
Indiana	2.00	2.02	2.01	0.85	0.91	0.93
Iowa	0.72	0.66	0.73	0.59	0.59	0.68
Kansas	0.37	0.36	0.37	0.40	0.42	0.45
Kentucky	1.16	0.99	0.89	0.70	0.59	0.53
Louisiana	1.29	1.18	1.59	0.91	0.86	1.16
Maine	0.36	0.39	0.36	0.41	0.44	0.41
Maryland	5.97	6.46	6.55	1.16	1.31	1.34
Massachusetts	11.90	11.50	10.19	1.56	1.61	1.46
Michigan	1.98	1.96	1.56	0.79	0.81	0.66
Minnesota	0.77	0.78	0.77	0.74	0.79	0.80
Mississippi	0.51	0.46	0.51	0.42	0.38	0.41
Missouri	0.99	0.90	0.77	0.68	0.66	0.57
Montana	0.06	0.05	0.06	0.23	0.24	0.28
Nebraska	0.30	0.26	0.29	0.54	0.53	0.60
Nevada	0.23	0.26	0.33	1.97	1.73	1.98
New Hampshire	1.81	1.69	1.47	0.70	0.69	0.60
New Jersey	17.53	16.87	15.60	2.03	2.05	1.95
New Mexico	0.20	0.15	0.16	0.64	0.45	0.47
New York	6.10	5.97	5.51	2.20	2.27	2.16
North Carolina	2.14	2.36	2.24	0.74	0.77	0.72
North Dakota	0.10	0.10	0.11	0.18	0.22	0.25
Ohio	3.45	3.22	2.73	3.20	0.98	0.85
Oklahoma	0.49	0.48	0.54	0.50	0.51	0.57
Oregon	0.45	0.42	0.50	0.90	0.91	1.09

Table 10.6: (Cont'd)

State	Based on total land			Based on developed land only		
	1997	2002	2007	1997	2002	2007
Pennsylvania	3.23	3.13	2.85	0.96	0.99	0.92
Rhode Island	10.82	12.57	11.39	1.42	1.73	1.60
South Carolina	1.33	1.37	1.19	0.49	0.50	0.42
South Dakota	0.13	0.16	0.15	0.28	0.39	0.37
Tennessee	1.58	1.61	1.43	0.65	0.70	0.61
Texas	1.07	1.06	1.26	1.08	1.06	1.22
Utah	0.28	0.31	0.34	1.01	1.08	1.19
Vermont	0.64	0.63	0.54	0.45	0.46	0.40
Virginia	2.06	2.37	2.24	0.81	0.95	0.90
Washington	1.10	1.13	1.19	0.88	0.94	1.01
West Virginia	0.62	0.56	0.53	0.40	0.36	0.35
Wisconsin	1.12	1.09	1.04	0.66	0.68	0.65
Wyoming	0.07	0.08	0.11	0.30	0.34	0.49

Alaska and Hawaii are excluded
[a] *Information sourced from the US Bureau of Economic Analysis, USDA Economic Research Service, with calculations by the author.*

of land controlled by the national government, but in Arizona, Utah and other western states the percentage is over 50 per cent. While these lands do see some economic activity, these states also tend to be very urbanized with the vast majority of population and economic activity concentrated in developed cities and towns. Consequently, including all land in the calculation of property tax capacity, particularly in western states, greatly underestimates the actual relative tax capacity of these states, and potentially overstates the capacity in areas with a higher percentage of developed land.

This point is made more clearly in Table 10.6 which reports the calculation of tax capacity of US states based both on total land area and developed land area only. As in Table 10.3, a value of 1.0 indicates that the tax capacity (GOS/km^2) in a state is equal to the average national GOS/km^2. The table columns headed 'Based on total land' report the capacity measure using total land area. Looking at the first two states listed, Alabama (2007 = 0.78) appears to be well ahead of Arizona (2007 = 0.60) in property tax capacity. Further down Table 10.6 the relatively urban states in the east (Connecticut, Delaware, Massachusetts, New Jersey and Rhode Island) all appear to have more than 10 times the national capacity average. Their apparently high averages are a result of the national average being so low because of the inclusion of federal and other largely idle land. Compared to Utah or Wyoming, the eastern states indeed appear to have very high capacity.

Table 10.7:   US state property tax effort

State	1997	2002	2007	2007 Rank
Vermont	207.8%	180.2%	228.6%	1
New Hampshire	191.4%	182.5%	202.0%	2
New Jersey	169.1%	164.8%	171.1%	3
Maine	232.2%	202.9%	168.2%	4
Rhode Island	186.1%	143.3%	152.4%	5
Michigan	117.3%	112.9%	150.2%	6
Wisconsin	147.0%	139.7%	136.7%	7
Florida	134.2%	117.9%	134.2%	8
New York	143.0%	121.4%	133.9%	9
Massachusetts	121.4%	123.9%	127.0%	10
Connecticut	136.5%	132.4%	123.2%	11
Illinois	124.6%	124.5%	120.1%	12
South Carolina	89.0%	95.8%	109.6%	13
Ohio	101.0%	103.1%	109.1%	14
Montana	166.9%	136.1%	107.0%	15
Pennsylvania	106.4%	99.1%	106.9%	16
Kansas	117.9%	110.7%	105.7%	17
Virginia	110.1%	91.3%	103.6%	18
Wyoming	109.3%	119.1%	103.5%	19
Nebraska	117.6%	110.4%	98.0%	20
Texas	99.7%	112.9%	94.8%	21
Maryland	113.1%	110.0%	94.1%	22
District of Columbia	98.8%	73.6%	92.7%	23
Minnesota	118.5%	106.9%	91.8%	24
Missouri	70.5%	79.8%	90.3%	25
Georgia	81.4%	77.9%	87.8%	26
California	82.5%	78.4%	86.0%	27
Washington	122.1%	98.3%	85.2%	28
Mississippi	89.8%	97.7%	85.0%	29
Arizona	89.0%	86.5%	84.0%	30
West Virginia	87.9%	86.4%	81.7%	31
Colorado	88.6%	81.6%	81.5%	32
Iowa	98.2%	99.2%	81.5%	33
North Dakota	120.0%	95.2%	81.4%	34
Indiana	121.2%	105.4%	78.3%	35
Oregon	100.8%	98.3%	75.0%	36
Nevada	68.0%	74.7%	71.6%	37
Idaho	103.7%	95.5%	70.6%	38

Table 10.7:   (Cont'd)

State	1997	2002	2007	2007 Rank
Tennessee	61.3%	66.1%	70.0%	39
Kentucky	56.6%	64.7%	67.0%	40
South Dakota	91.7%	68.8%	66.7%	41
Utah	80.4%	72.1%	66.3%	42
North Carolina	62.5%	60.1%	61.2%	43
Arkansas	50.7%	50.4%	50.2%	44
New Mexico	36.5%	53.5%	48.9%	45
Alabama	45.5%	46.9%	48.2%	46
Oklahoma	55.9%	57.5%	47.3%	47
Louisiana	44.0%	48.5%	34.8%	48
Delaware	28.2%	24.8%	23.7%	49

Information sourced from the US Bureau of Economic Analysis, US Census Bureau, with calculations by the author.

However, if the calculation is based on land which is more likely to be taxable and which generates the bulk of economic activity, the picture becomes much more consistent across the country. The columns in Table 10.6 headed 'Based on developed land only' report the calculation of relative capacity using only the developed land area in each state. Alabama now appears to be substantially below the national average capacity, while Arizona is slightly above. The eastern states mentioned above still appear to have greater capacity than the national average, but now the levels are 1.5 to 2.5 times the national level rather than 10 to 15 times higher. The impact of economic development and growth is also more apparent with this approach, as the number of states above the national norm increases slightly each year.

Calculating property tax effort is not sensitive to the land inventory used since only taxes collected and GOS are required for each state. Table 10.7 reports the calculation of property tax effort for each state (except Alaska and Hawaii), and the states are ranked by their 2007 effort level. Thus, Vermont exhibited the highest property tax effort in 2007 at over twice the national average effective tax rate. At the other extreme, Delaware had the lowest effort level at less than one-quarter the national rate.

The potential revenue implications of these figures are striking. In Utah, for example, 60 per cent of property tax revenue is dedicated to public education, schools are growing rapidly and funding levels are comparatively low. In 2007, Utah's tax effort by the measures developed here was about one-third below the national average rate. If the effort level were raised to the national average, the result would be an additional $1 billion per year or about $600 million for education each year.

In many developing countries and for many communities, however, the issue of revenue estimation is much more local. The next section takes up the question of revenue potential at the local level, particularly when data and resources are scarce.

Estimating local revenue potential

Estimating revenue potential for a given community is challenging, especially if the information currently available is limited. The case of Hargeisa, Somaliland is helpful in illustrating alternative approaches and demonstrating that even with limited resources measures can be developed (UN-Habitat, 2006; UN-Habitat, 2011). In 2001, development indicators placed Somaliland among the poorest and least developed regions in the world, with GDP per capita estimated to be US$200. After years of conflict, the damage to the physical and institutional infrastructure meant that the land registration system was largely destroyed.

Hargeisa is the capital of Somaliland with a population of about 396,000 in 2005. With the assistance of UN-Habitat, Hargeisa undertook a property survey intended to produce an improved fiscal cadastre. Beginning with satellite images of the city, staff produced digitized maps showing all buildings, roads, rivers, airports etc. Field teams then went throughout the city to collect and record property attributes. The amount of data collected was kept to a minimum:

- physical characteristics of the property (dimensions, use, building materials and access to infrastructure)
- occupier
- number of residents living in the building.

The entire process took about eight months (July 2004 to March 2005) and the end result was that the fiscal cadastre increased from 15,850 properties to 59,000 properties. Of course, before undertaking such an effort, community leaders would likely seek some estimate of what the revenue potential would be in order to justify the effort of building the cadastre and implementing the tax.

Three fairly straightforward methods can be employed to make rough estimates of potential revenue. The first method is based on the strong correlation between population and property values. If the national GOS per capita is known and a reasonable estimate of the local population is available, an estimate of revenue potential can be obtained by multiplying GOS per capita by the population. Absent a reasonable estimate of GOS, GDP can be used though it is likely to be somewhat less accurate. An estimate of 1 per cent of GDP is a reasonable target. For example, in the Hargeisa case, national GDP per capita was known to be US$200. As a by-product of the land survey, city population was determined to be 396,000. Multiplying these two figures and taking 1 per cent of the result yields an estimated revenue potential of US$792,000 per year. A number of national and international organizations produce population estimates for urban areas even if current survey data is not available.

A second approach is to divide the city population by the average number of people living in a household to obtain an estimate of the number of households in a city. To continue the example from Hargeisa, suppose that the average household size is estimated to be seven persons. Then the estimated number of dwellings in the city would be the city population divided by seven or 396,000/7 = 56,571 dwellings. If the expected average tax per household is US$15, then the revenue potential would be 56,571 multiplied by US$15, or US$849,000.

An estimate of the number of structures can also be obtained either from reasonably current satellite images or from a physical survey of a sample of properties. The survey approach would work by dividing the city into districts of approximately equal land area. The survey team would then randomly select some proportion of the districts. Each district selected would then be visited and a count of structures completed. The assumption is that the randomly selected districts are representative of the larger city and that the counts found in the sample could be applied to other districts. Thus, if surveying a random sample of 10 per cent of the districts yields a count of 5,000 structures, then the number of structures in the entire city would be estimated at 5,000 divided by 10 per cent, or 50,000 structures. Again, if the estimated tax per structure is US$15, then the estimated revenue potential would be US$750,000.

Another approach to obtaining an estimate of the number of structures in a city is to request from local utility companies a count of the number of customers or meters the company has on their records. This count of customers or meters can then be multiplied by the expected average tax bill per parcel, as above, to obtain an estimate of revenue potential. The best approach would apply several of these methods and compare the results. In the example used here, three estimates were generated:

- US$792,000, based on GDP per capita and estimated population
- US$849,000, based on estimated population and the number of persons per household
- US$750,000, based on a survey of sample areas within the city.

These values could be averaged to obtain an estimate of US$797,000, or a more conservative approach could be taken that takes the lowest reasonable estimate. The final estimate will depend heavily on the amount of confidence placed in the underlying data. The important consideration is reasonable consistency in the estimates. Any one value that is extremely different from the others should probably be discarded. In this example, all values are between US$750,000 and US$850,000, so the final estimate would also fall within that range.

It should be remembered, however, that these are crude estimates, intended only to give decision makers a rough estimate of the revenue potential from a property tax during initial discussions of strategies, alternatives and potential.

More refined estimates can be generated as the system design emerges. And actual revenues will depend on how well implemented and managed the property tax system is.

Conclusion

This chapter has briefly reviewed concepts of fiscal capacity and fiscal effort in an attempt to estimate the revenue potential of the property tax in several settings. It was noted that past conceptual approaches fall short in the context of the property tax either because they assume the availability of the very information that is sought (the base for the property tax), or because the income concepts are too distant from real property. A novel approach was introduced using the national income accounting concept of gross operating surplus and the income approach to property valuation. The approach was implemented for 26 OECD countries and for the states in the USA. A summary of more simplified approaches was also presented which can be implemented at a more local level.

Whatever the approach to estimating potential revenue or revenue enhancements, it is helpful to keep in mind that a well-administered property tax is likely to yield 1–2 per cent of GDP. And it should be borne in mind that administration is critical in achieving revenue levels at such levels. It is one thing to estimate capacity, and quite another to fully tap that capacity.

References

Appraisal Institute (2001) *The Appraisal of Real Estate*. 12th Edition, Chicago, IL: The Appraisal Institute.

Bucovetsky, S. and Smart, M. (2006) The Efficiency Consequences of Local Revenue Equalization: Tax Competition and Tax Distortions. *Journal of Public Economic Theory*, 8(1): 119–144.

Chernick, H. (1998) Fiscal Capacity in New York: The City versus the Region. *National Tax Journal*, 51(3): 531–540.

Compson, M.L. (2003) Historical Estimates of Total Taxable Resources for US states, 1981–2000. *Publius – the Journal of Federalism*, 33(2): 55–72.

Davis, M.A. and Heathcote, J. (2007) The Price and Quantity of Residential Land in the USA. *Journal of Monetary Economics*, 54(8): 2595–2620.

Fox, D.R. and McCulla, S.H. (2010) *Concepts and Methods of the US National Income and Product Accounts*. Washington DC: US Bureau of Economic Analysis.

Hy, R.J., Boland, C., Hopper, R. and Sims, R. (1993) Measuring Revenue Capacity and Effort of County Governments: A Case Study of Arkansas. *Public Administration Review*, 53(3): 220–227.

IMF (2008) *Government Finance Statistics: Yearbook 2008*. Washington, DC: International Monetary Fund.

Kincaid, J. (1989) Fiscal Capacity and Tax Effort of the American States: Trends and Issues. *Public Budgeting and Finance*, 9(3): 4–26.

Rodgers, H. R. (2005) Saints, Stalwarts, and Slackers: State Financial Contributions to Welfare Reform. *Policy Studies Journal*, 33(4): 497–508.

Sirmans, C. F. and Slade, B.A. (2011) National Transaction-Based Land Price Indices. The *Journal of Real Estate Finance and Economics*: 1–17.

Tannenwald, R. (2002) Interstate Fiscal Disparity in 1997. *New England Economic Review*, 3: 17–33.

Tannenwald, R. and Cowan, J. (1997) Fiscal Capacity, Fiscal Need, and Fiscal Comfort Among US States: New Evidence. *Publius – the Journal of Federalism*, 27(3): 113–125.

UN-Habitat (2006) *Better Information for Better Cities: The Case of Hargeiza*. Nairobi, Kenya: United Nations Human Settlements Programme.

UN-Habitat (2011) *Housing the Urban Poor in African Cities: Quick Guide 3*. Nairobi, Kenya: United Nations Human Settlements Programme.

11

Taxing Public Leasehold Land in Transition Countries

Yu-Hung Hong

Introduction

Tremendous efforts have been put into reintroducing property taxation to countries in transition (Bird and Slack, 2004, 2006; Malme and Youngman, 2001; Šulija and Šulija, 2005). Aside from other personal and immobile property taxes collected at the time of transfer, policymakers and analysts are particularly attentive to the levy on the possession of real estate. In most cases, an *ad valorem* property tax that is applied to both land and buildings is treated as the standard model. Although creating such a property tax system seems proper in transition countries where fiscal decentralization and restitution of private property are progressing rapidly, its implementation is not without problems. Challenges abound. At a conference co-organized by the Lincoln Institute of Land Policy and the State Council Research Development Center of China in 2005, Professor Roy Bahl highlighted seven challenging issues for the proposed real property tax reform in China. They include: (1) restructuring intergovernmental fiscal relations, (2) assimilating the proposed property tax into the existing fiscal system, (3) revising public accounting procedures and regulations, (4) coordinating cooperation among different public agencies for information exchanges, (5) nurturing a positive public attitude toward property taxation, (6) assessing impacts of property taxation on land resources allocation and utilization and (7) designing a property tax system that is in accord with the existing land tenure arrangements. The final point is the subject of this chapter.

A Primer on Property Tax: Administration and Policy, First Edition.
Edited by William J. McCluskey, Gary C. Cornia and Lawrence C. Walters.
© 2013 Blackwell Publishing Ltd. Published 2013 by Blackwell Publishing Ltd.

Public leasehold is a common land tenure arrangement in many transforming economies in which the state owns a majority of the land and assigns its development and use rights to private entities by long-term leases. Taxing land under public leasehold systems is an important, though often neglected, issue related to real property taxation in transition countries. The focus is on three questions:

1. To what extent would the idea of imposing a 'property tax' on land that is not private property be acceptable to would-be taxpayers in transition economies?
2. Under public leasehold systems where interests in land are shared between a government and the lessee, who will shoulder the final economic burden of the property tax?
3. When a uniform tax is imposed on both land and buildings, to what extent would the varied durations of land leases complicate the process of valuing property for tax purposes?

Answers to these questions can affect the legitimacy and operation of a property tax system, thereby influencing the level of compliance and, subsequently, administrative costs. Before discussing each of these questions in detail, which forms the three major sections of this chapter, it will be useful to provide a brief description of public leasehold systems at the outset.

Public leasehold systems

The idea of leasing public land is founded on the notion that property in land can be considered a bundle of rights (often referred to as a 'bundle of sticks' in the legal literature). Each element of the bundle can be assigned to and controlled by different parties. Using this logic, we can treat public leasehold as a system that allows government and private parties to negotiate the delineation and assignment of multiple land rights through contractual arrangements. For instance, a government that is the owner of public land can retain the land title and lease the right to use, develop, transfer, inherit and benefit from land to private entities. These lessees can enjoy the assigned land rights for a specified time and as stipulated in their land contracts.

In many transition countries where land is largely state-owned, public officials have been experimenting with leasing, so as to minimize the political tension generated by land reforms. They hope that leasing public land could be a means to meet both the communists' desire to uphold public land ownership and the reformists' demand for increasing private property rights in their economies. In theory, public leasehold does appear to be a compromise, because the system allows the state to remain as the landowner and lease the development and use rights of land to private individuals.

In practice, whether the government or private landholders have the real control over land will depends on how lease conditions are constructed. Lease conditions specify what the lessee can and cannot do with the leased land rights;

how much money and at what interval (or on which occasions) the lessee must pay the lessor to maintain the land rights; and what penalties the lessor will impose on the lessee if the latter breaches the land contract. These lease conditions, which are designed according to a set of constitutional rules and legislation, are the basic guidelines for delineating property relations between a government lessor and the lessee.

Lease conditions are formulated in diverse ways because legal and political institutions are seldom the same among nations. In countries where public land leasing is practiced, lease terms vary from 50 to 99 years (Hong and Bourassa, 2003). Most systems allow lessees to renew their land contracts for at least another term if there is a term limit. One important lease condition that is particularly relevant to the discussion here and differs among varied systems is the lease payment method. There are generally two kinds of lease payment – 'land premium' (sometimes referred to as a leasing fee) and annual land rent. The land premium is a lump sum payment that lessees pay to the government to obtain, modify or extend their land rights. Analysts refer to a leasehold system as a **premium system** if a government relies primarily on lump sum payments to collect leasehold charges. Examples include the public leasehold systems in Canberra (the capital of Australia), China and Israel.

Not all land leasing schemes are structured as a premium system, however. For instance, the Finnish, Polish, Russian, Swedish and Ukrainian systems, just to name a few, require lessees to pay mainly an annual land rent. Analysts call these **land rent systems**. In the Netherlands, municipalities also allow lessees to pay at the beginning of the lease term all yearly rental payments in a lump sum discounted to their present values. This option, if available, blurs the distinction between the premium and land rent systems (Needham, 2003).

One point should be emphasized here: not all public leasehold systems collect the lease premium and land rent from users at market value. Only the more developed systems may be able to do that. In some transition economies, payments for using public land are either low or even nil. Under these situations, property taxation may be designed to serve the purposes of collecting leasehold charges from land users and raising funds for financing public goods. Although it is convenient to combine all land related levies into one payment, this may lead to the problem of confusing land tax with rent – an important issue that I will discuss later. The fundamental issue is: should the lessee who has already paid the government leasehold charges either in the form of land premium or an annual land rent be liable for additional tax payments?

Land ownership and taxation

In the western world, the conceptualization of real property taxation is usually founded on the premise that land and buildings are privately owned. This is best illustrated by a statement made by Youngman and Malme (2004): 'perhaps the most important effect of a property tax is its reservation of a portion of private real estate value, importing a public element into the basic structure of [private] property right.'

This is certainly correct in the West where private property is the predominant mode of real estate ownership. Yet, to what extent could this perception be applied to countries where real estate (especially land) is publicly owned? Undoubtedly, some governments in eastern Europe are pushing for the privatization of state assets. However, it remains common that the ownership of most land is still in the hands of the state. For example, in Russia where the state is supportive of land privatization, only selected cities, such as Novgorod, Tver and Saratov, have a large portion of their land sold to private individuals (Krupa *et al.* 2006). In fact, out of all the land being privatized, about 90 per cent is located in just one city (Saratov).

In China, the government has so far not shown any intention to privatize land. The major change that the government has made was in 1987 when it allowed private individuals to lease land use rights from local governments for a definite time and with the payment of land leasing fee. In 1988, the Chinese National People's Congress amended the Constitution to legally acknowledge the transferability of land use rights between private entities (Development Research Center of the State Council, 2005). Another amendment to the Chinese Constitution was made in 2004, recognizing legally that buildings erected on leasehold land are private property (Constitution of the People's Republic of China, Chapter 1, Article 13). Hence, a person who possesses a piece of real estate in China is by legal definition the owner of the house (or apartment) but only the user of the land.

Given these unique property relations in some transition countries, policymakers who decide to adopt a 'western style' property tax system may have to reconcile the implicit assumption of private ownership embedded in the approach with the non-private land tenure arrangements in their economies. This issue is not trivial. For instance, during field research in China many objections were encountered from would-be taxpayers when they were asked to express their opinions about a proposed property tax. All too often, they questioned the rationale of paying a property tax on land that they do not own. If taxpayers do not feel obligated to pay their taxes, compliance could become an issue. There are at least three possible ways to mediate this problem.

First, property relations may be altered so as to accommodate a new property tax system. More specifically, land could be privatized. It then follows by an imposition of a property tax on real assets after private property rights have been legally established. This is the approach employed by the government in Russia where owners of real property pay property taxes, and land users pay rents (Krupa *et al.*, 2006). As this country is moving gradually toward a complete privatization of land ownership, the dual system will eventually be phased out, replacing land rents with property tax payments. As argued later, for public leasehold systems in general, from an economic viewpoint, there is no reason to treat land rent and tax as mutually exclusive. In Russia, the decision to collect either the land rent or tax, but not both, might have been largely driven by concerns about political opposition and citizens' ability to pay both levies. Limitations of this approach must be acknowledged, however. Coupling property tax reform with the transformation of land tenure arrangements could restrict the revenue-generating ability of the new tax. Because land reform is controversial and usually takes a long time to complete, the government may at best allow a few pilot cities, where privatization is in an advanced stage, to collect the property tax. Since taxable properties are restricted to land and buildings that have been privatized, tax collections will be less than it would have been, had the new tax been levied on both leasehold and freehold interests.

More importantly, if the payment of property tax is higher than that of land rent, incentives for private individuals to become owners of real estate may be hampered. This would thwart the progress of land reform. Lack of progress in privatization may keep the tax base narrow, thereby forcing the government to set a high effective tax rate in order to raise sufficient revenue to justify the costs of initiating the new tax system. A high effective tax rate, however, may further discourage private citizens from acquiring public property, and so forth and so on, until the government breaks the circle by either lowering the effective tax rate or giving away land to private entities at low costs. Neither of these actions appears fiscally prudent.

In addition, non-private land tenure arrangements in some countries (or communities) may serve special social and political functions. Converting a longstanding collective ownership of land into individuals' private property for tax purposes may run into conflict with customary rules or national ideologies, both of which are vital for maintaining political and social stability. For some countries, like China, privatization of public land is simply not an option at least in the foreseeable future. Due to constraints imposed by the Constitution, private land ownership is illegal. Not until changes to these formal rules are made could privatization become a viable option to facilitate the adoption of the property tax.

Analysing the issue from a broader perspective, the property tax is merely an instrument that may help local government achieve certain policy goals, such as raising public funds to finance local infrastructure and services. If preconditions for property taxation are absent, advocating drastic changes in property relations for the purpose of taxing real estate may not be a wise approach, because these modifications are often politically and legally testing. Public officials should broaden their search for alternative fiscal tools that match existing contexts rather than predetermine that the property tax is the right instrument.

The second way is to treat leasehold rights as private property. As explained before, under a public leasehold system, the government owns land, and leases other attributes of the bundle of land rights to private entities. So long as privileges and obligations of holding the leased land rights are fully delineated and recognized, both legally and by the society, there is no reason why leasehold rights cannot be regarded as private property. In most matured public leasehold systems, there are explicit provisions in their constitutions that acknowledge public leaseholds as private property and empower the state to establish special legislation for protecting the leased land rights (Hong and Bourassa, 2003). In this situation, leaseholds are as secure as if they were freeholds. The only difference is that the former grants land users the privilege to possess and use selected attributes of the bundle of rights for a specific time, whereas the latter bestows on freeholders all elements of the bundle for a perpetual use, limited only by government regulations. In this way, the proper interpretation of imposing a property tax on leasehold land is to tax the leased land rights held by land users. If this interpretation is deemed reasonable for all parties involved, the implicit contradiction in levying a property tax on public land would be reconciled.

One complication of this approach is that constitutional amendments may have to be conducted to reflect the legal status of leasehold rights. Constitutional rules in most countries are, by design, difficult to change. It normally requires a supermajority vote from legislators to amend the constitution, if a country is operated under a democratic system. Depending on the legal, political and social circumstances, any changes of the constitution related to public and private property rights may trigger contentious public debates. Especially, in some transition economies where the legacy of communism is still lingering on, political opposition to privatization could remain strong, thereby impeding the necessary constitutional amendments to make leasehold rights private property.

If the leased land rights are taxed as if they are private property, it is extremely important to educate would-be taxpayers and public officials as to the distinction between leaseholds and freeholds. Although lessees are paying property taxes, they must recognize that they possess only the leased land rights that are not designed to last in perpetuity. Otherwise, any confusion could complicate future land and tax reforms. For example, in Israel and Canberra, lessees are requested to pay the entire leasehold value up front and thereafter an annual property tax (or rates in Australia) for leasing public land. Lease terms in both cases are long and renewable – 99 years in Canberra and 49 years in Israel with four automatically renewable terms totalling 196 years (Neutze, 2003; Alterman, 2003). This method of collecting leasehold charges and property taxes is tantamount to the payment system for land in countries where land is freehold. Due to this similarity, lessees have developed the wrong perception that they own their lands.

This view, albeit legally a fiction, has engendered the expectation that any attempt by the government to exercise its rights as the landowner to retake land for public uses or to demand additional payments from lessees for enlarging or extending land use rights would constitute an infringement of private property. This expectation has added conflict to government efforts to redistribute land and land value between private landholders and the public. As Neutze (2003) argued, had the Canberra government provided enough public education about its leasehold system, it would have spared the Australian capital from many intractable disputes over land ownership. The above experience is particularly relevant for countries where the state has no immediate plan to give fee simple deeds to private landholders. Suppose these governments collect all leasehold charges up front and then levy a property tax on both land and buildings, they may be at risk of creating the same mistaken expectation. On the one hand, the state believes that it is the legal owner of land and should have the right to take land back when the lease expires, and on the other hand, lessees have been paying a property tax for years and may think erroneously that the government, by collecting this property tax, may have recognized them as the de facto landowners. This wrong perception of property relations, if it prevails, may put the government and lessees at odds with each other when there is a later need to reallocate land from private to public uses. Designing a property tax system that will not add more complications to the already unsettling land tenure arrangement is an important task that policymakers should never overlook.

The third, and final, way is to label property taxes on land and buildings distinctly. Setting aside the economic incidence for later discussion, not all property tax systems are based on the premise that the statutory incidence should always fall on property owners; occupiers are sometimes liable for tax payments. In some countries, such as Australia, the Netherlands and the UK, taxes paid by occupiers are referred to as rates, a council tax or a user tax to avoid any confusion. Despite the different names, the calculation of these levies is still based on either the capital or rental value of the property, which is similar to that of the *ad valorem* tax.

As discussed earlier, if the ownerships of land and buildings are not the same, two different taxes – a property tax on buildings and a use tax on land – may be created to tax these real assets separately. In most cases, because the government has the legislative power to impose taxes on citizens, it is conceivable to have one tax on the leased land rights and another on the improvements. In fact, this is the most straightforward way of dealing with the issue. Although this approach seems tenable, many countries, such as China, that currently tax land and buildings separately, are contemplating the possibility of moving toward a uniform tax system in which the two objects will be combined into a single tax base. One possible explanation for this trend is that the selling price of a piece of real estate comprises the values of both the land and the improvements; hence, it is convenient to use the market price of the entire property as the tax base, instead of having two separate components. Additional costs of taking extra steps to assess the land and building values separately might have deterred policymakers from taxing land and its improvements differently.

Despite possible savings, policymakers should not ignore the potential efficiency gained by taxing land more heavily than buildings. It has been accepted by scholars, at least in theory, that a two-rate property tax system would encourage intensive land use (Bourassa, 1987; England, 2003; Netzer, 1998; Oates and Schwab, 1998). Economic and social benefits generated from an efficient land use may outweigh the additional costs of assessing the land and building values individually. Policymakers must conduct a thorough analysis that accounts for all direct and indirect benefits and costs before deciding whether or not to tax land and buildings uniformly.

Land rent, property tax and tax incidence

In designing a new tax system, the most fundamental issue is its economic incidence, that is, who actually bears the burden of the tax, as opposed to who is legally liable to make the payment, as indicated earlier. To simplify the discussion, let us assume that only a land tax is in question and that the supply of land (or land use rights) is fixed in the short run. The standard argument of tax incidence under this situation is: under a public leasehold system, the government owner will bear the ultimate economic burden even if the statutory incidence falls on land users. The reason is that the new tax imposes additional costs – future tax liabilities – on land users and, *ceteris paribus*, will reduce the demand for land use rights. As illustrated in Figure 11.1, the demand curve will shift from D to D'. With lower demand, the amount of premium and land rent that the government can charge lessees for leasing the use rights will fall if the leasing fee and rental level are determined by the market. Because the supply of land use rights is perfectly inelastic (fixed at QL), the rental level will continue to drop until the reduced rental payments are equal to the present values of all future tax liabilities that users must pay to the government (the rectangle RL_0 A B RL_1). In other words, lessees are able to transfer the entire economic incidence of the new land tax to the government. It also implies that any new tax collections generated through property taxation may be annihilated by the decrease in the lease income.

In an ideal world where the 'capitalization' of the discounted present values of future tax payments into land prices occurs fully and instantaneously, taxing public leasehold land may in the short term lead to two outcomes. First, there may be a transfer of the control over the land revenue from one branch of government to another. For instance, in some countries, central and local

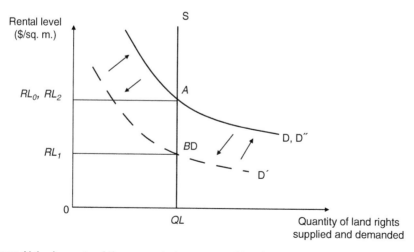

Figure 11.1 Impacts of the property tax on rental level

land bureaus are normally the government units that monitor land resource allocation and are therefore responsible for leasing public land and collecting lease payments. Tax policy and collection, however, falls within the jurisdiction of the ministry of finance and tax administrative agencies. If a land tax converts a portion of the land leasing fee into tax payments, it will imply a reshuffle of the power over the lease revenue from the land bureaus to the tax agencies. Depending on how important this income is in government budgets, this kind of interdepartmental transfer of responsibility could create rivalry between agencies.

A land tax could also alter fiscal relations between the central and local governments or between different levels of subnational government. Suppose further that tax collections have to be shared between different levels of government, whereas the lease income does not. If the revenue is collected in the form of lease payments which can be treated as an off-budget item, local officials will be able to retain 100 per cent of these funds for local uses. On the contrary, if it is in the form of tax payments, the local government that collects the revenue must surrender a portion of the collections to its superior units. This fiscal arrangement will not provide the right incentive for local officials to support property tax reform, thus rendering the implementation arduous.

Second, under the premium systems, taxing leasehold land will mean a deferral of a portion of the immediate lease payments to later years due to the capitalization of tax liabilities into leasehold values. This postponement implies that the current government will have less revenue to defray local spending at least at the beginning of the reform. If the lease revenue accounts for a major share of local government budgets, officials will not be enthusiastic about taxing leasehold land. One potential solution is to allow local governments to borrow funds from public or private financial intermediaries to cover any fiscal shortfalls caused by a property tax reform, using future tax collections as collateral. All tax payments may be deposited into a special fund account to ensure that they will be used to repay the related debts. As illustrated, capitalization of tax liabilities into leasehold values could determine the immediate impacts of a land tax on different involved parties. In reality, a land tax may be under- or over-capitalized depending on the expectations of different players in the property markets. Capitalization in transition economies is particularly unpredictable because their real estate markets are still in a developing stage. When market information and the knowledge of property investment is lacking, it will be hard to forecast when and how much capitalization will take place. Thus, whether government budgets will increase, decrease or stay the same when a land tax is first introduced must be evaluated on a case-by-case basis. What this analysis has illustrated is the question that all policymakers must face when contemplating property taxation under a public leasehold system: if additional property tax collections are to be offset by a decrease in the lease revenue, how can the scant financial benefit, if any, justify the high costs of initial capital investment and of reorganizing the intergovernmental fiscal relations needed for property tax reform?

So far, this analysis does not consider another type of capitalization that may also occur when a government levies a property tax. In most cases, the aim to collect the tax is to raise public funds for financing local infrastructure and services, such as schools, parks, local road networks, libraries etc. These public investments can improve the amenities of the neighbourhood and therefore boost the property demand in the community. As a result, the demand for land will also increase, as portrayed by the shift of the demand curve from D' to D", which raises the rental level from RL_1 to RL_2 in Figure 11.1. This assumes that the increase in public expenditures, holding other factors constant, has a capitalization effect that offsets entirely the impact of property tax liabilities on leasehold values. In reality, the net capitalization effect may not necessarily be zero. Whether the net effect will keep leasehold values the same will depend on many factors, such as the homogeneity of residents within a community with respect to demands for local public services, the mobility of the residents, location-dependence of residents' income and the variety of local government services available to satisfy diverse tastes (Mieszkowski and Zodrow, 1989; Tiebout, 1956). These preconditions may be attainable through binding zoning (Hamilton 1975; 1976).

Suppose that the net capitalization effect is zero, property tax collections would no longer be generated at the expense of the lease income. Leasehold values will rise back up to the pre-reform level due to the increase in public expenditures. And so will the rental level and leasing fee. At this point, tax collections will become an additional income because there will be no reduction in the lease revenue. As argued by many proponents of the 'benefit tax' view of property taxation, a tax on real assets can be treated as a payment for public services received (Fischel, 2001; Oates, 1969). When the property tax revenue is reinvested in local infrastructure and services whose benefits will be capitalized into property prices, real estate taxes are benefit taxes in the sense that they are similar to user charges for public goods provided. This financing mechanism in theory will have no effect on housing consumption (Zodrow, 2001, 2006). The benefit view is certainly not the only perspective on the effect of property taxation on housing consumption. The alternative is the 'new' or 'capital tax' view, which argues that the property tax is a tax on the use of capital and thus can create distortions by reallocating investment from high tax to low tax jurisdictions. According to this view, the property tax will reduce per capita housing consumption as taxpayers attempt to avoid the tax (Zodrow, 2006).

The validity of the above argument is based not only on whether or not capitalization of tax liabilities and public expenditures will take place but also on the timing of the two processes. Assume that the capitalization of tax liabilities will occur immediately after the government announces the new scheme, whereas a corresponding increase in public expenditures will only be capitalized into land values upon the completion of a proposed project, which is estimated to take three years to finish. All else being equal, the government will receive a smaller amount of lease revenue in the beginning, owing to lower leasehold values caused by the capitalization of tax liabilities. Not until the increase in public expenditures induces higher leasehold values could property tax collections be considered extra revenue for financing public services.

Another issue related to the timing of capitalization is that a new land tax may create certain horizontal inequity in the initial stage of reform. Using the above example, existing lessees who leased land in the past might have paid the entire leasehold charges up front without anticipating the possibility of paying a new property tax. In this case, these lessees did not have the chance to adjust their leasing fees (or land rents) downward, so as to account for the extra tax liabilities for using land. For lessees who plan to lease land after the reform, the situation will be different. Knowing that they will have to pay property taxes in the future, new lessees will lower their offers for leasing public land, so as to compensate for future tax expenditures. In other words, these new lessees will pay lower leasehold charges than did existing land users.

This problem may be mediated if the government collects an annual land rent instead of the entire leasehold charges up front. Under a land rent system, the government may be able to adjust the rental level annually according to changes in the fair market value of land. This way, both existing and new lessees will be charged at the same rental level regardless of when they acquired their leasehold rights. If collecting a land rent is not a viable option, the government may minimize this horizontal inequity by pledging to use the property tax revenue for specific infrastructure projects. By showing a reasonable goodwill to land users that improvements in land will be implemented in the near future, new lessees may be willing to pay a higher leasing fee for the land use rights, thereby narrowing the discrepancy in leasehold charges before and after the tax reform. Certainly, this method will only work if the government has a good reputation of keeping its promise and the competency to actually execute the planned investments. In an environment where taxpayers are not fully informed about how their tax contributions are used or what benefits they can expect from paying taxes, it is hard to imagine that new lessees will be willing to pay a higher leasing fee for promises that may not be materialized. To some extent, it is about trust in the government, which can shape expectations and thus the capitalization rates.

These relationships between the lease revenue and property tax collections are in accord with the general consensus among scholars and practitioners that the two levies are not the same and should be collected separately. The former is a payment to the landowner – the state under a public leasehold system – for leasing the land use rights to a private individual; and the latter should be considered a payment for local services and infrastructure provided by the government. The amount of land rent that lessees pay to a government lessor should be determined by the supply and demand of land use rights; and the amount of the property tax should be based on the quality and quantity of local services received.

Public land leasing is similar to the situation in which a private owner lets their property to a renter and collects a monthly rent for allowing this tenant to occupy the premises. It will be unreasonable to argue that the tenant should not pay rents to the landlord if the government levies a tax on the use of the property. But this is precisely what many analysts in China have advocated; they believe that the government should abolish the leasing fee after the adoption of a new property tax. One reason for this misconception is that the parties who collect the leasehold charges and property taxes belong to the same government under a public leasehold system, whereas these payments are made to two non-affiliated entities (a private owner and the state) when the leased property is privately owned. Undoubtedly, these two levies are interrelated, but they are far from being the payments for an identical service. Hence, their collection should not be considered mutually exclusive.

Valuing public leasehold for tax purposes

Another issue related to taxing land and buildings under public leasehold systems is property valuation for tax purposes. Aside from the familiar problems found in some transition countries, such as the underdevelopment of real estate markets, inadequate sales data and cadastral records and lack of administrative capability, we need to focus on a specific issue that has not been given enough attention in the literature: assessing leasehold value using mass appraisal methods. There are at least two challenges.

First, the value of leased land is highly sensitive to the lease term and provisions of the land contract. These contractual arrangements vary significantly from one land lease to another. At this moment, time-tested mass appraisal techniques for assessing large numbers of leasehold sites do not exist. In principle, an assessor can design an econometric model to estimate how the duration of the land lease contributes to property value based on historical sales data. Yet, before constructing such a model, additional information about the relationships between property value and lease term is required. Are their relationships linear or non-linear? Are impacts of the lease term on property value unidirectional? For instance, the duration of a lease may have very little influence on the property value at the beginning of the term but may gradually become a determining factor when the contract is approaching its expiration. A long-term lease may add value to the user's interest if the economic activity conducted on the site is location specific and has a long production cycle. Because relocation will cost the user dearly, a long-term lease will be preferable to a short-term lease, thereby allowing the former to increase the leasehold value in this situation. By contrarst, if land is used for a short-cycle production of a generic nature, a long-term commitment to a specific site may restrict the user from moving to another location in the future where production costs may be lower. In this scenario, a long-term lease may at best have no effect, or at worst lower the leasehold value due to the potential penalty for terminating the lease before it expires. Not until assessors have a good understanding of these relationships between lease term and leasehold value can current mass appraisal techniques be applied to property tax assessment under public leasehold systems. More research is needed on this topic.

Second, assessors may overcome the above valuation problem by using the rental value based method. In this approach, appraisers will estimate the annual fair market rental value of the property in question. Because the goal is to come up with an estimated rental value of the property at its highest and best use in a particular year, the lease term will not be a determining factor. It matters only when we want to know the capital value of the property by summing up the discounted present values of all annual rental incomes over the remaining term of the lease. In this case, the duration of the lease is important.

The major difficulty of using the rental value based approach is the divergence between 'fair market rent' and 'contract rent'. Fair market rent represents the land rent that a lessor can expect to obtain in the open markets by letting the property to a lessee for the highest and best use. Contract rent is the amount specified in the lease that the lessee must pay to the lessor in order to remain as the user of the property. For long-term public leasehold systems, leases established years ago may have a contract rent that falls far below the fair market rent, if periodic adjustments to the rental level are not incorporated as a part of the contractual agreements. If property taxation on land and buildings is based on the fair market rent, which is higher than the contract rent, it may open the door for legal and political challenges from taxpayers. In transition countries where governments have been leasing state-owned land to private individuals at low (or zero) charges, setting up a property tax system where payments are calculated based on the fair market rental value of the property could be a difficult task.

Conclusions

This chapter has examined three issues related to taxation on public leasehold land in transition countries. The first issue is the conceptual consistency of imposing a property tax on land that is not privately owned. Besides the common approach of privatizing land to facilitate the adoption of a property tax system, it suggests two additional options: (1) recognizing leasehold rights as private property and (2) taxing land and buildings separately with the tax on the non-privately owned land labelled as a land use tax. The selection among these options should be based on the political, social and economic contexts of the country in question. If privatization of state-owned land is progressing rapidly and without strong resistance, instituting a property tax system in which privately owned real estate will be subjected to taxation, as it is done in the West, seems plausible. Yet, for countries where there is still strong ideological and political supports for retaining public land ownership, the other two approaches seem more tenable than does land privatization. By amending the constitution to recognize the leased land rights as private property and legislating special laws to enforce these individuals' rights, levying a property tax on leasehold rights appears logical. Another way is to tax land and buildings separately, if their ownership structures are not the same. A land use tax may be created to tax leasehold rights, whereas a property tax can be used to tax the improvements that can be owned by private entities. All in all, property taxation under public leasehold systems should be acceptable to would-be taxpayers so long as policy-makers are mindful of the unique property relations between the government lessor and lessees and take the necessary steps to modify the legal and adminis-trative requirements for taxing leasehold rights.

The second issue is the economic incidence of a land tax under public leasehold systems. In the near term, one immediate impact of collecting a tax on leasehold land is that lessees may be able to shift the tax burden to the government lessor, if the supply of land use rights is fixed. The government will receive new land tax collections but, at the same time, earn a lower lease income because of the decrease in the leasehold charges caused by the capitali-zation of tax liabilities into land prices. Whether or not the increase in tax collections could offset the reduction in the lease revenue will depend on the capitalization rate.

Moreover, existing lessees who paid the entire leasehold charges up front and did not anticipate the future liabilities of a land tax might have overpaid for their leased land rights. Had they leased these rights after the implementation of the new tax, they would have offered a lower leasing fee or land rent to the government, so as to account for the future tax payments. If these lessees transfer their land rights to another party at the lower value, they will suffer a financial loss. If one adopts the benefit view of property taxation to analyse the situation, the above impacts on the government lessor and existing lessees may disappear when the new tax collections are reinvested in local infrastructure and social services. These public expenditures will be capitalized into land prices. Higher land prices will in turn increase the lease income for the government and raise the leasehold values for existing lessees. In an ideal world where tax liabilities and public expenditures are fully capitalized into property prices and where the net capitalization effect is zero, a property tax on leasehold land will be similar to the benefit tax in the sense that residents who receive the benefits of public goods financing by the tax revenue will pay for the services through property tax payments. Unfortunately, impacts of property taxation and public expenditures on land prices are difficult to assess in transition countries. Data sets with all the required control variables are not yet available. Thus, these assertions should be considered hypotheses whose validity must be proven by future empirical research.

The third issue is the possibility of using mass appraisal techniques to value leasehold rights for tax purposes. Although complications involved in valuing large quantity of leasehold sites are not insurmountable, care must be taken to understand the relationships between lease term and leasehold value. If the rental value based approach is employed to assess leasehold values, the distinction between fair market rent and contract rent should be made explicit.

Given the increasing popularity of real property taxation in transition countries where land may be leasehold, more work in this area is clearly needed. This chapter has only identified a few issues out of many challenges that may emerge from taxing leasehold land. Designing a property tax approach that suits the institutional environments of transforming economies promises to be a fertile topic for future research.

References

Alterman, R. (2003) The Land of Leasehold: Israel's Extensive Public Land Ownership in an Era of Privatization. In: Bourassa, S.C. and Hong, Y.H. (eds.), *Leasing Public Land: Policy Debates and International Experiences*, Cambridge, MA: Lincoln Institute of Land Policy, 115–150.

Bird, R.M. and Slack, E. (2004) *International Handbook of Land and Property Taxation*, (eds.), Northampton, MA: Edward Elgar.

Bird, R.M. and Slack, E. (2006). *Taxing Land and Property in Emerging Economies: Raising Revenue…and More?* Paper presented at The Conference on Land Policies for Urban Development, Cambridge, MA: Lincoln Institute of Land Policy.

Bourassa, S.C. (1987) Land Value Taxation and New Housing Development in Pittsburgh. *Growth and Change*, 44–55.

Constitution of the People's Republic of China, (1982) http://english.people.com.cn/constitution/constitution.html.

Development Research Center of the State Council, (2005) *China's Real Estate Taxation System*. Working Paper WP06CT1, Cambridge, MA: Lincoln Institute of Land Policy.

England, R.W. (2003) State and Local Impacts of a Revenue-Neutral Shift from a Uniform Property to a Land Value Tax: Results of a Simulation Study. *Land Economics*, 79(1): 38–43.

Fischel, W.A. (2001) Municipal Corporation, Homeowner, and the Benefit View of the Property Tax. In Oates, W.E. (ed.), *Property Taxation and Local Government Finance*, Cambridge, MA: Lincoln Institute of Land Policy.

Hamilton, B.W. (1975) Zoning and Property Taxation in a System of Local Government. *Urban Studies*, 12(2): 205–211.

Hamilton, B.W. (1976) Capitalization of Intrajurisdictional Differences in Local Tax Prices. *American Economics Review*, 66(5): 743–753.

Hong, Y.H. and Bourassa, S.C. (2003) Why Public Leasehold? Issues and Concepts. In: Bourassa, S.C. and Hong, Y.H. (eds.), *Leasing Public Land: Policy Debates and International Experiences*, Cambridge, MA: Lincoln Institute of Land Policy, 3–37.

Krupa, O., Mikesell, J.L. and Zorn, C.K. (2006) *Land Value Taxation for Local Government Finance in the Russian Federation: A Case Study of Saratov Oblast*. Working paper WP06KZ1, Cambridge, MA: Lincoln Institute of Land Policy.

Malme, J.H. and Youngman, J.M. (2001) *The Development of Property Taxation in Economies in Transaction: Case Studies from Central and Eastern Europe*. Washington, DC, World Bank.

Mieszkowski, P. and Zodrow, G.R. (1989) Taxation and the Tiebout Model: The Differential Effects of Head Taxes, Taxes on Land Rents, and Property Taxes. *Journal of Economic Literature*, September, 27: 1098–1146.

Needham, B. (2003) One Hundred Years of Public Land Leasing in The Netherlands. In: Bourassa, S.C. and Hong, Y.H. (eds.), *Leasing Public Land: Policy Debates and International Experiences*, Cambridge, MA: Lincoln Institute of Land Policy, 61–83.

Netzer, D. (1998) *Land Value Taxation: Can It and Will It Work Today?* Cambridge, MA: Lincoln Institute of Land Policy.

Neutze, M. (2003) Leasing of Publicly Owned Land in Canberra, Australia. In: Bourassa, S.C. and Hong, Y.H. (eds.), *Leasing Public Land: Policy Debates and International Experiences*, Cambridge, MA: Lincoln Institute of Land Policy, 39–60.

Oates, W.E. (1969) The Effects of Property Taxes and Local Public Spending on Property Value: An Empirical Study of Tax Capitalization and The Tiebout Hypothesis. *Journal of Political Economy*, 77(6): 956–961.

Oates, W.E. and Schwab, R. (1998) The Pittsburgh Experience with Land-Value Taxation. In: Ladd, H.F. (Ed.), *Local Government Tax and Land Use Policies in the USA: Understanding the Links.* Northampton: Edward Elgar and Cambridge, MA: Lincoln Institute of Land Policy.

Šulija, V.and Šulija, G. (2005) *Reform of the Property Tax and Problems of Real Estate Appraisal for Taxation Purposes in Transitional Economies of Central and Eastern Europe.* Working paper WP05VS1, Cambridge, MA: Lincoln Institute of Land Policy.

Tiebout, C.M. 1956. A Pure Theory of Local Expenditures. *Journal of Political Economy*, 64(5): 416–424.

Youngman, J.M. and Malme, J. (2004) *The Property Tax in a New Environment: Lessons from International Tax Reform Efforts.* Paper presented at the Andrew Young School Fourth Annual Conference on Public Finance Issues in an International Perspective: Challenges of Tax Reform in a Global Economy, Georgia.

Zodrow, G.R. (2001) Reflections on The New View and The Benefit View of The Property Tax. In: Oates, W.E. (ed.), *Property Taxation and Local Government Finance.* Cambridge, MA: Lincoln Institute of Land Policy.

Zodrow, G.R. (2006) Who Pays The Property Tax? And What Does Capitalization Tell Us About Who Pays? *Land Lines*, April: 14–19.

12

Property Tax and Informal Property: The Challenge of Third World Cities[1]

Martim Smolka and Claudia M. De Cesare

Introduction

Rampant informality, so emblematic of large cities in the developing world, poses many challenges for property taxation. Informality refers in general to activities outside the formal rules or procedures determined from time to time by the government (Payne, 1997). At first glance, taxation of informal settlements violates many of the premises on which property tax systems are based. Tenure rights are obscure or even of unknown origin. Building often takes place progressively, and housing units may never be entirely finished. In addition, a property's value depends on vague or intangible factors such as the security provided by the community organizations. Occupants, or even the legal owner, may be too poor to pay for their own survival. As a result, no ability-to-pay is identified. The administrative costs of tax collection, as well as assessment costs, in informal areas exceed those in formal areas. Finally, public investments in informal settlements are unlikely in most cases.

In essence, this is the conventional wisdom about informal settlements and the reasons why public authorities in general, and fiscal administrators in particular, ignore these areas for taxation purposes. These attitudes are, however, heavily charged with misconceptions and prejudices. This has created a vicious circle wherein informal settlements fail to gain public attention because they

A Primer on Property Tax: Administration and Policy, First Edition.
Edited by William J. McCluskey, Gary C. Cornia and Lawrence C. Walters.
© 2013 Blackwell Publishing Ltd. Published 2013 by Blackwell Publishing Ltd.

do not contribute to public revenues, and they remain informal and off the tax rolls because of public officials' neglect.

This chapter examines some of these common biases and their consequences for property tax collection. As argued here, collecting property taxes from residents of informal settlements may not only be possible under certain circumstances and within well defined limits, but it may also be desirable as an ingredient in a more effective urban policy to mitigate informality.

This study is necessarily exploratory in nature because of the limited data available to analyse the interrelations between the property tax and informality. Indeed, this topic is largely absent in the academic literature and in public debates on either housing policy or taxation issues. The analysis looks at informal occupations in general, using the specific case of Latin American cities as illustration. In most instances, the arguments point to promising directions for further analysis rather than to conclusive findings.

The rest of this chapter is divided into five sections. The first explains the phenomenon of informal land occupations and presents the myths that surround these areas and the people who live in them. The second analyses the impact of informality on the collection of property taxes, and explores some of the implications for establishing and administering property tax policy. Then we examine the potential of the property tax to break the vicious circle of informality. The discussion addresses the theoretical and practical impacts of the property tax on land use and occupation, and outlines alternative tax treatments that authorities might consider. The next section takes a longer and perhaps more critical view of the challenges involved in implementing more effective property tax policies in informal settlements. Then we have some final remarks summarizing the major findings and suggesting some directions for further research.

The phenomenon of informal land occupations

The first image of informality that usually comes to mind is one of slums. The term 'slum' refers generically to settlements that originate from a process of informal occupation of land, often through invasions (Duhau, 2003). However, there are several social and/or physical forms of informality, ranging from pirate subdivisions (usually characterized by market sales of land having no clear title) to areas where land is not used according to urban standards and regulations. Although the terms 'informal', 'illegal', 'irregular' and 'clandestine' occupations are often used interchangeably, they refer to slightly different conditions.

- Illegal occupations are generally associated with fragile land tenure and/or fiscal violations.
- Irregular occupations are related to noncompliance with urban regulations, particularly in relation to land development plans and building codes.

• Clandestine settlements are areas that officially do not exist, that is, areas with no title deed filed at the public registry. The term also applies to occupations of public areas.

In the strictest sense, all of these terms imply some type of deliberate act to break the law. But for most families living in these areas, informal settlements are the only choice available. As such, they may have a legitimate right to occupy the areas. This ambiguity reflects the fact that legality and legitimacy do not necessarily overlap.

For our purposes here, informality includes situations where property rights (not necessarily freehold tenure) are transferred through private contracts that are not publicly registered. Informality also refers to situations where land developers comply with urban standards and regulations but do not register the properties to avoid paying fees, taxes and other costs.

As synthesized by Barross (1990) the sequence of informal land development is the opposite of classical formal land development (see Figure 12.1).

Formal land development begins with planning and ends with the occupation of fully finished houses, which invariably occurs after urban services are in place. Informal land development, in contrast, typically begins with occupation of a land parcel through a series of market transactions involving the landowner, the developer (or subdivider) and future residents. Buyers purchase the right to occupy a piece of land through a private contract that may or may not be recognized in the public registry. The building process begins immediately even if plot boundaries and street layouts are only roughly delimited. The need to ensure possession encourages occupants to build rapidly with whatever materials are available (Abramo, 2003). The level of public services and infrastructure provided varies enormously, although these investments are normally made after the land occupation. Occasionally, government authorities may establish a plan to redevelop the area to improve settlement conditions.

When the landowner acts as the informal developer, he or she is simply seeking to maximize profit and therefore ignores the need to comply with urban

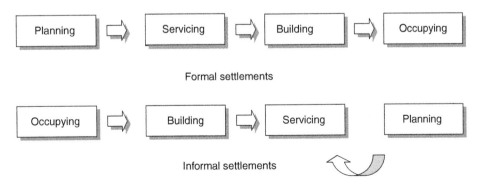

Figure 12.1: Typical processes of land development: formal vs. informal settlements
Source: Barros (1990). Reproduced by permission of UN-HABITAT.

standards, regulations or building codes. The buyers purchase the illegal plots in good faith, even though the properties meet neither urban regulations nor the necessary conditions to guarantee the property title. When an official inspection finally occurs in the area, the houses are usually partially built, and the community is organized to prevent eviction. Public authorities are rather tolerant toward informal settlements because there are no other housing options for the low-income segment of the population.

Widespread informality in third-world cities is projected to continue on a massive scale. The latest UN-Habitat estimate (UN-Habitat, 2003) shows that 928 million people, some 32 per cent of the world's urban population and 43 per cent of the population in developing countries – live in settlements with precarious urban infrastructure and public services. If current trends and policies continue, the report projects that the slum population will increase by 37 million a year to a total of 1.5 billion people in 2020. Although Latin America is home to only 9 per cent of the world's population, it accounts about 14 per cent of people living in slums. Estimated shares of informal settlements in specific Latin American cities include 39.5 per cent of households in Rio de Janeiro, Brazil (Instituto Pereira Passos, 2002); and 39 per cent of the population of Caracas, Venezuela (Angel, 1999).

Why is informality a problem?

Although certain scholars and public officials extol the virtues of informality as either an ingenious solution or an expression of popular creativity, the reality is much grimmer. Informality distorts how urban land markets function because illegal, irregular and clandestine operators reap higher profits by avoiding the costs of taxes, protecting the land from invasions, or providing mandatory infrastructure and public services (Smolka, 2003).

Contrary to expectations, land prices in informal settlements are often higher than in formal areas, when discounting for the costs of providing water, public lights, drainage, sewerage and other public equipment and services. This is an example of the so-called cigarette effect, where street vendors sell each cigarette above its pro rata value to those who cannot afford the whole package. In informal settlements, the reduction in lot size according to the buyer's purchasing capacity thus results in a higher sales price per square metre.

It is noteworthy that prices in informal markets are formed through similar mechanisms to those in formal markets. Nevertheless, the attributes associated with land values are distinct. For instance, in informal settlements, a premium is paid for 'urban freedom', for the expectation of future regularization and upgrading benefits, and for a more flexible, albeit draconian, form of payment. The term originally conceived by Turner and Fichter (1972) and revived by Abramo (2003) refers to noncompliance with urban standards, regulations and building codes. Because buyers have no access to formal credit (due to lack of property title, among other factors), sellers are often willing to allow instalment payments. The buyer and seller are complicit in an arrangement where the former accesses land relieved of the costs related to urban and building requirements, while the latter is compensated for bringing land to the market.

In addition, informality is expensive for society. The application of curative policies – that is, the cost of upgrading irregular settlements in terms of providing adequate urban infrastructure and public services – is higher than the cost of new land development. The typical cost of regularization programmes varies from USD$2,500 to $3,500 per family, or two to three times the cost of urbanizing formal areas (UN-Habitat, 2005). The UN-Habitat Annual Report (2005) estimated the cost of improving slums at $670 dollars per person.

In addition, informal development offers fewer social benefits than formal land development. For instance, formal developments must donate approximately 35 per cent of the land area to public spaces such as green areas, streets and public schools. Furthermore, informality has indirect social costs such as the proliferation of crime, not to mention the hazards related to natural disasters. The lack of hygienic conditions in informal settlements also imposes an excessive burden on public health systems.

Causes of informality

As Durand-Lasserve and Clerc (1996) argue, the geographic distribution of urban poverty tends to overlap with the pattern of informal settlements, but poverty cannot entirely explain the magnitude and persistence of informality. As Smolka (1991) has demonstrated, not all occupants of such settlements can be considered poor.

In Latin America, the proportion of illegal or irregular settlements is typically much higher than the number of families living below the poverty line. Similarly, the growth rate of informal occupations is higher than that of poverty. Attributing the increasing number of informal settlements to poverty is therefore simplistic.

One obvious explanation for informality is the lack of social programmes providing housing alternatives for the poor. According to Fernandes (1997) part of the growth of informal settlements reflects the absence of an effective and comprehensive housing policy at all government levels. Moreover, governments in developing countries have been incapable of providing urban infrastructure and public services in poor areas. Durand-Lasserve and Clerc (1996) conclude, 'The lack of infrastructure and services and the difficulties encountered in overcoming this area, even more than insecure tenure, are the main criteria for defining irregular settlements.'

Land use regulation is frequently identified as another source of informality in that the majority of the population cannot comply with established regulations. In a laxer regulatory context, less informality would thus be expected. Nevertheless, stricter regulations are imposed precisely to prevent undesirable land use. In other words, as long as society deems certain land use patterns as unacceptable, a regulation is needed. Achieving the right balance is not straightforward: over-regulation creates exclusive high-priced zones, while under-regulation creates an opportunity for unscrupulous agents to pursue predatory practices. Finally, it must be noted that informality begets informality. This is easily inferred from the fact that the high profits accruing to informal developers provide an incentive to expand such developments.

Myths of informality

The conventional wisdom surrounding informal settlements and their residents often reveals the following misconceptions which have helped to support the argument against instituting property taxes in informal areas.

- Informal settlements are homogeneous entities that are clearly distinct from formal settlements. In fact, informality takes many forms. Formal and informal developments are not dichotomous categories but instead exist along a continuum. Moreover, there are numerous differences among settlements that fall within the same category, as well as great heterogeneity within a single settlement. Rich and poor sectors exist side by side in informal settlements just as they do in formal areas.
- Only unemployed and informal workers live in informal settlements. This perception has been challenged ever since publication of The Myth of Marginality in the 1970s (Perlman, 1976). Many studies have found that residents of informal areas are heterogeneous, some of them work, and some of them have formal sector jobs. For instance, many automotive workers in São Paulo, Brazil, live in informal settlements.
- Occupants of informal settlements are poor. Several studies have found that consolidated, well-located informal settlements are hardly ghettos of the poor. As Smolka (1991) has demonstrated, there is ample evidence of poor people living in formal areas and non-poor people living in informal areas. The findings of a recent study conducted by the Institute Pereira Passos in Rio de Janeiro (2002), based on the Census of 2000, indicate that about 64 per cent of the population classified as poor (per capita income of less than a minimum salary of about US$200) did not live in informal settlements (see also, Smolka, 1992).
- According to Abramo (2003) family ties influence the decision to remain in the community even after individual income rises. The exchange of favours and services among neighbours in informal settlements is an important benefit. Moreover, the complex socio-political and economic organization of informal settlements – which tends to require the presence of owners to rent or sell rooms and second homes and to run local businesses – also prevents residents from leaving.
- Occupants of informal areas are neither willing nor able to pay property taxes. Not only are residents usually willing to pay, but they are also able to

do so in many instances. Payment of the property tax is a way to legitimize their right to public services and other urban improvements. It is also important to note that occupants of new land developments have already paid the equivalent of a property tax in the form of higher prices. As explained later, the revenue from property taxes in formal areas is capitalized into lower land prices. Moreover, Latin American tax administrators do not perceive the rich as necessarily better taxpayers than the poor (De Cesare *et al.*, 2003).

- Occupation of informal settlements does not occur through market transactions. Access to land at the urban periphery – and even to a large extent in the more consolidated informal areas – is no longer gained primarily through land invasion. Instead, as Tachner (2003) observes, no matter what type of land use or quality of houses are produced, there is a market where irregular plots and houses are advertised, sold and rented. Even when land is invaded, the organizers of the invasion collect a fee as a way of selling the right to occupy the area.
- Formal property title facilitates access to credit. Property ownership does not necessarily guarantee access to credit. For example, occupants of informal settlements in Lima, Peru, have received more access to credit (albeit at a modest level) from private financial agents than owners of regularized properties. This evidence, first published by Calderón (2002), suggests that formal workers holding informal properties may be more successful in getting credit than informal workers who live in formal housing.

Moving away from these misperceptions is an important step toward instituting the property tax in informal settlements.

Property tax performance in cities with extensive informality

In most Latin American countries, the property tax has been fully implemented for more than a century. This long tradition contrasts with the poor performance of the property tax systems in the region. Lack of universality, low effective rates, inequities in assessment and low collections have limited the social, financial and urban benefits from such a tax (De Cesare, 2002, 2006). Indeed, local officials generally admit that there is ample room to improve property tax administration.

The importance of the property tax as a source of revenue is still marginal. Based on data collected from 2000 to 2003 (De Cesare, 2006), Uruguay is the only Latin American country where property tax revenue represented more than 1.0 per cent of GDP. In Colombia, the share was 0.71 per cent, Chile 0.68 per cent, Argentina 0.58 per cent and Brazil 0.57 per cent. The share for Brazil takes into account two taxes: the tax on urban property and the tax on rural property. In the other countries cited, the share takes into account only the revenue collected by the urban property tax.

In Panama, Mexico, Honduras and the Dominican Republic property tax revenues made up less than 0.50 per cent of GDP. At the same time, the property tax represented 3.8 per cent of the total tax burden in Chile, 2.7 per cent in Argentina, 1.3 per cent in Brazil and 1.0 per cent in Honduras.

By comparison, in the 1990s property taxes represented on average 1.44 per cent of GDP in OECD countries (Bird and Slack, 2004). The revenue collected from the property tax is highly important in Australia, Canada, the UK and the USA, where the revenues contributed 2.5–3.0 per cent of GDP.

One common explanation for the poor performance of the property tax in Latin America is the presence of rampant informality. Nevertheless, the following analysis finds no empirical support for this claim. As suggested later, the relation between property tax performance and informality is much more complex.

Informality and property tax collection

This section presents a preliminary attempt to relate property tax performance to the presence of informality. The database was obtained from a survey on issues concerning local government performance in Brazil carried out by the Instituto Brasileiro de Geografia e Estatística (IBGE) in 1999 (IBGE, 2001). The first criterion for classifying municipalities was the existence of slums. Slums are identified as 'subnormal agglomerations' and must satisfy the following conditions: (a) form a group of more than 50 housing units; (b) occupy the land illegally; and (c) exhibit a disorderly pattern of urbanization and/or lack essential public services. Because the municipality defines whether a block is subnormal or not, political concerns may influence the definition. The second criterion was the existence of any type of irregular land development (including slums). As Table 12.1 shows, slums existed in approximately 28 per cent of Brazilian municipalities, while irregular land developments were present in approximately 44 per cent.

The existence of slums appears directly related to the size of the city. Indeed, municipalities with slums are much larger than average (or than cities with no slums). The same generally holds true for the presence of irregular settlements. Notwithstanding the limitations on data quality, the performance of the property tax as a revenue source seems to be better in the municipalities where slums and irregular land developments exist. The data thus does not support the hypothesis that property tax revenues per capita are lower in municipalities with informal settlements. However, it should be kept in mind that tax performance among municipalities varies widely in terms of actual and expected (assuming no tax evasion) tax revenue per capita.

The evidence also suggests that local authorities in Brazil have little capacity to monitor and control informality. Local cadastres included information on slums in only 52.5 per cent of the municipalities where slums were present (see Table 12.2).

Moreover, in 61 per cent of the cases, local administrators recognized that records for slum areas were not fully accurate and/or complete. In only 39 per cent of the cases were slum properties fully recorded in the cadastre (see Figure 12.2).

Table 12.1 Property tax revenue vs. informality

		All cases	Slums			Irregular land development		
			No	Yes	Not informed	No	Yes	Not informed
Number of Cases		5,506	3,971	1,520	15	3,077	2,418	11
Cases (%)		100	72.12	27.61	0.27	55.88	43.92	0.20
Property Tax Revenue per Inhabitant — Expected	Mean	22.32	19.30	29.68	16.99	15.18	30.09	256.39
	St. deviation	134.19	150.31	83.44	14.84	86.04	172.20	355.02
	COV (%)	601.06	778.77	281.13	87.36	566.84	572.26	138.47
	Minimum value	0.00	0.00	0.00	0.11	0.00	0.00	5.36
	Maximum value	7,227.46	7,227.46	1,675.32	44.65	3,179.04	7,227.46	507.43
Property Tax Revenue per Inhabitant — Collected	Mean	9.51	7.44	14.51	7.95	6.54	12.67	170.90
	St. deviation	28.18	20.00	41.37	9.36	20.20	33.99	238.06
	COV (%)	296.27	269.00	285.08	117.73	308.68	268.29	139.30
	Minimum value	0.00	0.00	0.00	0.08	0.00	0.00	2.56
	Maximum value	938.97	502.43	938.97	26.59	502.43	938.97	339.24
Income per inhabitant 1996	Mean	173.60	169.08	184.96	189.71	155.52	195.92	148.63
	St. deviation	96.15	90.58	108.29	96.87	88.90	100.01	89.26
	COV (%)	55.38	53.57	58.55	51.06	57.16	51.05	60.06
	Minimum value	28.38	28.38	30.43	51.55	28.38	30.43	55.93
	Maximum value	954.65	954.65	809.18	364.21	954.65	809.18	315.41
Population 2000	Mean	28,196.19	13,716.45	66,087.52	21,810.80	14,410.57	45,816.30	11,187.00
	St. Deviation	173,130.98	21,021.30	324,780.00	28,830.78	50,757.57	13,798.50	15,040.52
	COV (%)	614.02	153.26	491.44	132.19	352.22	30.12	134.45
	Minimum value	754	754	1,404	4,388	754	1,089	1,119
	Maximum value	9,839,066	438,986	9,839,066	112,712	1,965,513	9,839,066	55,033

Note: The existence of slums and irregular land developments was not informed in 15 and 11 municipalities respectively. The property tax revenue is provided in the Brazilian currency at the 1998 values. Reproduced by permission of UN-HABITAT.

Table 12.2:   Occurrence of slums in Brazil

Slums	Cases	%
Yes	1,520	27.61
No	3,971	72.12
Not informed	15	0.27
Total	5,506	100
Inclusion of Slums in the Cadastre	**Municipalities**	**%**
Yes	798	52.50
No	684	45.00
Not informed	38	2.50
Total	1,520	100

Reproduced by permission of UN-HABITAT.

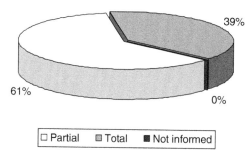

39%

61%

0%

☐ Partial   ▨ Total   ■ Not informed

Figure 12.2:   Coverage of the cadastre in slums: 798 municipalities
Source: Survey undertaken by the Instituto Brasileiro de Geografia e Estatística *(IBGE).* O Perfil dos Municípios Brasileiros. *Rio de Janeiro, Brazil (1999). Reproduced by permission of UN-HABITAT.*

Table 12.3:   Occurrence of irregular land development in Brazil

Occurrence of Irregular Land Development	Municipalities	%
Yes	2,418	43.92
No	3,077	55.88
Not informed	11	0.20
Total	5,506	100
Inclusion of Irregular Land Development in the Cadastre	**Municipalities**	**%**
Yes	1,220	50.45
No	1,133	46.84
Not informed	65	2.69
Total	2,418	100

Reproduced by permission of UN-HABITAT.

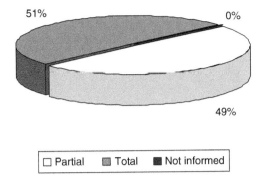

51%   0%

49%

☐ Partial   ▨ Total   ▪ Not informed

Figure 12.3   Coverage of the cadastre in irregular land development
Source: Survey undertaken by the Instituto Brasileiro de Geografia e Estatística *(IBGE).* O Perfil dos
Municípios Brasileiros. *Rio de Janeiro, Brazil (1999). Reproduced by permission of UN-HABITAT.*

As mentioned, irregular land developments are found in about 44 per cent of
the municipalities in Brazil (see Table 12.3).

They are partially recorded in the cadastres in approximately 49 per cent of
the municipalities and totally recorded in 51 per cent (see Figure 12.3). In most
cases, municipal officials recognize that their records of informal areas were
incomplete.

Based on data for municipalities with complete information, multiple
regression analysis was used to test the influence of informality on property tax
revenues per capita. The relationship was controlled with other attributes,
including average income per capita, size of the population and a set of variables
associated with the role of the local government in urban development.

The model was specified selecting variables with the most appropriate functional form, higher explanatory power and lower standard errors. Minimization
of the number of independent variables for the achieved goodness-of-fit was also
sought. Given these requirements, the final model excluded municipal
population size. Following standard procedures, the model includes only
variables that were statistically significant at the 5 per cent level (Table 12.4).
The dependent variable and the average income per capita were transformed into
a natural logarithm.

The model explains approximately 72 per cent of the variation in property tax
revenues per capita. The residual variance can be attributed to non-observed
factors omitted from the analysis and to measurement errors. The F-statistic
(1,139.77) is significant at both the 5 and 1 per cent levels. Based on this model,
the following factors proved to be influential in explaining either an increase
or a decrease in the property tax collected.

- Establishment of urban regulations and lot size not regulated. The findings support
  the argument that municipalities with a more complete regulatory framework
  were able to collect more property tax per inhabitant. At the same time, property
  tax revenues per capita decreased in municipalities requiring no minimum lot size.

Table 12.4:   Analysis of determinants of property tax collection

Dependent variable: Property tax revenue collected per inhabitant in 1998, ln(x)

Independent variables:	Description	β	St. error
Intercept	—	−29.8938	7.01505
Urban legislation	Indicates the establishment of urban regulations in the municipality, including development planning, urban zoning, zoning of areas for social interest, zoning of areas for special interest and building code. It varies from '0' to '8' indicating from the absence of this kind of regulations to the presence of all of them respectively.	0.05892	0.00998
Lot size not regulated	Dichotomous variable that is equal to '1' when no minimum lot size is established in the urban legislation, otherwise it equals zero.	−0.27936	0.038784
Update of property cadastre	Year of last general update of the property cadastre	0.008944	0.003516
Update of cadastral maps	Year of last general update of the cadastral maps	0.000265	0.000045
Use of digital maps	Dichotomous variable that is equal to '1' when digital maps are available, otherwise it equals zero	0.186164	0.057880
Inclusion of informal property in the cadastre	Dichotomous variable that is equal to '1' when informal properties are recorded by the local government, no matter its degree of coverage, otherwise it equals zero	0.107899	0.036951
Occurrence of slums	Dichotomous variable that is equal to '1' when slums are identified in the territory, otherwise it equals zero	0.251655	0.035109
Collection ratio	The percentage of the tax effectively collected in relation to the revenue that would be expected in case of non-evasion.	0.01417	0.00063

Table 12.4 *(Cont'd)*

Independent variables:	Description	β	St. error
Average income: ln(X)	Indicates the average income per inhabitant at the municipal level divided by the national average income per inhabitant, varying from 0.12 to 1.53	2.260726	0.038880
Data	3,966	R	0.8494
Adjusted $\bar{R}^2$[%]	72.088	F	1,139.77
DW	1.91	Standard error of estimate	0.96501

Reproduced by permission of UN-HABITAT.

These results indicate that the presence of land use regulations has a positive impact on property tax performance, just as their absence has a negative effect.

- Update of property cadastre and maps. As expected, municipalities that recently updated their property cadastre and maps tended to have higher property tax revenues per capita. The results of the model also show that municipalities using technology more intensively (as measured by digital mapping) were likewise able to collect more property tax per capita than others.
- Inclusion of informal property in the cadastre. The results confirm the importance of a more universal tax base. This is reflected in the better performance of the property tax when local governments recorded informal properties in the cadastre.
- Occurrence of slums. As reported in earlier studies, municipalities with slums have higher property tax revenues per capita. As Rolnik *et al.*, (1990) suggest, a plausible explanation for this fact is that informality is more prevalent in industrialized and/or economically dynamic cities. Assuming this is the case, the revenue collected in high-income areas and from commercial and industrial properties is likely to offset lower property tax revenue associated with informality.
- Collection ratio. As expected, municipalities with less tax evasion tended to collect more property tax per inhabitant.
- Average per capita income. Also as expected, the average per capita income (which is strongly correlated with property values) is a key factor. Indeed, it is the most important variable in the equation, explaining about 42 per cent of the variation in property tax revenues per capita.

As noted above, population was excluded from the final model specification given the low correlation between population size and property tax revenues per capita. This is due in part to the wide variation in property tax revenue among municipalities of similar size. This confirms findings from previous studies (De Cesare, 2005; Villela, 2001) that indicated that property tax performance reflected more political will than other factors related to the size or economic conditions of jurisdictions. That is to say, other determinants clearly account for the considerable variance in the property tax collected per inhabitant.

In addition to level of income, the results underscore the importance of effective property tax administration. Even in the presence of informality, municipalities achieved better results by maintaining updated cadastres and maps, including informal properties in the cadastre, and providing a broad framework of urban regulation.

In summary, when focusing strictly on property tax performance, the major cause of concern is not the presence of informality per se but rather the way public officials deal with it for property tax purposes. Further analysis should be undertaken to identify whether other factors explain the results reported here.

The property tax as a tool for reducing informality

As noted previously, informality is largely a result of an insufficient supply of serviced land at affordable prices. This section addresses the proposition that a more vigorous property tax system may actually expand access of poor families to serviced land.

The property tax constitutes (at least potentially) the most important source of local revenues that could be used to provide urban infrastructure and services. Furthermore, the portion of the property tax levied on land value is believed to help force more serviced land to the market. In effect, a tax that significantly reduces the economic return of vacant land addresses both components of land supply, that is, production of new serviced land and the use of vacant parcels. The land value tax can be viewed as a natural incentive to develop land to its highest and best use, discouraging owners from delaying development in the hope for higher prices (McCluskey and Franzsen, 1999; Oates, 1999).

This conventional argument regarding local service provision establishes a necessary, but not sufficient, condition for a policy on informality. It is important not only to spend more on urban infrastructure and services, but also to make the right type of public investment in the right place. Moreover, the land to be forced to the market must also be in the proper location, as discussed in the following sections.

Benefits of taxation of informal areas

The following discussion describes the major benefits of imposing a property tax in informal settlements.

Re-orienting the provision of serviced land

Third-world cities have a sad history of over-investing in high-income areas and neglecting low-income areas. Given the relative scarcity of serviced areas and associated land price differences, there are strong incentives for certain landowners to directly or indirectly influence decisions about which areas receive services. As a result, the process by which land gets serviced becomes a hot political currency even in informal areas.

Communities where the property tax is not collected are particularly vulnerable when it comes to public services. Residents may either sell their votes through different forms of clientelism or voice their demands in social protest movements. But this style of governance overlooks the fact that, more often than thought, low-income families in developing countries are willing to pay property taxes when doing so prompts the provision of needed public services in the neighbourhood. Moreover, fair and equitable allocation of tax revenues provides the government greater legitimacy for levying the tax.

Gaffney (1999) adds another twist to the argument by suggesting that imposition of land value taxes is redistributive because it opens up more land to the poor. The differential capitalization effect that benefits informal land markets is likely to increase the bidding power of the poor, enabling them to encroach on lands held by the rich. As a result, a land value tax tends to have a levelling effect across income groups, allowing the poor to move to better-quality land and live in less crowded conditions.

Reducing land prices

The prices of serviced land and informal land are extraordinarily high in third-world cities. Reducing land prices is fundamental to the achievement of sustainable social and economic policies (IAAO, 1997), and a property tax may be one mechanism to accomplish this goal. Bahl and Linn (1992) neatly state the argument as follows:

> Urban land prices are frequently so high that low-income groups cannot afford to purchase land, given their disposable incomes and the prevailing capital market conditions, which prevent access to mortgage credits at affordable interest rates. To the extent that the revenue from property taxes is capitalized into lower current land values (since the tax reduces the expected future private yield on the land), it partially expropriates land ownership rights from the present owner and also constitutes a loan to future owners, who can now acquire the land at a lower price but will have to pay property taxes in the future. If low-income groups cannot buy land because they lack liquidity and access to capital markets, property taxation may be one of the policy instruments to improve their access to land ownership.

The capitalization effect is particularly important because buyers of informal plots usually acquire land in instalments, at interest rates that are much higher than in the formal market. Thus, a land value tax has potential relevance as a surrogate credit system for acquiring serviced land.

Improving the efficiency of serviced land

As Furtado (1993) observes, it is common in third-world countries to see extensive areas at the urban periphery that have services but remain unoccupied, as well as extensive unserviced areas that are informally occupied. One possible explanation for this pattern is the common strategy for marketing and servicing land, known as leapfrogging. Both formal and informal developers often leave vacant land between old subdivisions provided with public services and their new subdivisions. As land parcels at the new site are sold and occupied, bus routes and privately provided services typically extend from the old site through the vacant area. The same applies to public services. To reach the new site, the services have to expand through the vacant areas, which immediately benefit from the new facilities (Cardoso, 1975).

This process explains both the profitability of peripheral development and the forces promoting urban sprawl, which raise the cost of providing public services and equipment. Imposing a strong land value tax would clearly deter the speculative component of leapfrog development. It would also likely encourage more compact cities and more rational development patterns, allowing more efficient use of the existing infrastructure (Brown, 1999).

Regularizing titles to informal land

Local government recognition of occupancy usually does not guarantee property titles at the public registry. However, as Rabello de Castro (2000) argues, relying on a cadastral registration number is a feasible way to certify tenure rights. Informal occupiers may thus perceive the property tax as a kind of a 'entry card' to access the legal world.

The city of Mauá at the periphery of São Paulo provides an illustration. This jurisdiction issues individual regularization certificates for occupants of pirate/clandestine subdivisions to regularize their plots regarding property tax contributions. Under a Municipal Act (Decree 6.692), occupants of informal areas decide whether or not to regularize their parcels by registering in the cadastre. Those that do not, are exempt from the property tax due from the whole area. In addition, occupants may now obtain a regularization affidavit to facilitate the eventual legalization of titling.

Providing a valuable information source

Another advantage of extending the property tax to informal parcels is the fact that its application requires basic knowledge of the area. The information necessary to collect taxes has immeasurable value to city management, as well as to the private sector if publication of the data is guaranteed. In addition, recognition of informal settlements may indirectly stimulate the interest of public authorities in the area, resulting in better provision of public services and expanded opportunities for low-income families.

Directions for improved property tax policy and administration

The Latin American experience offers several lessons about the challenges that informality poses to property tax administration, including the need to design feasible and politically acceptable procedures. The following lessons are presented in the form of policy recommendations.

- Extending tax liability to alternative forms of secure tenure. Limiting the tax liability to property title holders reduces the tax base in countries with widespread informality. Conventional wisdom now holds that the legal incidence of a tax falls primarily on the person liable for its payment. The owner's liability is usually combined with the public authority's right to seize and dispose of the property when the tax is unpaid. This prerogative is an effective sanction to enforce payment since the tax is secured by the property. Thus, there should be no major impediment to considering alternative forms of secure tenure to improve universality of the property tax.
- Bypassing assessment difficulties posed by progressive housing. Most Latin American countries define the capital value (including land and improvements) as the tax base, often regardless of tenure status or degree of irregularity. Implementation of this approach is likely to be problematic in informal areas where self-production of houses is common and improvements are often made gradually. Consequently, proper taxation of informal properties would require more frequent inspections.

Given this challenge, other approaches may be preferable. A strong argument for using site value as the basis is that it would reduce the burden of frequent inspections. Indeed, many jurisdictions in Baja California, Mexico, have switched to a full site value tax base to reduce exactly this administrative burden. In addition, site value taxation is arguably ideal from an economic point of view since it is uniquely non-distorting (see, for example, Brueckner, 1986; Lichfield and Connellan, 1997; Harriss, 1999; and Tideman, 1999).

Another approach to dealing with progressive housing is to rely on self-reporting schemes, passing responsibility for declaring what property improvements have been made on to taxpayers. Given the high cost of controlling the accuracy of self-reports, however, this approach may be unfeasible for local authorities. It may thus be necessary to involve other agents in the task, such as neighbourhood associations or community organizations. These groups are motivated to confirm property values in that their demands for public services depend on the legitimacy of their tax contributions. In other words, the benefits shared within the community would help make the tax acceptable, which in turn may induce taxpayers to declare their property improvements accurately. The reliability of self-reporting schemes would also improve if municipalities earmark revenues for investments in the neighbourhoods where the tax is collected.

Adjusting the tax burden on the poor. Although the number of informal occupiers with the ability and willingness to pay the property tax is often higher than expected, many families do not meet the affordability criteria. Measures that are widely applied in formal areas to reduce or eliminate the tax burden on the poor should be extended to informal areas. This tax relief may include individual deductions according to property value, family income or both, as well as the use of progressive rates starting at a symbolic value and moving up according to classes of assessed values. This is known as the homestead exemption. Similar to progressive tax rates, the approach provides greater benefits to taxpayers occupying low-valued properties than to those occupying high-valued properties despite a lower effective rate. However, the homestead exemption is simpler and benefits all taxpayers.

- While having no impact in terms of revenue, symbolic tax payments are likely to contribute to the creation of fiscal culture.
- Updating urban cadastres. In informal areas, establishing and maintaining the cadastre system are major obstacles to property tax implementation. Over and above issues related to determining the tax liability for properties with unclear tenure rights is the critical problem of recording irregular plots, land subdivisions and buildings. Conventional cadastral procedures and techniques often cannot keep up with such physical and legal idiosyncrasies. More flexible solutions at low cost may therefore be required. One option would be to partner with organizations that provide public services or social programmes in the area to collect the information necessary to update the cadastre system. In addition, neighbourhood associations and the community in general may have to share responsibility with public authorities for keeping property records current.
- Assessing informal property. There are many reasons for concern about the accuracy with which properties are assessed in Latin America. Overly long assessment cycles, inconsistencies in the standard assessment model, and lack of systematic control over assessed values have resulted in low assessment levels and a low degree of uniformity even in formal markets (De Cesare, 2006). Assessing informal property poses even greater challenges, including the need to take into account atypical determinants of property values (such as the value of urban freedom) and non-traditional sources of information (such as neighbourhood association records on property transactions).
- As Abramo (2003) has demonstrated, however, informal areas generally have vibrant property markets and the analysis of land price determinants is as feasible there as it is in formal markets. In addition, as the experience in Colombia, Costa Rica, Guatemala, Mexico and Peru attests, a self-assessment approach may be workable. The benefits include a high degree of acceptability, elimination of objections and appeals, a low-cost solution to lack of information, simplicity, reduction in assessment time and cost, and development of a fiscal culture. Perhaps the most well-known success story is Bogotá, Colombia, where self-assessment scheme has increased assessment levels and expanded tax rolls significantly (Puentes, 2002). It has also improved cadastral coverage (Dillinger, 2000).

Minimizing tax evasion. Contrary to common perceptions, tax evasion is more likely to occur among owners of high-valued properties than among owners of low-valued properties. Local officials repeatedly state that poor families are quite willing to have their properties included in the fiscal cadastre and to pay the property tax.

Establishing a fiscal culture. As in formal property markets, a sustainable and efficient tax system in informal markets requires a sensible adjustment of the tax burden according to ability to pay, demonstration of the public benefits related to the payment of taxes, promotion of educational programmes explaining the rights and duties of citizens and imposition of effective and fair penalties in cases of non-payment. Indeed, the higher administrative cost of taxing low-valued properties can be offset by the benefits of strengthening fiscal culture throughout the city.

Conclusion

Many Latin American countries with widespread informality have in fact implemented some of the initiatives described here, including the imposition of higher tax rates on vacant sites, use of progressive tax rates and introduction of self-reporting schemes and even self-assessment. These policies have been largely ineffective, however, in great measure because of poor property tax administration and lack of judicial support. Indeed, inequities and inefficiencies in property tax administration distort distribution of the tax burden and, in most cases, result in poor revenue collection.

Practical measures to improve administration of the property tax include: reducing the assessment bias; integrating cadastres with other databases managed by organizations responsible for social policies and public services; involving taxpayers as partners in updating cadastral data; minimizing political influence in primarily technical matters (e.g. property assessments and value maps); and educating magistrates about the social, economic and financial impacts of matters related to land regulation, regularization and taxation.

Transparency and dignified treatment of potential taxpayers are essential in both formal and informal areas. Broad acceptance of the property tax can be fostered by sound public investment policy to reduce social inequality and provide universal access to public services and equipment, as well as by extending cadastre coverage to include informal properties. Creating an environment where low-income families have access to basic public services would certainly increase their willingness to pay the property tax.

An effective property tax system does, however, conflict with the current structure of land markets in developing countries. Patrimonialism is still emblematic of Latin American societies, with control over land providing a cash cow for many powerful stakeholders. Thus, resistance to imposing the property tax in informal areas is less likely to come from the low-income residents of those areas than from wealthy individuals and businesses owning large tracts of underdeveloped land or high-valued properties. Change in this state of affairs is no easy task, but the benefits of instituting a vigorous tax on real estate property would certainly justify the effort.

This chapter provides evidence that collection of property taxes in informal areas may not only be possible but also, under the right circumstances and within well-defined limits, an attractive way to pursue a more effective urban policy. That is, implementing a vigorous property tax system would potentially mitigate informality and its negative effects on society in general and on occupants of irregular settlements in particular.

The part of the property tax levied on land value could help to minimize the distortions observed in land markets with extensive informality. At best, these benefits include stimulating land development, deterring land speculation, reducing land prices, increasing the supply of serviced land, promoting more efficient provision of urban infrastructure and services, encouraging more compact development and creating a more rational pattern of growth.

The empirical analysis presented here confirms the importance of sound property tax administration. The findings support the argument that, even in the presence of informality, municipalities can pursue measures to improve property tax performance.

In summary, when focusing strictly on property tax performance, the major cause of concern is not so much informality itself but the way public officials treat it. Introducing the property tax into an environment with rampant informality requires special caution. The challenges are many, including the need to understand the informal market, curb land ownership interests, improve administrative capabilities, and demonstrate how tax revenues can result in social benefits for the poor.

Overcoming the prejudice and ignorance of public officials regarding informality is also essential. Interestingly, imposing an efficient property tax system in informal areas would also likely contribute towards reducing informality.

Finally, there is urgent need for empirical research on the critical relations between the multiple forms and manifestations of informality, fiscal alternatives and regulatory treatments. Future research should also examine the relationship between land price formation in formal and informal markets. Another topic of concern relates to the impacts of changes in property tax collection practices and land prices, as well as property prices that take improvements into account. Finally, case studies and comparative analyses of innovative approaches to property tax management are essential to overcome the current limitations on aggregate data analysis such as the one presented in this chapter.

Note

1 This chapter is based on previously published work by the authors in *Property Tax and Informal Property*, published in Innovative Land and Property Taxation, (2011), UNHabitat, Nairobi, Kenya, 8–28.

References

Abramo, P. (ed.), (2003) *A cidade da informalidade: O desafio das cidades Latino-americanas. Librería Sette Letras*, Rio de Janeiro, Brazil: Lincoln Institute of Land Policy.

Angel, S. (1999) *Housing Policy in Venezuela: Diagnosis and Guidelines for Action.* Washington DC: The Inter-American Development Bank.

Bahl, R.W. and Linn, J.F. (1992) *Urban Public Finance in Developing Countries.* Washington DC: World Bank, Oxford University Press.

Barross, P. (1990) Sequencing Land Development, the Price Complications of Legal and Irregular Settlement Growth. In: Baross, P. and van der Linden, J. (eds.), *The Transformation of Land Supply Systems in Third World Cities.* Aldershot, England: Ashgate Publishing Ltd.

Bird, R.M. and Slack, E. (2004) *International Handbook of Land and Property Taxation.* Cheltenham, UK: Edward Elgar.

Brown, H.G. (1999) Land speculation and land-value tax. In: Wenzer, K.C. (ed.), *Land Value Taxation: the Equitable and Efficient Source of Public Finance*, London, Shepheard-Walwyn Ltd: 46–57.

Brueckner, J.K. (1986) A Modern Analysis of the Effects of Site Value Taxation. *National Tax Journal*, 39(1): 49–58.

Calderón, J.C. (2002) *Property and Credit: Property Formalization in Peru.* Working Paper WP02JC1, Cambridge, MA: Lincoln Institute of Land Policy.

Cardoso, F.H. (1975) The City and Politics. In: Hardoy, J.E. (ed.), *Urbanization in Latin America: Approaches and Issues*, New York, Anchor Books/Doubleday.

De Cesare, C.M. (2002) Toward More Effective Property Tax Systems in Latin America. *Land Lines*, 14(1): 9–11.

De Cesare, C.M. (2005). O Cadastro como instrumento de política fiscal. In: Erba, D.A., de Oliveira, F.L. and Junior, P.N. (eds.) *Cadastro multifinalitário como instrumento da política fiscal e urbana, Diego.* Rio de Janeiro, Brazil: 39–70.

De Cesare, C.M. (2006) Características generales del impuesto a la propiedad inmobiliaria en América Latina, in *Nuevas Tendencias y Experiencias en Tributación Inmobiliaria y Catastro*, Tomo II. INDETEC, Guadalajara, México, 413–439.

De Cesare, C.M., Silva Filho, L.P.C., Une, M.Y. and Wendt, S.C. (2003) *Analyzing the Feasibility of Moving to a Land Value-based Property Tax System: A Case Study from Brazil.* Working Paper WP03CD1, Cambridge, MA: Lincoln Institute of Land Policy.

Dillinger, W. (2000) *Brazil, Financing Municipal Investment: Issues and Options.* Report No. 20313-BR, Brazil Country Management Unit – Finance, Private Sector and Infrastructure, Latin America and the Caribbean Region, World Bank.

Duhau, E. (2003) Programas de regularización y mercado de suelo para vivienda popular en la Ciudad de México. In: Abramo, P. (ed.), *A cidade da informalidade: O desafio das cidades Latino-Americanas*, Librería Sette Letras, Rio de Janeiro, Brazil: Lincoln Institute of Land Policy: 43–78.

Durand-Lasserve, A. and Clerc, V. (1996) *Regularization and Integration of Irregular Settlements: Lessons from Experience.* Working Paper No.6, Nairobi, Kenya: UNDP/ UNCHS(Habitat) and World Bank.

Fernandes, E. (1997) *Access to Urban Land and Housing in Brazil: Three Degrees of Illegality.* Working Paper WP97EF1, Cambridge, MA: Lincoln Institute of Land Policy.

Furtado, F. (1993)*Urbanização de Terras e Ocupação do Solo Urbano – Elementos para a Análise do Processo de Crescimento das Cidades Brasileiras. Unpublished Master's thesis, IPPUR/URFRJ.*

Gaffney, M. (1999) Tax Reform to Release Land. Land-Value Taxation. In: Wenzer, K.C. (ed.), *Land-Value Taxation: the Equitable and Efficient Source of Public Finance.* London, Shepheard-Walwyn Ltd, 58–99.

Harriss, C.L. (1999) Fundamental and Feasible Improvements of Property Taxation. Land-Value Taxation. In: Wenzer, K.C. (ed.), *Land-Value Taxation: the Equitable and Efficient Source of Public Finance*. London, Shepheard-Walwyn Ltd, 100–108.

Instituto Brasileiro de Geografia e Estatística. (2001) *Perfil dos municípios Brasileiros: Pesquisa de informações básicas municipais 1999 (MUNIC)*, IBGE, Brazil.

Instituto Pereira Passos, Prefeitura da Cidade do Rio de Janeiro. (2002) *Evolução da população de favelas no Rio de Janeiro: Uma reflexão sobre os dados mais recentes*. <http://www.rio.rj.gov.br>

IAAO, (1997) *Standard on Property Tax Policy*. Chicago, International Association of Assessing Officers.

Lichfield, N. and Connellan, O. (1997) *Land Value Taxation in Britain for the Benefit of the Community: History, Achievements and Prospects*. Working Paper WP98NL1, Cambridge, MA: Lincoln Institute of Land Policy.

McCluskey, W. and Franzsen, R.C.D. (1999) *Land-value Taxation in Australia, Jamaica, Kenya, New Zealand and South Africa*. In: Proceedings of the IRRV Fifth International Conference on Local Government Property Taxation, Cambridge, MA.

Oates, W.E. (1999) Local Property Taxation: an Assessment. In: *The Value of Land: 1999 Annual Review*. Cambridge, MA: Lincoln Institute of Land Policy, 4–11.

Payne, G. (1997) *Urban Land Tenure and Property Rights in Developing Countries*. London, UK IT/ODA.

Perlman, J.E. (1976) *The Myth of Marginality: Urban Poverty and Politics in Rio de Janeiro*. Berkeley, CA, UC Press.

Puentes, C.R. (2002) *Evaluación del impuesto predial como instrumento para el logro de objetivos de política pública en Bogotá*. Alcadia Mayor de Bogotá, Colombia (resumen ejecutivo).

Rabello de Castro, S. (2000) *Habitação: Direito e governança – Duas sugestões para ação governamental*. Fundação João Ribeiro. Cadernos de Textos 2: 321–338.

Rolnick, R., Kowarick, L., Somekh, N. and Amaral, A. (1990) *São Paulo: Crise e mudança*, Prefeitura de São Paulo, São Paulo, Brazil.

Smolka, M.O. (1991) *Dimensões intra-urbanas da pobreza*, Rio de Janeiro, Brazil, IPPUR Convention/Ministry of Social Action.

Smolka, M.O. (1992) Expulsando os Pobres e Redistribuindo os Ricos: Dinâmica Imobiliária e Segregacao Residencial na Cidade do Rio de Janeiro. *Revista Brasileira de Estudos Populacionais*, 9(1): 3–21.

Smolka, M.O. (2003) Informality, Urban Poverty and Land Market Prices. *Land Lines*, 15(1): 4–7.

Tachner, S.P. (2003) O Brasil e suas favelas. In: Abramo, P. (ed.), *A cidade da informalidade: O desafio das cidades Latino-americanas*. Librería Sette Letras, Lincoln Institute of Land Policy. Rio de Janeiro, Brazil, 13–42.

Tideman, T.N. (1999) Taxing Land is better than Neutral: Land Taxes, Land Speculation, and the Timing of Development. In: Wenzer, K.C. (ed.), *Land-value Taxation: the Equitable and Efficient Source of Public Finance*, London, UK, Shepheard-Walwyn Ltd: 109–133.

Turner, J.F.C. and Fichter, R. (1972) *Freedom to Build: Dweller Control of the Housing Process*. New York: Macmillan.

UN-Habitat. (2003) *The Challenge of Slums: Global Report on Human Settlements*, London, Earthscan Publications Ltd.

UN-Habitat. (2005) *Annual Report*. Nairobi, Kenya.

Villela, L.A. (2001) Subnational Taxation: the Property Tax and the Challenges for its Modernization in Brazil. *Journal of Property Tax Assessment & Administration* 6(3): 45–62.

13

Non-market Value and Hybrid Approaches to Property Taxation

William J. McCluskey and Riël Franzsen

Introduction

Chapter 2 discussed market-value approaches to determine a tax base for the property tax. In this chapter the determination of property tax bases, using approaches other than market or cadastral values, is discussed. The first section describes non-market value approaches and the second a number of hybrid approaches, in terms of which some form of 'value' is used as the basis for the property tax, is discussed. The next looks at so-called flat taxes, and finally some conclusions are drawn.

Non-market valuation approaches

There are several assessment approaches that do not rely on market sales data or other transactional evidence, to determine a tax base for the property tax. These approaches are used (or in some instances necessitated) because such evidence is not available, its reliability is questionable or the property market is simply not mature enough to provide the body of evidence required for a value-based property tax.

Some of the alternatives detailed here are those based on, for example, the size/area of the property (both land and buildings) and/or the use of property (Bell *et al.*, 2008; Almy, 2001).

A Primer on Property Tax: Administration and Policy, First Edition.
Edited by William J. McCluskey, Gary C. Cornia and Lawrence C. Walters.
© 2013 Blackwell Publishing Ltd. Published 2013 by Blackwell Publishing Ltd.

Area based assessment

Area based formulae are commonly used as a means of determining an assessed 'value' for property, particularly where the property market is not functioning properly or where it has not reached a sufficient state of maturity (McCluskey and Plimmer, 2007). Area based systems tend to use the size of buildings and land as the underlying basis. This area is often adjusted, for example, to reflect number of floors in a building and the net usable area as opposed to gross area (Bell *et al.*, 2008; Brzeski, 1999; McCluskey *et al.*, 1998).

Area based systems tend to persist in a number of countries within central and eastern Europe (e.g. Czech Republic, Poland, Slovakia) (Bell *et al.*, 2008; McCluskey and Plimmer 2011), Central Asia (e.g. Georgia, Tajikistan) as well as in some countries in Francophone Africa (e.g. Burundi, Democratic Republic of the Congo, Madagascar). Undeveloped property markets, as well as limited cadastral and property registration systems have to a large extent curtailed the imposition of value-based systems (Malme and Youngman, 2001). In Hungary, for example, the land parcel tax or plot tax is based on the area of the land, and the buildings tax is based on the useful surface area or the market value of the building (Peteri and Lados, 1999). Currently, almost all municipalities opt for the area based assessment (Szalai and Tassonyi, 2004). In Albania, the property tax is levied on buildings according to their age and in which 'value' zone they are located (Dhimitri, 2003).

While area based systems are often regarded as 'simple' solutions for jurisdictions with limited resources, they do suffer from several significant and serious drawbacks. A principal drawback is that they tend not to reflect the value and other spatial benefits that the location offers to property. Well-located buildings and land will pay the same as less well located property of a similar size (Brzeski and Franzsen, 1999; Youngman and Malme, 2004). Compliance with the concepts of vertical and horizontal equity therefore becomes difficult. Buoyancy of the tax revenue under an area system is primarily afforded by altering the tax rates. This is because the assessed 'value' comprises the area of property which tends to remain relatively fixed over time (Rao, 2008; Cornia, 2008). In some jurisdictions there may be political resistance to increasing tax rates, with the result that tax revenues stagnate and – in real terms – actually decrease over time.

Because an area based property tax does not account for the differences in value due to property location, it also distorts land markets (Brzeski, 1999). In effect, it does not put a 'scarcity' value on the individual parcel. By applying the same rate to all types of land and not taking into account any value in that land such as services, amenities or location, the government treats all land the same, thereby discouraging the most productive and efficient use of land. As a result, land that typically commands high market value due to its prime location (e.g. in the centre of a city), will not be recognized as such and may be left to an inefficient use (such as industrial).

The main advantages of the area approach generally relate to lower administrative costs in that self assessment and/or self declaration of property areas and the tax payable in relation thereto can be provided by the taxpayer (e.g. in Czech Republic and India). Data requirements are much less than with a typical *ad valorem* system; trained valuers are not essential; and area based techniques can indeed be modified to reflect aspects such as location and quality of structures (Zorn *et al.*, 2000). The methodology adopted can be viewed as a preliminary step towards a value-based system (Cornia, 2008; Rao, 2008).

In the following paragraphs a brief overview of area based systems employed in India, Slovenia, Czech Republic and Israel is provided.

India

Property tax (called 'rates') in India is levied in terms of state legislation. After independence in 1947, the colonial rating system, inherited from the British, was retained. Properties were taxed on the basis of the annual rent, which was defined as, 'that which such land or buildings were reasonably expected to be let from year to year'. Over time issues were raised concerning this system in terms of the inequity (since it created wide disparity in levels of property tax of similarly placed properties in the same locality), subjectivity in assessments and excessive litigation. A further problem in most states in India is the existence of strict rent control legislation. Rents, fixed by rent control, no longer resembled actual market rents.

In the 1990s and early 2000s, various cities in India (such as Ahmedabad, Bangalore, Delhi and Pune) followed the example of Patna Municipal Corporation and opted for an area based system (Rao, 2008). According to Rao and Ravindra (2002), property tax revenue increased by some 40–60 per cent following the shift to an area based system. Central to the administration of this new system is the fact that property owners can self-assess their tax. The property tax is based on determining a unit area value per square metre of covered space. The tax for a particular property is based on the annual value of the property arrived at by multiplying unit area value assigned to the localities by the covered area of the property and then adjusted by multiplicative factors for occupancy, age, structure and use (Rao, 2008).

Two examples are briefly discussed, namely Delhi and Bangalore.

Delhi

To calculate the annual value the following formula is used in the case of Delhi Municipal Corporation:

$$\text{annual value} = \text{unit area value} \times \text{covered area} \times \text{multiplicative factors}$$

where the multiplicative factors include an occupancy factor (if not owner-occupied), age factor, structure factor and use factor.

Table 13.1: Recommended unit area values

Category	Unit area value (in Rs per sq metre)
A	630
B	500
C	400
D	320
E	270
F	230
G	200
H	100

Self assessment of land and buildings has been effected on the basis of use (in the case of buildings), as well as localities (e.g, with regard to street width), structural characteristics (buildings), age (buildings) and occupancy.

The rates of tax on the annual value of vacant land or covered space of the building for respective categories are for:

Residential property
• 10 per cent for categories A to E
• 6 per cent for categories F to H

Non-residential properties
• 10 per cent

The range of areas/localities has been classified into eight categories from A to H, with the base unit area value being category D. Multiplying factors of greater than 1.0 would be used for those categories above D and less than 1.0 for those categories below D. Table 13.1 shows the prescribed unit area values.

The multiplicative adjustment factors were considered appropriate in order to refine the assessed values to reflect various aspects that could be deemed to affect property value.

Occupancy factor (residential)

Owner-occupied	1
Tenanted	2
Flat factor	(less than $100\,m^2 = 0.9$; greater than $100\,m^2 = 1.0$)

Structure factor

Structures are classified into three categories of buildings, i.e. *kutcha*, semi-*pucca* or *pucca* with factors of 0.5 for *kutcha* structures, 0.7 for semi-*pucca* and 1.0 for *pucca* structures.

Age factor

Post 2000 properties: 1.0
1990–2000: 0.9
1980–1990: 0.8
1970–1980: 0.7
1960–1970: 0.6
Pre 1960: 0.5

Use factor

Medical institutions, religious, schools   1
Industrial (vacant), utility, telecommunication   2
Industrial (occupied), museums, theatres, schools   3
Business, retail   4
Hotels, towers   10

Where vacant land constitutes more than 75 per cent of the total plot area, the base unit value is computed at a factor of 0.3.

Bangalore

Bangalore, in Karnataka State, has a unique property tax system, called the 'Self Assessment Scheme' (SAS). It is a hybrid between a value-based and an area based system. In 2000 the Bangalore City Corporation successfully negotiated with civil society that a renewal of the outdated annual value property tax system was required. Although the SAS was introduced as an optional scheme, 90 per cent of taxpayers opted for 'self-assessment', in reality self-declaration (Rao, 2008). Information was readily available which made it transparent, public meetings were held and most importantly, it was backed by politicians and the media. More than 60 per cent of taxpayers filed their declarations within the prescribed 45-day period. The city corporation promised that no changes would be effected until 2005 – i.e. clarity and transparency were key features to obtain public support.

The Karnataka State Legislature introduced capital value by law in 2002. However, the city was of the view that the capital value system was fatally flawed as only the built-up land area was to be considered when determining land values and the maximum values in respect of buildings were fixed. This coincided with a court case which ruled in favour of the SAS and suggested that it should be made mandatory, rather than merely optional. All political parties agreed that it would be prudent to rather retain and revise the SAS than enforce capital values. The extension of the city's boundaries in 2007, which created the new Bruhat Bengaluru Mahanagara Palike (BBMP), necessitated a revision of the SAS system and saw the introduction of so-called 'unit area value' (UAV) taxation. UAV is determined with reference to the average rate of expected returns from a property per square foot per month, depending on the location and use of the property.

The whole BBMP area has been classified into six value zones (for residential and non-residential properties) based on published guidance values produced by the Department of Stamps and Registration. These values are adjusted regularly, ensuring some measure of buoyancy as evidenced by the continued annual growth of property tax revenues in Bangalore in recent years.

For residential properties the steps are as follows (SAS, 2008):

1. built-up area × unit area value × 10 months = **Total₁ (T₁)**
2. T_1 – applicable depreciation = T_2 (i.e. taxable annual value)
3. $T_2 \times 20\% = T_3$ (property tax)
4. $T_3 \times 24\% = T_4$ (cess)
5. $T_3 + T_4 = T_5$ (gross property tax payable)
6. $T_5 \times 5\% = T_6$ (rebate for early payment)
7. $T_5 - T_6$ = net property tax payable

The 'total built-up area' means the total area covered by buildings immediately above the 'plinth level' (i.e. the base or platform upon which a column, pedestal or structure rests). Courtyards, gardens, drainage, culverts and boundary walls are excluded from total built-up area.

Slovenia

In Slovenia the basis of the tax is the value of the buildings according to a 'point' system where each building is allocated a number of 'points' according to prescribed criteria which reflects the age, location, condition and any building equipment (McCluskey and Bevc, 2007; Bevc, 2000). The value is determined as follows:

- number of points × value of the point/m^2 = value of the building/m^2
- value of the building/m^2 × useful area in m^2 = value of the building

The value of the 'point' is determined each year by the municipality and adjusted annually by reference to the cost of living index (Bevc, 2000).

Czech Republic

The buildings tax adopts various rates per square metre depending on the type and use of the building. For example, dwellings have a tax rate of 1 CZK per m^2 of built area, holiday homes attract a rate of 3 CZK per m^2 and garages 4 CZK per m^2. Buildings used for agriculture operations are assessed at 1 CZK per m^2, industrial at 5 CZK per m^2 and other business/commercial buildings at

Table 13.2: Adjustment coefficients by population of municipality

Coefficient	Municipal population
1.0	Less than 1,000
1.4	1,000 – 6,000
1.6	6,000 – 10,000
2.0	10,000 – 25,000
2.5	25,000 – 50,000
3.5	Greater than 50,000
4.5	Prague

10 CZK per m². The basic tax on buildings or land is then adjusted by a coefficient which is determined by the size of a municipality in terms of its population (Rochlickova, 1999). Table 13.2 shows the various coefficients.

Other non-value approaches

Israel

The 'arnona' is the property tax levied by municipalities in Israel and is an excellent example of a non value based approach. The tax is levied on residential and non-residential properties as well as undeveloped and agricultural land. In general the arnona is determined by reference to four criteria: actual use (rather than zoned use), location, type and the age of property (Darin, 1999). Municipalities tend to be divided into residential and non-residential value zones. Within each of these zones specific arnona rates per m² are determined by the municipality for the different types of property according to their age, size and type (Portnov *et al.*, 2001).

In terms of this approach, the arnona is highly correlated with the location of the property. However, location is rather broadly determined. For example, Tel Aviv has five residential and also five non-residential zones to cover a city with a population exceeding 400,000. Furthermore, the arnona is paid by the user of the property, rather than the owner (Darin, 1999). The arnona is an important source of local revenue and tax rates are determined annually by local authorities, ensuring some buoyancy.

Hybrid alternatives that use a form of value as the basis for the property tax

There are several assessment methodologies that use a form of property value as the basis of the property tax. This section provides an overview of some of the 'hybrid' approaches adopted.

Acquisition value basis

Acquisition value is really a means to create a property tax assessment limitation. Essentially, it is a mechanism to curb or limit the increase in assessed value (Sjoquist and Pandey, 2001). Thus, the assessed value can only be changed annually in line with some predetermined growth rate such as inflation or a specified increase. Generally speaking the assessed value is the purchase price of the property, and that value, subject to any annual changes, will remain the assessed value until the property is sold.

Possibly the most well known of the assessment limitation measures is Proposition 13 in California. On 6 June 1978, California voters overwhelmingly approved Proposition 13, an amendment to California's constitution which was the taxpayers' collective response to dramatic increases in property taxes (Youngman, 2006). Under Proposition 13, the property tax on a residential property is limited to 1 per cent of its assessed value, until the property is resold. The resale price then becomes the new assessed value. However, this 'assessed value' may only be increased by a maximum of 2 per cent per year. In addition, Proposition 13 fixed the assessed values for real property at their 1975–76 market value levels. This particular measure was largely adopted to counteract ever-increasing property tax bills fuelled by inflation-induced property assessments.

Under Proposition 13, similar properties can have substantially different assessed values based solely on the dates the properties were purchased. Disparities result wherever significant appreciation in property values has occurred over time (O'Sullivan *et al.*, 1994). Long-time property owners, whose assessed values generally may not be increased more than 2 per cent per year, tend to have markedly lower tax liability than recent purchasers, whose assessed values tend to approximate market levels. If the property's market value increases rapidly, say by more than 10 per cent per annum, or if inflation exceeds 2 per cent, the differential between the owner's taxes and the taxes that a new owner would have to pay can become quite large (Sexton *et al.*, 1999). Despite the glaring inequities created by Proposition 13 over time, where neighbours in basically identical properties pay vastly different taxes on the basis of their respective dates of acquisition, it was found to pass constitutional muster by the USA Supreme Court in 1992 (Youngman, 2006) and remains popular among the majority of Californian voters (Sheffrin, 2010).

Property value banding

A property value banding system relies upon the concept of dividing properties into different categories according to an estimate of their capital or rental value for the purposes of determining a property tax bill. Rather than valuing the properties to a discrete figure and assigning them to a band, the property values are estimated according to a range of values or bands (Plimmer *et al.*, 2002a). It is of course possible to value to a discrete figure and then to place the property into the appropriate value band. Banding is presently only utilized in Great Britain and while there is thus little current international practice of jurisdictions using banding, there appears to be a growing international interest, particularly for developing countries (Plimmer *et al.*, 2002b). The banding approach can also be used as an integrated tax system, because the tax liability can be (and is in Great Britain) built into the system on a per property basis.

Property value banding: the theory

There are essentially three key elements in a banded system: first, the number of value bands, second, the band widths and third, the tax multiplier (or tax ratio) per band. The final element is essentially the tax liability for each owner or occupier of taxable property. These elements can be modified in different ways to examine whether a banding system can perform adequately in terms of progressivity, a key factor in assessing the fairness of a tax (McCluskey *et al.*, 2004). This aspect is of particular importance as any change to the tax basis is likely to have a considerable redistributive effect.

Property value banding system in Great Britain

A banded property value/tax system (known as the council tax) for domestic (i.e. residential) property was introduced in Great Britain in 1993 (DoE, 1991). The council tax came into force in April 1993 and was based on property values as at 1 April 1991. The Department of Environment Green Paper (1991) laid out the basic underpinnings of the banded system:

- There were eight valuation bands (categorized as A through H).
- A 3:1 tax ratio between the bill paid by owners of property in the highest value band (H) and those with lowest (A); in other words if a taxpayer owned a property in Band A and paid $1,000 then the owner of a property in the highest value band would have to pay $3,000.
- Band D was selected to represent the reference band from which the tax paid for the other bands is mathematically calculated.
- A system of 'ninths' was used to determine the relevant tax multipliers per band, with band D representing 'nine ninths' or one (see Table 13.3).
- The starting point for band A was 'six ninths' or 0.66.

Table 13.3 provides an example of the tax liabilities for properties in each value band, based on eight bands and a tax ratio of 3:1 on ninths. Band D is taken as the reference band with a liability of say $500. The overall tax ratio is 3:1 as shown by the fact that band A property pays one-third ($333) of property in band H ($1,000). The tax to be paid for property in the other bands is shown in Table 13.3.

It must be remembered that the number of bands, their value widths and the tax ratio are variables. Any one or more of these can be changed in order to 'fit'

Table 13.3:   Banding structure

Band	Tax ratio (based on 'ninths')	Tax liability ($)	Tax to be paid ($)
A	6/9	500 × 6/9	333
B	7/9	500 × 7/9	389
C	8/9	500 × 8/9	444
D	9/9	500 × 9/9	500
E	11/9	500 × 11/9	611
F	13/9	500 × 13/9	722
G	15/9	500 × 15/9	833
H	18/9	500 × 18/9	1000

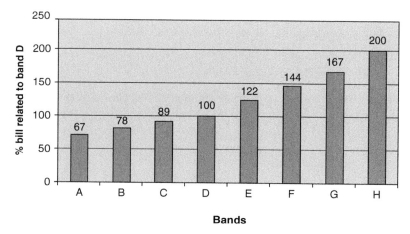

Figure 13.1:   Tax bills in relation to band D

in with the property market of the jurisdiction or to meet other issues of tax progressivity. The banding system finally adopted in Great Britain is depicted in Table 13.4. Tax is payable in the proportions on the eight bands A to H. The banding system means that the amount of tax payable will vary according to the value of the property but only within a limited range (Hills and Sutherland, 1991). Taxpayers in the lowest band of property will pay about two-thirds of those properties in the middle bands in that area; those in the highest band will pay three times as much as those in the lowest band (see Figure 13.1). Figure 13.1 illustrates the tax bill progressivity, in that the bills increase as the value of property increases, in this case a tax ratio of 3:1 applies.

A feature of Great Britain's value banding system was the establishing of a series of value bands developed by reference to the average value of dwellings in the different regions; therefore bands are distinct for England, Scotland and Wales (see Table 13.4).

Table 13.4: Valuation bands in Great Britain

	Range of values			
Valuation band	Scotland (£)	England (£)	Wales (£)	Proportion of band D bill payable
A	Up to 27,000	Up to 40,000	Up to 30,000	6/9
B	27,001–35,000	40,001–52,000	30,001–39,000	7/9
C	35,001–45,000	52,001–68,000	39,001–51,000	8/9
D	45,001–58,000	68,001–88,000	51,001–66,000	9/9
E	58,001–80,000	88,001–120,000	66,001–90,000	11/9
F	80,001–106,000	120,001–160,000	90,001–120,000	13/9
G	106,001–212,000	160,001–320,000	120,001–240,000	15/9
H	Over 212,000	Over 320,000	Over 240,000	18/9

Advantages of a property value banding system

The strength of a banding system rests on the robustness of the valuation of the property on which it is levied. The banding system is designed to place properties into wide valuation bands. This means that there would have to be major changes in relative property prices before significant numbers of properties were being unfairly treated (Plimmer *et al.*, 2002a). A large part of the appeal of banding lies in the simplicity of its structure, the low cost and the relative ease of valuation. In the long run this is undoubtedly true; properties, as opposed to people, are relatively immobile, and the problem of evasion is therefore diminished (Plimmer et al, 2000). Banding at least partly mitigates the need for the individual valuation of every property. A further advantage of banding is that property improvements and small changes in capital values resulting from the vagaries of the property market need not lead to changes in a property's valuation band and thus unpalatable increases in yearly tax bills. Revaluations therefore become much less of an administrative and financial burden because the period between revaluations can be as much as ten years (currently for Great Britain the interval is some 20 years). The challenge for many jurisdictions will be to what extent fully discriminating capital value property tax systems can be justified in terms of such issues as cost of introduction, annual maintenance, human resource capacity and expertise. The UK government in its White Paper, *Modern Local Government: In Touch with the People* (DoE, 1998), stated that the council tax was working well as a local tax as it had been widely accepted and was generally well understood.

Disadvantages

Weighted against these attractions is the fact that, as with any system of banded rather than continuous taxation, decisions at the margin become more contentious.

For example, some taxpayers on band boundaries may face a substantial difference in payments, depending on the band into which their properties fall. In addition, banding may result in a regressive tax system, which could well lead to costly and time-consuming appeals. A further disadvantage is that you cannot apply a flat tax rate to arrive at a tax bill.

Proposed value banding option for Ireland

The *Report of the Commission on Taxation* (2009) in Ireland provides an illustrative model for an annual, self-assessed, property tax based on the valuation of a residential property. The Commission proposed that properties be grouped in eight valuation bands (five bands of €150,000 each from zero to €750,000 (i.e. upto €150,000 and €150,001 to €300,000, etc.); €750,001 to €1,000,000; €1,000,001 to €1.5 million; and over €1.5 million) with properties being taxed at the midpoint of the valuation band. Based on suggested tax rates of 0.25 per cent and 0.3 per cent, using house price date from 2004, the Commission estimated that the 0.25 per cent rate would yield €1.231 billion (gross of reliefs and based on approximately 2 million dwellings) it was estimated that the 0.3 per cent rate would yield €1.476 billion gross; no yield was estimated for properties valued over €1.5 million because values for those properties were not available. The advantages of this proposal were seen to include the following:

- It is perceived as 'fairer' than a flat-rate charge on all households.
- Self-assessment allows a relatively easy and fast collection of valuation data.
- Unlike other options, it is not based on unavailable information.
- Over time, the system could be developed into a more accurate system.

The disadvantages of this proposal include the following:

- Self assessment is likely to lead to inconsistent estimation of property values.
- While self assessment has advantages, a relatively small portion of the population is currently subject to self assessment, so imposing self assessment on basically the entire population is likely to pose problems (although these problems could be addressed through audit checks by the agency administering the system).
- It does not allow for future improvements to accuracy.
- Information about building use is not currently available, which would hinder the enforcement and compliance of the tax.
- There are potential difficulties with valuing properties which are close to the edges of the bands.
- Any tax based solely on valuations would probably be higher in the Dublin area and, to a lesser extent, other urban areas, so the tax could be open to similar criticisms to the previous residential property tax.

Indexation

Few countries and taxable jurisdictions are able to maintain their statutory obligation to undertake revaluations according to the prescribed frequency. Typically, revaluations are postponed, or indeed cancelled, and then at some future date a major effort is mobilized to revalue all properties. The objective of the revaluation is to move assessed values more into line with current market values. An alternative to a major revaluation is to develop indices which are market based and then apply them to the previous assessed values, thereby moving the assessed values into line with the market.

Indexation is a mechanism to alter assessed values either on an annual basis or at some other predetermined interval, such as every three years. The indices can be determined directly from property market evidence (as in New Zealand) or can be developed on the basis of property types and by location (i.e. market area). Or alternatively, surrogate indices can be used, for example the general rate of inflation or the retail price index (as is the case in Brazil).

The most appropriate approach would be to develop market-based parcel indices by market area, and differentiated by land use type. Market areas are effectively neighbourhoods of similar properties of similar value and therefore theory would suggest that such property values would tend to move at the same rate and in the same direction.

In essence the procedure is relatively straightforward:

$$\text{Base value} \times \text{Index} = \text{Assessed value}$$

The base value should normally be determined in accordance with standard valuation principles (manual or CAMA-based). This discrete base value would capture the particular, unique characteristics of the parcel and it is this value that would be indexed. The base value during the currency of the valuation roll would be revised subject to any physical changes which would affect the value.

It is essential that during the currency of the valuation roll, transactions are continually reviewed to ensure that the base value established is uniform and correct. Once the valuation date has been determined, at for example 31 December, then sales around that date can be gathered and analysed. Normally sales would be gathered over a 12- to 24-month period prior to the valuation date. The sales should be analysed by market area and from this an index for each market area can be determined.

Flat-rate residential property charge

This approach represents a uniform flat charge per property regardless of size and value. This format is typically more akin to a 'charge' than a 'tax'. A flat-rate residential property charge would have the following advantages:

- It is easy to administer and understand, although the lack of a property register might mean that many properties could go unregistered and therefore would escape the charge.
- It would give an immediate yield.
- Significantly less information is needed to administer the tax.
- Inspections would only be required to verify the existence of a residence.

Notwithstanding the administrative advantages, there are also several disadvantages to consider:

- A flat-rate tax would be perceived as inequitable because the same amount of tax would be levied on expensive and inexpensive properties – this perception could be mitigated by the application of waivers, reliefs and exclusions.
- Given its application to all residential property regardless of valuation or size, some allowance would have to be included for low income households.
- Introducing and maintaining a simple system does not assist with the collection, the collation and the use of valuable property-related data which could contribute towards the future migration to a more buoyant and sustainable system.

The level set for the charge would be important, to ensure that it is not perceived as a nuisance tax and that it is financially worthwhile to follow up with delinquent taxpayers.

In July 2009, a new local authority charge was introduced in Ireland. It is a charge levied on every residential property (unit) that is not the main residence of the owner. The charge has remained at €200 per annum since its introduction. The charge is per dwelling – so a block of 30 apartments owned by one person or company – will incur a charge of €6,000 per taxable year. The charge is payable by non-residents as well as Irish residents.

In New Zealand, local government has the right to levy a 'uniform annual general charge' (in addition to a general rate or property tax). This is a fixed amount per rating unit, or per separately used or inhabited part of a rating unit, for all rateable land within the council area. For example, this would mean that each shop within a shopping centre, would be liable for a uniform annual general charge. The same would apply to a farm with more than one dwelling, (e.g. worker accommodation), or a residential property with a separate fully self-contained unit (e.g. a flat or cottage for tourist/visitor accommodation).

Greece

In September 2011, the Ministry of Finance in Greece announced that a special property tax would be introduced and would apply to all properties in Greece, raising an estimated €2–3 billion. The tax is likely to affect approximately 5.1 million properties. The tax is based on three factors: size of the property, location and age. Properties are assigned a zonal rate according to location and street type. It is interesting that the size and zonal rate of properties are currently listed on

Table 13.5: Typical euro charge based on prescribed zonal rates

Zonal rate	Euros per sq. metre
For vulnerable group	0.50
0–500	3
501–1,000	4
1,001–1,500	5
1,501–2,000	6
2,001–2,500	8
2,501–3,000	10
3,001–4,000	12
4,001–5,000	14
5,001 and up	16

Table 13.6: Age and surcharges

Age (years)	Multiplier	Surcharge (%)
26 and older	1	None
20–25	1.05	5
15–19	1.1	10
10–14	1.15	15
5–9	1.2	20
0–4	1.25	25

the electricity bills of the power companies (see Table 13.5). The government is indeed planning to use these companies as agents to collect the property tax.

Properties 0–25 years old will be assessed a surcharge of 5–25 per cent, inversely proportional to age. The newer the property, the higher the surcharge and vice versa (see Table 13.6).

Therefore, the computation of the tax is relatively straightforward. For example, in respect of a 10-year old property of 120 m² and with a zonal rate of €3,000 per m², the property tax calculation would be:

$$120 \times €10 \times 1.15 = €1,380 \text{ for the relevant tax year.}$$

Flat-rate taxes

A flat-rate property tax is a rather blunt revenue-raising tool and is largely based on the idea that property users or owners should contribute at least a minimum amount of tax. In Australia and New Zealand, these taxes are commonly referred to as uniform annual general charges, which are set as a fixed amount irrespective

Table 13.7:   Flat rates for residential properties in Temeke Municipal Council for 2002

No.	Description of rateable property	Main building gross external area (m²)	Tax assessment category shillings
1	Residential low density	up to 100	30,000.00
2	Residential low density	100–150	45,000.00
3	Residential low density	over 150	75,000.00
4	Residential medium density	up to 75	23,000.00
5	Residential medium density	75–100	25,000.00
6	Residential medium density	over 100	30,000.00
7	Residential high density	up to 50	10,000.00
8	Residential high density	50 m² – 75	12,000.00
9	Flat prime area	up to 50	25,000.00
10	Flat prime area	over 50	30,000.00
11	Flat secondary area	up to 50	20,000.00
12	Flat secondary area	over 50	25,000.00

Source: Schedule to the By-laws published in Government Notice No 336 on 12 July 2002.

of the use or value of the property. A similar tax is also charged by the Accra Metropolitan Assembly in Ghana.

New Zealand

So-called uniform annual general charges are generally levied across entire taxing jurisdiction or within a defined area or areas within such a jurisdiction. It provides for the payment of a minimum amount which is levied at the same amount for all properties. Without this minimum payment, many small, low-valued properties would otherwise not contribute enough to cover the costs of levying the tax. This is particularly noticeable, for example, in some of the lower-value rural settlements in New Zealand (McCluskey, 2001).

One of the problems of such an approach is that of equity and fairness, especially as flat-rate-per-property taxes may impact more heavily on poorer households and therefore be regressive.

Tanzania

The flat-rate tax, as its basis, measures the property use and size, and in some instances also the location of the property. In terms of section 15(1)(e) of the Local Government Finances Act of 1982, a rate may be levied as a 'rate based on the fact of ownership of immovable property situated in a specified area or at a specified place within the area of the authority'.

Municipalities have some freedom in designing their own flat-rate systems, with some municipalities having more than 60 property categories, thus introducing administrative complexity into an otherwise simple system (McCluskey and Franzsen 2005). As an example, Table 13.7 lists 12 categories of residential properties for the Temeke Municipal Council in Dar es Salaam in 2002.

Conclusions

It is evident that not all countries or jurisdictions use a property tax that is based on market price transactions. In fact, there are a significant number of countries that use assessment approaches that are not directly related to prices derived from the property market. Various options to the *ad valorem* approach exist and include a simple area (pre-2007 Cameroon) or an adjusted area basis (Israel), flat-rate property charges simply based on a per property basis (Ireland) or derivatives that use some measure of value such as banding (Great Britain), indexation (Brazil) or broad zonal rates for land and/or buildings (Greece).

There is a rich source of descriptive and analytical information contained in several international country- or regional-specific surveys on property tax systems. Some of the more recent comparative studies or compendia include (in chronological order): McCluskey (1991), Youngman and Malme (1994); Rosengard (1998); McCluskey (1999); Almy (2001); Brown and Hepworth (2001); Malme and Youngman (2001); McCluskey and Franzsen (2001); Bird and Slack (2004); De Cesare (2004); Franzsen and McCluskey (2005); McCluskey and Plimmer (2007); Bell *et al.* (2008). What is patently clear from an international perspective is that there is no such thing as 'one size fits all', but rather pragmatic solutions that are largely tailored to meet the specific country's objectives at a given point.

References

Almy, R. (2001) *A Survey of Property Tax Systems in Europe*. Report prepared for the Slovenia Department of Taxes and Customs, Ljubljana, Ministry of Finance.

Bell, M., Yuan, N. and Connolly, K. (2008) *A Compendium of Countries with an Area Based Property Tax*. Working Paper WP09KC1, Cambridge, MA: Lincoln Institute of Land Policy.

Bevc, I. (2000) Property Tax in the Republic of Slovenia. *Journal of Property Tax Assessment & Administration*, 5(4): 57–62.

Bird, R. and Slack, E. (eds.), (2004) *International Handbook of Land and Property Taxation*, Northampton, MA: Edward Elgar.

Brown, P.K. and Hepworth, M.A. (2001) *A Study of European Land Tax Systems*, Working Paper, Cambridge, MA: Lincoln Institute of Land Policy.

Brzeski, J. (1999), Real Property Taxation in Poland. In: McCluskey, W.J. (ed.), *Comparative Property Tax Systems: An International Comparative Review*, Aldershot, UK: Avebury Publishing Limited, 411–418.

Brzeski, J. and Franzsen R. (1999) Making the Case for Ad Valorem Reform in Transitional Economies: The Non-Fiscal Benefits. *Journal of Property Tax Assessment & Administration*, 4(1): 29–38.

Commission on Taxation (2009) *Report of the Commission on Taxation*. Dublin: Stationery Office.

Cornia, G.C. (2008) Commentary. In Bahl, R., Martinez-Vazquez, J. and Youngman, J. (eds.), *Making the Property Tax Work: Experiences in Developing and Transitional Countries*, Cambridge, MA: Lincoln Institute of Land Policy, 307–312.

Darin, D. (1999) A Politician's Appraisal of Property Taxation: Israel's Experience with the *Arnona*. Working Paper WP99DD1, Cambridge, MA: Lincoln Institute of Land Policy.

De Cesare, C.M. (2004) *General Characteristics of Property Tax Systems in Latin America*, paper presented at the 7th annual conference of the International Property Tax Institute, Guadalajara, Mexico.

Department of the Environment, (1991) *The New Tax for Local Government: A Consultation Paper*. London: Department of the Environment.

Department of the Environment, Transport and the Regions, (1998) *Modern Local Government: In Touch with the People*. London: Department of the Environment, Transport and the Regions.

Dhimitri, J. (2003) Property Taxation in Transition Countries: The Case of Albania. *Journal of Property Tax Assessment & Administration*, 8(1): 19–32.

Franzsen R.C.D. and McCluskey, W.J. (2005) An Exploratory Overview of Property Taxation in the Commonwealth of Nations. Working Paper WP05RF1, Cambridge MA: Lincoln Institute of Land Policy.

Hills, J. and Sutherland, H. (1991) The Proposed Council Tax. *Fiscal Studies*, 12(4): 1–21.

Malme, J.H. and Youngman, J.M. (2001) (eds.), *The Development of Property Taxation in Economies in Transition: Case Studies from Central and Eastern Europe*. Washington DC: World Bank Institute.

McCluskey, W.J. (ed.), (1991) *Comparative Property Tax Systems*. Aldershot, UK: Avebury Publishing Limited.

McCluskey, W.J. (1999) (ed.), *Comparative Property Tax Systems: An International Comparative Review*. Aldershot, UK: Avebury Publishing Limited.

McCluskey, W.J. and Franzsen, R.C.D. (2001), Land Value Taxation: An Empirical Study of Five Countries, *Journal of Property Tax Assessment & Administration*, 6(2): 3–44.

McCluskey, W.J. (2005), Property Tax Systems and Rating in New Zealand. In: W.J. McCluskey and R.C.D. Franzsen (eds), *Land Value Taxation: An Applied Analysis*, Ashgate Publishing Group, Aldershot, England, 115–146.

McCluskey, W.J., Almy, R. and Rohlickova, A. (1998) The Development of Property Taxation in the New Democracies of Central and Eastern Europe. *Journal of Property Management*, 16(3): 145–159.

McCluskey, W.J. and Bevc. I. (2007) Fiscal Decentralisation in the Republic of Slovenia: An Opportunity for the Property Tax. *Property Management*, 25(4): 400–419.

McCluskey, W.J., Davis, P and Lim, L.C. (2004) Residential Property Taxation: A Capital Value Banding Approach. *Journal of Property Tax Assessment & Administration*, 1(3): 51–64.

McCluskey, W.J. and Franzsen, R.C.D. (2001) Land Value Taxation: A Case Study Approach. Working Paper WP01WM1. Cambridge, MA: Lincoln Institute of Land Policy.

McCluskey, W.J. and Franzsen, R.C.D. (2005) An Evaluation of the Property Tax In Tanzania: An Untapped Fiscal Resource or Administrative Headache. *Property Management*, 23(1): 43–69.

McCluskey, W.J. and Plimmer, F. (2007) The Potential for the Property Tax in the 2004 Accession Countries of Central and Eastern Europe. *RICS Research Paper Series*, London: Royal Institution of Chartered Surveyors.

McCluskey, W.J. and Plimmer, F. (2011) The Creation of Fiscal Space for the Property Tax: the Case of Central and Eastern Europe. *International Journal of Strategic Property Management*, 15(2): 123–138.

O'Sullivan, A., Sexton, T.A. and Sheffrin, S.M. (1994) Differential Burdens from the Assessment of Proposition 13. *National Tax Journal*, 47(4): 721–730.

Peteri, G. and Lados, M. (1999) Local Property Taxation in Hungary. In: McCluskey, W.J. (ed.), *Comparative Property Tax Systems: An International Comparative Review*, Aldershot, UK: Avebury Publishing Limited, 419–439.

Plimmer, F., McCluskey, W.J. and Connellan, O. (2000) *Equity and Fairness within Ad Valorem Real Property Taxes*. Working Paper WP00FP1, Cambridge, MA: Lincoln Institute of Land Policy.

Plimmer, F., McCluskey, W.J. and Connellan, O. (2002a) Valuation Banding – An International Property Tax Solution. *Journal of Property Investment & Finance*, 20(1): 68–83.

Plimmer, F., McCluskey, W.J. and Connellan, O. (2002b) Property Tax Banding: A Solution for Developing Countries. *Assessment Journal*, March/April, pp 37–47.

Portnov, B.A.; McCluskey, W.J. and Deddis, W.G. (2001) Property Taxation in Israel: a Non Ad Valorem Approach. *Land Use Policy*, 18,351–364.

Rao, U.A.V. and Ravindra, A. (2002) *Reforming the Property Tax System in India*. United Nations Development Programme, New Delhi, India.

Rao, U.A.V. (2008) Is Area Based Assessment an Alternative, an Intermediate Step or an Impediment to Value Based Taxation in India? In Bahl, R., Martinez-Vazquez, J. and Youngman, J. (eds.), *Making the Property Tax Work: Experiences in Developing and Transitional Countries*, Cambridge, MA: Lincoln Institute of Land Policy, 241–267.

Rochlickova, A. (1999) Property Taxation in the Czech Republic. In: W.J. McCluskey (ed), *Comparative Property Tax Systems: An International Comparative Review*, Aldershot, UK: Avebury Publishing Limited, 440–454.

Rosengard, J. (1998) *Property Tax Reform in Developing Countries*. Norwell, MA: Kluwer Academic Publishers.

Self Assessment Scheme (2008) *Property Tax Self Assessment Scheme Handbook: Block Period 2008–09 to 2010–11*. Bruhat Bangalore Mahanagara Palike.

Sexton, T.A., Sheffrin, S.M. and O'Sullivan, A. (1999) Proposition 13: Unintended Effects and Feasible Reforms. *National Tax Journal*, 52(1): 99–112.

Sheffrin, S.M. (2010) Fairness and Market Value Property Taxation. In Bahl, R., Martinez-Vazquez, J. and Youngman, J. (eds.), *Challenging the Conventional Wisdom on the Property Tax*. Cambridge, MA: Lincoln Institute of Land Policy, 241–262.

Sjoquist, D.L. and Pandey, L. (2001) An Analysis of Acquisition Value Property Tax Assessment for Homestead Property. *Public Budgeting and Finance*, Winter, 1–17.

Szalai, A. and Tassonyi, A.T. (2004) Value Based Property Taxation: Options for Hungary. *Environment and Planning C: Government and Policy*, 22: 495–521.

Youngman, J.M. (2006) *Property Valuation and Taxation: Cases and Materials*. Cambridge, MA: Lincoln Institute of Land Policy.

Youngman, J.M. and Malme, J.H. (1994) *An International Survey of Taxes on Land and Buildings*. Amsterdam: Kluwer.

Youngman, J.M. and Malme, J.H. (2004) *The Property Tax in a New Environment: Lessons from International Tax Reform Efforts*, paper presented at Andrew Young International Studies Program, University of Atlanta, 1–32.

Zorn, K.C., Tesche, J. and Cornia, G. (2000) Diversifying Local Government Revenue in Bosnia-Herzegovina through an Area Based Property Tax. *Public Budgeting and Finance*, Winter, 63–86.

14

Computer Assisted Mass Appraisal and the Property Tax

William J. McCluskey, Peadar Davis,
Michael McCord, David McIlhatton
and Martin Haran

Introduction

Mass appraisal or computer assisted mass appraisal (CAMA) are terms that tend to apply to the valuation of real property for property tax purposes. The greatest change in assessment practice over the past 30–40 years has involved the use of computers and mathematical formulas to establish a relationship between property characteristics and transaction prices, thereby permitting an estimate of the market value of other properties not subject to a recent sale. Site characteristics such as size and location are important elements of these mathematical models, raising the possibility of estimating the effect of location on parcel value. This chapter is divided into a number of sections. The first provides a brief introduction to the concept of computer assisted mass appraisal (CAMA). In the second, we offer a detailed review of the main concepts in CAMA. The next section examines the main CAMA techniques used, followed by a section applying a multiple regression analysis case study, and the final section comprises a number of concluding remarks.

The history of CAMA can be traced back to the mid 1960s in the USA when pilot studies were undertaken in California and New York to test the applicability of computer based assessments (Shenkel, 1968). Developments in computer processing capacity heralded the ability to automate data processing, comparable selection and assessments based on cost and market prices. At the same

A Primer on Property Tax: Administration and Policy, First Edition.
Edited by William J. McCluskey, Gary C. Cornia and Lawrence C. Walters.
© 2013 Blackwell Publishing Ltd. Published 2013 by Blackwell Publishing Ltd.

time, appraisers were evaluating the potential role of applying statistically based predictive models to determine assessments. Early studies into the use of multiple regression analysis proved that such techniques could replicate the economics of the market to produce realistic assessed values. Mass appraisal in essence evolved out of the need to provide uniformity and consistency in *ad valorem* valuations. An equally important aspect was the ever increasing financial burden of undertaking single manual appraisals, particularly at times of revaluations, where several millions parcels needed to be assessed at the same time. According to Silverherz (1936) the reappraisal of St Paul, Minnesota, marked the beginning of scientific mass appraisal. Developments in mass appraisal accelerated in the 1950s with the introduction of computers. Renshaw (1958) had this to say about scientific appraisal:

> While it may be hopeless to isolate all the factors which buyers take into consideration when purchasing property, it is possible to establish a correlation between real estate values and a select subset of determining variables. Although the choice of the function and its mathematical form is somewhat arbitrary, it is not necessary to choose the best possible function, but only the one which predicts real estate values with sufficient accuracy in a statistical sense, for the type of appraisal under consideration.

So what exactly is CAMA modelling? The International Association of Assessing Officers (IAAO) defines a model for appraisal purposes as 'a representation (in words or an equation) that explains the relationship between value or estimated sale price and variables representing supply and demand' (IAAO, 2011).

A CAMA model can in the alternative be more accurately described as an automated valuation model (AVM). According to the International Association of Assessing Officers, it is:

> A mathematically based computer software program that produces an estimate of market value based on market analysis of location, market conditions, and real estate characteristics from information that was previously and separately collected. The distinguishing feature of an AVM is that it is an estimate of market value produced through mathematical modeling. Credibility of an AVM is dependent on the data used and the skills of the modeler producing the AVM. (IAAO, 2011)

Mass appraisal has been defined as the systematic appraisal of groups of properties as of a given date, using standardized procedures and statistical testing (Eckert, 1990). It differs from single property appraisal only in terms of scale. In mass appraisal modelling, the aim is to try to replicate the market within which real estate is traded and to derive a representative mathematical model which achieves this aim (Eckert, 1990; Fibbens, 1995). Thus, valuation models developed for mass appraisal purposes must represent supply and demand patterns for groups of properties. The model must be firmly established within micro-economic theory which would support the underlying rationale of the model. Appraisal judgments for mass appraisal must relate to large groups of properties rather than to single properties. However, the ultimate objective is the same whether the approach is mass or single valuation: an accurate assessment of the value of many properties or of a single property. The methods of valuation which the valuer uses are essentially the same, the main differences between the approaches being in the areas of market analysis and quality control.

Concepts of CAMA and quality control issues

Quality control is measured differently across the two approaches. In mass appraisal, given the scale of valuations, statistical methods are used to measure accuracy and variations in the assessed values from actual sale prices. For most mass appraisal models, if the average deviation from sale prices falls within a predetermined range, the model and quality are considered good. In single property appraisal, quality can usually be measured by direct comparison with specific comparable sales. In both approaches the valuer will be required to defend their assessment of value, and as one would expect this is somewhat easier in the single property appraisal than in the mass appraisal situation. Nonetheless the model needs to be capable of explanation, to demonstrate how the value was achieved.

Within the mass appraisal system the dual components of predictive accuracy and explainability are extremely important. Predictive accuracy can be assessed through quality control measures as noted previously, but explainability, not being capable of being statistically measured, is therefore more difficult to assess. Gloudemans and Miller (1976) suggested that there are at least seven issues related to explainability within a mass appraisal system:

1. simplicity of the design of the models in terms of functional form and rationale of the variables used in the models
2. reasonableness of the monetary value assigned to the property attributes; the effect on the estimated price of a property of a particular attribute must conform with a priori expectations
3. consistency between submodels which means that submodel equations produce accuracy between as well as within property groups in terms of the values assigned to particular attributes
4. consistency of time, which ensures that values for individual properties do not change inexplicably from one year to the next
5. decomposition of value between land and improvements, which may be important in those jurisdictions where land and buildings are taxed at different rates
6. ease of explanation of the underlying models to the tax payer, or rather demonstrating in simplistic terms how the assessed value was arrived at rather than showing the mathematical functional form of the models
7. comparable transactions, which have traditionally provided the main source of evidence in defending assessments.

Table 14.1: Number of assessed properties (millions)

Ontario, Canada	4.70
British Columbia	1.88
Jakarta	1.60
São Paulo	2.76
Bogota	1.78
Kuala Lumpur	0.46
Bangalore	1.16
Johannesburg	0.81
Hong Kong	2.35
Western Australia	1.90
Cape Town, South Africa	0.73

As a result, explanatory mass appraisal systems enhance taxpayer under-standing and general acceptance of the property tax system through concepts such as fairness and equity.

Today it is commonplace in most property tax assessment jurisdictions to use fully automated processes and procedures across the whole spectrum of property tax administration. Given the scale of the valuation task and the frequency of reval-uations, from a logistical perspective the use of automated approaches is essential. Table 14.1 illustrates the point in respect to the large numbers of properties that must be valued to a common valuation date. Also, a related issue is the quantity of data required on each property. This inventory of property characteristics can create issues in terms of data collection and data maintenance. For example, if the tax base consists of one million properties and for each property ten variables are collected, this creates an inventory data base of 10 million pieces of information.

The mass appraisal process typically includes the following steps:

- identify properties to be appraised
- define the market area in terms of consistent behaviour on the part of property owners and would-be purchasers
- identify characteristics of supply and demand that affect the creation of value in the defined market area
- develop a model structure that reflects the relationship among the character-istics affecting value in the market area
- calibrate the model structure to determine, among other attributes, the con-tribution of the individual property features affecting value
- apply the conclusions reflected in the model to the characteristics of the properties being appraised
- validate the adopted mass appraisal process, model, measurements or other readings including the performance measures, on an ongoing basis and/or at discrete stages throughout the process
- review and reconcile the mass appraisal results. (IVS, 2007)

Mass appraisal value definitions often apply to the unencumbered value of landed property, that is, the value of the hypothetical fee simple estate in land. Under these circumstances, all subsequent interests such as leasehold and reversionary interests are excluded. This is an established administrative practice due to the very complicated and time-consuming process of establishing the value of fractional interests/time shares in land/property.

The IAAO Standard on Mass Appraisal of Real Property (IAAO, 2011) states that market value for assessment purposes is generally determined through the application of mass appraisal techniques, with mass appraisal being defined as the process of valuing a group of properties as of a given date using common data, standardized methods and statistical testing. The International Valuation Guidance Note 13 describes mass appraisal as, 'The practice of appraising multiple properties as of a given date by a systematic and uniform application of appraisal methods and techniques that allow for statistical review and analysis of results' (IVS, 2007).

All these definitions share the common elements of:

- valuing homogeneous groups of properties simultaneously
- incorporating statistical testing and analysis of results.

The strengths of the mass appraisal process include the following:

- providing reasonably accurate valuations at low cost
- the ability to produce a large number of valuations in a short space of time
- the ability to design a system which should improve in consistency and accuracy over time.

Weaknesses of the mass appraisal process include:

- less accurate than traditional methods of valuation
- heavily reliant on the availability of suitable transaction/sales data
- reliant on a high quality database of property information.

In some jurisdictions the methods used are highly technical, using advanced statistical methods such as multiple regression and multivariate analysis, but the methods used for statistical review and analysis are remarkably similar.

The property tax has never been a popular tax and has always been subjected to criticism and scrutiny. Given the relative importance of the tax, it has become important for jurisdictions involved in valuation/appraisal to be able to measure and verify their appraisal performance. Early ratio studies focused primarily upon measures of overall assessment level. In the 1950s, greater effort was given to the other important aspect of assessment performance, known as equity or uniformity. Since 1934 the IAAO has served as the major professional organization for assessors in the USA. In 1976, the IAAO began to study the equity issue in greater depth, and in 1980 released its first Standard on Ratio Studies. This document is currently one of the 12 technical standards developed by the IAAO over the last 20 years to serve professionals involved with mass appraisal and assessment administration. The Standard on Ratio Studies has been revised several times with the most recent revision in 2010.

The Standard on Ratio Studies provides recommendations on the design, preparation, interpretation and uses of ratio studies for a variety of purposes. The generic term 'ratio study' can be used to describe any orderly programme to evaluate mass appraisal performance through a comparison of appraised or assessed values for tax purposes with independent proxies of market value. In most cases, sales of property in a competitive, free market can serve as the best indicators of market value. A ratio study is an investigation of how closely the appraisals that underlie property tax assessments approach market values, and how consistent those appraisals are across all property. There are two principal concerns: first, *level* – do the assessments meet some predetermined standard? For example, if the standard is 100 per cent of market value, then, on average, how close are the assessments to market value? And, second, *uniformity* or *consistency* – how close are individual assessment ratios to assessment ratios across all property in the jurisdiction or by property type?

A ratio study is a form of applied statistical analysis. This means that conclusions are drawn about the overall quality of assessments on the basis of data about a sample of properties, that is those that happen to have sold on the open market.

A ratio is formed when the assessed (or appraised) property value is divided by an indicator of true market value. For example, a property that was assessed at $200,000 and sold for $250,000 has a ratio of 0.80 (or the assessed level is 80 per cent of market value).

Ratio studies can be designed to accomplish a variety of goals. From an oversight perspective, this may result in adjustments resulting in the bringing of assessed values up or down to a required level. Sales or transaction evidence is at the heart of the ratio study. It is important to recognize that absolute accuracy of all assessments in any jurisdiction is unattainable, simply because that would require all property to sell in the open market over a given period of time (Gloudemans, 1999). Therefore, the accuracy of a ratio study depends upon the reliability of a sample of sales collected for analysis. Since the data will be used to make statistical inferences, it is important to prepare a sample that is representative of all property in the jurisdiction. Not only must the sales serve as a small model of the jurisdiction, they must also represent market value (IAAO, 2010a). Each sale considered for the study must be verified, inspected and adjusted if necessary.

It is essential that the property sold or transacted is matched to the same property held at the same location or address by the assessment jurisdiction. Therefore, it is important to know what legal rights have been transferred: is it the whole property or only part. An inspection of the sale property will attempt to record the physical characteristics. For the ratio study, the physical characteristics should not change between the time the property is valued and the date it is sold. A property that has been significantly altered due to, for example, major construction or demolition after the valuation date and before the sale, is of limited use. The process of matching sales to property requires a well-maintained cadastre, spatial (GIS) and aspatial databases that can locate property by a variety of search parameters.

The process of dividing properties into subgroups for analysis is known as stratification. If a sufficient number of sales are available for a ratio study, stratification can lead to a more complete and detailed picture of appraisal performance. The initial analysis involves the calculation of a ratio for each sale (calculated by dividing the appraised value by the sale price). Sales with unusually high or low ratios (called outliers) should be subjected to further review and verification.

Assessors should be concerned with two important aspects of mass appraisal performance. The overall level of assessment is usually the first performance measure evaluated. In a statistical study these indicators are sometimes referred to as measures of location or central tendency. The other aspect of appraisal performance that should be examined involves uniformity. This measure is often considered to be more important because it relates to equity and fairness. In a statistical environment these measures often describe qualities of scale, dispersion or variability about a measure of central tendency. The most common measures of assessment level and uniformity will be discussed later in this paper.

Consistency

The principle of consistency is that properties with similar values should have similar valuations as at the valuation date, and that if properties are generally over- or under-valued then this same level of over- or under-valuation should apply to each property. The effect of this principle should be that the burden of rates or tax will be borne equitably. What is interesting is that the requirement is not that the valuations are accurate; if they are inaccurate then they are equally inaccurate.

Accuracy

While accuracy is important, there is an underlying principle that over-valuation is more of a problem than under-valuation. Over-valuation can create additional costs such as defending values through objection and legal appeal processes. The purpose of the statistical measures employed in the mass appraisal process is to monitor the performance of the process at the appropriate point (i.e. as close as possible to where the individual valuations take place). Due to possible data limitations, this is usually accomplished at either the component level or by land use type in each location. Standards are imposed to ensure that, as far as possible, the principles of consistency and accuracy are satisfied as well as possible and consistent with the discussion above.

Equity

Measures of variability tend to relate to 'horizontal' or random dispersion among ratios in a sample, regardless of the value of individual properties. Another type of inequity can be related to systematic differences in the valuation of high-value and low-value properties; this is referred to as 'vertical' inequity. In essence, when low-value properties are valued at greater percentages of market value than high value properties, the assessment is regressive. When low-value properties are assessed at smaller percentages of market value than high-value properties, the situation is referred to as progressive.

The price related differential (PRD) measures the vertical equity of valuations. As such, it is not a measure of location, but behaves more like a measure of variability/consistency. The PRD aims to measure whether the Valuation Ratios are consistent between lower valued and higher valued properties. The statistic should be close to 1.0. A PRD below 1.0 would indicate progressivity and a PRD greater than 1.0 would indicate regressively.

Measures of uniformity

The most common measure of appraisal uniformity is the coefficient of dispersion (COD). It is a specialized measure of variability that is not often seen or used outside the assessment industry. The COD is sometimes referred to as a measure of horizontal or random dispersion. It provides information about uniformity across a class of property or the entire jurisdiction. The COD is a relative measure of how much the value ratios differ from the median ratio. As it involves differences from a typical value (the median) for the set of ratios, the COD is a measure of variability. As such, the COD is *not* a measure of accuracy, but rather a measure of uniformity or consistency. Since the COD is calculated from the absolute value of the differences, it cannot be negative and can only be zero if all the ratios are identical. It is also a relative measure (the median ratio also appears in the denominator), so the larger the COD, the greater the inconsistency in the value ratios. The 15 per cent standard is arbitrary, and different jurisdictions use slightly different standards for COD, but values above 15 per cent are certainly starting to indicate reasonably substantial differences in the value ratios and inconsistency in the comparison of valuations to adjusted (land) prices.

Performance standards

The performance standards established by the IAAO are a result of surveys, forums and discussions over a period of many years. They represent a consensus of opinion among assessors, oversight authorities and other appraisal professionals. The Standard recommends a median ratio within ±10% of the statutorily

Table 14.2:   COD by property class

Property class	COD standard
Single-family residential	
Newer, more homogeneous areas	10 or less
Older, heterogeneous areas	15 or less
Rural residential or seasonal	20 or less
Income-producing properties	
Larger, urban jurisdictions	15 or less
Smaller, rural jurisdictions	20 or less
Vacant land	20 or less

mandated level of assessment. In jurisdictions where the standard is full market value, compliance with the standard would require the median ratio to fall between 0.90 and 1.10. Uniformity standards have been defined in terms of the COD and specified property classes (see Table 14.2).

The price related differential (PRD) should fall in the range 0.98–1.03. If the PRD is above 1.03 the assessment process may be regressive. A PRD below 0.98 suggests that the assessments may be progressive.

Mass appraisal techniques

Mass appraisal and automated valuation techniques

Mass appraisal modelling techniques have continued to evolve since their earliest use in the 1930s (Silverherz, 1936). This evolution has seen significant progress in the application of statistically advanced techniques that incorporate elements of location such as geographic weighted regression, interpolation techniques such as kriging and other spatial expansion models. According to Kauko and d'Amato (2008) the quantitative, multiple regression analysis (MRA) based methodology may be referred to as the 'orthodox' approach to mass appraisal valuation. Research during the 1980s and 1990s explored different and often more mathematically complex approaches in an attempt to provide more 'accurate' estimates of value. Again, Kauko and d'Amato (2008) suggest that these methodologies are dubbed as 'heretic' because of their different theoretical basis from MRA, the dominant approach in mass appraisal. Model-free estimation techniques such as neural networks, self organizing maps (Kauko, 2008) and fuzzy logic/systems have been introduced to bring some flexibility to the property value calculations, without neglecting the mathematical rigour (Lin and Mohan, 2011; Peterson and Flanagan, 2009; González, 2008). As a result, the value model becomes more powerful than its formal regression-based and completely crisp counterpart. Pattern recognition is yet another relatively untried approach within this realm. Indeed, a number of contributions here offer ingenious and pragmatic, if not totally transparent, modeling methodology (Jenkins *et al.*, 1999: McCluskey and Anand, 1999).

Notwithstanding this development, from an industry perspective, all of the modelling techniques are required to meet the dual objectives of first, being able to attain acceptable industry driven standards of predictive accuracy and second, to facilitate explainability and defensibility of the assessed values.

The various modelling approaches achieve these objectives with varying degrees of success, some scoring highly in both while others forego one to achieve better than average results in the other. It could be argued that predictive accuracy is more important and therefore models should be as comprehensive as possible in achieving high levels of accuracy, notwithstanding that such models are not taxpayer friendly in explaining how the values were determined (IAAO, 2010b). Ultimately the application and use of particular modelling techniques depends on several factors including data availability and accessibility, data characteristics, the basis of value and the objectives of the assessment jurisdiction. Thompson (2008) contends that the performance of automated models is related to a number of factors, the principal one being the quality of the data and its fitness for use in the modelling/valuation process. This applies not just to the attributes, but also to the coding of the sales or market transactions as to their appropriateness for use in the market analysis and valuation processing. Data is crucial to the mass appraisal process and often the sources of the data need to be investigated so as to have confidence in its quality, accuracy and applicability.

This section outlines some of the main modelling paradigms which have been developed in terms of the appraisal of property for property tax purposes. It cannot be totally comprehensive, since with continuing research new modelling techniques and hybrid approaches are continually being developed.

Rule based expert systems

A rule based expert system is a computerized technique representing human expertise which can emulate and perform the functions of an expert and/or perform tasks which require a certain level of expertise (Czernkowski, 1989; Kilpatrick, 2011). Nawawi and Gronow, 1991) states that the general objectives of any rule based expert system are to ascertain a body of knowledge in a particular domain, to be able to apply this knowledge to given situations (often in situations of incomplete or uncertain information), to deliver effective and efficient solutions and to provide explanations and justifications for these solutions. Bonnet *et al.*, (1988) provide the following as a typical definition of an expert system: 'It is a program that contains a large body of knowledge concerning one specific field, this having been provided by one or more human experts in that field, and able to achieve the same performance in problem solving as those experts.'

Expert systems draw from Bayesian estimation, and constitute a maximum likelihood estimator of value, which results in the same coefficients as the least squares estimator derived from a hedonic model, but approaching the problem from a different perspective (Kilpatrick, 2011). The knowledge elicitation process is central to the success or failure of a rule based expert system. Thus the system is not merely a representation of data but more accurately a simulation of the expertise and knowledge of the expert valuer. Unlike multiple regression analysis which begins with a predetermined model, the rule model discovers the expertise. Knowledge can be directly or indirectly derived from the expert or a team of experts. McCluskey and Anand (1999) were among the first to thoroughly outline the application of such expert systems as they apply to mass appraisal. Nawawi et al (1997) outlined models that would simulate appraisal expertise. Further developments in this area included Boyle, (1983); Nawawi and Gronow (1991); and Nawawi *et al.*, (1997). McCluskey and Anand (1999) also present, and dismiss, what they call the 'domain expert' model. In this model, relative weights and factors are determined by an expert, who has prior knowledge of the valuation equation. They state that the principal shortcoming of this model is that it requires an 'expert' and thus is not self-learning.

Nawawi *et al.* (1997) argue that the greatest feature of rule based expert systems is their ability to encapsulate rules of thumb or heuristics and generalities. One of the problems of this technique is that they do not inherently learn but merely mirror the actions of an expert; therefore, provided the problem to be addressed is one in which information is already contained within the parameters of the elicited knowledge, then the expert system should be able to deduce a solution. One additional problem is that the behaviour of large rule based systems can be difficult to predict, because although individual rules may be easy to understand on their own, interactions between rules are not obvious. Increasing amounts of data were being stored in relatively easily accessible databases. Researchers were interested in a variety of data analyses, including classification, discovery of associations, pattern identification, temporal modelling, deviation detection, dependency modelling, clustering and characteristic rule discovery (Kilpatrick, 2011; Schiller and Weiss, 1999).

Artificial neural networks

Artificial intelligence is a subfield of computer science concerned with the use of computers in tasks that are normally considered to require knowledge, perception, reasoning, learning, understanding and similar cognitive abilities (Rumelhart and MacClelland, 1995). Therefore, one could consider artificial intelligence to be concerned with intelligent behaviour involving complexity, uncertainty and ambiguity (Benitez *et al.*, 1997). It represents techniques which have strong problem-solving components such as synthesizing a set of attributes to achieve a goal and powers of deduction. The ability of people to make accurate generalizations from a few scattered facts or to discover patterns from within a collection of observations is a primary research focus of artificial intelligence. The development of a number of conceptual tools have made it relatively easy to structure and manipulate symbolic databases. The notion of representing information in the form of networks or nodes and links is one of the major contributions of artificial intelligence research and in particular the development of artificial neural networks (ANNs).

ANNs take their name from the network of nerve cells in the brain. Traditional neuroscience has identified two key functions of the brain: first, the ability to learn from experience and second, the ability to create internal representations of the world in the form of internal data maps. Research has now been able to harness these powerful abilities into computer programs, which are currently being applied to a wide range of practical problems. Neural networks excel at problems involving patterns including, pattern mapping, pattern valuing, financial prediction and so forth (Borst, 1995).

Neural networks utilize a parallel processing structure that has a large number of processing elements and many interconnections between them. A typical structure for an ANN would have on the left side the inputs to the processing unit. Each interconnection has an associated connection strength or weight, denoted as w_1, w_2, ... w_n. The processing unit performs a weighted sum of the inputs and then uses a non-linear threshold function (sigmoid function) normally utilizing a back propagation algorithm to compute its output. The calculated result is then denoted as the output of the network.

ANNs are not programmed but rather they 'learn' by example. A network is presented with a training set of data from which it can learn the underlying pattern. The most common approach to training the network is to process input data with its associated output, in other words property characteristics including the known sale price. The forward pass through the network will result in the connection weights being adjusted in an attempt to minimize the error between the output of the network and the actual desired result.

In recent years ANNs have been critically compared to hedonic models to test their efficacy and broad applicability. A number of the research studies include for example, Borst (1991); Do and Grudnitski (1992); Kathman (1993); Tay and Ho (1994); Evans *et al.*, (1995); Worzala *et al.*, (1995); Lenk *et al.*, (1997); McCluskey (1996); Kauko (1997); Lewis *et al.*, (1997); McCluskey and Borst (1997); Bonissone *et al.*, (1998); McGreal *et al.*, (1998); Cechin *et al.* (2000); (2000), and Nguyen and Cripps (2001).

González (2008) argues that artificial intelligence based methods are easier to apply than the spatially extended hedonic regression based methods in the sense that the latter require much more specialized statistical training. Kauko (2008) deals with two modelling techniques: first, the self-organizing map (SOM, also known as the Kohonen Map) and second, the analytic hierarchy process (AHP, also known as the Saaty method of elicitation). While being fundamentally different the two methods potentially complement more conventional methods of data analysis. The research discussion shows the possibilities and limitations for using the two proposed approaches for 'heretic' mass appraisal. González contends that the approaches put forward are better suited for situations where the marketplace is affected by frictional factors, monopoly price or other circumstances, when various externalities or simply human behaviour are suspected to have an effect on values, but the extent of which is yet to be comprehended and assessed in monetary terms.

Fuzzy rule-based systems

There are several studies about fuzzy logic in other domains but very little on real estate. Byrne (1995) proposed to apply fuzzy logic considering the risk and uncertainty presents on real estate appraisal. Bagnoli and Smith (1998) used fuzzy logic to handle vagueness and imprecision in the subjective measures of property attributes. Bonissone *et al.*, (1998) used fuzzy logic in real estate appraisal, in two subsystems.

The use of regression techniques in mass appraisal is a common practice. Real data has several sources of error or imprecision, such as the lack of correct specification of model format, multiple simultaneous relationships among the explanatory variables, and not clear transitions between submarkets – this generating difficulties for constructing mass appraisal models. An alternative to develop more flexible and comprehensive models is to use fuzzy systems (Castro *et al.*, 2002). However, fuzzy systems may not learn market characteristics alone, and generally fuzzy systems are developed jointly with other techniques, such as ANNs and genetic algorithms (GAs), providing hybrid systems (Goldberg, 1989; Kosko, 1992; Liu *et al.*, 2006).

Multiple regression analysis

Hedonic modelling or regression analysis is today the widely accepted or ortho-dox technique applied within the *ad valorem* assessment process. Numerous studies and research have been undertaken which demonstrate the potential of the technique in terms of both explanation and predictive capabilities (Gloudemans and Miller, 1978; Mark and Goldberg, 1988). Hedonic price modelling is therefore the dominant method for determining how various property characteristics affect values (Can, 1992). It is based on the assumption that amenities such as property size, parcel size and amenities have a cumulative effect on the value of the property. Regression analysis isolates and quantifies the contribution of a single given amenity to the additive price effect. This technique has been criticized for a variety of reasons, including the smoothness assumption of a linear and continuous market mechanism, where the value formation is seen in a static equilibrium of supplied and demanded quantities of each characteristic in the housing bundle (Kauko, 2008).

It might be useful at this point to give a brief overview of the technique. Simple regression is concerned with describing how one factor or variable behaves in relation to another; in other words, it seeks to study the statistical relationship between one dependent variable Y and one independent variable X. To study the relationship between Y and several independent variables, multiple regression analysis is used.

Thus if Y is the land value and $x_1 \ldots x_n$ are the various attributes or factors influencing that value, the multiple regression equation takes the form:

$$Y = a_0 + b_1 x_1 + b_2 x_2 + \ldots + b_n x_n + \varepsilon$$

Where,

a_0 is the regression constant; it indicates the contribution to value of the property by factors not considered in the regression model, either because the valuer did not know them or left them out of the analysis

$b_1 \ldots b_n$ are the regression coefficients; they indicate the relative importance of each factor in the valuation model

ε is the error term; it indicates the difference between the predicted value and an independently observed value such as the transaction price.

Multiple regression will find the best numerical values for $a, b, \ldots b_n$ etc. by the method of least squares. The basic objective of MRA, therefore, is to develop a strong predictive relationship between property characteristics and value, so that the latter can be estimated through knowledge of the former (IAAO, 2011). There are two broad types of MRA used in mass appraisal standard linear regression models and non-linear regression techniques.

The increasing availability of relatively large sets of sales data has been instrumental, along with increased computing power, in facilitating appraisers' movement toward the use of hedonics. However, a problem with basing a regression analysis on a large data set is that a single pricing model in unlikely to have relevance over a geographical area sufficiently wide to provide a substantial quantity of observations. The analysis might produce positive *spatial autocorrelation*, meaning that similar values would be attributed to properties simply because they are located 'near' to each other. As Tobler (1979) states, 'Everything is related to everything else, but closer things more so'. Spatial statistics and spatial econometrics consider the data's geographical references as the most important feature of the property due to the large amount of information it contains. Spatial econometrics differs from traditional econometrics in two main respects: first, it considers the spatial dependence among sample variables and second, it attends to spatial heterogeneity in the model parameters, which change across space.

Explicit and implicit use of location

There are several techniques that use the x, y coordinates as variables within the model. The most direct is to include linear, quadratic, cubic and higher order terms of x and y including cross product terms such as xy, $x^2 y$, xy^2

and x^2, y^2. Foster (1991) presents model formulations that contain x, y coordinates explicitly. Response surface methodology uses an implicit location specification. It emerged from the assessment community in the early 1980s. Initially it referred to the application of a location based correction factor to a base value determined via MRA or similar multivariate technique without explicit incorporation of location in the model structure. O'Connor and Eichenbaum (1988) and Eichenbaum (1988) provide additional insight as to how to incorporate 'value influence centres' into the development of the correction factor. Ward *et al.*, (1999) detailed the use of GIS to develop a surface of normalized sale price per square foot of living area. The normalized factor derived from the surface was utilized as an independent variable in a hedonic model. McCluskey *et al.*, (2000) and Ward *et al.*, (2002) provide further examples of the method.

Advanced model specification methods

A number of studies report the use of advanced modelling techniques as part of the method used to model the influence of location. One characteristic of these methods is that they do not lend themselves to calibration by one pass of ordinary least squares techniques. These methods include hierarchical and random coefficient models, models with spatially varying parameters and spatial autocorrelation models. Dubin (1988) presented a formulation with spatial autocorrelation, modelled in the error term. Dubin (1998) provides a further breakdown of the methods used to model the error dependencies. She observes that there are two commonly used methods to model the spatial autocorrelation structure (in the errors term) found in housing prices. The first is to model the process itself, the weight matrix approach. The second is to model the covariance matrix in the error terms directly, which is called the geostatistical approach, or 'kriging'. Kriging methods represent best use of the structure of the spatial dependence that arises in residential property prices in order to predict the value at a non-observed location. This is kriging's main advantage compared to other interpolation techniques such as inverse distance weighting, splines and polynomial regression.

Clapp (2003) and Case *et al.*, (2004) describe the theory for a local regression model (LRM), and characterize it as a *semi-parametric* approach to estimating a location value surface. In addition, Fotheringham *et al.*, (2002) describe a model formulation in which the coefficients become spatially dependent. They use geographically weighted regression (GWR) to calibrate the model. This GWR approach incorporates the application of housing parcel centroid coordinates (Brunsdon *et al.*, 1996), which is a special case of the locally weighted regression (LWR) modelling. The GWR approach is non-parametric, thus not requiring any assumptions to be made regarding the underlying distributions of values of the predictor variables and therefore has the ability to handle highly skewed and categorical predictors. As a technique, GWR has expanded substantially across many disciplines. Within the property context, it has two core uses: as an exploratory tool to understand varying tastes and preferences for different property attributes and as a statistical technique to enhance estimation of property price with a given set of attributes taking into account the effects of location.

Unlike the global perspective offered by MRA, which contains a one-model-wide set of regression coefficients, the geographically weighted regression technique produces a different set of coefficients for every property processed through a series of weighted least squares (WLS) regressions (Moore and Myers, 2010). This weighting is determined by nearest neighbours distance analysis (bandwidth) which results in a combination of many small weighted MRAs that are performed around each subject property. This weighting function is premised on the (x, y) coordinates of the regression point and the data points in the proximity. Therefore, the peak of the surface is the regression point with sample points under the surface being attributed a weight based on the height of the surface at that specific point. Significantly, this results in the GWR approach being considered as a function of location as it is a local modelling approach that explicitly allows parameter estimates to vary over space (Brunsdon *et al.*, 1996; Fotheringham *et al.*, 2002). These separate estimates are constructed through the incorporation of the dependent and explanatory variables falling within the bandwidth of each target feature, allowing for the production of 'local' regression results. The output is a set of spatial statistics which denote local relationships (Huang *et al.*, 2010).

The GWR model extends the traditional regression framework by allowing the parameters to be estimated locally so that the model can be rewritten as:

$$y_i = \alpha_{0i}(u_i, v_i) + \sum \alpha_k(u_i, v_i) x_{ki} + \varepsilon_i,$$

where (u_i, v_i) denotes the coordinates of the *i*th point in space and $a_k(u_i, v_i)$ is the continuous function $a_k(u_i, v_i)$ at point *i*, indicating that the spatial variations between the relationships provide a mechanism for measurement (Fotheringham *et al.*, 2002). In this regard, the coefficients are deterministic functions of other variables (location in space). This estimation process is a substitution between bias and standard error which assumes that data points in close proximity to *i* influence the estimation of $a_k(u_i, v_i)$ more so than data located further away. Huang *et al.*, (2010) indicate that the result is that this measures the relationships inherent in the model around each node *i*, using weighted least squares. Hence, an observation is weighted in accordance to proximity to point *i*, resulting in it no longer remaining constant. In matrix notation the model parameters are:

$$\alpha(u_i, v_i) = \left(X^T W(u_i, v_i) X\right)^{-1} X^T W(u_i, v_i) y,$$

where $W(u_i, v_i)$ is the spatial weighting matrix. As observed in Bitter *et al.* (2007) the Gaussian function specifies *d* to signify the Euclidian distance between the regression node and observation point, with h denoting the bandwidth as follows:

$$W_i(u_i, v_i) = \exp(-d/h)^2$$

As highlighted by Fotheringham *et al.* (2002), and more recently by Bitter *et al.*, (2007), the findings of GWR are sensitive to bandwidth estimations, which can distort variances in the estimators. The adaptive approach permits nearby properties to be afforded more weight than properties further away, following Tobler's (1979) first principle of geography and the backbone of the comparative appraisal method. Indeed, this approach observes the weight function applied to all sale properties as a sliding neighbourhood around each property in which a local regression specific to a number of sale properties is variable (Moore and Myers, 2010). In essence, distances differ, and the allocation of nearest neighbour remains the same. The most common adaptive bandwidth weighting approach as suggested by Brunsdon *et al.*, (1999) is the bi-square function given as:

$$w_{ij} = \left(1 - (d_{ij}/b)^2\right)^2, \; d_{ij} \leq b$$
$$w_{ij} = 0, otherwise$$

where d_{ij} is the geographic distance between the ith subject property and its jth neighbouring sale property, and b is equal to the bandwidth.

In a typical application of multiple regression analysis one equation is calibrated on a given set of sales, each of which is weighted equally. GWR, on the other hand, is a computationally intensive technique that weights each point in the dataset, based on its location. The introduction to the concepts involved in GWR often includes description of moving window regression. In this case, the sample points within a fixed distance of a given point are included in the regression, all with equal weight, and all others are excluded. In GWR, the weight is a function of location, and diminishes with the distance from the regression point. The weighting function, referred to as a spatial kernel, can either be fixed or variable in spatial extent before it effectively diminishes to zero.

There are several techniques that use the x, y coordinates as variables within the model. The most direct is to include linear, quadratic, cubic and higher order terms of x and y, including cross product terms such as xy, x^2y, xy^2 and x^2y^2. Foster (1991) presents model formulations that contain x, y coordinates explicitly. Response surface methodology uses an implicit location specification.

Comparable sales analysis

The comparable sales method of valuation (CSM) is widely used in the USA for valuing residential properties (Todora and Whiterell, 2002; Gau *et al.*, 1992). There is an identifiable relationship between CSM as practiced by mass appraisers and the recent developments in spatially aware valuation models. A modified CSM (MCSM) is shown to be a special case of a spatially lagged weight matrix model. There is a less formal but clear relationship with geographically weighted regression as well (Borst and McCluskey, 2008a; Borst and McCluskey, 2008b).

The comparable sales method of valuation as implemented in a mass appraisal setting has gained widespread use in North America. These techniques, according to Borst and McCluskey (1996), are certainly among the best, if not the best methods for mass appraisal. The main processing steps within the method include: find the n most comparable sales properties; compute an adjusted sale price for each; weight these estimates according to their similarity to the subject; and sum the weighted comparable sales estimates to get the final estimate (Vandell, 1991). Now, finding the most comparable sale is equivalent to finding the least dissimilar, and the actual dissimilarity measure can be based on physical separation, differences in physical characteristics, date of sale and the neighbourhood to which the comparable sale belongs.

The storage and rapid retrieval capabilities of computer databases can readily be used to select 'comparables' which are then used to determine the value of a subject property. The approach is for the system to select comparables closest to the subject, which obviates the necessity of the valuer having to search through data sales to find comparables and secondly to adjust them for comparability. The computer based adjustments are made to the selected properties by deletions and additions of dollar amounts to make the comparable a notional physical replica to the subject. The approach utilizes distance to establish a measure of comparability between the subject and the comparable. This 'distance', sometimes referred to as Mahalanobis distance, is used to identify the closest or most similar comparables whose price is then adjusted to reflect what the sale price of each would have been if the physical characteristics of the sale property had been the same as the subject. This adjusted sale price, together with the adjusted prices of the comparables, is used to value the subject (Todora and Whiterell, 2002; Fraser and Blackwell, 1988).

The comparable sales analysis approach lends itself to produce defensible assessed values; its output is traditional in that actual comparables are used, so one can see how the value of the subject was arrived at (Moliver and Boronico, 1996). This is in contrast to MRA where, due to variable transformations, the coefficients can be difficult to interpret.

Adaptive estimation procedure

Adaptive estimation procedure (AEP), otherwise known as 'feedback', was developed by Carbone and Longini (1977). The method derives its name from the way in which the data is processed. In the case of estimating the selling price of real estate, sale transactions are processed one at a time in the sequence in which the sales took place. The feedback model is one that learns by experience.

If the predicted value of the first property is higher than the actual value, it is reasonable to assume that the assigned weights and values for each attribute were too high and should be reduced. The model alters the assigned weights and the next sale is then processed, with the predicted value again being compared to the actual value. The two values will not match exactly, so again the coefficients in the equation will be adjusted to minimize the error. The coefficients are associated with various property characteristics such as lot size, number of rooms, garage, floor area etc. The alterations made to the coefficients are made in a way that extreme changes in the associated weights do not occur, therefore the modifications are smoothed out.

AEP can be visualized as 'curve tracking' with information constantly being fed into the model which alters in order to improve the level of accuracy. This is in contrast to MRA which involves 'curve fitting' with all data being processed simultaneously. Within the AEP model, property characteristics are classified as being either qualitative or quantitative (Schrieber, 1985). For example, lot size would be a quantitative variable, and type of construction would be a qualitative variable.

It has been suggested that AEP has a number of advantages over MRA including the ease of the model to incorporate both types of variables which have an additive and a multiplicative effect on value. As a result the variable coefficients tend to have a realistic appearance which is more readily accepted by property owners/taxpayers.

The feedback system is not optimal in the sense of minimizing a pre-specified mathematical form. This is in contrast with regression analysis which seeks to fit an equation to data in order to minimize the sum of the squared errors.

Because AEP coefficients are continuously refined each time a sale is processed, it is considered that there is little likelihood of there being unexplainable year-to-year fluctuations in value estimates, a problem which can occur with MRA. Also, there is no need to store old sales data, since the prior year's formula can be easily updated using current sales. This feature makes it suitable in situations in which properties are not sold frequently or in large volumes.

This section is not meant to be totally comprehensive in its analysis of the various techniques, but rather to highlight the state of the art in relation to computer assisted mass appraisal systems and techniques. From an international perspective there is a growing trend in the application of mass appraisal within property tax systems. There are added benefits in having such computer assisted approaches including mass valuing, but also data analysis, quality control, administrative, financial and economic efficiency arguments, as well as recognizing that the future does not rest in manually based valuation systems. Notwithstanding that, mass appraisal models are tools which assist valuers and complement their other appraisal skills. They equip them with the technical ability to perform their job more efficiently while also recognizing that it is the valuer who must ultimately defend the assessments before the taxpayer, valuation tribunal or court.

Case study: MRA modelling

As mentioned earlier, multiple regression analysis (MRA) modelling is the traditional approach used for replicating the economics of the market to produce
realistic and accurate assessed property values. This section proceeds to describe
the development of MRA modelling through an empirical example of property
valuation from an urban region within the UK. This is achieved through a series
of steps which begin with a basic ordinary least squares (OLS) regression model
which then proceeds to encompass a spatial dimension. Two broad classes of
hedonic specifications are examined: first a parsimonious specification which
relates to the transaction price to property size and numerous characteristics;
and second an expanded specification which encompasses the locational aspect.
The models are then assessed for performance accuracy using the tests for equity
and uniformity described earlier.

The data

The data was obtained from a government assessment authority (the Land and
Property Services, a division of the Department of Finance and Personnel,
Northern Ireland). The sample consists of 2,695 residential properties sold
between 2002 and 2004, with all extreme outliers, inaccurate and incomplete
property records excluded. The data includes various property attributes and
characteristics such as age, type, glazing, size and, in the more expansive model,
spatial (locational) proxy characteristics, such as the electoral ward within
which each property is located. For descriptive statistics, see Table 14.3.

Data transformation

Natural logs are often used in regression modelling when applied to property valuation. As property data is often highly skewed and leptokurtic it is possible to
transform the distribution (usually of sale price) by subjecting it to a simple alge-
braic operation. This process can help improve residuals with improved normality
within linear regression modelling. The logarithmic transformation is the most
widely used method to achieve normality when data is skewed. This data transformation applies a deterministic mathematical function to each point in a data
set, that is, each data point z_i is replaced with the transformed value $y_i = f(z_i)$,
where f is the function. These transforms are usually applied so that the data fits
the assumptions of statistical inference for improved interpretability (Figure 14.1).

The logarithmic transformation is based on the equation $x = a^y$, where the
value of $y = \log_a x$ with two constraints; $a > 0$ and $a \neq 1$. Two of the most widely
applied logarithmic bases are the common logarithm (10) and the natural logarithm (e), which has an infinite number of decimal places (similar to π) with an
approximate value of 2.718281828459. The symbol for depicting the natural

Table 14.3: Data descriptive statistics

	Minimum	Maximum	Mean	Std. deviation
TASP	23324.86	630909.43	125353.33	59000.09
size	46.0	300.0	116.682	41.2363
garage	1.00	4.00	2.1759	1.13752
beds	1	8	3.16	0.666
Type	111	121	112.40	3.466
subtype	1.00	3.00	2.1158	0.77639
glaze type	1.00	2.00	1.8504	0.35674
ward	1	30	14.37	8.441
travelwork	6.77	21.23	13.0815	3.85058

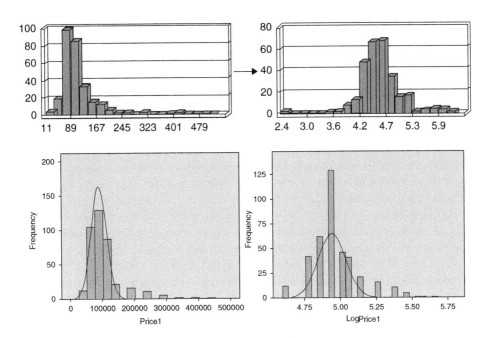

Figure 14.1: Data transformation using logarithmic form

logarithm is '*In*'; for example, as evidenced in Table 14.4, a property valued at £85,000 has a natural log$_e$ of 4.93, whereas, a property with a value of £115,000 has a logarithmic value of 5.06.

Analysis is then performed on the *transformed* variable. Indeed this, when substituted into the multiple regression formula algebraically, is:

$$In(Y) = a_0 + b_1 x_1 + b_2 x_2 + \ldots + b_n x_n + \varepsilon$$

where *In(Y)* is equal to the natural log$_e$ of price.

Table 14.4: Logarithmic transformation of property value

Property value	Logarithmic value (*ln*)
40,000	4.6020599
85,000	4.9294189
90,000	4.9542425
105,000	5.0211893
115,000	5.0606978
140,000	5.1461280
190,000	5.2787536
240,000	5.3802112
290,000	5.4623987
340,000	5.5314789
390,000	5.5910646
440,000	5.6434526

Adjusting for the temporal aspect of sale price (time adjusted sale price)

There are a number of approaches applied within regression modelling to account for time. It is necessary to analyse the sales data to identify the underlying time trend and adjust to a common valuation date. This is the approach suggested by Gloudemans (1999) and is commonly adopted in the practice of CAMA modelling worldwide. The key question for analysis purposes is the identification of an appropriate basis upon which to undertake the indexation – that is, should the data be subdivided to derive and deploy a number of different indices and, if so, on what basis should the data be subdivided. The key theoretical aspect is to identify submarkets within the general market, whereas the key practical aspect is to ensure that there are sufficient data points for meaningful regression analysis to take place. An initial consideration is the common date to be adopted. When determining the time adjustment, this would ordinarily be the 'tone date' or (antecedent date of valuation) for the revaluation exercise. Initial analysis should be undertaken to determine the temporal spread of the sales data in the sample, which can be carried out by determining the percentage of sales in each of the relevant months. This step is necessary to identify the effective start month and end month, a requirement to ensure that the index is appropriately calibrated. The spread of sales is then analysed using a cross-tabulation between the sale year and sale month attributes and an appropriate date range selected to ensure an acceptable number of sales in each month.

The subsequent step necessary is to create an attribute in the database (e.g. Salemonth) which represents a continuous numbering of months from the first to the last month. From this the indexation frame can be established to reference all sales to the reference date for the mass appraisal exercise. This is achieved by setting the reference month to month zero in a new attribute (e.g. MOS), by the process of:

$$MOS = Salemonth - number\ of\ months\ prior\ to\ reference\ month.$$

This creates a range around the key valuation date, negative numbers indicating prior to the date, positive numbers indicating post the date. The index itself is created by regressing Price (dependent) with Salemonth (independent) and dividing the Salemonth unstandardized *beta* coefficient by the mean price. It is now necessary to calculate a time adjustment factor (TAF), which indicates how much adjustment is to be made, according to the index and the month of sale (e.g. MOS), following the basic formula:

$$TAF = 1 - Index \times MOS$$

The process is completed by calculating a new time adjusted (or indexed) sale price (TASP) formulated by multiplying the sale price by the time adjustment factor (TAF). This results in a new attribute in the data which is a time adjusted sale price, indexed to the tone date for the appraisals. Having accounted for the temporal nature within the data, the TASP can therefore be applied as the dependent variable within MRA.

OLS regression model

In order to examine the role that various property characteristics play in determining accurate predictions of market value, the typical multiple regression equation is applied, given by:

$$Y = a_0 + b_1 x_1 + b_2 x_2 + \cdots + b_n x_n + \varepsilon$$

The hedonic price model therefore takes the form:

$$Y = a_0 + b_1 SIZE + b_2 TYPE + b_3 SUBTYPE + b_4 BEDS... \\ + b_5 GARAGE + b_6 GLAZE + \cdots + b_n x_n + \varepsilon$$

Where Y is the price at which the property is sold (TASP); *SIZE* is the floor area of the property in square metres; *SUBTYPE* is a set of dummy variables that depict the type of property as follows:

Det is 1 if the property is detached, 0 otherwise;
Sdt is 1 if the property is semi-detached, 0 otherwise;
Ter is 1 if the property is terraced, 0 otherwise

TYPE is 1 if the property is a private dwelling and 0 if a public dwelling; *BEDS* is a set of dummy variables that depict the property as follows:

BEDS1 is 1 if the property has 1 bedroom, 0 otherwise;
BEDS2 is 1 if the property has 2 bedrooms, 0 otherwise;
BEDS3 is 1 if the property has 3 bedrooms, 0 otherwise;
etc.

GARAGE is a set of dummy variables that depict the property as follows:

AttachedGar is 1 if the property has a garage attached, 0 otherwise;
IntegralGar is 1 if the property has a garage integrated, 0 otherwise;
DetachedGar is 1 if the property has a garage detached, 0 otherwise;

and GLAZE is 1 if the property has double-glazing, 0 otherwise. This is a similar procedure for any variable used through the dummy approach. Consequently, the model form for a detached property built within the last year with a garage is:

$$Y = a_0 + b_1 SIZE + b_2 Det + b_3 PRIVATE + b_4 BEDS \ldots$$
$$+ b_5 GARAGE + b_6 GLAZE + \cdots + b_n x_n + \varepsilon$$

where the gradient of the relationship between house price and floor area is given by adding the estimate of b_1, and the intercept is given by the estimate of a_0. It is important to note that the lack of overall functional form for the hedonic specification is a widely debated topic (Fleming, 1999). Nonetheless, this is generally overcome as a result of the additive nature of the regressive model which makes interpretation of each parameter estimate highly intuitive (Fotheringham et al., 2002).

OLS model results

The complete model from the hedonic model was calibrated using ordinary least squares (OLS) to produce the parameter estimates evidenced in Table 14.6. The findings, denoted by the coefficient of determination (R^2) show that the parameter estimates explain 77.6 per cent of the variation in property price in the sample (see Table 14.5). When adjusted to the general population, using the adjusted R^2 statistic, the level of explanation reduces to 77.5 per cent, leaving 22.5 per cent of the variance in price unexplained. This adjusted R^2 statistic is important as it will only increase when a new variable is in excess of the expected increase in R^2 that would occur with the introduction of an irrelevant variable (Wolverton, 2009).

The baseline model used for the regression analysis is a semi-detached, private, two-story property with three bedrooms and a detached garage, which is four years old. The floor area (SIZE), coefficient indicates that, *ceretis paribus*,

Table 14.5:   OLS model summary

Model	R	R²	Adjusted R²	SE mean
1	0.881	0.776	0.775	27979.697

Table 14.6:   OLS regression parameter estimates

Model	B	Std. error	Beta	t	Sig.
(Constant)	795.188	3627.089		0.219	0.826
Size	1024.536	21.792	0.716	47.014	0
Det	23420.37	1619.06	0.191	14.465	0
Ter	−7838.14	1624.264	−0.057	−4.826	0
Beds1	23635.72	8944.433	0.024	2.643	0.008
Beds2	10659.23	1891.264	0.058	5.636	0
Beds4	6367.472	1733.466	0.046	3.673	0
Beds5	5524.12	4390.329	0.013	1.258	0.208
Beds6	22617.36	12845.74	0.017	1.761	0.078
Public	−19389.7	1850.669	−0.114	−10.477	0
AttachedGar	5276.09	2031.468	0.025	2.597	0.009
IntegralGar	7172.673	1759.779	0.042	4.076	0
Glazetype	1400.278	1546.422	0	0.009	0.993

an additional square metre adds £1,025 to the average value of a property in the sample area (Table 14.6).

In addition, the presence of double-glazing adds £1,400 to the value of the property, with the presence of six or more bedrooms adding £22,617. In the sample area, a detached property adds £23,420 compared to a terrace property which decreases in value by £7,838. This is also similar for the type of property, as a publicly subsidized dwelling reduces a property's value by £19,390. The t-statistics clearly identify floor area ($SIZE$) to be the most important contributor to the model, and therefore price, significant at the 99 per cent level ($t = 47.01$, $p < 0.01$), followed by the detached property type (14.47, $p < 0.01$). Only three coefficients are not statistically significant (Beds5; Beds6 and Glazetype).

The expansive OLS model

The parsimonious OLS model can include an expanded hedonic specification which encompasses numerous additional spatial characteristics to help account for location when modelling property price. The more expansive 'locational' model simply adds to the traditional OLS which comprises property attributes by including various neighbourhood characteristics and submarket information; in this example, electoral ward districts. The expansive OLS model is therefore written as:

$$Y = a_0 + b_1 SIZE + b_2 Det + b_3 PRIVATE + b_4 BEDS \\ + b_5 GARAGE + b_6 WARD \cdots + b_n x_n + \varepsilon$$

where *WARD* is a set of dummy variables that depict the area in which the property is located as follows:

WARD01 is 1 if the property is located in this area, 0 otherwise;
WARD02 is 1 if the property is located in this area, 0 otherwise;
WARD03 is 1 if the property is located in this area, 0 otherwise;
etc.

The addition of the electoral wards 'locational' variable has added to the level of explanation within the OLS model framework. The adjusted R^2 show that the additional ward parameter increased the level of explanation of property price to 82.8 per cent, an increase in explanation of 5.3 per cent (see Table 14.7). The parameter coefficients show relatively similar findings to the OLS model; for example, size is still the most significant predictor of price ($t = 46.43$, $p < 0.01$), and increases by £1,021 per square metre. The introduction of the electoral ward parameter further shows the non-stationarity and complexity of location within valuation. The parameter estimates for the electoral wards indicate that a property located in ward 3 will add value of circa £18,634, whereas, if located in ward 6, value will decrease by £14,337.

Predictive accuracy testing

To assess and compare the predictive accuracy of the OLS approaches, the predicted prices from both the parsimonious model and the expansive models were compared with the observed market value (Table 14.7). This is easily achieved by comparing within the analysis output the unstandardized predicted residual values (denominator) with and the time adjusted sale price (numerator). Based on the internationally recognized IAAO standards, the results indicate quite clearly that the price related differential (PRD) scores for both models are very close to the generally accepted middle benchmark range. The PRD ratio for the OLS model shows marginal regressivity, whereas the OLS spatial model illustrates a slight progressivity; nonetheless, they are generally consistent between lower- and higher-valued properties. The COD figures indicate that both models fall within the IAAO benchmark for heterogeneous residential property of 15. It can be seen that the expansive model, by including a spatial component, better explains the uniformity and variability across the sample class of properties, as it scores lower than the parsimonious OLS model (see Table 14.8).

The findings clearly demonstrate that the addition of the locational/spatial proxy variable can add to the accuracy level within automated valuation, a finding

Table 14.7: OLS regression model with spatial parameter estimates

Model	B	Std. Error	Beta	t	Sig.
(Constant)	1168.285	3634.576		0.321	0.748
Size	1021.533	22	0.714	46.433	0
Det	23084.82	1616.478	0.188	14.281	0
Ter	−9094.96	1641.475	−0.067	−5.541	0
Beds1	26397.21	8899.894	0.027	2.966	0.003
Beds2	10788.02	1886.424	0.059	5.719	0
Beds4	6227.697	1731.161	0.045	3.597	0
Beds5	4207.194	4361.677	0.01	0.965	0.335
Beds6	23412.52	12768.48	0.017	1.834	0.067
Public	−18093.7	1880.22	−0.106	−9.623	0
AttachedGar	5064.004	2026.593	0.024	2.499	0.013
IntegralGar	7156.92	1756.29	0.042	4.075	0
Glazetype	428.463	1536.5	0.003	0.279	0.78
Ward1	−15718.5	2974.667	−0.049	−5.284	0
Ward2	−3647.8	2616.195	−0.013	−1.394	0.163
Ward3	18633.64	5713.551	0.03	3.261	0.001
Ward4	−319.631	2081.274	−0.001	−0.154	0.878
Ward5	3027.768	2827.67	0.01	1.071	0.284
Ward6	−14337	5421.597	−0.025	−2.644	0.008

Table 14.8: Ratio statistics for model accuracy

Ratio Statistic	OLS	Spat. OLS
PRD	1.004	0.994
COD	0.138	0.131
Adj. R^2	0.775	0.825

which can be built upon with the use of spatial econometric approaches such as geographically weighted regression and other spatial approaches made possible by the growth in GIS and spatial referencing generally.

Conclusions

In broad terms, this chapter has sought to examine the framework around which automated valuation approaches can be used to deliver high quality valuation assessments at realistic cost. The use of computer assisted valuation techniques is applied worldwide in most assessment/valuation departments in local, state and national government as well as in the private sector. From a review of the literature and practice it is clear that the trend would be to apply forms of multiple regression analysis (MRA). While other techniques are being used, such as expert systems and artificial intelligence, the fundamental components of high predictive accuracy and high levels of explainability are more consistently met with MRA. That is not to say that other approaches do not have merit; on the contrary, artificial neural networks are strong predictors, in this case of property value, but have limited explainability. As all assessments can be legally challenged, it is important that transparent models of predicting value are used, which can be easily interpreted by tribunals and courts.

Innovation in value modelling techniques is an important advancement for what is a global industry. Strong advancements in knowledge have been made in terms of incorporating property location within MRA techniques and using geostatistics within geographic information systems. Clearly, for new techniques to become 'successful' there needs to be an acceptance by industry and all the other key players within the property tax assessment process.

References

Bagnoli, C. and Smith, H.C. (1998) The Theory of Fuzzy Logic and its Application to Real Estate Valuation. *Journal of Real Estate Research*, 16: 169–199.

Benitez, J.M., Castro, J.L. and Requena, I. (1997) Are Artificial Neural Networks Black Boxes? *IEEE Transactions on Neural Networks*, 8(5): 1156–1164.

Bitter, C., Mulligan, G.F. and Dall'erba, S. (2007) Incorporating Spatial Variation in Housing Attribute Prices: A Comparison of Geographically Weighted Regression and the Spatial Expansion Method, *Journal of Geographical Systems*, 9(1): 7–27.

Bonissone, P.P., Cheetam, W., Golibersuch, D.C. and Khedkar, P. (1998) Automated Residential Property Valuation: An Accurate and Reliable Approach Based on Soft Computing. In: Ribeiro, R., Zimmermann, H., Yager, R.R. and Kacprzyk, J. (eds.), *Soft Computing in Financial Engineering*. Heidelberg: Physica-Verlag.

Bonnet, A., Haton, J.P. and Truong-Ngoc, J.M. (1988) *Expert Systems: Principles and Practice*. England: Prentice Hall.

Borst, R.A. (1991) Artificial Neural Networks: The Next Modeling/Calibration Technology for the Assessment Community? *Property Tax Journal*, 10(1): 69–94.

Borst, R.A. (1995) Artificial Neural Networks in Mass Appraisal. *Journal of Property Tax Assessment & Administration*, 1(2): 5–15.

Borst, R.A. and McCluskey, W.J. (1996) Artificial Neural Networks. In: Flaherty, J., Lombardo, R., Morgan, P. and De Silva, B. (eds.), *Quantitative Methods in Property*, Australia: Royal Melbourne Institute of Technology: 659–679.

Borst, R.A. and McCluskey, W.J. (2008a) The Modified Comparable Sales Method as the Basis for a Property Tax Valuations System and its Relationship and Comparison to Spatially Autoregressive Valuation Models. In: Kauko, T. and d'Amato, M. (eds.), *Mass Appraisal Methods: An International Perspective for Property Valuers*, United Kingdom: Wiley-Blackwell: 49–69.

Borst, R.A and McCluskey, W.J. (2008b) Using Geographically Weighted Regression to Detect Housing Submarkets: Modeling Large-Scale Spatial Variations in Value. *Journal of Property Tax Assessment & Administration*, 5(1): 21–51.

Boyle, C. (1983) An Expert System for Valuation of Residential Properties. *Journal of Valuation*, 2: 271–286.

Brunsdon, C., Fotheringham, A.S. and Charlton, M., (1996) Geographically Weighted Regression: A Method for Exploring Spatial Non-stationarity. *Geographical Analysis*, 28: 281–298.

Brunsdon, C., Aitkin, M., Fotheringham, S. and Charlton, M. (1999), A Comparison of Random Coefficient Modelling and Geographically Weighted Regression for Spatially Non-stationary Regression Problems, *Geographical & Environmental Modelling*, 3:1, 47–62.

Byrne, P. (1995) Fuzzy Analysis: A Vague Way of Dealing with Uncertainty in Real Estate Analysis? *Journal of Property Valuation & Investment*, 13(3): 22–41

Can, A. (1992) Specification and Estimation of Hedonic Housing Price Models. *Regional Science and Urban Economics*, 22: 453–474.

Carbone, R. and Longini, R. (1977) A Feedback Model for Automated Real Estate Assessment. *Management Science*, 24(3): 241–248.

Case, B., Clapp, J., Dubin, R. and Rodriguez, M. (2004) Modeling Spatial and Temporal House Price Patterns: A Comparison of Four Models. *Journal of Real Estate Finance and Economics*, 29(2): 167–191.

Castro, J.L., Mantas, C.J. and Benitez, J.M. (2002) Interpretation of Artificial Neural Networks by Means of Fuzzy Rules. *IEEE Transactions on Neural Networks*, 13(1): 101–116.

Cechin, A.L., Souto, A. and Gonzalez, M.A.S. (2000) *Real Estate Value at Porto Alegre City using Artificial Neural Networks*. Sixth Brazilian Symposium on Neural Networks, Rio de Janeiro: SBRN.

Clapp, J.M. (2003) A Semi-parametric Method for Valuing Residential Location: Applications to Automated Valuation. *Journal of Real Estate Finance and Economics*, 27(3): 303–320.

Czernkowski, R.M.J. (1989) Expert Systems in Real Estate Valuation. *Journal of Valuation*, 8: 376–393.

Do, A.Q and Grudnitski, G. (1992) A Neural Network Approach to Residential Property Appraisal. *The Real Estate Appraiser*, December: 38–45.

Dubin, R.A. (1988) Estimation of Regression Coefficients in the Presence of Spatially Autocorrelated Error Terms. *The Review of Economics and Statistics*, 70(3): 466–474.

Dubin, R.A. (1998), Spatial Autocorrelation: A Primer, *Journal of Housing Economics* 7, 304–327.

Eckert, J.K. (1990), *Property Appraisal and Assessment Administration*, Chicago, International Association of Assessing Officers.

Eichenbaum, J. (1988) *Incorporating Location into Computer Assisted Valuation: Progress in New York City*. Paper presented at the World Congress III Computer-Assisted Valuation and Land Information systems Assisted Valuation, Cambridge, MA: Lincoln Institute of Land Policy.

Evans, A., James, H. and Collins, A. (1995) Artificial Neural Networks: An Application to Residential Valuation in the UK. *Journal of Property Tax Assessment & Administration*, 1(3): 78–92.

Fibbens, M. (1995) Australian Rating and Taxing: Mass Appraisal Practice. *Journal of Property Tax Assessment & Administration*, 1(3): 61–77.

Fleming, M. (1999) Growth Controls and Fragmented Suburban Development: The Effect on Land Values. *Geographical Information Sciences*, 5: 154–162.

Foster, S.A. (1991) The Expansion Method: Implications for Geographic Research. *Professional Geographer*, 43(2): 131–142.

Fotheringham, A.S., Brunsdon, C. and Charlton, M. (2002) *Geographically Weighted Regression*. United Kingdom: John Wiley & Sons Ltd.

Fraser, R.R. and Blackwell, F.M. (1988) Comparable Selection and Multiple Regression in Estimating Real Estate Value: An Empirical Study. *Journal of Valuation*, 7(3): 184–201.

Gau, G.W., Lai, T.-Y. and Wang, K. (1992) Optimal Comparable Selection and Weighting in Real Property Valuation: An Extension. *AREUEA Journal*, 20(1): 107–123.

Gloudemans, R.J. and Miller, D.W. (1976) Multiple regression analysis applied to residential properties: A study of structural relationships over time. *Decision Sciences*, 7(2), 294–304.

Gloudemans, R.J. and Miller, D.W. (1978) Multiple Regression Analysis Applied to Residential Properties: A Study of Structural Relationships Over Time. *Decision Sciences*, 7(2): 294–303.

Gloudemans, R.J. (1999) *Mass Appraisal of Real Property*. Chicago, IL: International Association of Assessing Officers.

Goldberg, D.E. (1989) *Genetic Algorithms in Search, Optimization, and Machine Learning*. Reading: Addison-Wesley.

Gonzalez, M.A.S. (2008) Developing Mass Appraisal Models with Fuzzy Systems. In: Kauko, T. and d'Amato, M. (eds.), *Mass Appraisal Methods: An International Perspective for Property Valuers*, United Kingdom: Wiley-Blackwell: 183–202.

Huang, B., Wu, B. and Michael Barry M. (2010) Geographically and Temporally Weighted Regression for Modelling Spatio-Temporal Variation in House Prices, *International Journal of Geographical Information Science*, 24(3): 383–401.

IAAO, (2010a) *Standard on Ratio Studies*. Kansas: International Association of Assessing Officers.

IAAO, (2010b) *Standard on Automated Valuation Methods*. Kansas: International Association of Assessing Officers.

IAAO, (2011) *Standard on the Mass Appraisal of Real Property*. Kansas: International Association of Assessing Officers.

IVS (2007) *Mass Appraisal for Property Taxation*. International Guidance Note 13, London: International Valuation Standards.

Jenkins, D.H., Lewis, O.M., Almond, N., Gronow, S.A. and Ware, J.A. (1999) Towards an Intelligent Residential Appraisal Model. *Journal of Property Research*, 16(1): 67–90.

Kathman, R.M. (1993) Neural Networks for the Mass Appraisal of Real Estate. *Computer Environment and Urban Systems*, 17: 373–384.

Kauko, T. (1997) *Exploring the Prices of Residential Apartments and Locality Features Within an Artificial Neural Network Approach: Evidence from Finland*. AREUEA International Conference. UCLA: Berkeley.

Kauko, T. (2008a) Utterly Unorthodox Modelling for the Purposes of Mass Appraisal: An Approach Based on Patterns and Judgements. In: Kauko, T. and d'Amato, M. (eds.), *Mass Appraisal Methods: An International Perspective for Property Valuers*, United Kingdom: Wiley-Blackwell: 203–219.

Kauko, T. and d'Amato, M. (eds.) (2008) *Mass Appraisal Methods: An International Perspective for Property Valuers*, United Kingdom: Wiley-Blackwell.

Kilpatrick, (2011) Expert Systems and Mass Appraisal. *Journal of Property Investment & Finance*, 29(4/5): 529–550.

Kosko, B. (1992) *Neural Networks and Fuzzy Systems: A Dynamical Systems Approach to Machine Intelligence*. Englewood Cliffs: Prentice hall.

Lenk, M.M., Worzala, E.M. and Silva, A. (1997) High-tech Valuation: Should Artificial Neural Networks Bypass the Human Valuer? *Journal of Property Valuation & Investment*, 15(1): 8–26.

Lewis, O.M., Ware, J.A. and Jenkins, D. (1997) A Novel Neural Network Technique for the Valuation of Residential Property. *Neural Computing and Applications*, 5(4): 224–229.

Lin, C.C. and Mohan, S.B. (2011) Effectiveness Comparison of the Residential Property Mass Appraisal Methodologies in the USA. *International Journal of Housing Markets and Analysis*, 4(3): 224–243.

Liu, J.-G., Zhang, X.-L. and Wu, W.-P. (2006) Application of Fuzzy Neural Network for Real Estate Prediction. *Advances in Neural Networks*, 1187–91.

Nawawi, A.H., Jenkins, D and Gronow, S.A. (1997) Expert system development for the mass appraisal property in Malaysia. In: McCluskey, W.J. and Adair, A.S. (eds.) *Computer Assisted Mass Appraisal: An International Review*, Ashgate Publishing Limited, England, 103–130.

Mark, J.H. and Goldberg, M.A. (1988) Multiple Regression Analysis: A Review of the Issues. *The Appraisal Journal*, 56: 89–109.

McCluskey, W. J. (1996) Predictive Accuracy of Machine Learning Models for Mass Appraisal of Residential Property. *New Zealand Valuer's Journal*, July: 41–47.

McCluskey, W.J. and Borst, R. (1997) An Evaluation of MRA, Comparable Sale Analysis, and ANNs for the Mass Appraisal of Residential Properties in North Ireland. *Assessment Journal*, 4(1): 47–55.

McCluskey, W.J. and Anand, S. (1999) The Application of Intelligent Hybrid Techniques for the Mass Appraisal of Residential Properties. *Journal of Property Investment & Finance*, 17(3): 218–38.

McCluskey, W.J., Deddis, W.G., Lamont, I. and Borst, R.A. (2000) The Application of Surface Generated Interpolation Models for the Prediction of Residential Property Values. *Journal of Property Investment & Finance*, 18(2): 162–176.

McGreal, S., Adair, A., McBurney, D. and Patterson, D. (1998) Neural Networks: The Prediction of Real Estate Values. *Journal of Property Valuation & Investment*, 16(1): 57–70.

Moliver, D. and Boronico, J. (1996) Unit Selection and the Sales Comparison Approach. *Journal of Property Valuation & Investment*, 14(5): 25–33.

Moore, J.W. and Myers, J. (2010) Using Geographic-attribute Weighted Regression for CAMA Modelling. *Journal of Property Tax Assessment & Administration*, 7(1): 5–29.

Nawawi, A.H. and Gronow, S. (1991) Expert Systems in Rating Valuation. *Journal of the Society of Surveying Technicians*, 18(8): 66–72.

Nawawi, A.H., Jenkins, D. and Gronow, S. (1997), Expert System Development for the Mass Appraisal of Commercial Property in Malaysia. In: McCluskey, W.J. and Adair, A.S. (eds.), *Computer Assisted Mass Appraisal: An International Review*, Ashgate: London: 103–130.

Nguyen, N. and Cripps, A. (2001) Predicting Housing Value: A Comparison of Multiple Regression Analysis and Artificial Neural Networks. *Journal of Real Estate Research*, 22(3): 313–336.

O'Connor, P.M. and Eichenbaum, J. (1988) Location Value Response Surfaces: The Geometry of Advanced Mass Appraisal. *Property Tax Journal*, 277–298.

Peterson, S. and Flanagan, A.B. (2009) Neural Network Hedonic Pricing Models in Mass Real Estate Appraisal. *Journal of Real Estate Research*, 31(2): 147–64.

Renshaw, E.F. (1958) Scientific Appraisal, *National Tax Journal* 11: 314–322.

Rumelhart, D.E. MacClelland, J.L. (1995) *Parallel Distributed Processing: Explorations in the Microstructure of Cognition*. Cambridge: MIT.

Schiller, R.J. and Weiss, A.N. (1999) Evaluating Real Estate Valuation Systems. *Journal of Real Estate Finance and Economics*, 18(2): 147–61.

Schrieber, J. (1985), A feedback Primer. In: Woolery, A. and Shea, S. (eds.) *Introduction to Computer Assisted Valuation*, Oelgeschlager, Gunn and Hain, United States.

Shenkel, W.M. (1968) Computer Valuation by Multiple Regression Analysis. In: *International Property Assessment Administration*, Chicago, International Association of Assessing Officers: 26–39.

Silverherz (1936) *The Assessment of Real Property in the USA*, Albany: New York State Tax Commission.

Tay, D.P.H. and Ho, D.K.H. (1994) Intelligent Mass Appraisal. *Journal of Property Tax Assessment & Administration*, 1(1): 5–25.

Thompson, J. (2008) Data Issues involved with the Application of Automated Valuation Methods: A Case Study. In: Kauko, T. and d'Amato, M. (eds.), *Mass Appraisal Methods: An International Perspective for Property Valuers*, United Kingdom: Wiley-Blackwell: 27–48.

Tobler, (1979) Cellular geography. In: Olsson, G.S. (ed.), *Philosophy in Geography*, Reidel: Dordrecht: 379–386.

Todora, J., and Whiterell, D. (2002) Automating the Sales Comparison Approach. *Assessment Journal*, 9(1): 25–33.

Vandell, K.D. (1991) Optimal Comparables Selection and Weighting in Real Property Valuation. *Real Estate Economics*, 19(2): 213–239.

Ward, R.D., Guilford, J., Jones, B., Pratt, D. and German, J.C. (2002) Piecing Together Location: Three Studies by the Lucas County Research and Development Staff. *Assessment Journal*, Sept/Oct: 15–48.

Ward, R.D., Weaver, J.R. and German, J.C. (1999) Improving CAMA Models Using Geographic Information Systems Response Surface Analysis Location Factors. *Assessment Journal*, 6(1): 30–38.

Wolverton, M.L. (2009) An Introduction to Statistics for Appraisers. Chicago, IL: Appraisal Institute.

Worzala, E., Lenk, M. and Silva, A. (1995) An Exploration of Neural Networks and its Application to Real Estate Valuation. *Journal of Real Estate Research*, 10(2): 185–201.

15

Geographic Information Systems and the Importance of Location: Integrating Property and Place for Better Informed Decision Making

David McIlhatton, Michael McCord,
Peadar Davis and Martin Haran

Introduction

Geographical information systems (GIS) and geographic information are terms often referred to in the mass appraisal of property for taxation purposes. While many people will have heard of such terms in the property taxation context, there is still a lack of real understanding of their business benefits globally. Indeed, there is a dearth of published literature identifying the importance of integrating GIS with appraisal methodologies such as computer-aided mass appraisal (CAMA) and the benefits that derive from such integration. Instead, most of the information available focuses specifically on how GIS and geographic information have been applied in CAMA and this, in many instances, falls short of illustrating why GIS should be written into property taxation related business cases. To address the shortfall in literature on this topic, this chapter will present an informative and evaluative discussion on both the importance of geographic information and the benefits of GIS based CAMA methodologies. This first section of the chapter provides a brief introduction to

A Primer on Property Tax: Administration and Policy, First Edition.
Edited by William J. McCluskey, Gary C. Cornia and Lawrence C. Walters.
© 2013 Blackwell Publishing Ltd. Published 2013 by Blackwell Publishing Ltd.

the concept of GIS, and the second section provides an overview of the importance of location based data and the main concepts of GIS. Then there is a section examining the role of GIS for CAMA and one which provides examples, while and the final section provides a concluding commentary.

The history of GIS is fairly aligned with that of CAMA, which dates back to the 1960s and 1970s. Indeed, their primary purpose was of a similar nature, in that they were both designed and developed to aid regulatory procedures, albeit in different disciplines – GIS was developed to facilitate land-use management and resource monitoring (Longley *et al.*, 2001) and CAMA was created for the purposes of making property taxation more streamlined and efficient (McCluskey and Adair, 1997). However, what is surprising is that it is only in recent decades (and even now it can be somewhat misaligned) that GIS and CAMA have been integrated to deliver an effective and efficient solution for mass appraising property. While the literature may suggest that their history predates this, it must be noted that in many cases of past research, a core GIS has not been used in the CAMA stage, but rather has used geographic information to model the spatial interactions that exist which affect the value. There is a distinct difference, but at least there is the acceptance that location is important, something which does not always exist in other sectors of property research.

Geographical information systems: the importance of location

The term 'geographic information systems (GIS)' is one that has manifested itself in nearly all aspects of business globally. Indeed, its application within built environment decision making, and more specifically, the property discipline, has been gaining momentum in recent years. Despite this, it would appear that the acceptance of the benefits of using GIS for improving valuation do not necessarily mean that such a methodological component will be adopted and therefore utilization falls somewhat short of where it could potentially be. However, this is not surprising given the relative lack of true explanation in the current literature base for mass appraisal of the importance of GIS. Indeed, it would also appear that there is a certain degree of ambiguity surrounding the difference between GIS and geographic information (GI) in the current thought process. While the two are intrinsically linked, there is a clear distinction and it is therefore the intention of this chapter to capture the dynamics of each, and illustrate how enhancing spatial awareness among decision makers can help leverage maximum benefits for both improving governance and property valuation.

Geographic information

The rationale for leading with an explanation of geographic information rather than with GIS could perhaps be challenged by those who do not fully appreciate the real benefits of geographic information and GIS. These are the people who you do not want coordinating your GIS. The reason for saying this is the fact that if you do not have timely, accurate and holistic geographic information specific to the valuation of property then there is not much point having a GIS embedded within the core business of your organization to model the spatial effects which influence property value. In other words, if the data going in is not right, then the results that will be coming out will not be as accurate and meaningful as they could be. While this may seem like a simplistic point to make, data quality and its temporality are critical issues for mass appraisal that even western countries haven't fully resolved or appreciated thus far and therefore often lose out financially as a consequence.

It is also often the case, especially in countries that are less economically developed, that the data they collect has little or no geographic reference attributed to it. This is sometimes difficult to comprehend considering that property can usually be referenced to some component of an address; however, this is not always the case and this can limit both the effectiveness and utility of the data. It is therefore prudent for those tasked with the mass appraisal of property to ensure that the quality and timeliness of their data is at optimum levels prior to conducting a GIS based mass appraisal methodology.

Geographical information systems (GIS)

While there is a general knowledge and understanding of the concept of GIS within the property valuation profession, it is more than likely that those working within the discipline do not have a strong theoretical underpinning of the methodological structure of GIS. This is, however, not a negative because many people tasked with making decisions do not wish to have such knowledge as their primary concern is based on how the application of GIS can help inform their business model. Indeed, being engulfed in the theoretical and infrastructural components of GIS can often result in the real business benefits being either ignored or not fully realized, but it is imperative that there is some appreciation of the technology informing your decision.

What is GIS?

There are many definitions that exist to explain what GIS is and does, but none that are universally agreed. To this end, such definitional ambiguity has perhaps led to a lack of appreciation of what GIS can actually do. Definitions for GIS such as, 'a platform for creating and visualizing data' or 'a tool for making maps' are fine for the general reader and for simple explanation to those that haven't come across the concept before, but they don't really capture the true essence of what GIS is and does. Table 15.1 gives some of the popular GIS definitions that currently exist. However, the diversity in nature and description of these definitions, in our opinion, does not capture a holistic, yet simple representation of what GIS is and does. As a consequence, we would like to provide a definition

Table 15.1:   Definitions of GIS

Source:	Definition
Dueker, 1979	A GIS is a special case of information systems where the database consists of observations on spatially distributed features, activities or events, which are definable in space as points, lines or areas
Burrough, 1986	a powerful set of tools for storing at will, transforming and displaying spatial data from the real world, for a particular set of purposes
Clarke, 1995	automated systems for the capture, storage, retrieval, analysis and display of spatial data
Longley *et al.*, 2001	a tool for performing operations on geographic data that are too tedious or expensive or inaccurate if performed by hand
Radke and Hanebuth, 2008	GIS is a system for input, storage, processing and retrieval of spatial data

of GIS that can draw comparisons with that of CAMA while maintaining all of the key components of GIS. We are able to do this due to the strong alignment that already exists between GIS and CAMA.

The authors of this chapter would advocate that any definition needs to illustrate the complexity involved in GIS (Figure 15.1), while maintaining an ability to clearly communicate effectively with those external to the GIS and information technology environments. Therefore, we would generally adopt the view that GIS is best explained by the following:

GIS involves the ***development and/or utilization of hardware and software*** for the ***collection, collation and governance of data*** that can be, or is, ***referenced to a location*** which can then be ***analysed, visualized and manipulated to generate further data, provide an evidence base and geographically represent information*** in an effective, efficient and accountable manner.

However, it must be noted that the adoption and utilization of a GIS is very much co-dependent on data and people. The organization must have people with the expertise in place to be able to deliver an effective, efficient and accountable service. This expertise can be through previous academic and/or professional experience or as a result of bespoke training. While it is not critically important where the expertise comes from, it is fundamental that somebody who knows what they are doing is managing and coordinating GIS based analysis. This may seem like a simplistic and elementary thing to highlight, but it is often the case that organizations bring GIS in (which effectively ticks the box to say that they have it), but are not necessarily leveraging its maximum potential, or as is often the case, not utilizing it at all. This is a very common phenomenon and usually stems from the fact that there isn't an advocate and/or expert in place internally to initiate the application of GIS or as a result of the

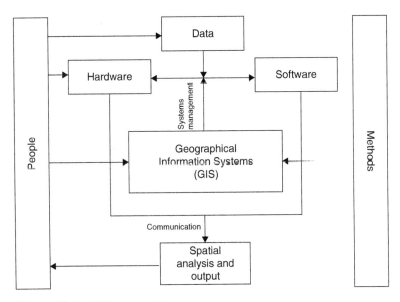

Figure 15.1:   GIS as a system

expert leaving their position, thus creating a void in the expertise. The point we are trying to make here is that an effective rollout of GIS, particularly in appraisal, is not just about having the hardware and software in place, but also having the proficient human resource base.

What must be remembered is that GIS has developed far beyond the function-ality and potentiality that it had in the early days of both GIS and information technology. Indeed, this evolution has seen its primary function move away from land management and simple cartographic methodologies to much more advanced analytical capabilities that have seen GIS turn into a global multi-billion-dollar industry that covers nearly all disciplines that are concerned with some aspect of location. The changes that have taken place have seen GIS move beyond simple functionality (such as feature creation and drawing maps) to being a centralized geo-database management system that has the ability to integrate with other parts of the system to provide a mechanism to model spatial data, conduct spatial analysis and produce meaningful and user-friendly output, as well as providing other decision support functionality.

In relation to data dependence, organizations must realize that it is their data that should be driving the answers that the GIS generates and not the hardware and software dictating what questions can be asked – something which the authors have realized, through past experiences, occurs in other disciplines and something which we are keen to ensure doesn't happen in the property valua-tion industry.

While defining GIS is not the core purpose of this chapter, it is integral to understanding the synergies that exist and how it can be integrated into prop-erty valuation methodologies. Firstly, if we look at the mass appraisal methods that exist, they are principally based on the use of **hardware and software** for the analysis of property data – information that can be **referenced to a location.** This geographic information is then statistically **manipulated and analysed** to **generate further data, provide an evidence base for valuation purposes and geographically represent the data.** Although common ground does exist between the functionality of traditional mass appraisal and GIS methodologies, it is the integration of the two that really generates the added value. The current literature on the integration of GIS and CAMA usually does not provide a detailed understanding of the rationale behind using GIS and it is potentially for this reason that many organizations responsible for property taxation do not fully include utilizing such a methodology in their business models. The following section highlights the potentiality of using GIS as part of the CAMA methodology.

Potentiality of GIS

There are many benefits that using GIS can produce for the property environment and it is the purpose of this section to help illustrate these. A review of the current literature on the topic shows that there is a lack of true knowledge and understanding of what GIS can actually bring to the CAMA market, with most of the focus directed at the use of geographic information and, to a lesser degree, GIS in the modelling of statistics spatially. There is nothing wrong with that, but if you are trying to understand the actual benefits that you are going to generate from integrating CAMA with GIS, then the current literature falls somewhat short.

Perhaps the most important benefit that GIS can bring to the CAMA market is efficiency. When we refer to efficiency, we are talking about more than just cost. There is always the upfront cost of implementing a GIS based CAMA solution – whether it's through creating a bespoke solution in-house or procuring software from vendors in the CAMA market – and it is unlikely that you will see a financial return on your investment straightaway; it is more likely that this will come over the short to medium term. Therefore, you have to speculate to accumulate. The main aspect of efficiency that we refer to is that of time. In the big bad world of economics, time equals money. Therefore, the more employee time you spend appraising properties, the more money it will cost. Utilizing a GIS within your CAMA will help to reduce the amount of time spent appraising and will help make the property taxation process more effective, efficient and transparent. Indeed, freeing up staff time will allow that resource to be allocated to other areas of priority within your organization, which in turn, can help to make your overall business model more efficient.

The second key benefit that can be derived from the integration of GIS and CAMA is that of the ability to improve the accuracy of the appraisal. While the CAMA can allow you to appraise based on the property information you hold, integrating a CAMA with GIS can enable you to model the effects of location on the property (e.g. the distance to a golf course, rail line, schools etc.) to provide a much greater analytical capability and a more accurate appraisal. Another benefit of using GIS within a CAMA is the enhanced visualization capability that you will have as a result. Many mass appraisal methodologies are primarily concerned with the resulting statistical analysis and not so much on the geographical representation of these results. By integrating CAMA with GIS, the ability exists to provide an enhanced visual representation of the data that can demonstrate the impact that the location of a property may have on its overall value. In many cases the results are presented through a map-based output which makes it much easier to communicate with those who do not necessarily have a background in mass appraisal (decision- and policymakers) and those who the mass appraisal affects (property owners/dwellers). This can help to make the system more accountable and transparent as it provides the mechanism to communicate more effectively.

The integration of GIS and CAMA also makes it possible to improve the analytical capabilities of the appraisal methodology by providing a mechanism to view, query, manage and model the spatial data. This allows a number of possibilities that do not exist without the integration, such as: augmenting the ability to identify patterns and potential outliers in the data which may impact upon the overall valuation model; the potentiality to carry out subregional analysis much more effectively; improve the overall management of the spatial data and, more importantly, the management of the properties that the appraisal will be carried out on.

Challenges facing uptake

With benefits come challenges. These are, however, more to do with making sure that the data you are wanting to analyse is fit for purpose and that the IT infrastructure that you have within your organization is able to accommodate the inclusion of a GIS.

Perhaps the most difficult barrier to overcome is not one of IT intelligence or knowledge of GIS, but one of getting your data right. We hear many stories of organizations having data that they are paying to collect and maintain, but are not necessarily able to use to its full utility as a result of not being spatially aware – a term that we usually refer to as 'not appreciating the effect that location has'. In regards to mass appraisal, being spatially aware can be attributed to 'realizing the effect that location can have on value', and this is something which is critical. As mentioned previously in this chapter, accurate and meaningful data is critical in the valuation process of residential properties. Indeed, without it the results that you will derive will be less effective and meaningful and will in turn provide the platform for challenge from those whom the valuation affects. Therefore, it is of paramount importance to ensure that the data you collect is able to answer the questions that are fundamental in your decision making process.

Another potential challenge facing the integration of GIS and CAMA is that of cost and time. Although the financial cost of implementing such a methodology in the appraisal process may be less restrictive than it once was, the length of time that it can take to calibrate, validate and apply such technology can be relatively high, which in turn can have indirect implications for the overall cost of the project.

Integrating CAMA and GIS

Integrating GIS and computer-assisted mass appraisal enables the property tax assessment function to be concurrent with spatial data that is relevant to the property tax valuation model. It also supports the creation and maintenance of a more accurate land records system using the tools and functions of GIS and provides a single repository of parcel geometry and descriptive data supporting workflow, updates and mass appraisal output.

GIS adds value to CAMA systems, such as a valuation model, which can place added value on property that has, for example, frontage onto a golf course or lake. Government tends to invest heavily in geospatial data and technology because almost everything in the public realm happens within the context of geography. Governments of all sizes need to use GIS to analyse complex situations and create solutions across disciplines. GIS helps them increase efficiency, reduce costs, improve coordination and deliver transparency and accountability.

The development of a geo-database for local government places this function at the heart of a GIS environment (URISA, 2009). The geodatabase supports such functions as data capture, data management and processing and information dissemination in an open environment that supports standards and interoperability with existing systems.

For many years valuers, assessors and appraisers have utilized CAMA technology to accurately assist them in their task to mass value large numbers of properties at the same time (McCluskey *et al.*, 1997; McCluskey *et al.*, 2002). The literature on CAMA techniques has long recognized the crucial roles of time, space and property characteristics in determining the value of real property. The ability to analyse location value has been greatly enhanced over the past 15–20 years by the development of GIS. A major development, which assisted those involved in mass valuation work, has been the assimilation of large amounts of property attribute data into extensive relationally focussed databases. These databases are potentially the most important sources of data for use within GISs. The ability to 'visualize' data and the results of a valuation model have created immense added value to the mass valuation process.

Linking of CAMA and GIS technologies is at the forefront of property tax valuation systems. Previously both technologies have tended to be essentially standalone but the synergies of having an integrated CAMA/GIS environment are fundamentally more powerful. Research into the benefits to the property tax

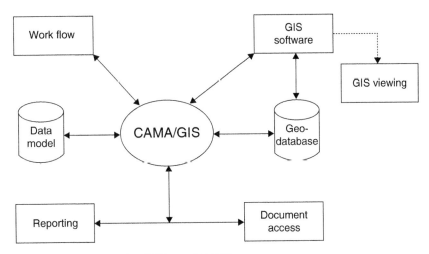

Figure 15.2:   Structure of a GIS based CAMA

industry of such an integrated approach has advanced at a significant rate. The GIS is essentially the graphical component of the GIS/CAMA unison (Figure 15.2).

The highest level of GIS and CAMA integration is referred to as 'true imbedded GIS/CAMA'. In this environment, GIS and CAMA are integrated together within a seamless application utilizing the strengths of both technologies. Not only is a common database used, but also a single application to merge spatial analysis functions into the CAMA functions. One of the key issues to full imbedded integration relates to the technical issues surrounding such aspects as non-relational CAMA databases, operating systems and database configuration, each of which must be resolved prior to full, seamless integration.

The benefits of full integration allow the valuer/assessor to create, distribute and analyse information in a much more detailed manner. Data creation includes the ability to develop products that are difficult to create with a manual system (Hensley, 1993). Data distribution includes creating custom maps, use of the internet and an intranet. The analysis capabilities extend the ability of the valuer to visualize patterns in data and to assist with both modelling and quality control.

The value of location for mass appraisal

The development of GIS has permitted valuers/assessors to create location-based analytical tools that can coordinate sales data with location. Early attempts to quantify location effects faced difficulties not only in defining and maintaining 'value neighbourhoods' or zones, i.e. contiguous areas of relatively homogeneous property values, but also in understanding the dynamics of the interactive and elusive locational factor. Approaches tended to be to develop different predictive models for each geographic region or 'market area' of properties with similar characteristics. However, these approaches could not capture the many complex, interrelated and significant micro-variations within any given neighbourhood or market area and could not reduce the determination of location value to an objective process.

CAMA based on statistical models and, in particular, multiple regression analysis (MRA) is used to value residential, commercial and industrial properties. In general, these appraisal models attempt to disaggregate property values into various 'contributing' attributes. For the CAMA models to be accurate it is essential that all the key attributes explaining value are properly accounted for in the model specification. Among these attributes, location has been considered as one of the most important in the real estate market.

In examining the effect of location on property values in CAMA models, one of the industry standard approaches is to develop a form of geographic stratification, that is delineating an area into neighbourhoods or broad market areas. In this way, it is assumed that properties within a neighbourhood have the same location value, which is that of the average typical property.

Although some subjective location qualifiers are specified for properties within the neighbourhood, this stratification method cannot properly account for the sudden and sharp value changes for similar properties on the boundaries of different neighbourhoods.

To improve the value measurement of location, a technique called location value response surface (LVRS) analysis has been investigated (O'Connor and Eichenbaum, 1988). The LVRS technique endeavours to better analyse the effect of location on property values, through the integration of GIS.

The response surface is a fitted three-dimensional surface that represents a percentage adjustment to land and/or improvements, based on a parcel's geocoded location (al-Murshid, 2008). Included in the analysis are geographic coordinates and distances from important features, such as other recent sales, institutions, amenities or other 'value influence centres'. This analysis results in a three-dimensional representation, with the height of the surface (z) at any specific x-y coordinate indicating the approximated location value of that parcel. This variable is then evaluated with others, such as land and building size, quality, condition and depreciation, to produce a total estimated value for the parcel.

The response surface differs from a mathematical equation in that it is developed through a spatial analysis process available in GIS to estimate the effects of location on value and to refine those estimates after comparing them with sales and appraisal data. This approach still relies on an element of appraisal and economic judgment in determining neighbourhood boundaries for location effects, but it can be tested and refined by observing the effect of different neighbourhood 'break lines' on the resulting three-dimensional value surface.

LVRS analysis has been tested with some degree of success in relation to the mass appraisal of single-family houses (Eichenbaum, 1989; 1995; Ward *et al.*, 1999; Gallimore *et al.*, 1996; McCluskey *et al.*, 2000). The technique was first comprehensively documented by O'Connor and Eichenbaum (1988), who developed the location value response surfaces by incorporating value influence centres (VICs), and concluded that the LVRS technique is superior to and sophisticated than traditional models such as the fixed neighbourhood approach, localized models or cluster analysis (Siu and Yu, 2001).

O'Connor and Eichenbaum (1988) criticized the traditional approaches for their inherent vulnerability to sharp changes in value over geographic space, the difficulty in explaining models to taxpayers and the resource-intensive nature of building and maintaining the models. However, the LVRS technique overcomes these problems by interpolating or 'smoothing out' a response surface as a function of location adjustment and thus eliminating value inconsistencies. Research by Eichenbaum, (1989) and (1995) has demonstrated the applicability of the technique in large diverse cities. The models were able to demonstrate extreme variances of location values from one part to another of the city, but were also able to detect subtle adjustments in relatively homogeneous areas. Research by Siu and Yu (2001) also illustrated the application of the technique for the valuation of high-rise office units for rating purposes in Hong Kong.

To be used successfully in mass appraisal, these sophisticated approaches must yield results that are reasonable, understandable and available to typical taxpayers.

Example: price modelling using GIS based statistical analysis

Chapter 14 identified the most widely used approach (MRA) for mass appraisal valuation prediction and price estimation purposes. By and large this approach is applied with mass appraisal due to its relatively easy applicability and cost-effectiveness. Increasingly, however, awareness has shifted focus towards more local non-parametric regression methodologies (geostatistical). These approaches have assumed greater importance due to flexibility in functional form and reduced error prediction (Lin and Mohan, 2011). In this regard, locally weighted regression specifications which account for locational variation and spatial heterogeneity in residential prices are now commonplace in the suite of CAMA tools available for utility by appraisers. In chapter 14, discussion surrounding the effectiveness of various local models and statistical approaches for increasing accuracy in price estimation was illustrated. This section applies a geographically weighted regression (GWR) model encapsulated within a GIS, in comparison to a spatial OLS traditional framework, to examine the development of the use and applicability of incorporating geographic information within mass appraisal. According to Fotheringham *et al.*, (2002) the advantage of this specific locally weighted spatial approach is premised upon a traditional regression framework which depicts local spatial relationships and is highly intuitive.

Table 15.2:   Data descriptive statistics

	Minimum	Maximum	Mean	Std. deviation
TASP	23324.86	630909.43	125353.32	59000.09
size	46.0	300.0	116.682	41.2363
garage	1.00	4.00	2.1759	1.13752
beds	1	8	3.16	0.666
Type	111	121	112.40	3.466
subtype	.00	3.00	2.1158	0.77639
glazetype	1.00	2.00	1.8504	0.35674
ward	1	30	14.37	8.441
travelwork	6.77	21.23	13.0815	3.85058

Global versus local

Applying an average statistic or measure uses equally weighted data which produces a global statistic or value summarizing data for the entire sample population. In contrast, utilizing local statistics, which are multi-valued due to local relationships being examined in a disaggregated form, can account for changes across a population. This is extremely beneficial for example when investigating horizontal or vertical equity for property taxation purposes. GI and GIS models that apply a global statistic are difficult to map and GIS-unfriendly (Fotheringham *et al.*, 2002). Local statistics, on the other hand, are GIS friendly and easily mappable to illustrate key spatial trends and hot-spots; these local statistics are therefore spatial with global statistics aspatial. Indeed, for mass appraisal this is significant in terms of accuracy and explanation.

Comparing MRA with GWR: empirical analysis

The geographically weighted model can be compared with a traditional hedonic regression model. The model specifications both encompass property characteristics and spatial variables with an additional number of spatial characteristics incorporated. Property characteristics include size, type, sub-type, storeys, garage, bedrooms, age and glazing, with spatial characteristics travel-to-work time and ward area. The descriptive statistics are shown in Table 15.2. The sample data is derived from a local government body at ward level, consisting of 2,695 residential properties sold between 2002 and 2004, after excluding all outliers.

Basic models

In order to account for more localized relationships and assess the degree of spatial variation in our sample properties the spatial variables are applied using electoral wards for the traditional OLS model specification, with the x-y coordinates used within the GWR model specification. To account for price non-stationarity within the data set, the following hedonic price model was constructed:

$$P_i = a_0 + b_1 + b_2 SIZE + b_3 SUBTYPE + b_4 AGE \dots$$
$$+ b_5 GARAGE + b_6 BEDROOM + b_7 STOREYS$$
$$+ b_8 GLAZING + b_9 TTW + b_{10} WARD + \varepsilon$$

where P_i is the price at which the property is sold, adjusted to a single sale date (TASP *see* chapter 14); SIZE is the floor area of the property in square metres; TYPE is the property classification either public or private market housing; SUBTYPE is the property type (detached, semi-detached or terraced); AGE depicts when the property was built; BEDROOMS accounts for the number of bedrooms the property has; STOREYS denotes the number of levels the property has; GARAGE illustrates whether the property has a detached, attached or integrated garage; GLAZING is the type of glazing, either singular or double; TTW is the average time, at electoral ward level, it takes to travel to work; and WARD depicts the ward in which the property is located.

The mechanics of the GWR methodology were previously discussed in chapter 14. As highlighted, this approach works on the basis of the traditional hedonic specification, nonetheless representing a continuous spatial process through a discrete weighting allocation (Fotheringham *et al.*, 2002). This therefore uses absolute x-y coordinates to specifically weight the similarity between prices, as each regression point is weighted by distance from the regression point through the spatial kernel as described in chapter 14. The GWR model specification in its simplest form is therefore:

$$P_i = \alpha_{0i}(u_i, v_i) + \sum \alpha_k(u_i, v_i) x_{ki} + \varepsilon_i,$$

where (u_i, v_i) denotes the coordinates of the ith point in space and $a_k(u_i, v_i)$ is the continuous function $a_k(u_i, v_i)$ at point i. This estimation process is a substitution between bias and standard error which assumes that data in close proximity to i influences the estimation of $a_k(u_i, v_i)$ more so than data located further away.

Table 15.3:   MRA results

Model	R	R²	Adjusted R²	Std. error of the estimate
1	0.912	0.831	0.828	24451.94

Model results

The base model applied within the MRA modelling applied a private market, semi-detached two-storey property with three bedrooms, double glazing and a detached garage. The R^2 for the global regression (Table 15.3) is 0.831 (83.1%) indicating a relatively high level of explanatory performance, with 16.9 per cent of the variance unexplained.

Examination of the coefficients illustrates that as the size of the property increases per square metre the price increases by £1,015, and for example the average value that an integrated garage adds to the price is £10,210 (Table 15.4). Scrutiny of the variance in property price across space (location) demonstrates substantial price differential within each electoral ward. These results nonetheless represent averages across each ward and can therefore mis-specify price estimation and exceptions due to location. To account for possible spatial variation each ward is included within the model creating in this instance 30 separate regression estimates for each ward producing 30 sets of parameter estimates which can then be analysed and mapped. For mass appraisal purposes this is time-consuming and tedious. In addition, a major statistical problem with this relates to sample size within each specific ward and the possible resultant elevated standard errors.

Examination of the GWR model shows a higher level of explanation 0.889 (increase of 6.1%) than the traditional OLS approach, serving to account for more local variability within the data. However, this is a 'pseudo' R^2 estimate produced by the analysis, as the GWR model produces an R^2 value for each property (Figure 15.3).

The main GWR findings are presented in Table 15.5. The output is a set of local estimates for each relationship. Due to it voluminous nature, only an indication based upon the summary of distribution statistics is presented. This shows the extent of the variability within the local parameter estimates and the substantial variation and non-stationarity of property price in the study region. For example, the parameter estimate for size suggests that the size of a property in one location only adds £375 per square metre, whereas in another location the same sized property adds £2,286 per metre square. This in comparison with the global parameter estimates which suggested that the average addition to the price of a property resulting from its size was £1,015. Therefore, the GWR technique appears to provide additional insight into the local variation in size and how it adds value. Importantly, in terms of assisting valuation, it helps reveal more complex patterns within the data.

Table 15.4: Global model parameter results

	Unstandardized coefficients		Standardized coefficients		
	B	Std. Error	Beta	t	Sig.
(Constant)	−45715.016	17536.498		−2.607	.009
size	1015.429	20.730	.710	48.983	.000
public	−13977.617	1929.037	−0.082	−7.246	.000
Gar_Integral	10209.986	1845.458	.059	5.532	.000
Gar_Attached	4983.508	2017.973	.023	2.470	.014
storeys1	15283.911	1626.557	.092	9.396	.000
storeys3	11034.845	5984.167	.015	1.844	.065
storeys4	214725.002	24773.586	.070	8.667	.000
Beds1	17757.424	7969.628	.018	2.228	.026
Beds2	6505.859	1787.319	.035	3.640	.000
Beds4	−4285.142	1582.963	−0.031	−2.707	.007
Beds5	−3053.272	3905.621	−0.007	−0.782	.434
Beds6	−23640.346	11328.660	−0.017	−2.087	.037
det	18478.194	1589.344	.151	11.626	.000
ter	−9329.053	1708.436	−0.068	−5.461	.000
age01	−81.064	2179.087	.000	−0.037	.970
age02	3777.299	2364.561	.016	1.597	.110
age03	1801.569	1621.792	.011	1.111	.267
age05	1371.229	1456.467	.011	.941	.347
travelwork	3061.604	1387.488	.200	2.207	.027
glazetype	2903.000	1389.504	.018	2.089	.037
ward1	−37744.254	10113.541	−0.117	−3.732	.000
ward2	−4555.529	2884.942	−0.016	−1.579	.114
ward3	3530.430	7987.306	.006	.442	.659
ward5	6967.389	3011.160	.023	2.314	.021
ward6	−5708.206	6611.412	−0.010	−0.863	.388
ward7	−69.019	2711.800	.000	−0.025	.980
ward8	−35701.605	8522.898	−0.111	−4.189	.000
ward9	32427.882	3461.927	.088	9.367	.000
ward10	29774.156	5277.303	.103	5.642	.000
ward11	−19825.853	5650.035	−0.062	−3.509	.000
ward12	1055.933	4270.307	.004	.247	.805
ward13	7636.511	7453.661	.021	1.025	.306
ward14	7444.604	4715.043	.019	1.579	.114
ward15	25560.729	7426.846	.074	3.442	.001
ward16	13026.868	5388.323	.024	2.418	.016

(Continued)

Table 15.4:   *(Cont'd)*

	Unstandardized coefficients		Standardized coefficients		
	B	Std. Error	Beta	t	Sig.
ward17	4392.537	4416.475	.013	.995	.320
ward19	14329.414	5214.898	.040	2.748	.006
ward20	2642.420	3373.010	.008	.783	.433
ward21	−22671.028	5030.425	−0.089	−4.507	.000
ward22	1646.080	3227.875	.005	.510	.610
ward23	−6920.962	5457.001	−0.027	−1.268	.205
ward24	−35187.987	12553.242	−0.153	−2.803	.005
ward25	−368.251	7707.349	−0.001	−0.048	.962
ward26	20249.883	7008.439	.053	2.889	.004
ward27	11692.981	7760.831	.024	1.507	.132
ward28	2164.500	5959.925	.006	.363	.717
ward29	8001.786	6254.130	.012	1.279	.201
ward30	25413.869	8329.398	.072	3.051	.002

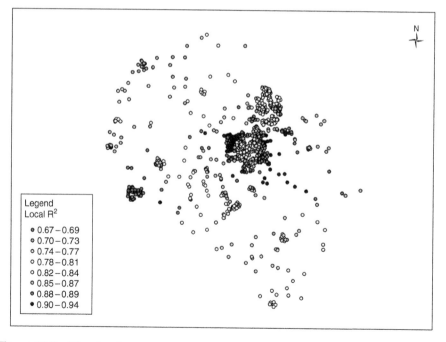

Figure 15.3 R^2 estimates

Table 15.5:   GWR summary of local parameter estimates

Variable	Minimum	Lower quartile	Median	Upper quartile	Maximum
Constant	−240956.217	62334.76	132254.6	198863.8	589133
ward	−4025.07229	−621.943	−162.169	458.0797	5897.705
travelwork	−9093.65791	−2292.56	702.5279	2525.81	20946
class	−3722.01058	−1498.59	−1141.62	−904.53	1654.133
subclass	−2814.70329	10303.46	15579.91	19310.69	28128.04
age	−15709.1188	−5527.67	−2439.71	1371.623	8005.552
storeys	−35172.3404	−13483.5	−7522.24	−3187.67	20444.78
beds	−28158.2022	−7263.73	−3503.1	219.99	16535.32
glazetype	−25646.5461	−269.852	1913.635	5117.373	20908.59
gartype	−10098.4976	2487.541	3399.921	4526.158	10212.27
size	375.17348	855.6434	970.2711	1118.767	2285.698
R	0.958				
R²	0.899				
Adj. R²	0.889				

Spatial function: bi-squared; adaptive kernel: 12% neighbours

The importance of the findings serve to highlight the applicability of using GI and GIS for estimating price within mass appraisal. The results show that for interpretability and analysis the application of local statistics and modelling can serve to enhance and improve accuracy and the understanding behind valuation.

Conclusions

The role of GIS has to a large extent transformed the way in which CAMA is being undertaken. To some extent the 'holy grail' of location and its value influence has been captured by the application of geographic solutions such as response surface analysis and geographic weighted regression to name but two techniques. Real property occupies geographic space and therefore its location is known, the skill is in delineating this location within an environment that can be adapted and used to improve value estimation. Two-dimensional mapping, satellite imagery, Google Earth and 3-D oblique photography are all now contributing to the array of tools available to the property tax assessor. Inventory management, once seen as expensive and time-consuming, is being re-engineered by the application of the above technologies.

The integration of GIS within a CAMA environment has created significant synergies and cost efficiencies. Seamless integration employs all the benefits of both technologies to provide the valuer/assessor with tools to develop estimation models that can provide intuitive information for the taxpayer.

The future for property tax assessment is clearly one based on technology. To some extent the 'art' of the value has been superseded by a more 'scientific' approach as Renshaw (1958) alluded to in his paper.

References

al-Murshid, A.H. (2008) *Modelling Locational Factors using Geographic Information System Generated Value Response Surface Techniques to Explain and Predict Residential Property Values*. Paper presented at 1st NAPREC Conference, INSPEN, Malaysia.

Burrough, P.A. (1986) *Principles of Geographical Information Systems for Land Resource Assessment*. Oxford, Oxford University Press.

Clarke, K.C. (1995) (ed.) *Analytical and Computer Cartography*. Prentice Hall Series in Geographic Information Science. Upper Saddle River, NJ: Prentice Hall.

Dueker, K.J. (1979) Land resources information systems: a review of fifteen years' experience. *Geo-Processing* 1(2): 105–128.

Eichenbaum, J. (1989) Incorporating Location into Computer-assisted Valuation. *Property Tax Journal*, 8(2): 151–169.

Eichenbaum, J. (1995) The Location Variable in World Class Cities: Lessons from CAMA Valuation in New York City. *Journal of Property Tax Assessment & Administration*, 1(3): 46–60.

Fotheringham S., Brunsdon C. and Charlton M. (2002) *Geographically Weighted Regression: the Analysis of Spatially Varying Relationships*. UK, John Wiley & Sons.

Gallimore, P., Fletcher, M. and Carter, M. (1996) Modelling the Influence of Location on Value. *Journal of Property Valuation & Investment*, 14(1): 6–19.

Hensley, T. (1993) Coupling GIS with CAMA Data in Johnson County, Kansas. *Property Tax Journal*, 12(1): 19–36.

Lin, C.C. and Mohan, S.B. (2011) Effectiveness Comparison of the Residential Property Mass Appraisal Methodologies in the USA. *International Journal of Housing Markets and Analysis*. 4(3): 224–243.

McCluskey, W., Deddis, W., McBurney, R.D., Mannis, A. and Borst, R. (1997) Interactive Application of Computer Assisted Mass Appraisal and Geographic Information Systems. *Journal of Property Valuation & Investment*, 15(5): 448–465.

McCluskey, W.J. and Adair, A. (1997), *Computer Assisted Mass Appraisal Systems*, Gower, Avebury, London.

McCluskey, W.J., Deddis, W., Lamont, I.G. and Borst, R.A. (2000) The Application of Surface Generated Interpolation Models for the Prediction of Residential Property Values. *Journal of Property Investment & Finance*, 18(2): 162–176.

McCluskey, W., Deddis, W. and Lamont, I. (2002), *Development of a Geographic Information System (GIS) Based Mass Appraisal System*, London, Royal Institution of Chartered Surveyors Educational Trust.

O'Connor, P.M. and Eichenbaum, J. (1988) Location Value Response Surfaces: The Geometry of Advanced Mass Appraisal. *Property Tax Journal*, 7(3): 277–296.

Radke, S.L. and Hanebuth, E. (2008), *GIS Tutorial for Homeland Security*, ESRI Press, California, United States.

Renshaw, E.F. (1958) Scientific Appraisal. *National Tax Journal* 11: 314–322.

Siu, K.K. and Yu, S.M. (2001) *Using Response Surface Analysis In Mass Appraisal To Examine The Influence Of Location On Property Values In Hong Kong.* Paper presented at the 7th Annual Pacific-Rim Real Estate Society Conference, Adelaide South Australia.

URISA, (2009), Urban and Regional Information Systems Association, Illinois, United States.

Ward, R.D., Weaver, J.R. and German, J.C. (1999) Improving CAMA Models using Geographic Information Systems/Response Surface Analysis Location Factors. *Assessment Journal*, 6(1): 30–38.

Index

A Primer on Property Tax: Administration and Policy, First Edition.
Edited by William J. McCluskey, Gary C. Cornia and Lawrence C. Walters.
© 2013 Blackwell Publishing Ltd. Published 2013 by Blackwell Publishing Ltd.

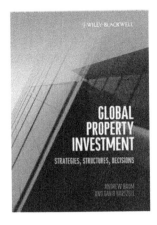

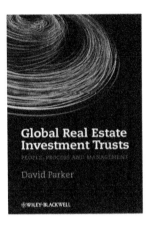
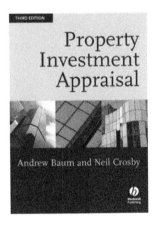
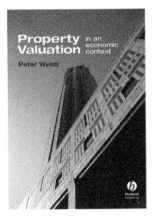

Printed and bound by CPI Group (UK) Ltd, Croydon, CR0 4YY